75

America Comes of Middle Age

Also by Murray Kempton

Part of Our Time:
Some Ruins & Monuments of the Thirties
The Briar Patch:
The People of the State of New York vs. Lumumba Shakur, et al.

America Comes of Middle Age

COLUMNS 1950-1962

by Murray Kempton

The Viking Press   New York

To Sally Ambler Kempton
and to her grandchildren,
Sally, Mike, Arthur, David and Christopher,
and TO BEVERLY

Foreword

The pieces joined here were written as columns for the *New York Post* between the summer of 1950 and the late fall of 1962.

It has seemed profitless to attach to them any general statement of the notions of craft and the ideas of man which went into their composition; they carry by themselves quite enough of a burden of their author's philosophy as it is.

Still, they are exercises submitted to a school from which I have since been graduated. There are worse schools than daily newspapers.

And, reading over these twelve years, I began to feel more and more that they formed most of the education I have. Those school papers are broken up according to the dictates of that feeling: eight sections and eight lessons.

Contents

I

Some Internal Exiles

The first lesson begins at the very bottom.

I was hired on first as a labor reporter. My credentials were the regular ones: I had never worked in a factory, but I had briefly worked for a labor union, and I knew labor leaders and arbitrators and statisticians; in other words, I was equipped to engage the shadow and no one complained much about the substance. It occurs to me that just twice in all those years I saw the inside of a factory; and once was with Nikita Khrushchev who was as affronted as I.

A theory suffused — I started to say informed — my work at the beginning. It was in sum the liberal theory. There was a continuing social revolution in the United States which had begun with Roosevelt, continued haltingly with Truman, and would end only with the triumph of God in America. The labor union, by this theory, was an instrument of providence. If Walter Reuther had not built Jerusalem in Highland Park, he would quite soon, if he were not stopped by the enemies of the light, who were the auto companies and the building trades unions and John L. Lewis and Robert Taft — or the devil masks they presented to my imagination — and, of course, poor souls, the Communists. We stood, in that theory, fighting the massed weight of General Motors and United States Steel on the one side and the massed weight of Miss Elizabeth Gurley Flynn on the other.

It was a dear kind theory, and I am only sorry that it did not prove useful for the long pull. I do not apologize for it; the late Philip Murray was the finest man I have ever known and any cause of his would still be good enough for me.

And I should hope that I should never cross a picket line; when men are cold and hungry, it takes someone more principled than I to insult them for no better reason than that they are wrong.

In those days, though, I belonged to one of the many clubs that make life comfortable in this eminently clubbable nation. The union professionals offer a club for labor reporters, as the police professionals offer a club for police reporters; there even seems to be a club for the better element in the White Citizens Councils, for which Mr. David Lawrence is editor of the bulletin. The club was good to me, and I was faithful to its legends: I walked every night in those days through the garment district to the Pennsylvania Railroad, regularly comforted by the thought that the International Ladies Garment Workers Union had abolished the sweatshop.

Like so many of the fallen, I can thank the Communists for getting me out of the club. It was not so much what they taught — which to the extent that it was consistent was seldom about reality — but what they turned out to be.

My club very early had thrown the Communists out of its garden. This expulsion was dictated only a little bit by the desire all persons who have risen in the world have to be recognized as respectable by members of other clubs. What was more important was our sense that the CIO — like other implements of established liberal providence — hadn't been doing too well; and we blamed the Communists who were alien. But, most of all, having made the mistake of exaggerating our importance in history, we exaggerated the Communists too.

And so the CIO threw them out, and, after they were gone, the CIO still did not do too well. Looking at them afterwards, it was obvious that they had in general been inadequate leaders of labor, but it is a profession where the average of adequacy is not high. Losing them did not damage the CIO; cleansing them did not improve it much either. The point was that those Communists who had held union jobs had been pretty much like other labor leaders, none as good as Reuther and Murray, none as bad as poor Joseph P. Ryan.

Then all respectable society arose and threw the Communists out of jobs and housing projects, off pensions, into tax courts. Men were honored for having spied upon them. A persistent complaint of liberals was that Joe McCarthy, by his inaccuracies, damaged the legitimate cause of anti-Communism. The legitimate cause expressed itself by sending old ladies to jail on the solemn finding that they were a clear and present danger.

This section is about some of the things we have done to the Communists to save our liberty. Many of the petty malignities put in process were never carried through, thanks, in large part, to a Supreme Court which, if it is not always even, has the saving grace to draw the line against truly petty and disgusting things.

I covered these troubles with a fascination which few of my colleagues seem to share. I think they were wrong, and that they neglected their education. We would be disillusioned less often if we did not so often confine our sympathy to those victims of society who seem blameless. Few victims of society turn out blameless upon inspection. (I think, quite seriously, that, if I had the choice of committing a murder or being murdered myself, purely from the point of view of reputation, I might be better off as the murderer. Any victim whose posthumous good name can survive a long murder trial is a noble specimen indeed.)

Newspapers are proud, as they should be, of the times when police have arrested the wrong man and they have rescued him. But what of the right man who is the victim of a harsh and malicious law? The people in this section were public Communists and therefore the right people; does the fact of proper identification justify what we have done to them?

It is argued of course — these matters are still considered controversial — that they would do worse to us if they had the chance. I cannot conceive an idler argument. Our laws deal with what a man has done, not with what he might have done given the chance. I am willing to concede — although I do not believe it — that J. Edgar Hoover has a purer heart than most of the Communists he hunts. But Mr. Hoover has power and they do not; and his public actions and not their private dreams are our business. We have quite enough to bother about when our government subsidizes a man to spy on his wife or takes down the names of the mourners at a Communist funeral without lying late into the night worrying about Gurley Flynn overthrowing the government.

The history of the American Communist Party is, of course, hardly free of personal malignities. But these are people who have paid far more than they deserved for whatever private damage they have done.

They have borne these troubles nobly and well and they have an honor as victims which they could never have had as figures of power. They have paid; and in any case I should not belabor them, because I should have no reason to except to protect my own reputation. And these things were done because enlightened, liberal government wanted to protect its reputation against the charge that it was soft on Communists.

The U.S. as Pickpocket

The United States government, in all its awe and majesty, has now descended in malignity to picking the pocketbooks of poor old women.

Alexander Bittelman is a sixty-six-year-old Communist Party official now serving a prison term under the Smith Act. Early this fall, someone discovered that Bittelman was receiving social security payments from the United States government.

Bittelman was getting $88.10 a month mailed directly to his cell in Atlanta. He used to take $10 out for cigarets and other sundries from the commissary and send the rest back to his wife, Eva, living without other income in Croton, New York.

Old Mrs. Bittelman appears to be the menace from which the Social Security Board rescued us yesterday when it announced that persons employed by the Communist Party and its affiliates are no longer eligible for old-age retirement benefits.

Her husband is a professional Communist and has had no other employer in the seventeen years he and the party have been paying social security taxes. The government is only the custodian of the social fund, which is supported by equal payments by employer and employe. When the government stops Bittelman's retirement checks, it is not saving its own money; it is stealing his.

A few months ago, the Communist Party of the State of New York applied to the Health Insurance Plan of Greater New York for medical insurance for its thirteen employes. H.I.P. replied that the party's application has been rejected by decision of its underwriting committee. An H.I.P. spokesman said that it does not have to give reasons for rejecting applications, and I suppose it hasn't.

I only know that, if a child is born to a secretary in the Communist Party office some time in the future, it will be a child born under free private enterprise, because its mother is debarred from health insurance, a benefit taken for granted by most workers in this town.

In the last decade we have developed a sort of common law of justice for Communists. That common law is now in its full flower; the Communist is taxed as an American citizen and denied any other blessing of citizenship except taxation. From the Communist Party's typist's child to old Mrs. Bittelman, these people have total insecurity, from the cradle to the grave.

There is always a regulation somewhere that will allow a government officer to do a malignant thing. That regulation serves two purposes; it gives an excuse to him and it gives an excuse to such bystanders as should be outraged and need to justify their silence.

Bittelman's experience summons to memory the whole Republican campaign of 1936. Social security was a big factor in that campaign; the Republicans argued that it was no insurance at all, and that the government would steal it from prospective beneficiaries whenever the whim touched it. The Republicans could not have dreamed then that their case would be proved nineteen years later by a worn-out Communist hack and with not one word of protest from them.

Eva Bittelman is an old woman; and I would not believe the government of the United States if it argued without further proof that she is a wicked or dangerous one. That is irrelevant; virtue is irrelevant to any concept of a basic American right. As Calvin Coolidge might say, we hired her husband's money and the Communist Party's, didn't we? And, when we refuse to pay it back, we are welshers on a debt.

There are very few people in America who would stand up and say without shame that they favor the suppression of ideas. Yet are ideas so much more important than people that our government can without shame make its wars on old women? We have a government, which without protest from any liberal Senator, has taken social security away from an old man and a disability pension away from an ex-soldier solely because they were Communists. Is there any better measure of a nation than the way it treats the helpless?

[December 15, 1955]

Maxwell Berman wrote the *Post* yesterday to dissent from my view that the government of the United States of America had stooped to picking pockets because it denied social security benefits to Alexander Bittelman, a convicted Communist, and his wife.

"We are," said Brother Berman, "a country of laws."

This is a splendid notion and one to be commended to the Department of Justice, the Social Security Board, the Bureau of Internal Revenue, and the Veterans Administration.

Brother Berman says that I should stop and reflect and not let emotion govern my thinking. It certainly plays hell with my writing. I got so worked up about poor Bittelman that I cheated the customers of the facts of his case.

The Social Security Board did not cut off Bittelman's old age pension because he was convicted under the Smith Act. Its order applied to all employes of the Communist Party. The Social Security Board found that, under the McCarran Act, the Communist Party has been found to be an agent of a foreign power, and, the board says, employes of a foreign government are ineligible for social security.

There are, it appears, two Alexander Bittelmans. There is Mr. Berman's Alexander Bittelman who tried to murder our government. That one is all right; he can get his social security. But there is another Alexander Bittelman; he is an employe of a foreign government and thus presumably enjoys a kind of diplomatic immunity from its taxes.

We are a government of laws; am I mistaken in the emotional notion that there is the same law for the Social Security Board and for other agencies of the government? Apparently I am.

George Blake Charnay is the state chairman of the Communist Party of New York. He makes $75 a week, all of it from the party. Under the social security law, he is an employe of a foreign government and exempt from social security tax. Charnay also served two years under the Smith Act and then got sprung for a new trial. During his stretch, he fell behind in his income tax payments, all on earnings paid him by the Communist Party. Does his diplomatic immunity extend to the Bureau of Internal Revenue? Of course not; Charnay is being harassed for taxes by its agents right now.

We are a government of laws. Saul Wellman is a Communist official convicted under the Smith Act for conspiring to overthrow the government of the United States. The Veterans Administration was paying him a disability pension for wounds suffered in Europe in World War II. Now that has been cut off. The excuse is that the statute provides that any veteran who gives aid and comfort to an enemy of the United States thereby loses his pension. The Wellman who tried to murder the government can be paid for his wounds; it's just this other fellow who gave aid and comfort to an enemy of the United States. And this is not, by the way, a charge for which Wellman has ever been tried.

We are a government of laws. A number of Communists convicted under the Smith Act have run enough of their course to be eligible for parole. The board asks them, as it asks all convicts, whether they repent of their crimes. These people, of course, deny they ever committed a crime; they propose to go on doing what they felt innocent of doing in the first place.

There is, of course, a relevant statute to deal with their attitude. Parole boards are abjured to make sure that a prisoner repents of his crime before considering his parole. This applies alike to bank robbers and sick old Communists. A sick old Communist does not repent of the crime he says he did not commit, and he — under the law, of course — is ineligible for parole.

We are a government of laws. Any laws some government hack can find to louse up a man who's down.

[December 21, 1955]

Big Brother No-Face

It would appear that the Treasury agents who seized the *Daily Worker* a few weeks back took away the following items:

(1) A New York City press police card issued to a *Daily Worker* reporter.

(2) A list of persons who have written the *Daily Worker* for trial copies or otherwise sought its wisdom.

(3) The foreign stamp collection of one Joseph Clark, an individual and city editor of the *Daily Worker*.

(4) The telephone operator's list of numbers frequently called.

(5) One egg of three left in a refrigerator by a do-it-yourself short order chef on the staff.

All these items, except the list of potential dupes, are reported still missing. They cast an interesting light on the Treasury's argument that it moved against the *Daily Worker* as it would against any delinquent taxpayer. The list of inquiring correspondents and the office telephone directory of the *Daily Worker* are hardly negotiable commodities unless we consider the chance that the Internal Revenue Service proposes to peddle them to the friends of Ben Schultz for the annual dinner.

They are, of course, not assets but intelligence documents and intelligence documents of a rather low grade; the names and telephone numbers of revolutionary conspirators are not usually listed for the convenience of office telephone girls.

And this was a search and seizure not of assets but of intelligence. It was also a rather formless and whimsical attempt at suppression by evasion. I have seen it compared to a Palmer raid, which is unkind to President Wilson's attorney general. A. Mitchell Palmer was occasionally brutal; he was never sneaky. He walked in the front door. But our government sidles through the side entrances. It enforces its notions of security through loopholes in laws that were written with no notion of security. It has thus become lawless, not as gangsters are lawless, but as their shysters are. Like the shyster, it uses the letter of one law to evade the spirit of all law.

The other day, I heard from the widow of a man who used to be a sort of janitor, handyman and mimeograph operator in the Communist Party office. All his social security credits came from wages paid him by the Communist Party. The Social Security Board had taken away the survivors' benefits of his widow. The excuse was that he had been an employe of a foreign power. In the same month, one agent of our government lands on the Communists as a political party subject to our tax laws and another cuts off a janitor's pension because the Communist Party which employed him is not a political party but the creature of a foreign power.

Will the same Solicitor General of the United States argue both those propositions in the same Supreme Court?

I miss the time when people we thought were the enemies of our freedom had faces you could point to. There were pictures in the prints of Donald Moysey, the public servant who ordered the *Daily Worker* raid — but who could recognize him on the street? Have you ever seen the face of the Social Security Board clod who cut off that widow's pension or of what's-his-name from the Veterans Administration who stopped Saul Wellman's disability benefits?

I know all about Joe McCarthy and Jim Eastland, but did either of them ever steal an egg out of a Communist's refrigerator? The government has become a shyster, and we do not even see its face. Tired and timid men sit up late at night seeking little dodges to harass the poor and the shabby; somehow a tyranny of cowardly pickpockets seems so much worse than a tyranny of bully boys, and Big Brother so much more terrible when he is not a face but an all-concealing blur.

[April 17, 1956]

Government Witness

Leonard Patterson is a kind of semi-pro backstop for the Department of Justice in deportation cases against aliens.

Patterson is an ex-Communist who has served as an expert witness against targets of the Immigration and Naturalization Service. In some cases, he drew $34 a day as a witness last fall, and when he was in the wholesale line he was drawing a $450-a-month retainer from the Justice Department.

He rates an expert's compensation. In reality he is a fact witness, which means that he is most valuable to the government's case because he asserts a cavernous memory equipped to recall faces from party meetings of twenty-five years ago. An expert witness gets paid more than a fact witness. It is a mark of the inflationary virtues of Patterson's memory that the government pays him the expert rate for "fact" testimony.

On three occasions in the last year government appeals boards have found testimony by semi-pro Patterson so contradictory on its face that they officially labeled it unworthy of belief. Catching witness Patterson at this sort of thing is hardly new or sensational, but it will be a tedious necessity so long as he remains an instrument of an agency calling itself Department of Justice.

Last November, Frank Ibanez, a local baker, was arrested and held for deportation to his native Cuba. Ibanez has been in this country more than thirty years. The charge was that he had been a member of the Communist Party when he left Cuba and afterwards.

Ibanez denies that he is or ever was a member of the Communist Party. He is on his face a proud left-winger, with a union record going back to the old Food Workers Industrial Union and a political record most conspicuous for support of the pro-Communist faction in the Spanish Republican government. These things did not, by themselves, constitute any proof of party membership.

What the government needed was two direct witnesses — we retain the shell of the ancient Anglo-Saxon principle that no man should be convicted on the testimony of just one witness. The two witnesses were Manning Johnson and Leonard Patterson.

Johnson is another ex-Communist, with a reputation for consistency to fact not substantially better than Patterson's. Johnson had known Ibanez in the Food Workers Union in 1934. It is his word against Ibanez's word. I have my personal views of the sort of government which would deport a man on the otherwise unsupported testimony of Manning Johnson, but he was telling the minimum truth when he said he knew Ibanez.

The other witness, as I have said, was Leonard Patterson. He testified somewhat murkily that he had met Ibanez first during the Food Workers' strike of 1930. And then, much more positively, he swore that he had seen Ibanez at the 1930 New York district convention of the Communist Party. Under cross-examination, he fixed the date as late April or May of 1930.

Ibanez remembered Johnson quite well, but Patterson was a stranger to him. His own reaction to the testimony was that it cooked him. He couldn't remember where he had been twenty-five years ago.

And then he checked his memory and found a very precise record. The 1930 New York district convention of the Communist Party had been held in the first week of May, six weeks before the party's national convention.

In 1930, Frank Ibanez had been working as a night clerk in the National City Bank. He had been in Wall Street when Patterson remembered him as a cafeteria striker. He was laid off in April, and on the fourteenth of the month sailed for Cuba. He was in Cuba when Patterson says he was in New York. The Cuban government's immigration service records show that Ibanez left Key West April 14, and returned from Cuba on June 17, 1930.

The Board of Immigration Appeals ordered Ibanez deported last April. He is in court now using the documents to prove that Leonard Patterson's memory has done it again. If he wins his appeal, the chances are that the government will bench semi-pro Patterson and use another witness in the rehearing. But you may be sure that Leonard Patterson will be back, and the government will offer him against some other poor soul.

[June 10, 1955]

Some Open Files

It is an occasion for mordant amusement in a week when the secret files of the FBI are being opened for commercial purposes in every bookstore and on every newsstand, to reflect that the government will start Monday on yet another attempt to send Steve Nelson to prison.

Steve Nelson's is a perennially open case in the FBI's files. He is the Western Pennsylvania chairman of the Communist Party. State and Federal agencies have been trying to send him to prison, with the FBI's cooperation, since 1951. Pennsylvania sentenced him to twenty years in prison for criminal sedition and a Federal judge to five for conspiring to overthrow the government of the United States. Both convictions were thrown out by the Supreme Court; now the government is trying again with the Smith Act.

It would be difficult to conceive a more melancholy record of FBI techniques than the successive trials of Steve Nelson. For purposes of economy let us consider only two of those trials. When Pennsylvania first convicted him of sedition in 1951 the witnesses attesting to his criminal acts included:

(1) Manning Johnson, whose testimony against the Communist Party before the Subversive Activities Control Board was later thrown out by the Supreme Court as "tainted." The government has not dared use Johnson as a witness since 1954, when he swore that Ralph Bunche was a Communist and was caught in flat disproof.

(2) Leonard Patterson, who, while lacking the Supreme Court's endorsement of his taint, has a record as a witness which differs from Johnson's only in farther extremes of fantasy. Testimony by Patterson has been characterized as unworthy of belief by at least one Federal judge and by the U. S. Board of Immigration Appeals.

(3) The late Paul Crouch, like Johnson described by the Supreme Court as a "tainted witness." Since the poor fellow is now at rest, that would seem characterization enough for charity.

(4) Matthew Cvetic, hero of Warner Brothers' *I Was a Communist for the FBI*, and an habitual government witness between ordeals of his whisky cure. The government's enthusiasm for Cvetic has diminished since July, 1955, when a United States Court of Ap-

peals unanimously described his testimony in a deportation case as "unbelievable and incredible."

It is only five years since that sad quartet was a team testifying against the enemy in court after court, their names written in gold in the files of the FBI. And, if the Supreme Court hadn't reversed Nelson's conviction on constitutional grounds, their word would have been enough to send a man to prison for twenty years.

In the summer of 1953, the Federal Government convicted Steve Nelson of conspiring to advocate the forcible overthrow of the government. This time, the FBI-sponsored witnesses included:

(1) Cvetic.

(2) Joseph D. Mazzei, for eleven years an undercover agent of the FBI. The Department of Justice subsequently admitted that Mazzei had given testimony so dubious in three separate cases since then that it now had "serious reason to doubt" his probity.

(3) Mrs. Mazzei, about whom the government expresses no doubt but who nonetheless gave evidence exactly like her husband's in one of the cases where his testimony aroused the Justice Department's suspicions.

Steve Nelson is fortunate in having his fourth chance. We have no way of knowing how much luckier he is than how many other people. Last summer, Nelson's lawyer was engaged in taking a deposition from Mazzei. He showed him a picture; Mazzei swore that he had never seen the subject before in his life. It was a picture of an alien about to be deported as a Communist; Mazzei had been one of the two main witnesses against him. Only that accident kept him off the boat.

And there you have six witnesses the FBI has provided the prosecution in five years of Steve Nelson's trials, and who cannot be available to it next month. The FBI has never apologized; the closest we have had to an apology came from Assistant Attorney General Tompkins who said, "You use the best you have." Their successors are now matters for the secret files of the FBI but what cause have we to doubt that they too will be open and we ashamed before too long?

[January 2, 1957]

To Save a Nation

The Veterans Administration, after long consideration, seems finally to have decided to take away the disability pension of any ex-soldier convicted under the Smith Act.

In the melancholy roster of Communist convicts, this rule applies to only two men. They are Robert Thompson, a former staff sergeant in the 32d Division at Buna, and Saul Wellman, a former corporal in the 102d Airborne at Bastogne. Those are geographical orientations not without a certain ring in the memory.

Both Thompson and Wellman were Communists when they entered the service. Both came out with 100 per cent disability. Wellman was wounded by 88's at Bastogne and spent nine months in the hospital.

Thompson was not wounded, which is by way of being a miracle because he was the kind of combat soldier who seldom survives wars without accident. He was a platoon leader at Buna. When it was all over, the Army gave him the Distinguished Service Cross and wanted to make him a captain. But, by then, he had TB and general malaria and was invalided home.

There has been no suggestion yet that the DSC be taken away from him, although you never know these days. If the committee is interested in who promoted Thompson, the answer, of course, is Douglas MacArthur, and that sentence is not conceived in irony. MacArthur would not, I think, reading that citation, be ashamed of anything he ever did for Staff Sergeant Thompson.

Thompson's pension was suspended in 1951, after he had been convicted under the Smith Act and skipped bail. The VA waited until 1954 to announce that this was a matter of policy. Last month Thompson's wife received a letter from the chairman of the Committee on Waivers and Forfeitures of the Veterans Administration saying that her last appeal but one had been denied.

Wellman was convicted last year and his pension has been stopped, too. Our government's policy rests on a clause in Public Law 144 which says a man can lose his veteran's pension for treason, espionage, and rendering aid to an enemy of the United States. So far as I can find out, he can lose it for no other cause. A murderer or a dope peddler gets it as long as he lives, and that, I think, is as it should be.

Thompson and Wellman argue that they were not convicted of treason but only of conspiring to advocate the overthrow of the government of the United States, which courts and legislatures alike conceived as something else and lesser. But that is a technical argument and somehow beside the point.

For we do not pay a disabled veteran a pension because he has a sound moral character; the sort of man he is or becomes has nothing to do with that. The Purple Heart is not even a medal for courage; it is a recognition of a wound. It says only that a man was hurt during the operations of combat; and, when the VA certifies 100 per cent disability, it says only that here is a man who stood on our ground and suffered there; that he came in one sort of man and left quite another.

We owe Wellman and Thompson a debt that pensions cannot pay or malice erase. We owe it to them because they earned it a long time ago when they were young and at the price of their youth; and no act or thought of theirs can change the account due them.

If Bastogne and Buna are glorious, these men, whatever their lives before or since, are glorious for that single moment they stood there and were targets. And, when we play them cheap, whatever their sins, we debase not them but the memory of that moment.

A long time ago, an old Sinn Feiner reminded W. B. Yeats that there are things a man must not do even to save a nation.

[May 6, 1955]

Comic

When John Howard Lawson was pastor of the Communist Party's Hollywood sheep, he said, with lips pursed, that Lionel Stander was a fine example of how a Communist should not act in public.

For Lionel Stander was always a hot rod. He hit Hollywood with the first wave of New York radicals; most of his good friends then became the old guard of the party's film section.

As a New York actor, he had always taken a special delight in those experimental atrocities where the worker stands up and spits in the boss's eye. He wanted to go to Spain and fight, an ambition which soberer heads in the party put down as the posturing to be expected of a ham.

Lionel Stander could never play the hero; there was no tenderness in those gravel accents, no charm in that bulging neck, no softness in those granite eyes; he was cast for the wise guy, the cynic and the heel; he was Caliban. And he was a political juvenile delinquent, an irresponsible who rasped that the party was too soft in its Popular Front period and then ran off to join Bundles for Britain during the Nazi-Soviet pact.

He was at least an intimate Communist fellow traveler, and John Howard Lawson and all the rest of them kept wishing that he would stop spitting on the floor and telling dirty jokes in the Pullman of the express train of history. When Harold Velde summoned him to New York yesterday, he was on the road with *Pal Joey*, cast as a black-mailer.

When he sat down to testify, the pro-Communists in his audience looked at him with utter detachment; he could not really be one of theirs, even if he paid them dues — emotional, unpredictable, spitting in everyone's eye. They had no reason to know what he would do.

And so Lionel Stander managed to do everything these poor hulks have dreamed so long of doing; he shouted and stormed and bellowed poor Harold Velde into the shakes. Most hostile witnesses tend to pirouette gently on the Fifth Amendment; Stander didn't just stand on it; he trampled all over it.

The Velde committee, which is customarily portrayed as an arm of the Third Reich, is probably the most remorseful agency of the American legislature. Counsel Frank Tavenner approaches his witnesses like an undertaker welcoming the prodigal son back to the funeral; his gentle, wheedling voice cries out for a little give, for just the semblance of remorse. He was no match for Stander.

He was pursuing a fugitive dream of how the hero acts in the great confrontation scene and Harold Velde could not stop him. Our forefathers fought for free opinion, grated Lionel Stander; do you remember the Alien and Sedition Acts, the deportation of the Jews from Spain, etc., etc.?

No one is ever really long miscast and poor Lionel Stander can never escape being a slightly comic figure. His long, unchallenged tribute to the rights of man came forth in that Broadway accent as if a character in *Three Men on a Horse* had suddenly been handed a Norman Corwin script.

Once Tavenner intervened to read testimony that Stander and his wife had been members of a Hollywood Communist cell in the Thirties. There was a silence and then Stander rasped, "Which wife"; try though he will, Caliban can only play comedy.

Harold Velde finally gasped and sweated and told Stander that he was still under subpoena and would be recalled. The party people, in a slight state of shock, broke into applause as he left. Velde put on Jay Gorney, the composer. Gorney, a disciplined Bolshevik, took refuge in the Fifth Amendment on all questions involving his past activities except writing the music for *Hey, Rookie*, which might have seemed to the layman sufficient cause to invoke the protections against self-degradation. Gorney was very polite; we were back to normal.

Outside the courtroom, Stander posed for photographs. His hand shook as he held the match; there was a sudden sense that all this had been very important to him. Then he spit one more time on the floor of the Pullman, and went back to Philadelphia to play the black-mailer.

[March 12, 1953]

The Victim

Philip Loeb, the actor, was found dead from an overdose of sleeping pills in the Hotel Taft early this month. There was no reason to doubt that he had committed suicide.

He had registered at the Taft under the name "Fred Lang," which he had told friends a few weeks before was the name he wished he owned, because, in German, it means "long peace." He had talked about death frequently in the weeks before he died; if he left no note, his silence at the end must have arisen, as the impulse to die did, out of simple exhaustion.

Loeb's most solid material success as an actor was five years ago when he played the father on the Goldberg show. He lost that part in 1952, after two years of struggle against "Red Channels," which had listed his Communist front associations. Gertrude Berg, who owns the show, fought gallantly to save Loeb; in the end, she had to surrender.

It was the tragedy of Philip Loeb that he thought that he had surrendered, too. His wife had died some years before; and he had been left with only his son, who, along with his work and the theatrical unions, was the major interest of his life. Three years ago, all these interests came into terrible conflict.

Some years ago, his son became a schizoid. The chief symptom of his illness was the delusion that unknown Communists were trying to kill him. It seemed by no means a hopeless case; and, when it began, Loeb was confident of a cure. He put his son in a private institution that had a history of success with schizophrenia.

The treatment cost $12,000 a year, the Goldberg show paid Philip Loeb a little better than $20,000. The stake for which he fought when his "Red Channels" trouble came was not just his chance to work but his son's cure.

In 1952, when Mrs. Berg gave up and he was dropped from her show, Loeb prepared to make a test case of his discharge. He believed, right or wrong, that his victory could destroy the television blacklist. He came to the fight with certain advantages: (1) he had always been an active militant in the theatrical unions, and many of his opponents there offered token support; (2) his was a clearcut case of a political discharge, and he had been fired when his contract had two more years to run.

Then, just at the moment when his unions were moving behind him, Philip Loeb gave in. Mrs. Berg offered him a settlement; reports were that it ran as high as $40,000. In the end it was much less; but in any case, it was enough to guarantee that his son could stay in a private hospital two more years.

Sam Jaffe, who was his oldest friend, said yesterday that Loeb made the settlement and then wept.

"It was," says Sam Jaffe, "the old question about, if you are in a fire, you save a baby or a priceless manuscript." But for Philip Loeb, it was much more, because this was his son, and because, whatever his enemies could say of him, he had worked without pay twelve hours a day for Actors Equity and the Television Authority. "This was the ground Philip Loeb had chosen." And, when he gave in, he sacrificed his posture in the union and lost his will to go on in it.

He had carried on for the last three years on the fringes of the theater. He testified before a Senate committee investigating his past connections with Communist fronts; he said he had never been a party member but intended to go on cooperating with anyone he thought was right. It was not a satisfactory performance.

He was hired for the road company of *Time Out for Ginger* at a reduced rate for a star. "Even though there is no blacklist in the theater," says Sam Jaffe, "they know they can get you a little cheaper." When that was over, he spent a season off Broadway at $87.50 a week.

By then, he had used up his credit and was hopelessly in arrears for his son's maintenance. In the end, he gave up and transferred his son to a state institution in Massachusetts. Two months ago, he got a letter from his son; it was a desperate, pathetic plea to get him back to a place where he might be cured.

Now Loeb is dead and his son is in that institution. As Sam Jaffe says, Philip Loeb had a hopeless choice to make and might have lost either way. He began in the early Thirties, fighting for a $50-minimum for actors, and his heart may have led him to affiliations from which his head should have held him back.

"I cannot look back," said Sam Jaffe yesterday, "and think of anyone Philip ever harmed." In the same way, his enemies did not even hate him, and we can be sure that no one of them ever thought it would come to this.

[September 13, 1955]

Daughter of the Furies

Victoria Wellman is the fourteen-year-old daughter of Saul Wellman, a leader of the Detroit Communist Party, and of his wife, Peggy, whom the government is trying to deport to Canada.

Last week Vicky Wellman was graduated from Hutchins Junior High School in Detroit wearing the Bronze Medal for Americanism awarded by the American Legion. The medal cited her for: "Courage, Leadership, Honor, Service and Scholarship."

Vicky's more-than-ordinary piquancy was compounded in this case by the circumstances of her father's business, and Detroit is very proud of itself, of the Legion, of its school system and of all concerned except, of course, her parents, who, after all, only brought her up.

The *Detroit Free Press* commented: "In spite of the home influence to which she must have been exposed, Vicki obviously acquired a deep sense of understanding of what it means to be an American citizen . . . [this] is a tribute to [the Legion's] sense of fairness which enabled it to judge Vicki's qualification on their own merits."

It is things like this which long ago made most civilized persons understand that, if there is a God in heaven, the average editorial writer in the average newspaper had better get to his knees and beg His compassion as fast as he can. I don't think anyone but an editorial writer would suggest that we are a great people because the American Legion abstains from demanding that children name names.

Vicky answered the telephone last night at her home, where, let us all hope, she was womanfully resisting the dreadful influence of her mother and father.

She is in high school studying dress design. "I want to be a hair stylist, but they don't have that course there." She has no particular favorite subject, and she supposes that swimming is her favorite pursuit. She likes Elvis Presley and Sammy Davis, Jr.

She had been quoted in the *Free Press* as saying: "I'm real happy that Daddy is proud of me." "Oh," she said last night, "they made that up, but I *am* real glad."

Was she in her turn proud of her father and mother? The answer was the obvious one that this was a silly question.

"I agree with them," she said. "I mean I think they're right, although I don't really care much about these things."

She said the excitement was "fun while it lasted." "I've put the medal away with my brother's." Her brother David won the Legion Americanism award at Hutchins in 1955, shortly after his father was convicted of conspiring to advocate the violent overthrow of our society.

Peggy Wellman was saying that, come spring, Vicky and David may face a pretty serious test of the qualities of courage and honor the Legion has certified in them. Saul Wellman could be in prison; and

Peggy Wellman could be deported by then. Once sent to Canada, under the Walter-McCarran Act, she is forever barred from returning.

"They may have to decide whether to go with me or stay here and visit their father in prison."

It is strange, as I have said all too often, how humanity tricks and taunts us. We write laws which are aimed at declaring that Communists are not people, and they bedevil us with the faces of children like Vicky who was ten years old when her father was first arrested, and who thinks he is right, and who wants to be a hair stylist.

Medals aren't for fourteen-year-old girls anyway. They are for grown men fighting for their country. We owe Vicky something much more important than a medal — the home she grew up in and the mother who raised her.

[January 29, 1957]

Present Danger

The ascension of Elizabeth Gurley Flynn to the chairmanship of the American Communist Party seems like an enormous joke on J. Edgar Hoover.

It is impossible to look at Miss Flynn without collapsing into the molasses of the American dream. She is the aunt Dorothy longed to get back to from Oz. She is seventy and looks marvelous, thanks to her Rumanian doctor and her vacation in the Soviet Union, which she makes sound like St. Petersburg, Florida.

If the old-fashioned virtues really had any impact on our culture, the disenchanted of our society would rush to this dear sister's bosom.

She is not quite Aunt Het, of course. She had a deliciously rough-house youth as an anarchist incendiary, and only a few years ago the government railroaded her to prison. But all these experiences have left her with a face that would be irresistible on the label of an apple pie mix.

She had a handsome turnout of the enemy press. They found her a strange spokesman for a party which, Mr. Hoover assures us, has practically entered the para-military stage. One television man asked her what plans she had for the revolution; and she answered, in the tone of a grandmother who loves the dear little things but whose feet do hurt sometimes standing in the kitchen baking all those pies: "I hope they don't work me too hard. After all, I am seventy."

She is, she said, like most Americans and has her fingers crossed about President Kennedy. "I am willing to wait and see. I'm neither prejudging the administration nor giving it a blank check." The picture of Lenin on the wall remained in place, but one felt it faintly trembling. She rather liked the idea of the Peace Corps. She was reminded that J. Edgar Hoover had announced that her party had twenty thousand members. The expression became that of the gentle, unlucky lady who owned the motel bypassed by the new toll road. "Oh, he always comes up with that when he needs a new appropriation."

She had read most of the stories about the Khrushchev–Mao Tsetung differences and found them distorted. The tone became that of the aunt talking about the nephew — no less beloved than the others — who had taken the family car without permission. The Chinese had not really trusted the possibilities of peace and co-existence, she said, and then had come to Moscow and been impressed by the unanimity of the Communist parties and then had voted with them.

Someone asked whether she had been impressed with the possibilities of dissent in the Soviet bloc. Why, asked Miss Flynn, would anyone dissent in a socialist society? Someone suggested that Gomulka had dissented in Poland, and had gone to jail. That, Miss Flynn pointed out gently, was under Stalin. The family had made mistakes. Now Gomulka was the leader of the country.

A Tass man asked how many leaders of the American Communist Party had been sent to prison for dissent. It seemed a fair hit, but the gentle Miss Flynn forebore to exploit it.

Looking around the *Daily Worker* office, one could find scarcely a face, except for the press, that did not belong to someone either convicted or tried under the Smith Act. There was no party member there under fifty; Jack Stachel, who was once the party's trade union secretary, was passing out press releases, a clerk's job. This is not said to suggest that Stachel has been downgraded; the point is rather that the party has no employes left and not many more members; it is nothing but leaders.

How tired they seem; how old; how out of history. This is not said to deride them — they've pulled their time and unjustly, and whatever they deserve, they have earned something more than mockery. The evil is not them, but a society which, when they have come down to the shadow of existence, demands a vast establishment of policemen, Congressional committees, and disgusting laws to protect us from them. You could sum up the domestic history of a dozen years just by printing a picture of Elizabeth Gurley Flynn and putting under it the caption: "From 1948 to 196– a great nation was afraid of this woman." But what generation unborn could possibly be expected to believe that?

[March 15, 1961]

Academic Pride

The administrators of the city colleges have joined in forbidding their students to invite Communists to speak on their campuses. The primary victim of this decree is Benjamin Davis, national secretary of the U. S. Communist Party.

The students are reacting with vigor. This, with all fondness for Ben Davis, could hardly be because they are so desperate to hear his voice. They simply know they are being cheated. Free education is for the underprivileged. Ben Davis can speak at Columbia University any time he is invited. Columbia University is managed by private industry, presumably reactionary. City College is managed by government, self-certifiably progressive. Ben Davis cannot speak at City College. City College students are wards of government; they have no rights. They are smarter than their elders; they protest not for Davis but for themselves.

The municipal college administrators explain their decree in part by saying that it is a function of education to obey the laws of the state and nation. This, of course, is the philosophy upon which Governor Patterson of Alabama expelled the Negro students who protested lunch counter segregation, a law of that state. The administrators also say that the students cannot be trusted to make up their own minds; this is the philosophy which Fidel Castro employed to house-break the University of Havana.

It is a function of government to invent philosophies to explain the demands of its own convenience. The administrators of the city colleges, of course, barred Davis to keep out of trouble, and then looked up a theory of education to justify their own cowardice. Davis had been invited to Queens; that college's Marxist Study Society had publicized his approach loudly enough to bring down the Catholic War Veterans. Public education is a second-class enterprise; the Catholic Church travels first class. The Jesuits bar Communists from their schools because they consider them atheistic and dangerous, but no Jesuit would accept instruction from the Catholic War Veterans. The Jesuits make their own mistakes. The municipal colleges allow free play to any idiot who wants to tell them what to do.

Yet these are great colleges with devoted and creative faculties. They are cursed only by their sense of inferiority; that curse dictates that history will always be harsh to them: City College of New York will be remembered as a great institution which once had a chance to have Bertrand Russell on its faculty and rejected him.

The municipal colleges feel, of course, that they can bar Ben Davis and be permitted thereafter to function without embarrassment. He becomes, by this act of policy, a sort of sacrifice to the ideal of academic freedom. The liberals cast out Davis and so save their own higher function. The Communists exist so we respectable people can point out their differences from ourselves.

But since Ben Davis is flesh and blood, he is no different from me. He has been convicted under an unjust and wicked statute and he has served five years in prison and he is quit; he has gone beyond paying his debt to America; he has paid more than he ever owed in the first place. I shall not degrade him further by discussing his politics. If I can become respectable only by denying that Ben Davis is my brother, then I must die beyond the pale.

We shall come out of all this sometime, and those who are children today will be our judges tomorrow. This may not matter but there is such a thing as pride. Scott Fitzgerald wrote once: "Does anyone think an angel of God appeared to George Washington and suddenly informed him that if he gave up all the allegiances that he had in Virginia and the entire caste to which he had been born, he would become a model hero to all the school children in 1933?" The municipal colleges might, in the usual absence of the angel of God, settle for a little pride.

[November 7, 1961]

The Saddest Story

Geraldine Gray was born in Mississippi and her mother brought her north to Chicago just after the First World War when the great migration began.

She became a Young Communist on the South Side in 1938, and after a year she married Claude Lightfoot, who was a comrade and has now become the Chicago leader of the Communist Party. Last month she died of cancer.

The saddest stories an American could read, if they were printed outside the Communist press, are the accounts of the funerals of American Communists.

I did not know Mrs. Claude Lightfoot, and I cannot report whether she was a good woman. In any case, one would think that those who hated her most, since they hated a Communist stranger more than a real person anyway, might suspend any judgment upon her the day she died.

Geraldine Lightfoot lived all her adult life in South Side Chicago, which is a Southern city. She was a regular communicant of the Mount Hebron Missionary Baptist Church and was buried according to its ritual. Four Negro ministers spoke, along with Benjamin Davis and William Patterson of the American Communist Party. The ministers reported her a good Christian and the party speakers reported her a good Communist. It was an odd mixture, and, at the present stage of our civilization, it may seem impossible that a woman could consider herself a good Christian and a good Communist. Persons expert in the conspiracy may assume that she joined the church as a Communist tactic to fool the South Side. But the South Side is not that easy to fool: she was always a public Communist, and she must have earned the friends who came to her funeral.

Some, of course, were Communists. But most of them seem to have been neighbors and fellow church members. There were three guest books at the funeral parlor and 696 visitors signed their names.

George O. Jones, the funeral director, reported afterwards that a young man, properly identifying himself as a member of the FBI, came to his establishment and asked to see the guest books. As a good citizen, George Jones was anxious to cooperate with generous and majestic government, but he could not. The Chicago police had already picked them up at closing time the night before.

We are all safer today because the Department of Justice has in its files a sheaf of photostats, labeled: "Guests at the wake of one Geraldine Lightfoot." It is not so precious as a Communist Party petition from 1941, but it has its uses.

The FBI and the Chicago police came to the funeral, of course, and took notes while the leader of the church choir gave her testament to Geraldine Lightfoot's virtues. Mrs. Lightfoot was buried in the village of Forest Park; a motorcycle policeman stood at the gate and copied down the license plate of each car that entered. "Maybe," said village Police Chief Joseph L. Cortino, "the FBI and the Chicago Police Department want them." Then Chief Cortino stood at the graveside, his revolver on, and heard the minister's final words and watched the coffin lowered and went back to lesser duties of law enforcement.

And that was a Christian burial in the United States of America, the great bastion of Christianity. In death as in life, a Communist is merely an object for police routine. And just what had that woman done that she and her friends should deserve this at the end? And what have we all done to make it possible for our country not to feel the shame it deserves for that moment?

[June 5, 1962]

II

Circus Animals

The circus animals of our journalism are those scoundrels who have crossed that shadow line beyond which they can no longer hope to sue for libel.

I was led away from the unions by chasing after their circus animals. The first was Joseph P. Ryan, president of the International Longshoremen's Union, then a federation of banditti ruling over peasants. What strikes me in recollection about Joe Ryan is that by the time I came to his pursuit the facts about his union had been set forth in enough volume to leave no excuse for ignorance.

Malcolm Johnson of the old *New York Sun* won a Pulitzer Prize in 1949 for writing everything of substance about Ryan that the Fifties were to proclaim in shock and disgust. Still he went on; and every spring civic leader and gangster sat down together to do him honor. I attended my first Ryan dinner in 1951 and have preserved the guest list — New York's sitting mayor, now a judge, was honorary chairman — because there is a lesson somewhere in it. The mayor knew, or should have been able to smell; the district attorney knew; the AFL could hardly not know; yet the Ryan dinner was a civic tradition and none of them would be the first to abandon it. Then a crime commission investigated Ryan; he crossed the shadow line; there were no more dinners.

I believed then that the labor racketeer — and Ryan is excluded from that general term because he was too slothful to be anything that active — was the servant of business. It seems fairer now to say that business accepted Joe Ryan because it found him when it got there and businessmen are reluctant to change systems that work.

There is a theory, of course, that labor leaders are crooked because crooked industry tempts them, and that businessmen tolerate dishonest labor leaders because they are easier to live with than honest ones. This theory, while comforting, is wrong, not because it underestimates the morality of businessmen but because it overestimates the social indignation of honest labor leaders.

I have, I hope, learned at least enough to know that, should I establish a business and want a labor leader who would not harass me, I should seek out one who was socially responsible and then trust time to make him my junior partner, unpaid.

The scoundrel exposed is otherwise chiefly of interest as a repository of persistent national myths. Dave Beck believed in the American executive. Jimmy Hoffa believes, I'm afraid, in the power of the Mafia; I am sure the Mafia doesn't; Hoffa's fidelity to this misconception is the only evidence I have that there is some innocence intact in him.

The Senate says, of course, that the Mafia controls an important section of our society. But I cannot think this a sincere belief; Congress, in the spirit which enforces the conception of un-American activities, has a duty to express the national faith that all sin is alien.

I also learned what I should have known already. There is a myth that hoodlums are romantic; they are in fact as narrow, as dull and mean-spirited as ordinary people. (One has to except Frank Costello, who cherishes the myth of the gentleman.) They are also not terribly important, excepting of course Jimmy Hoffa, to the ceremony of whose public exposure we owe a President, an Attorney General and, by extension, a junior Senator from Massachusetts.

Mixture as Before

The Joseph P. Ryan Association, unblushing, unlaundered and un-bowed, held its annual spring gambol Saturday night. There are, thank the Lord, some institutions still proof to the ravages of reform.

Present were Police Commissioner Monaghan and Fire Commis-sioner Grumet and New York County Republican Chairman Curran. The association is bipartisan; it is also, if there's such a word, bi-legal.

The master of ceremonies was Phil Regan, the chanteur, who last exhibited the social dexterity required of a pillar of our association by arranging an assignation between Jersey City's Mayor Kenny and mobster Tony Bender.

Manhattan Borough President Wagner was chairman of the ar-rangements committee and enjoyed the assistance of such model con-stituents as Michael Climenti, a convicted bootlegger, and Austin Furey, a Ryan lieutenant once unfrocked by the AFL Teamsters for conduct unbecoming even to them and a man of such keen social perception that a Brooklyn chippie once had him unsuccessfully in-dicted for breaking her jaw and breaching her honor in the same eve-ning.

Tammany Hall's Carmine DeSapio was vice chairman of the recep-tion committee; his assistants included Jimmy Clifford, a convicted bank robber. An anchor of the entertainment committee was Willie Cox whose capacity for innocent enjoyment was especially marked on the evening long ago when he used his dentures to denude a friend of his right ear.

It must have been an occasion of more than social interest to the Police Commissioner. For the guest list included Jerry Anastasia, mas-ter of the pier from which the Schuster gun was snatched; Tony Cheese Marchitto, the reform president of Jersey City Longshore Local 1247, who is currently under indictment for assault; and, ac-cording to unconfirmed rumor, one Jay Sullivan, now facing trial for interrupting a barroom discussion to work two disputants over with a baseball bat.

Another guest, warmly greeted by a host of fellow-celebrants, was William Ackalitis, brother of Albert, the most amiable assassin of them all. Albert was recently released from Dannemora and his urge to improve himself is a subject of some trepidation to the association's weaker brethren. While Albert was ravening in the bucket, his brother Bill was his transmission belt to the docks and is thus a man difficult to snub.

Social tolerance is not the Ryan dinner's only virtue. For one thing there are no speeches, and jugglers and Irish reelers are a conspicuous improvement over William Green. The menu is unvaryingly sumptuous and solid; it always features sliced roast beef as thick as Ryan's hand and a dessert called *bombe praline*, a somewhat tactless bit of nomenclature for the Jersey City delegates but a superb confection all the same.

Ryan is not a man to change his sense of the proper and the decent. For years now, the association has gone on printing a guest list blending the lawful and the larcenous, and it proceeds that way unashamed. Old Joe has lost a few judges and all his district attorneys with the years; but he has kept his borough presidents. He even has a governor of the Stock Exchange and a sometime acting mayor, City Council Majority Leader Sharkey.

When your agent left, Ryan was sitting in his dinner jacket with the fine needlework on the cuffs watching the jugglers, at home among his friends, be they the Police Commissioner or Jerry Anastasia. Time and his enemies have not shaken him; neither the jitters nor the sense of sin is at his back; the years will go on and every spring they will troop loyally to honor him. He will, I suspect, survive you and me, a huge invulnerable god of brass.

Another guest was Sanitation Commissioner Mulrain. He was, I am sorry to say, obviously not there in any professional capacity.

[April 28, 1952]

Friendship

Mike Clemente is a longshoremen's labor leader — "pier hoodlum" is, I believe, the word favored in even the more conservative prints. John W. McGrath is an employer of longshoremen, a solid citizen, the past president of the National Association of Stevedores.

Mike Clemente began life carrying bananas on the East River piers with intervals of what he calls "trouble," the most serious being a 1943 conviction for bootlegging. In the last ten years, Mike has come to be something of a figure on the East River; his Local 856 is a well-managed affair by ILA standards and his longshoremen like him.

John W. McGrath and his family started life on a shoestring and they have also prospered mightily. McGrath is a realist; and he has borne the code of the waterfront with notable fortitude and no little profit. His West Side piers are under the sway of the waterfront's least restrained mobsters. When he was competing for a municipal pier lease in Jersey City, he admits being sophisticated enough to understand that local custom required him to pay off Mayor Kenny's son-in-law and to spend over $5,000 entertaining the Mayor and other Jersey statesmen.

Mike Clemente knows a lot of people; his list of acquaintances includes an unashamed mixture of priests and mobsters; he will do a favor for anyone. He helped his friend Albert Anastasia find a job for his brother Tony; he is a pillar in the fund-raising efforts of the church across the street. But best of all, he likes Jack McGrath.

Mike Clemente doesn't talk about it but the District Attorney knows that McGrath and Clemente used to have breakfast at Schrafft's and lunch at the Downtown Athletic Club regularly. Mike likes to mix his friends and once he made a luncheon date for Mc-Grath with C. Don Modica, the professor who tutored Willie Moretti's children. In this business, it is best to touch all bases.

In recent years, John W. McGrath has done well on the East Side and being assured of pleasant relations with Mike Clemente could hardly be a handicap. They are friends; they eat together and they go to each other's houses. But Mike Clemente hasn't got a very good name; he has a record; and he is, as he says, very good copy for the papers. I would not argue that he is without sin, but he makes a very nice fall guy.

On Sunday morning, the District Attorney indicted Mike Clemente for extorting $100 a week from John W. McGrath, an employer. They came to get Mike just as he was about to go to church; the cops wanted him right away.

It wasn't very easy for Mike to believe that it would come to this, but least of all could he believe that his friend John W. McGrath had gone to the District Attorney and complained about him. But it was there in the paper Monday morning with suitable compliments to McGrath as a friend of a better moral code on the waterfront.

There should, Hogan said, be more stevedores like McGrath; if there were, there'd be less crime on the waterfront. Mike Clemente went down to his dusty South Street office as usual, a full-faced man with a face of untrammeled innocence wearing his double-breasted brown suit of neat and unobtrusive weave, walking the streets he loves.

They talk about me, he said, like I was the Al Capone of the East Side. Mike Clemente, always Mike Clemente; Mike Clemente's good copy, so they write about him and bring him to this, where his children would rather not go to school.

But there was, he said, one consolation. Jack McGrath had called up that morning and said that he hoped Mike didn't believe what he had read in the papers. He hoped Mike understood that it wasn't so and that Mike was still his friend, and Mike answered that he would rather know that Jack felt that way than anything else.

I cannot argue whether the Clementes and the Florios and all the other fall guys belong in jail. But where were John McGrath and all the other respectable folks before the heat was on? Living with the system and liking it.

Hello Mike, hello sucker. Merry Christmas, with all my heart.

[December 24, 1952]

Solidarity Forever

Joseph Fay, fourth vice president of the International Brotherhood of Operating Engineers (AFL), went to Sing Sing for seven years in 1947. He was convicted, after years of substance and non-interference, of shaking down two building contractors for $180,000.

He was, and is, the Grand Panjandrum of all labor skates, and any poor fish any crime commission ever nets will be a minnow beside him. He was also convicted of peddling labor peace — an act of treason in the labor movement. But it loves him still.

Joseph Fay, Sing Sing SSP number 106-825, was visited in his cell by the following persons, all identifying themselves as "friends," between February 20, 1948 and June 22, 1951:

Richard J. Gray, president of the Building Trades Department of the American Federation of Labor, adviser to President-elect Eisenhower, and a close also-ran for the office of Secretary of Labor.

John V. Kenny, mayor of Jersey City.

Meyer Ellenstein, former mayor of Newark, identified as "attorney."

Thomas A. Murray, president of the New York State Federation of Labor.

Joseph Madden, business agent of the Jersey City Common Laborers and an anti-Kenny candidate for sheriff of Hudson County.

William De Koning, president of the Nassau County Central Trades and Labor Council.

Frazier Holtzlohner, then president of the Newark Building Trades (AFL).

Louis P. Marciante, president of the New Jersey State Federation of Labor.

Frank J. O'Connor, international representative of the AFL painters union for New Jersey.

To gain admittance to Fay's presence, the aforementioned and a dozen lesser AFL officials signed their names in the warden's book as "friend." Neither the frequency of any man's visits nor their purpose is, of course, available from the Sing Sing record.

The presumption is that, in a number of cases, they were simply not turning their backs on a fallen friend, although a man convicted of selling strike insurance is a special kind of friend for a labor leader to retain. But there are also indications that not all these visits were entirely social; Joe Fay is a man with many active interests; imprisonment might confine him; it could hardly immobilize him.

Fay can still transact a little business, if Mayor Kenny can be believed. The mayor visited Sing Sing and saw Fay right in the middle of his 1951 primary campaign. When the State Crime Commission taxed him with this fact, Kenny said that he had just run into Fay while he was there on another errand. The mayor confessed himself mystified by the commission's information that he had signed in to see Fay and that he had spent two hours with him. "First time I ever spoke to the man in my life," said Kenny.

Kenny said that he might have spent three or four minutes with Fay. That was enough to throw an interesting sidelight on our lost leader's visitor roster.

Fay told Kenny that just the other day one William Ackalitis, of an AFL longshoremen's checkers' local, had come to see him about Jersey. Kenny was keeping his brother Albert — the assassin — out of Jersey City, William had complained. Fay just thought he'd mention it.

Fay also told Kenny that he had just seen or would soon see Joe Madden, AFL leader and pro-Hague candidate for Hudson County sheriff. He would, Fay volunteered, tell Madden to stay out of politics.

For a visitation to a crypt, a call on Joe Fay would seem to contain an abnormally high quotient of businesslike chatter about the here and now. Any problems, fellow worker? Take them to Sing Sing SSP number 106-825.

[December 30, 1952]

In His Fashion

They threw Joe Ryan to the mastiffs last week; all the respectable people he calls by their first names: William J. McCormack, his best friend, and the shipowners he served so long.

Joe was an expensive bauble for the longshoremen; in six years he took no less than $200,000 from them in salary, expenses and tips. But he came very cheap for McCormack, the most powerful employer in the port of New York.

"Joe Ryan don't cost Bill McCormack much," a fallen waterfront racket guy said. "He gets him with a smile and a little Christmas present."

Friday morning, in his own darkening hour, Bill McCormack showed the door to poor Joe Ryan as to an old hound gone in the teeth. Joe had believed that McCormack was his best friend but McCormack told the State Crime Commission different. He had been to Joe's house, but Joe hadn't been to his. Joe had asked him about the problems of his union; but Bill had never stooped to ask Joe's help in his business.

He had put Joe up for membership in the Winged Foot Golf Club; the vision of Joe lifting his cloudy eyes across the fairways of Westchester would not down all day. And he had been chairman of the annual Joseph P. Ryan dinner, but hadn't been active for five or six years now.

And on Thursday morning, for the shipowners, John V. Lyon, redolent of sanctity, had blamed all the mess on Joe Ryan's union, and said, in effect, that since the present company union had become an embarrassment, the SCC should be careful to put another company union in its place.

And Friday Joe Ryan was a better man than those he had served. For there were men who had served him and were now in odorous repute; but Joe did not turn *his* back on the Ed McGraths and the Eddie Florios and the other bandits he had protected so long.

Time and self-indulgence have turned old Joe into a ravaged monument with a patina of old brandy patches, but shame will never bow that head. The SCC walloped him for three hours; counsel Theodore Kiendl asked him whether he had checked Ed McGrath's record for grand larceny when he hired him as an organizer.

"No, sir," said Ryan, the great face a mass of righteous indignation at the suggestion that he, Joe Ryan, could have done his duty.

Ed Florio was as much his friend before he was convicted of extortion. Kiendl asked him whether he had known that Florio was an old bootlegger when he hired him. "No, sir," roared Joe. "I violated the prohibition law myself."

Judge Proskauer finally asked him please to answer the question. Joe Ryan turned to Proskauer with the warmest of smiles. "I guess you think I'm an earbender, don't you, Judge?"

Kiendl asked him about Alex DiBrizzi, the bookmaker's runner who owns the Staten Island docks, and Joe said, "They got production down there; any employer will come up and tell you." He knows, if the commission doesn't, the respect due a union man who does his duty to the bosses.

Then, very late in the afternoon, Kiendl turned to the union's secret anti-Communist fund, administered by Ryan himself and financed by contributions from employers. In six years, Kiendl said, Joe's private journal showed he had withdrawn $48,725.18 to fight the Bolsheviks in ways like these:

Golf club charges, $2,331.60; personal insurance premiums, $10,-774.85; repairs to Cadillac, $942.30; cruise to Guatemala, $460.00;

shirts from Sulka's, $222.00; a luncheon at the Stork Club, then anti-
union, $546.15.

Kiendl asked him whether constant attendance upon the barricades
required him to buy his shirts at Sulka's, and old Joe — convicted out
of his own mouth of gluttony, sloth and every other sin of omission
— smiled and said, "You ought to allow me a few vices."

The weight of his vices would have crushed anybody else; and Joe
Ryan walked out carrying them like a feather. He stood before the
cameramen, the pale gray fedora set forward on his head, a friendly
smile on his face, waiting. He may be false to a lot of things; but say
of him this at least: He is true to himself and to his own.

[February 2, 1953]

The Forces of Light

Tony Anastasia, the little shepherd of Erie Basin, stood on a Brooklyn
sidewalk outside his club last night and watched his flock march in to
hear him proclaim their emancipation.

He was wearing high-draped pants, a soft pale green shirt and
brown suede shoes and was smoking a costly cigaret; no person of
vaster social graces has taken upon himself the burdens of the toilers
since Corliss Lamont's first trip to Russia.

He waved his hand at the crowd of longshoremen around him and
said, "They're the bosses; they're the people who got to elect their
own officials. If they want me to, I'll resign my job in five minutes. So
will the other officers."

He paused and turned to push at one of his bosses.

"All right," he said. "All right. Get over everybody, get over to the
other side of the street."

A new inner light may fill your stomach, but it is hard to revise the
habits of twenty-five years. The heart of Tony Anastasia bubbles with
love for the enchained, but they had better move along when he tells
them the first time.

Tony had called the Brooklyn longshoremen together to proclaim
a peaceful, legal and ineffably holy war on Joseph P. Ryan. The little
shepherd believes that any man, even a former material witness in the
Murder, Inc., case, has the right to be a reformer. A few weeks ago he

had quit his $12,000-a-year job as a Jarka hiring boss, and got himself elected business agent of an AFL dock local with the proclaimed intention of freeing all the Brooklyn longshoremen from the grip of corruption, insecurity and gangster rule.

"I gave my life voluntarily to God," continued Tony, a man not subject to coercion even from the Almighty. "In my mind I never was with the company. My heart was with labor. These men need somebody able to risk his life. I live and die for labor."

Ryan, of course, has enough trouble with reformers of every description, let alone Tony's. He had warned the Anastasia group to quit their union jobs or face forcible ejection. Then he softened up and let it be known that peace was possible. But last night Tony called his troops together to tell them that he would stand or die, that it was him or Ryan and that, if Ryan did not yield, he would "proclaim the independence of the port of Brooklyn."

Maybe seventy-five loyalists stood around the platform Tony had put up outside his Court Street headquarters; another thousand longshoremen stood across the street, silent and obviously neutral. Anastasia's fellow business agent in the reform administration in Local 527-1 is a huge young fellow named Charley Bananas, who once beat a murder rap.

Tony himself was so busy holding up the dazzling mirror of his soul for the attendant press that Charley Bananas had to take over the assignment of shoving the guests across the street, which he did with sufficient vigor to leave the doubtful assured that a reform business agent pushes you just as hard as an unregenerate one.

The assemblage was greeted at last by Joseph Pepito, counsel for Tony Anastasia, who explained the background of this struggle for decency and principle in the conduct of the ILA's affairs.

"You are tired," Pepito cried, "of being ruled by thugs and goons and the fact that your union has been an eyesore in the labor movement . . . determined to clean up the waterfront . . . [to remove] the shapeup system with its inherent evils . . . your future and your children's future."

The State Crime Commission and a Senate committee, Pepito shuddered, had both proclaimed the shame of the docks and condemned the ILA's decadent officials.

Jerry Anastasia stood beside the platform; when Pepito mentioned

"Mr. Anthony Anastasia," he and Tony led off the extended applause from close in. Across the street there was silence.

After a while, the chairman said that he would "now introduce to you our leader," and Tony stood up.

"If I live or die," he said, "I'm determined to clean up the waterfront.

"As for Ryan," he said, "we'll make the punk die of a broken heart. For years he has kept the Negroes and the Italians slaves." And, if Ryan chooses to fight, "I will declare the independence of the union in the port of Brooklyn.

"We don't need nobody. We don't need Joe Ryan . . . this is your local . . . I'd like to hear one voice from you people . . . I want you to believe that I am very very proud and that I will fight to the end."

There was a sudden, shocking sense that he believed it. Tony Anastasia has been a strikebreaker; he is the favored brother of Albert Anastasia, a multiple assassin; he is a brawler and a gambler and a jungle animal. The name Anastasia is like Cain; whatever Tony does, the headlines have only to print it and conjure up nameless, infinite crimes.

But he is not a confidence man; he cannot say words that he does not mean. And he would stand his ground — almost alone. Pepito had announced in advance that all the Brooklyn locals would be there to back him up, but only one of them showed up. The army of ten thousand of the outraged oppressed he conjured up was a shadow, but he would stand and assert the feudal right of an Anastasia to be the Grand High Reformer if the hour of reform had come.

The chairman called for a resolution. Someone in the crowd moved "that all our —" and then stopped in confusion having forgotten his script. The chairman finished for him; the brother had obviously intended to move that the local pledge its officials, its fortune and its honor for justice, honesty and the fight to the death against corruption. It has been so long since a rank-and-filer has had a chance to make a motion in Brooklyn that you could hardly expect him to avoid an attack of lockjaw.

[July 28, 1953]

Monkey on His Back

Marcel Proust says somewhere that passion, whichever way it takes, is the only truly interesting subject. If a man leaves his wife because he is in love with a bus conductor, that, Proust says, is a love story like any other, and should be measured for its passion and not for its deviation from convention.

To sit all day here listening to the tangled, tawdry financial affairs of Dave Beck is to think of Balzac and his obsessed collectors. There is a novel in Dave Beck as there was a novel in the Baron de Charlus. The mere promise of a $100 bill acted upon this man as the love dream worked on Tristan and Isolde. He was consumed by passion; you can no more fit his story into any consideration of labor racketeering than you could fit the troubles of Hart Crane into the framework of an armed services committee investigation of morals in the Brooklyn Navy Yard.

We deal here with a vast unrequited love. I am convinced, by hunch alone, that Dave Beck is broke as every man who risks all for love ends up with nothing.

The truly passionate are little boys. In 1947, when Dave Beck was at the onset of his affair with the monetary system, he acquired a Seattle financial adviser named Fred Loomis. Loomis is a spare man, with his own passion for the financial realities and for caution and propriety. His advice had as much effect on Beck as a Seagram's exhortation to moderation has on me.

Loomis remembers the frequent occasions he told Beck that it was time to devote himself to "simplifying his financial operations and get out of his business and clear his debts." In 1952 Beck signalized his election to the presidency of the Teamsters and assumption of trust for its treasury by entering into a working arrangement with Don Herlund, a Seattle mortgage broker, to handle the union's real estate investments.

Loomis had heard that Beck proposed to become Herlund's partner in National Mortgage for a share of the profits from its transactions with the Teamsters. Loomis says he reminded Beck that he was in a fiduciary position and that the responsibility of a trustee is extremely high.

The lawyer who wrote Paul Gauguin to come back from Paris and the art warrens and support his family must have been a reasonable man like Fred Loomis. After five years, Loomis heard that Dave Beck had taken $2,500 personally to approve a $2,000,000 Teamsters loan to build an apartment in Honolulu. Loomis wrote in deep shock and announced his resignation.

Beck, like any victim of an obsession, made a pathetic effort to tell Loomis, who represented respectability to him, that he was at worst a man who could take it or leave it alone.

In 1953, after one Loomis appeal to him to come home, Beck wrote an answer which was a model of the self-deception of the possessed. He said that he would not be in National Mortgage as a partner; "it would be in another name.

"I repeat," he said then in a horrible echo of Sam Gompers, "that I can see no valid objection to our rewarding our friends with our business instead of just acquaintances . . . It [the treasury] has to go through some broker, so the Int. Union is not injured, whether it be through Don's associates or some other mortgage company."

It was pleasant for a change to find that Fred Loomis rather liked Beck still; we had spent the morning with the Anheuser-Busch officials, who had granted Beck a plush distributorship and who retained the animus dope pushers have for free-loading addicts. In 1947, Beck, as a sachem in the union which bargains for more Anheuser employes than any other, had convinced the company to give his son — apparently a dummy in the word's full sense — the Washington distributorship for Budweiser.

He began with a great splash, announcing that Governor Wallgren "is one hundred per cent with us" and bullying the *Seattle Post-Intelligencer* into putting a model of the brewer's big horses atop its building.

As ever, his promises were delusive. The Budweiser salesmen reported Dave Beck, Jr., "an overgrown small boy," was taking an extortionary cut of the Alaska sales figures, and generally botching the business. By 1950, the firm was casting desperately around for some way to get out without incurring the rancor of "his majesty, the wheel." That year, there was some hope that a man named Dewey Busch could take over the Tacoma distributorship and "that the

Becks will lose interest in the operation due to the comparatively small return and will decide to sell."

That didn't work out, and by 1954, John C. Wilson, executive vice president of Bud, was willing to pay $80,000 to buy Beck out entirely. It was, Wilson confessed unhandsomely, an abnormal relationship with a distributor. One needs the goodwill of union officials, bankers, security underwriters; "it doesn't pay to antagonize anyone."

And all the rewards were not one-sided. In January, 1954, Anheuser-Busch's new plant in Los Angeles was threatened with a building trades jurisdictional fight. Wilson went to bus.ness associate Beck for "advice." He got a good deal more than that, judging from the telegram of reply Beck sent: "Our People in LA working hard on your situation. There will be no tie-up."

The brewers who used him and Loomis, who liked him, are alike unhelpful on the character of this victim of passion. He was gouging Anheuser in 1947; Loomis does not remember the face of rapacity until 1954.

"He was compartmented, I guess. One person knew just so much. He was an adept at keeping straight the differences in what he said." The old skill of the obsessed. "But I remember telling my wife in 1954 that there had been a change of personality. The fun had gone out of him." The monkey was all the way on his back.

[Washington, D.C., May 10, 1957]

The Man Who Knew Jim Duff

The adjective "jaunty" seldom runs its course in our language unaccompanied by the adverb "pathetically," and, with that understanding, let it be noted that Dave Beck was especially jaunty when he came to run his course before the Senate yesterday.

He arrived fifteen minutes early, fairly reeking greed for the cameras, accompanied by a long, melancholy reed of a lawyer named Arthur Condon, who looked so expensive and so genteel that one might have thought that this was Ruggles and poor Beck some Western butcher who had won him as butler in a poker game.

He stood for a long time indulging the photographers, his china-blue eyes like a doll's at F.A.O. Schwartz's, his air the hollow empty geniality that is the shabby cloak left over from the days when he was taken seriously as a man of affairs.

He is sixty-three years old, yet his skin is untouched by sun, wind, or experience; the hair of his eyebrows is like the hair on a three-month-old baby. The years show only in his chin, which was unpromising in his prime and is withering now; his neck is almost ravaged; he has the face of a middle-aged midget.

There sat upon him a dreadful parody of assurance; if it had been anyone but Beck, I would have thought him fortified with juice. The brave posture did not survive the day. A fellow reduced to taking the Fifth Amendment as to whether he'd snitched $14 from the petty cash fund to buy himself a custom-made tie has taken himself beyond the protections of the libel statutes.

The story of Dave Beck is above all an American story, and it must be said of him that he has come to the shadows a true American, who loved his Constitution and its Bill of Rights more when he needed them than when he didn't.

His lawyer carried an obscenely swollen briefcase which was identified as the personal financial records the committee wanted; Beck refused to hand them over. John McClellan leaned — the very embodiment of Salem — across the table and asked the president of the International Brotherhood of Teamsters if he believed in his heart that "if you made those records available, they would reflect information which would incriminate you."

"Yes," said Dave Beck after a while, "I think very definitely." He had hired former United States Senator James Duff as his counsel, and he seems to have thought in his innocence that the name of this bit of clay was a magic spell. Poor Duff did not lend his presence but Beck cited Duff as authority for his position all morning on occasions countless but running upwards of seventy-five.

Beck said that the Senate of the United States should be the last body on earth to infringe on Constitutional rights, and "impugn upon" the motives of any patriotic American and that "there are millions of American citizens as good as you and I," and as spokesman for these heresies he reiterated the name of James Duff. Dave Beck has shown us the way to make the Senate conscious of the glories of the Bill of Rights: first beat a Senator, and then give him a fee from a wealthy victim of the inquisition.

Even so, it was an awful degradation for Dave Beck to take the Fifth. He began citing the first three articles of the Constitution of the United States to the effect that the Senate was without jurisdiction in these matters, which amounted to an assertion that the minimum-wage law is unconstitutional. McClellan stripped that from him; and with Condon tugging at his elbow, Beck finally switched to a dreary euphemism, and then, when the prospect of going to jail for contempt was set before him, turned the color of marbled chuck steak too long in the heat of the day and settled for: "I refuse to give testimony against myself and invoke the Fifth Amendment."

Poor Beck has only one method of debate, which is to come as close as possible to apoplectic seizure, and he exercised that terrifying talent as far as he needed to yesterday afternoon; he was still baying himself purple when counsel Robert Kennedy set him down and asked the chairman to call one Nathan Shefferman, and there was a sudden sense of how well Kennedy has done his homework.

Shefferman is a labor relations man, whose clients are all employers; he began with the Labor Board in 1939 and has so many customers now that he cannot remember whether there are 150 or 200. He has twenty assistants servicing them, which leaves him free to roam the country with Dave Beck.

His function, Shefferman said with piety, is "bringing about more wholesome relations between labor and management." This pursuit of the Holy Grail, according to the files of the Senate investigating committee, occasionally involves bringing strikebreakers through picket lines, a holy work in which the friendship of the Teamsters is occasionally valuable.

We had been transported to a better world. This was obviously a man who would not lower himself to steal $14 from any treasury. Dave Beck is, said Shefferman, attentive to his friends and generous to his folks.

Shefferman had also helped the Teamsters, for $61,000, to set up a new bookkeeping system, which on the record of these hearings is not recommended for wider use. In 1950, grateful for a better America and mindful that he had reached a higher tax bracket, Nate Shefferman decided that Dave Beck was "entitled" to some reward. He gave him $24,500.

Dave Beck had ended his day in extreme indignation over the suggestion that he resign as a vice president of the AFL-CIO. He stood up now and put on his hat. The smile was as intact as the misty marble blue of the eyes; he was observed in jaunty progress towards the new $11,000,000 headquarters — decorating consultant Nathan Shefferman — of the Teamsters Union. He does not know what he has done or what it has done to him.

[Washington, D.C., March 27, 1957]

Snapping the Leash

There is a raging tiger inside every man whom God puts upon this earth. Every man worthy of the respect of his children spends his life building inside himself a cage to pen that tiger in. There is this raging tiger inside Jimmy Hoffa and he has never thought of his duty to build a cage for it.

He and the mob he is leading to its own damnation here this week are brothers because they have no interior moral curbs. They have to hire lawyers to explain just what might appear to the public to be proper conduct. Jimmy Hoffa's lawyers convinced him Tuesday night that he might be considered, by some outsider among the army of his persecutors, to have observed the shell of proper procedure if he forced his mob to listen to the bill of particulars on his sins filed by the executive committee of the AFL-CIO.

And so Dave Beck was deputed to shock everybody present yesterday afternoon by announcing that the findings of the ethical practices committee would now be intoned by the reading clerk.

The reading clerk was Lawrence Steinberg, president of the Toledo Teamsters. As he arose to do his dreadful office, there were a few dull boos and Jimmy Hoffa shook his head as a signal that they should take this dose, if not with grace, at least without overt demonstration of the beast within them. And so they sat while Steinberg read the indictment. Afterwards, three Hoffa delegates came up and told him that he ought to be ashamed of himself because he read the findings of their sins aloud carefully enough to be audible to anyone who might have been listening and thus had committed the objective treason of communicating the truth about this pack of thieves in open convention.

It was an occasion of horror that cannot be communicated. Dave Beck sat through the recital of his various affronts to the most minimum moral code with his eyes on the middle distance. It was obvious that nothing could be said about him which would touch any spark to glow faintly with the impulse to arise and tell the delegates what he had done with the money. They didn't care and he didn't; they knew he had stolen it.

Jimmy Hoffa sat there with his storms all over his face, maintaining his vigilance against the spontaneous reaction of some proud friend of his who might throw a chair at the innocent Steinberg. When Steinberg read off the minor thieveries of his good friend Bert Brennan, shortly to be anointed a vice president, Bert Brennan smirked. Most of the delegates looked at the floor, their square paper Hoffa hats on their heads, their Hoffa placards between their legs.

In the middle of the ordeal, one Joe McCarthy of Boston demanded that this monstrous comedy cease and that Steinberg sit down and everything he had said up to that point be wiped from the record. Dave Beck ruled out of order this statement of the majority, and thereafter such persons as were too sensitive for further endurance began arising to walk out in the free air.

The rest writhed like children forced through a concession to good manners. When poor Steinberg expired, Weldon L. Mathis, of Atlanta, arose boiling with outrage to say this un-American document must be stricken from the record of this convention.

A delegate named Bolling demanded that the delegates be given this chance to express their belief in the integrity of Vice President Hoffa. He did not mention Dave Beck, who stood there without a shred of pride to assert his protest. Mike Singer, of the milk drivers, demanded that we vote our thanks to our "wonderful executives."

Tom Haggerty of Chicago, who is running against Hoffa, stood up to ask for the floor. Dave Beck looked desperately around for someone else to recognize. He picked out a young man with glasses who radiated the impossibility that he could ever damage anybody.

The delegate said that he was from Oakland, California, and that his name was Jeffrey Cohelan. And then he teased the animals and they boiled from their paper cage and ran riot before all witnesses.

This, said Jeffrey Cohelan, was a matter which this convention was charged with investigating. Locals have passed resolutions demanding that something be done. His own local had written the executive board and gotten no reply. "If we do this thing now, we stand indicted before the country."

The word "indicted" woke Dave Beck the way some key phrase arouses a sleepwalker. He screeched to Jeffrey Cohelan to be fair. The mob moved and pitched and bellowed, and Jeffrey Cohelan stood there, alone in the possession of his dignity. You and I have seen that face; its glory is imperishable in our memories. It is the face of the colored child who walks through a crowd of the sort of people who come to a Southern high school to shout "nigger" at children. I do not say this to make propaganda against a majority of the delegates to this convention; I am past caring. I say it only because there is no other way to describe this scene with precision; the largest union in America is in the hands of people indistinguishable from the Kluxers who carry their hates to Southern high schools on the day of integration. I assume the mob at Little Rock was worse, but the mob at Nashville was hardly as bad.

I am glad that I am no lawyer condemned to advise people on the appearance of decency. It is an appearance that can only be sustained by people who accept a minimum standard of proper conduct out of the sense that somewhere an avenging God is watching. These people have no such sense. To advise them to go on parade is to risk full exposure of the animal in them. Their instinct against proper behavior is so unbounded as to explode against any suggestion of restraint. To ask them to behave is to make them worse. Yesterday, Jimmy Hoffa attempted a piece of hypocrisy, and succeeded only in showing the face of what is more hideous than ever before. I would strongly suggest that his advisers counsel no more parades.

[Miami Beach, Florida, October 3, 1957]

Hail and Good-By

An observer — by now a violently detached observer — was wandering the floor of the Teamsters convention in the dying moments of waiting for the cab that would carry him to an airport and someplace where children smile and mothers complain.

It was over for him. Dave Beck was burbling at the microphone. But it was all past tense; the screw could be turned no tighter; nothing could touch or shock the sensibilities any further. These people and their damnation were less a fact than a memory; they were only a bitter thought.

Ed Woods of the *St. Louis Post-Dispatch* said good-by. He envied anyone, he said, in a position to escape. "After all," he finished, "it's all over but the looting."

And then the voice of Dave Beck penetrated the callus of the sensibilities. He said he had raised the salaries of his organizers higher than they had ever been before. When he came in, Beck said, there had been no welfare plan for labor skates. "Now," he said, the staff has a "marvelous welfare plan." By God, we had come at last to the dying declaration. Dave Beck was justifying his stewardship. The departing chairman of the board was telling his associates that, despite all criticism from the stockholders and the public, he had served the directors well.

Even to talk of Dave Beck, let alone make fun of him, is an act of necrophilia for which I apologize. But he began as a laundry driver forty years ago; he is a brother, by equity if nothing else, of the Ludlow martyrs and the bearded men who walked the streets of Flint. And he was saying farewell to the fraternity of the toilers and remembering the great moments that made him proud.

"I have had," he told them, "a little experience in finance." When he began in 1952, the union had a poor investment picture. It is always necessary to protect the liquidity position, of course. But the debt market can create situations where it is less important to consider liquidity positions than earning power of collateral. Of course this policy occasionally produced flecks in the big picture and — the phrase recurred in what was to come — "moments of temporary financial stringency." These had occurred, but they were tiny clouds on an endlessly unfolding horizon. And he said that if anyone present doubted Dave Beck's service, "Just take back what I have said and ask your banker about it." Before you judge the retiring president of our largest union, don't ask a priest, don't ask a truck driver; ask a banker.

He went on to explain those loans to Teamsters locals for the building of Byzantine palaces. They had occasionally jumped salty; there had been those periods of "temporary financial stringency." But these were, he said, "the finest facilities"; the mortgages were "solid as a rock." They may say I took the petty cash box with me, but by God, no man shall criticize the portfolio I left behind me. Dave Beck, after forty years in labor, stood — and almost wept as he stood — on the judgment of your banker.

When it was over, there was a dreadful moment while Dave Beck said he would get out of the way right away to let his successor, whoever he may be, take over at once. Perhaps the convention would be kind enough to let him take a leave of absence. Whoever his successor may be, in this case James R. Hoffa, made the motion to grant Beck a leave of absence, and mumbled a few graceless words of formal appreciation.

One wishes somehow that Jimmy Hoffa could find in himself a little mercy and Dave Beck a little sense of sin. There remained, ridiculous as it seemed to any reasonable imagination after the last week, a further turn of the screw in these two moral lepers; something compelled them to prove that James Hoffa could learn nothing from triumph at the very moment when Dave Beck was showing that he had learned nothing from disaster.

So it ended. At moments of revolutionary terror, one can be consoled only by satisfaction with the posture of its victims. Dave Beck was being devoured by his children, and his last words were that he remained — the phrase is his — "an A-number-one credit risk."

You can judge a man by the manner of his passing. As the visitor stood there, emptier than even he could ever have thought he could be, Frank Brewster came over to say the good-bys. "Would you fellows check up on me too hard," he said with a smile, "if I borrowed a little money from my local to buy some placards to run again for vice president?" He will run just to defy Jimmy Hoffa, even though he knows he will lose. Here at the end, he will lift — if he can find the cash — his banner of the Imperial Guard.

He was saying, I suppose, stay awhile, and see how a marshal of France dies. He was thinking, there at the end, not of his future but of his past, of the ashes of his fathers and the altars of his gods. The visitor stood in the rubble of that battlefield, and saw, not Frank Brewster, but General Cambronne forming the remnant of the Imperial Guard.

"Mr. Brooster," said the visitor — Frank Brewster smiled at the reminiscence of Bobby Kennedy's pronunciation — "steal what you need if you can, and, if you can't, send the bill to your grandchildren. What your memory will be to them is a thing worth paying for. If I could be here tomorrow, I, who will never march in a convention parade again, would stand and march one last time under any standard you raise." So long, Frank Brewster, so long, soldier. And, otherwise, farewell the sewer.

[Washington, D.C., October 4, 1957]

The Professor

It is hard to believe all this talk about our new national respect for the intellectual, what with C. Donald Modica idle in Hasbrouck Heights with no responsibilities for the life of the mind beyond shopping for his wife.

For poor Don Modica's is the odyssey of the intellectual in America, a constant series of bookings on ships that are wrecked. The last rock upon which he broke was that ultimate enemy of all inquiring minds, the state.

He was educational director of the Greater New York Cartmen's Association when the McClellan Committee called him last November. Before that he was best known as private tutor to Albert Anastasia's children.

The Greater New York Cartmen's Association is an agency for gouging the public with the assistance of the Teamsters Union. It has been described by Senator McClellan as a $50,000,000-a-year racket; as house intellect, Don Modica was on a salary of $100 a week. The intellectual's share was thus under the Medicis and always will be.

Modica was sent to the Cartmen's Association by Albert Anastasia, who counted it as part of his estate. He entertained the promise that, as watchdog for Anastasia, he might have a real part in making history, and, in the wistful hope that it could be a demonstration of his moral authority and accessibility to power, Modica set up a blackboard in the office where visiting cartmen might glimpse him teaching calculus to Albert Anastasia, Jr.

Jimmy Squillante, Anastasia's surrogate as director of the cartmen's shake, always referred to Modica as "the professor" or "the pro." He thought it, we may assume, a term of respect; it was, of course, a man of action's term of contempt for the intellectual; you can judge a society by the way its enemies ape its standards in caricature.

Long before he took the Fifth Amendment before the McClellan Committee and thus rendered himself unemployable, Don Modica had been shoved aside by Jimmy Squillante. In 1953, when he undertook the assignment, he addressed the membership of the Cartmen's Association on the subject:

"The three E's—education, engineering, and enforcement."

By 1956, Squillante, as man of action, had taken over all the enforcement and engineering, thank you, and left Don Modica with the education. This is a traditional experience with intellectuals in the labor movement, but it is always a shock in individual cases.

He was permitted to edit the cartmen's journal: *The Hired Broom.* The hopes, dreams and visions in this project are best described by the title of its lead editorial of October, 1956: "Out of Garbage There Grows a Rose."

Jimmy Squillante was, of course, not in the rose-planting business. Modica's position was hardly improved by the public ventilation of his Lorenzo de Medici, Albert Anastasia, at the Park-Sheraton. His own reminiscences of the day of that disaster are a vignette of the essential difference between men of the intellect and men of action:

"I went over to Anastasia's house to succor his wife and children. Not one person called all that day to express condolences. And he had so many friends in his lifetime."

Modica is, of course, much too delicate to talk about Jimmy Squillante; his most extreme characterization is "provincial." Squillante, of course, had as little respect for progressive management techniques as he had for Albert Anastasia after decease.

When Don Modica came to the Cartmen's Association, he had great hopes for making it a vehicle to spread effective interest in "industrial hygiene, traffic safety, and occupational diseases" and for his own great general hope of teaching management "to teach the proletariat how to get along with him better." When he left, this vision was no farther along than it had been, and there were no roses in that garbage truck.

Through the eighteen years of the odyssey, it has always gone like this. Don Modica was teaching the philosophy of education at NYU in 1939; he left because of low teacher's salaries. He met Albert Anastasia at a club where he was pursuing his sociological interest in the roots of the criminal temperament, and became tutor to the children of the Adonises, the Morettis and the Anastasias.

These fellows are no more generous to education than society is; Don Modica's fee for teaching their children everything from Socrates on was, he says, no more than a turkey at Christmas and an occasional ham.

He sits in Hasbrouck Heights like Grant in Galena and, from time to time, commercial publishers try to buy his memoirs of his former patrons. It saddens him that these offers all seem to arise more from "larceny in the heart" than from any interest in the sum of twenty years of the mind's pilgrimage.

What he would like to write is a synthesis which would correlate the three great elements of our sickness: "Progressive education, delinquency and subversive influences such as communism." But so far he has no takers. It is the eternal fate of the intellectual that he is summoned only for the wrong reasons.

[January 14, 1958]

The Big Cheese

Joseph Profaci, the *principe* of olive oil, was observed yesterday wandering, a plucked owl among the television cables, at the Senate Mafia hearing, in search of an audience with Robert Kennedy.

"I got to get home," he said. "I pray to God that the sickness that's happening to my kid should not happen to yours. Do you want to see their pictures?"

He reached into his back pocket and took out a vast display of his six children, sleek, plump, rosy and lovely as six pimientos. Joseph Profaci is billed here as a member of the grand council of the Mafia, and he is certainly the oldest surviving delegate to its convention in 1928.

"Mafia, Mafia," said Joe Profaci, "it's a fantastica storia. They say I was in Cleveland, because they arrest me there in a card game. I coulda been in the Mafia. In my village in Sicily, when I was thirteen years old, I didn't even belong to the Knights."

Instead Joe Profaci became a grocer in Palermo, and then in Chicago; he was twenty-seven years old when he came here from Sicily loosely pursued by its *carabinieri*.

He settled in Brooklyn, and since then his troubles with the terror of the total state have been those to be expected by any simple businessman, the conviction for adulterating the olive oil and for dodging his taxes. He looks like what he is, a squat Sicilian grocer, harried by, but resistant to, the importunities of the starving; he was our largest importer of olive oil, and his grip on tomato paste was so universal that wholesale grocers, faced with the choice between their love of country and their sense of civic virtue, began buying the stuff in Hungary, where it was cheaper.

"How do I know they were labeling my olive oil wrong?" said Joe Profaci. "I never bought any olive oil in my life in my own name. I don't even know the name of the ship. It was the broker. He put it in barrels. I didn't know whether it was 75 per cent or 25 per cent oil; it was olive oil, wasn't it?

"Now they close down fifty-two of my businesses. They took my home. I live on rent. In Bath Beach. I got nothing.

"And what do they say about me? Cocaine." Joe Profaci pulled at his nose and sniffed. "What I know about cocaine? I hope a man should die if he messes with cocaine. It's dishonest.

"And look what they say about me. After the war, I send $3,000 over to Italy to bring five nuns over here. Now they say it was for cocaine. And one of the five nuns was my niece. Look, you go to Italy; you ask the secretary to the Pope. I give you a letter."

He believes in the saints and he believes in the Mafia, being a simple man, large of hope at night, mean of spirit by day. Even when he owned the mass of the provolone on the Brooklyn docks, Joe Profaci lived in Bath Beach in Brooklyn. The brigands of the Internal Revenue Service took away his house and the farm in Hightstown; he moved down the street to a rented apartment. "Heroin," he says to curious strangers, "I don't know what heroin is. Don't they call it cocaine?"

Joe Profaci's day away from his children had been spent largely watching his social inferiors. The Senate Rackets Committee has been studying the mob's Apalachin conference; in deference to its jurisdiction, most of the delegates it canvassed were labor skates, with a corresponding lack of social stature.

There may not be a Mafia, but there is an America, and it is divided on class lines. There were labor delegates to Apalachin and there were employer delegates; the difference between them, in our affluent society, is indicated by the fact that the labor delegates served most often as chauffeurs for the employer delegates.

Rosario Mancuso, one such chauffeur, was described as a former official of the Utica hod carriers union who had occupied those hours free of commitment to the toilers as a bouncer in a gambling house. I cannot say, on the basis of observation, whether Rosario Mancuso is a steward I would approach with less confidence as a dues-payer seeking enforcement of my rights or as an oppressed plunger questioning the absolute fidelity of the wheel. He looks like a man who, in either case, would be working for the house.

There was also John Charles Montana, delegate to the New York State constitutional convention in 1937, president of the Van Dyke Taxi Co., and member of the Buffalo Zoning Commission, who brought considerable pain to the committee of citizens who had named him Buffalo man of the year in 1956 by being caught in the

Apalachin house of Joseph Barbara last November when the state police descended upon Barbara's fifty-eight guests. Montana explained his presence on this melancholy occasion in a fashion which I will summarize because it is entirely logical and might have happened to you and me:

Montana was driving his three-month-old Cadillac to Pittston when the brakes failed because it was raining and he bethought himself of his old friend Joe Barbara who has fifteen mechanics who hang around the house for just such emergencies as this, so he drove to Barbara's house and he was wet from fixing the windshield wipers which had also broken down, and Mrs. Barbara made him a cup of tea to take the chill off his bones and then Joe Barbara came in and said there was a roadblock outside, so John Montana did what any respectable citizen would do and cut out to the woods and that was absolutely all there was to it.

For some reason or other, after this description of a routine moment in the life of an honest enterpriser, John Montana was dismissed by his interrogators with a noticeable sniff, and was free to go back to Buffalo and service as a director of the Erie County ASPCA. He left with a few ill-chosen Anglo-Saxon words about the witnesses against him. He couldn't be a member of the Mafia. Joe Profaci wouldn't use words like that.

[Washington, D.C., July 2, 1958]

Soft Drinks

We now know all that good society can claim to know about last November's Apalachin conference, hitherto described by our organs of public information as the "Mafia grand council," "the summit meeting of the international underworld," or, if you prefer decisive detail, by the *Daily News*, as "the big meeting of gangsters Vito Genovese called at a Western New York crossroads to decide what to do now that ambitious punks are pushing 'the Old Guard' out of organized crime."

As his last act of public office, State Commissioner of Investigation

Arthur L. Reuter filed with Governor Harriman a sixty-four-page memorandum on the findings of his study of this latest manifestation of the invisible government.

It is, of course, generally known that the invisible government is responsible for all the woes of our society not directly traceable to Soviet weather experiments.

The peril — I should say the accomplished national strangulation it represents — is well described in the following dialogue between two members of the United States Senate last fall:

> Senator McClellan: "We've got to find out if the government is bigger than the hoodlums and crooks, or if they are running the country."
> Senator Ives: "We've got to beat this thing if it's the last thing we do."
> Senator McClellan: "We've got to, we have to, or the hoodlums are going to take over the country."

Senators Ives and McClellan were at the time preparing to confront the horror of underworld infiltration of the Long Island garbage industry. Since then, the nation has staggered under the revelation that the invisible government also controls Utica, New York, and Pittston, Pennsylvania, and is advancing remorselessly towards Kingston.

Commissioner Reuter's report on Apalachin is a notably conscientious and dutiful performance right down to the itemization of a $432.81 prime steak order placed with Armour and Co. for the nutriment of the guests and charged to the Canada Dry Bottling Co. of Endicott, New York.

It is, however, seriously lacking in prodigies of speculation. Reuter was legislated out of office at the last session of the State Assembly of our visible misgovernment. That fact appears to gall him; in listing possible subjects of discussion at Apalachin, he suggests: "Arrangements and expenses for lobbying, including political contributions." I take this to indicate that Reuter feels that the invisible government got him. Respectful though I am of the i.g.'s omnipotence, it seems much more likely that Reuter departed because he lacked the lurid imagination without which no law enforcement official can hope to survive in the United States.

For what would the invisible government be without the creative powers of us journalists and the generally anonymous spinners of dreams who toil in police station and narcotics bureau? The narcotics agent who told the *Tribune*, after Apalachin, that he is convinced "that the Mafia still operates under a single leader in Italy. We have an idea who it is." And the other narcotics agent who told us, "There are no elected chiefs or leaders, no word or sign that would make one member recognize another."

This kind of speculation is the essence of law enforcement. Its value for avenging wrong was nowhere better demonstrated than by the 1956 death, by heart attack, of Jack Dragna, described in his obituaries as "dreaded Mafia boss" and "chairman of the board of the West Coast crime syndicate." A copy of a biography of Lucky Luciano, written by a crime reporter on information supplied by law enforcement officials, was found opened beside his bed. Obviously Jack Dragna laughed himself to death, and good riddance too.

Even so, for all its failures of imagination, the Reuter report is a workmanlike document, with a great deal to tell any moderately skeptical observer about the real nature of the invisible government.

It is, first of all, a portrait of a convention of businessmen, who happen to be of Italian origin. They are not so much businessmen as the sort of proprietors Carlo Levi describes as *signori* in small Italian cities. They are padrones, and they live off the *contadini* or peons or peasants or what you will.

Many of them began as labor contractors who transported the labor code of pre-Fascist Italy to Pittston or the Brooklyn waterfront. Since they had their seat in an ancient culture strongly resistant to Methodist intolerance of light wines, they became bootleggers during Prohibition. Most of them lived then, and still do, off an Italian community which, as it becomes more and more Americanized, has less and less to offer them. Even so, they remain rooted in the *contadini*.

Vito Genovese, allegedly the most powerful delegate to Apalachin, is credited with some scrappy waste paper interests, but, most of all, is "said to receive $20,000 weekly from the Italian lottery in New Jersey." That is living off one's own.

Joseph Profaci's chief resources are the Mama Mia Olive Oil Co. and the Carmella Mia Packing Co., both of Brooklyn. These two enterprises catered largely to Italo-Americans until recently when all of us became conscious of their delights. It is obvious that, since Profaci's major concerns are olive oil and tomato paste, the largest portion of our national tribute to the invisible government went last year for buying pizza.

Since he is a businessman, the great hope of any Apalachin delegate is obviously to get a soft-drink franchise. It is steadier, more lucrative and much less chancy than, say, heroin. The cops, Reuter reminds us, were first tipped off about Apalachin when Joseph Barbara, Jr., son of the host, told the proprietor of the nearest motel that he was running "a convention of Canada Dry men." That, of course, is what every delegate wishes he were.

[May 6, 1958]

N. Y. vs. Sonny

There is something wonderful in the persistence of New York State's struggle against Sonny Liston.

This is perhaps the last gasp of the grand old progressive notion that government, properly enlightened, can do anything. The Russians won't go away; Castro won't go away; the institution of the direct primary produces results as bad as Ross Barnett and seldom visibly better than Charley Buckley. But can't government at least give us a suitable heavyweight champion?

So yesterday the Joint Legislative Committee on Professional Boxing continued its heroic effort to prove that government can do what poor Floyd Patterson was unable to do.

Its main witness was Cortez Stewart, a tall young heavyweight of such obvious integrity and articulation as to be the perfect candidate for an office which every impulse of social planning seems to indicate should henceforth be appointive. Stewart testified that he had been offered a job as Liston's sparring partner only last April under a bridge in the dark of the night by Frank Palermo, the hoodlum who used to manage the new champion. Liston has repeatedly insisted that he long ago severed all connections with Palermo and traded him for three priests.

Stewart's testimony about Palermo was a minimal surprise. It merely indicated that Sonny Liston still entertains the superstition that the mob controls all American society. That is a superstition, of course, properly to be expected from a man whose experience with American society has been confined to the Teamsters Union, prison and the sport of boxing.

Stewart was more interesting for himself than for the sensation he offered. He had won twenty-three out of twenty-four fights with no visible interest from boxing's establishment. Then his manager had sold a piece of him to a group of Philadelphians; it is the tribute which innocence pays to reality in this business, Philadelphia being the financial capital of boxing. Eddie Gayles, his Philadelphia manager, had brought Stewart to Palermo. Stewart had asked $50 a day to work out with Liston; Palermo had answered that instead of cash he and Liston could offer only a limitless future beginning with a spot on the Patterson card. The mob, of course, invented the credit card; it never pays cash.

Stewart had turned his back on this promise, and, presumably, on his career. It was suggested yesterday that, in testifying, he had put his life in danger. This, of course, is not the real condition; the mob will not shoot him; it will just never trust him with a fight again. Afterwards someone asked him if he was not frightened; he answered that he was a man who would rather get what was coming to him and live than play safe and not live. He talked with the grace and articulation which Joe Louis made the pattern for heavyweight champions, and which was true to the man but somehow false to the subject. The Negro heavyweights, as Negroes tend to do, have usually given that sense of being men above their calling. Floyd Patterson sounded like a Freedom Rider. We return to reality with Liston.

We have at last a heavyweight champion on the moral level of the men who own him. This is the source of horror which Liston has aroused; he is boxing's perfect symbol. He tells us the truth about it. The heavyweight championship is, after all, a fairly squalid office.

But Sonny Liston is as bad as anyone around him. He will therefore take care of himself. He also can, if he is as true to his essential character as he shows every sign of continuing, be a heavyweight champion who will be the discredit his profession has needed all these years. He has already helped us grow up as a country because he is the first morally inferior Negro I can think of to be given an equal opportunity. He will help us grow up further if he destroys the illusion that a man whose trade it is to beat another man senseless for money represents an image which at all costs must be kept pure for American youth.

[October 3, 1962]

III

The Way We Live Now

The Way We Live Now is a favorite title for novels written in the middle age, gently disillusioned, of novelists whose readers generations later think of them with affection rather than awe. It is a title of fraternal criticism; men who employ it are not after blood.

It seems strange, having mentioned my beginnings, that most of what I have left to say about the unions should come to rest under this label of faint reproach.

Still I think it describes a permanent condition. Many years ago, when American radicals were more passionate and in a poetic sense closer to reality, they used to debate the question of who would have to collect the garbage under socialism. Questions like that did not occur to us who hoped for more from the labor movement than it could ever provide; we assumed that a man could collect garbage all day and live under an industrial democracy.

I learned something of the reality quite by coincidence in two days in Detroit in the summer of 1958. One day I went to an auto plant.

I had never before bothered to see the conditions under which the members of the best union in America work. The next day I talked to an unemployed member of the United Auto Workers. He had been laid off after fourteen consecutive years with Ford; in Detroit men are laid off according to seniority; Ford had been forced to cut back to the class of 1932. The man was not sure about his birthday; he was doubtful about his birthplace. He had, in fact, just one number in his mind: his seniority date. That was his only possession.

I should, of course, have known this all along; could anyone who did not know this write intelligently about men who work? Of course not; and, going through what I had written about labor before then, I found very little that did not have to be thrown out.

The way we have always lived has been that there are persons who own property and persons who work for a living. Unions can do certain things for those persons who work for a living; they can bring some order into their workday and protect them against whimsical, personal injustice. But they cannot change that fundamental condition; we may complain about a union leader because he deceives him-

self that he has changed it, but it is ridiculous to call him a traitor because he had not done what no union can do. John L. Lewis, the
largest of all our labor leaders, in his last years made a cold and delib-
erate decision which indicated his understanding of this condition.
Having despaired of ever making a coal mine a decent place to work,
he set out to reduce employment; the best thing you could do for the
grandchildren of coal miners was to abolish the job.

There were, of course, the New York subway motormen who struck
in 1958 against their union leadership, the socialist monopoly which
was their employer, and the fact-finders who had misinterpreted the
facts about their case. I include a piece on them because their strike
was so old-fashioned and so beautiful that I do not know a reporter
who saw them who does not cherish their memory. There was no
room for the end of their strike, which was an example of the way
we live now. They were broken, of course; they were spied on by the
liberal in charge of the Transit Authority's labor relations — he is, according to what is becoming a chorus, now a judge; all of organized
labor 'joined to defend the brother who had a license as their proprietor; all the devices society has set up to protect labor were employed
to deny them an election. Now they are gone.

Their leader ended by going to work for the union administration
against which he had revolted. He had, I really think, no more honorable course open to him. These were the years — they still are —
when our society was wealthy enough, if not to clothe its poor and
educate their children, at least to pay those of us who complained for
the amusement of our complaints.

"He Hasn't Come in Yet"

William J. Hynes, president of District Four of the United Mine Workers, wasn't available last weekend. Every time you called his hotel, the clerk said Mr. Hynes hadn't come in and he didn't know when to expect him.

Billy Hynes has lived at that hotel most of his later years, and there was a suspicion in most of those who knew him that the clerk was following orders. For Billy Hynes's district had gotten loose from him, and it wasn't anything he enjoyed talking about.

There was something about the name Hynes that sounded familiar. Something in a story Philip Murray told once.

The story went back forty-five years to when Murray was eighteen years old. The mine he'd worked in had been closed about three months when Murray gave up hope for it and went looking for work somewhere else in the fields.

He had just enough cash to pay his fare to West Fayette on one of the rusty, chilly trolleys that still lurch around these hills.

And Murray got off at last that black night in 1905 with a carpetbag filled with nothing but his pit clothes. The road to the mine patch went up a hill and, as he walked it, the sound of hot words came down to him.

West Fayette had just one street light, and miners were standing under it in a little cluster, listening to a little, wizened-up man pouring on a flaming socialist speech.

"And that," said Murray forty-five years later, "was the first time I ever heard a Hynes."

Pat Hynes was a delegate to the first convention the United Mine Workers ever had. That was in 1890, and Pat Hynes spent the rest of his life dragging that threadbare frame around the rutty street-corners of the mining towns speaking his revolutionary piece to whatever crowd would listen.

Somewhere along that lonely road he died and his son Billy took his place. Billy grew up like the old man; now he, too, is leathery and stringy and wizened; last week, an old miner said in Vestaburg that when Billy Hynes speaks and throws that long pointed finger out he reminds you of Eugene Victor Debs.

But somehow Billy Hynes was never lucky. He lived, for one thing, on the wrong side of the river. Cross the Monongahela only a few miles from Uniontown and you're in District Five of the UMW. The miners there have been unionized for fifty years.

But across the river in District Four was the area of United States Steel paternalism and the way of a missionary like Billy Hynes was rocky. It was 1934 before any of the Frick mines around here were organized and it was 1941 before the UMW finally won the Ronco mine.

Through all these years and these bloody heads, Billy Hynes fought on around Uniontown. Through the late Twenties and the early Thirties you didn't eat much on an organizer's pay, but he was always a "half-baked socialist" and the Hynes harangues went on.

Then they gave Billy Hynes a break. In the Thirties John Lewis and Philip Murray made him president of District Four. He has ruled it ever since. John Lewis is a hard master and Billy saw some of his friends go out, and none of it was quite like the flaming sword that he and Pat had flourished at the trolley stops.

Two weeks ago, after eight months of the three-day week, District Four lost its nerve. Its big mines began the "Five-day week or nothing" push, and no word Billy Hynes could say about loyalty to John Lewis and their union made any difference.

He dragged his tired body to Brownsville last Thursday a week ago to talk the Maxwell miners back into the pits. And they lay back in their seats and they booed him and men who'd worked in non-union mines when Billy Hynes was crying on his soapbox shouted that he was eating good and they were starving and to hell with him.

And young punks who'd never heard of Pat Hynes took up the cry Billy Hynes could do nothing with them. He went to Washington and laid his problem before John Lewis, a man very short with mistakes that aren't his own. And after that he came back here to his hotel and told the clerk to say he was unavailable.

When I was growing up, I used to think of the miners the way you do of the Yankees. No matter how dark the night, there was DiMaggio and there was always the hit with the men on bases.

But the labor movement isn't the Rover boys and there are no Di-

Maggios in it. Sometimes there is only defeat and the cracking of the tabernacle and the shadows coming in and the four walls in a hotel room where your only defense is a clerk who'll cover up and say you haven't come in yet.

[Uniontown, Pennsylvania, January 31, 1950]

The Ghosts

Michael Angelo Musmanno was a thirty-year-old lawyer in Pittsburgh in 1927 when the Sacco-Vanzetti case approached its final agony. He went running to Boston as so many others did. There he was delegated to visit Supreme Court Justice Oliver Wendell Holmes near the last hour in a desperate clutch at a stay of execution.

Holmes turned him down, and, as Musmanno was leaving, he looked at the clock in the justice's hall; it was after midnight and he knew that Sacco and Vanzetti were dead. And then Mike Musmanno sat down and wept. Long afterwards, when he himself was a politician and a judge, he was bitterest of all at old Judge Thayer, who had said, "Did you see what I did to those anarchist bastards?"

Who can say what Steve Nelson was doing the night Musmanno wept for Bartolomeo Vanzetti? He was then named Steve Mesavich and was a carpenter, infrequently employed, around Philadelphia. Sometime in the late Twenties, he became a Communist.

Ever since, he has lived the life of the professional revolutionary in America, a vocation which, when it is not pernicious, is one of massive social non-utility. He went to Moscow to the Lenin school; and came back to be the party's leader in the anthracite coal district. He went to Spain and was wounded as a political commissar.

When he got home, the party sent him to Berkeley, California, as an open Communist organizer. His duties brought him into association with Vassili Zubilin, a Russian agent, and with two or three young physicists who were working on atomic energy at the University of California. It was afterwards said before Congressional committees, but never proved, that one of the physicists gave Nelson a secret formula which he copied down and passed on to Zubilin for shipment to Moscow.

In the end the case died; he could not be indicted with any promise of success; and the party sent him to Pittsburgh, still as its open organizer.

He sat there for two years, in a public office across the street from the Allegheny County courthouse, and directed a fearsome legion of seven hundred Western Pennsylvania Communists. There, in 1950, he was discovered by Mike Musmanno.

Musmanno was by now a county judge with an approaching primary and ambitions to be the Democratic nominee for lieutenant-governor. In August, 1950, he walked across the street and bought a few pamphlets at Steve Nelson's office. Thus armed, he moved the next day as a private citizen to file a criminal information against Steve Nelson under Pennsylvania's ancient sedition law.

Running against Steve Nelson, Musmanno lost his bid to be lieutenant-governor of Pennsylvania. But he stayed on the bench, and assigned the judge who tried Nelson; Musmanno was the main witness, and his nephew was prosecuting attorney.

There were too many calls on Steve Nelson's time to make a quick trial possible. The government indicted him under the Smith Act, and, in May, 1951, he was badly cut up in an auto accident. Musmanno was then running for the State Supreme Court, and badly in need of a healthy opponent. In June, in Philadelphia, he came into the boarding house where Nelson was recuperating, rushed up to his bed and shouted, "When are you going to come home to be tried, Steve?"

At last Steve Nelson was brought to trial in 1952; he was being tried for his ideas and the documents he sold; but those headlines about atomic espionage didn't hurt any. The jury was out twenty-six hours; at the end Nelson got twenty years for criminal sedition from a judge who had publicly demanded his indictment.

Last January, the Pennsylvania Supreme Court threw out his conviction on the grounds that the Smith Act takes precedence over all the sedition acts which afflict the statute books of twenty states. The U. S. Supreme Court will begin hearing an appeal from this decision next month; if Nelson wins, all the state sedition laws will die.

Nelson is in town this week looking for a conservative lawyer, a ghost with the menace out of him, and with no hope except to avoid twenty-five years in prison. Mike Musmanno is a ghost, too, looking at his empty, used-up enemy and saying, I presume, "Look what I've done to that Communist bastard."

[March 10, 1955]

Serpents on the Nile

The Legion of Decency seems determined to increase the already immoderate estates of Elia Kazan and Tennessee Williams by crying *Baby Doll* through the streets and all on the theory that these people are purveyors of dangerously adult entertainment.

Poor Williams has never outgrown the cornsilk stage in his attitude towards sex, and Kazan is an habitual abetter of his adolescence, and there should be a law against outsiders grade-labeling their product in such a way as to seduce a sentient high-school student into the theater on the promise of showing her life in the raw.

This sort of thing is also rather hard on old Cecil B. deMille, who was peddling flesh — honest, tinted, sandalwood-anointed flesh — before Tennessee Williams's mother first showed him the French Quarter.

DeMille is serving up flesh in pots in *The Ten Commandments* at the Criterion right now. Yesterday's audience was a little thin, but I hope that when this report on the bacchanales around Mount Sinai is finished, the Legion will come to his rescue, too.

Like all truly respectable orgies, *The Ten Commandments* consumes nearly four hours, and has the expert supervision of three lower Protestant divines, who could teach Tennessee Williams more than something about conjuring up visions of sin unbridled. One does not attend this movie; one enlists in it; yesterday afternoon there were families parting amid tears. The souvenir counter was selling children's coloring pencils.

"Watcha want, Protestant, Jewish or Catholic?" the butcher asked. Your agent replied, "Call me Ishmael" and settled for the Protestants.

A kid's pencil bearing the strange device "Thou Shalt Not Commit Adultery" is a novelty item any collector would want to be the first to have.

The Ten Commandments, after a little routine sadism, gets down to matters with the discovery of the infant Moses by the Egyptian Princess Birhiah. This gives deMille his chance for the swimming-pool scene, bulrushes by Petronius Arbiter. The Princess's attendants wear white bathing suits styled like Gussie Moran's tennis dresses. For reasons of security the princess orders the chorus to go to the dressing room; the master lingers like the artist he is over the business of their taking their legs out of the water.

Moses, like all strong men, is tempted; without temptation, there could be no religious films. He is tempted most of all by Miss Anne Baxter as the Princess Nefertiti — it is deMille's old-fashioned Baptist notion that Little Egypt came from Chicago — a nymph so advanced in mania that, if she did not cover her cleavage with a little bit of blue stuff at one point, I doubt if even the Methodists at Lake Junaluska would clear her for a summer afternoon. She smokes and reeks desire all four hours.

Even near the end, when Moses returns bearded and smelling of sheep dip, Miss Baxter, her armpits drowned in myrrh, pushes against him in her boudoir and wonders if the shepherd girl he married has lips like hers ("Pomegranates," stupid) or whether they are dried and parched by the wind.

This last is a dreadful knock on Yvonne De Carlo, who plays Mrs. Moses, since Wally Westmore has anointed her with rose lipstick and left her just as greased with cosmetics as any Egyptian princess. She has otherwise taken the veil for this one, and refuses to participate in the libidinous dance at which her six sisters — a chorus billed as "Jethro's Daughters" — shake their veils for Moses' favor. Hard as Miss Baxter tries, she does not get to fall.

The only soiled dove — the phrase does come up — is Debra Paget, a water-bearer to the Hebrew slaves who is passed among such of her masters as Vincent Price, only to fall into the hands of Edward G. Robinson, who is straight out of the Jelke case and economical enough to bring her forth for the consummation of his evil enterprise in the same gold dress that poor Price had bought her.

Robinson puts a white lotus in her hair — "for purity," he leers — and listens unregenerate to her suggestions that God would not look with favor on this union.

At last he says: "You would do anything to save Joshua's life, wouldn't you?"

"Anything," she answers.

To hell with you, Williams; deMille delivers.

The grand climax comes, of course, with the golden calf. Moses is up on Mount Sinai dodging the lightning bolts with which God is writing that one shall not covet, while the children of Israel are falling from grace all over what had hitherto been the barren plain below. No religious film is complete without a sequence of worshiping false gods, and no one caters like Satan. You will not find Lucullan delights like these in an advertisement for the Sans Souci in Miami: the desert blossoms with purple lotus; the mountains turn to cheesecake; girls rip their skirts and jump on grapes and wriggle in the arms of brown-limbed men.

They are wriggling still when Moses comes down the hill, so I assume no permanent damage is done.

Moses breaks up this festival of concupiscence by hurling the tablets on the golden calf, which falls into an abyss. Each brown-limbed boy leaps with his burden across to safety with Moses. The girls are wriggling still and it's consoling to know that there are as many kicks in salvation as in perdition.

[December 18, 1956]

The Face of Time

The thing that's happening to baseball should finish the economic interpretation of history once and for all. The ballplayers were never richer, never more comfortable, never higher on the social scale, and never more neurotic. Duke Snider pops a customer in Cincinnati; and Ted Williams, majestic in shame as he is majestic in glory, spits in the face of those who love him.

"Sometimes," Williams told Milton Gross yesterday, "you get it up to here."

The Red Sox pay him $100,000 a year. He has the royalties from the endorsement of the Ted Williams casual sport shirt, he has the fishing tackle business in Florida, and he is baseball consultant for the Wilson Sporting Goods Co. But what does this all have to do with the artist's sense of the meaning of his art? Williams looms larger in our economy than the average president of the average corporation;

yet he is unhappy; it is very sad to have it all made and still have a terrible Western trip.

The reason for being C. E. Wilson is not the money, but the hushed tones which greet your presence. Ted Williams is an economic mammoth, and any Boston Irishman is entitled, for $2.10, to hurl the foulest imprecations at him. The last chance our unshirted have to tell a capitalist off is to sit in the left field stands and abuse Ted Williams. Let him spit; they have it coming; what did the entire baseball staff of the Boston press hit the last time they went West?

I am indebted for the above information on Ted Williams's Dun and Bradstreet average to "The Baseball Player" — an economic survey by Professor Paul M. Gregory of the University of Alabama. It's a book without much point, but it has a great subject. Gregory reminds us that some sportswriter or other was disturbed because Babe Ruth made more money than Herbert Hoover. "What the hell has Hoover got to do with it?" said Ruth. "Besides I had a better year than he did."

There is this wonderful arrogance; but what can they pay you to endure the baseball fan? I speak as one myself: we are creeps. Every sportswriter in the business psychoanalyzes Ted Williams; if I read one more piece about a $100,000-a-year man who is unhappy because he came from a broken home, I'm going to feel that I owe it to the kids to break up my home. But does anyone ever try to analyze a man who will sit in the grandstand and curse a ballplayer and then take up a collection to pay the fine the target gets when he spits back? They don't do it because it's impossible.

Gregory passes on a wonderful story about Yogi Berra's off-season function as a clothing salesman in 1951. A daddy creep and a little boy creep came in to buy a suit and the little boy creep asked Yogi how come he dropped the foul ball on the last out of Allie Reynolds's no-hitter against the Red Sox.

"For a moment," says Yogi, "I forget about the customer always being right. I guess the kid got scared, the way he backed up. Even the smile disappeared from his old man's face. Then I remembered that you gotta be nice to the customers, and I told him . . . he's got nothing to worry about and if he wants I'll autograph both sleeves for him."

What must it be like to be Ted Williams and have to endure the democratic judgment of customers who are such hopeless squares that, whether they're for you or against you, they're wrong. If a man is the idol of people like that, he has a serious moral problem: he can say thank you or he can spit. I think it's his duty to his art to spit. Someone has to spit on the triumph of the herd man, and I'm for Williams; he doesn't cop the Fifth; he spits forth that the committee has no jurisdiction.

The first baseball union ever formed, Gregory tells us, came into being because Ty Cobb was suspended for punching a fan who provoked him. The Detroit team walked out in the only real strike baseball players ever conducted. This was when the owners of baseball were so rapacious that Ban Johnson suspended the Most Valuable Player award because the recipient had too much bargaining power on next year's contract. Yet they never struck against that; in baseball the true class enemy is not the boss, but the fan.

[August 10, 1956]

Private Enterprise

Nella Bogart is a melting, rosy-cheeked continental and altogether compliant young lady with a smile forgiving all, understanding all, and keeping all secrets. She is a delightful contrast to Fortune's horrible portrait of the corporation wife. She was a corporation chippie.

Nellie was delegate-at-large to one of last summer's dealers' conventions of the August General Electric Sales Corporation as a stimulant to good will and sales. Nellie was allegedly booked by G.E. officials across state lines, and G.E. paid her hotel expenses. It would, of course, be unthinkable for the United States Government to try our fourth largest industrial firm for corporate pimping, so the burden of these sins has fallen upon this poor working girl and she is being tried in a federal court here as a madam.

The two G.E. executives who hired her were dragged in to testify this week, and their stories are a sobering lesson in how badly the Harvard Business School neglects the teaching of important aspects of industrial procurement.

Lewis E. Rinker, former advertising director of G.E. Supply in Newark, testified:

"My duty as advertising manager was to set up dealer shows. I was requested by the sales manager to call Miss Bogart and ask her if she would come over to Newark and bring a young lady with her. I did it because it was part of my job."

Rinker appears to have been somewhat wanting in executive equipment, because he registered his salesladies into the hotel as Nella Bogart and daughter, Hotpoint Co., for all the FBI to see. G.E. paid the bill for the installation, but there was serious question about the service charge. Sales Manager J. W. Murray told Rinker: "If they want to go upstairs, then they will pay for it."

This policy appears to have been a serious blow to corporate good will. Shortly after Pat D'Amico, Nella's associate, set up her exhibit, there were signs of disturbance from her booth, and the advertising manager arrived to find Pat in the uniform of her trade arguing with one of the dealers. "I discovered that the gentlemen were under the impression that we were going to pay."

By August, Sales Manager Murray had compiled such a dazzling record as to be promoted to Buffalo. His successor, a democrat, offered a new model and more liberal credit terms. He instructed Rinker to call Nella and find out if she knew a blond. "Anybody," he said handsomely, "can have her who wants her." There appeared Miss Lynne Phillips, paid $100 on petty cash.

Henry Singer, Nella's attorney, asked Rinker: "You were using the body of this woman to advance the financial interests of the company?" Rinker replied that he guessed that was so, and went on to dilate upon the expanding horizons of the new capitalism: "This is a public relations thing. It creates good will. It has nothing to do with sales."

Rinker has been fired and J. W. Murray's career appears to have been blighted, although he retains Nella's good will, which is worth more to me than Ralph J. Cordiner's. From G.E. come only bleats of outrage about unauthorized applications of the sales budget.

Yesterday, the jury heard from Lynne Phillips, now a regenerate in the interest of the feds and a witness against little Nella. Her testimony was of minor interest except for its reiteration of the melancholy fact that loose women get along as badly together as proper ones do. Said Nella: "They don't like me because I'm prosperous. It's just a vicious campaign against a poor little DP who's trying to make a living." She came here to escape a class society, and, if the Senate Small Business Committee doesn't care what's happening to G.E.'s small contractors, I hope someone does.

[February 22, 1957]

Is This All?

Before I say another word about Billy Graham's opening, I should like to say that, if Jesus Christ crucified for our sins was good enough for Johann Sebastian Bach and Fyodor Dostoevski and Georges Rouault He is much too good for the likes of me, and I shall make no sport of any honest prophet of His.

Billy Graham is a decent, honorable man — although a feeble preacher by any proper standards — and he is much too decent to be forced by his commitment to Christ to live even six weeks in a town whose stores hang dirty Christmas cards in their windows in December. The faithful who walked down Eighth Avenue from the Garden last night passed, blessedly unseeing, by a store which displayed the Holy Bible, Stanley High's book on Billy Graham, some bookkeeper's rewrite of various epistles of Saint Paul, and the latest vision of Norman Vincent Peale side by side with works geared more to its ordinary clientele like Are You Over Sex-ty? and Sex-ation, 1957.

It is not my recollection that the money-changers were peddling Cretan postcards on the side; I think the risen Jesus would have thrown a brick through that store window, and, if I have a complaint about Billy Graham, it is that he is too timid.

Billy Graham finished his message a little after nine fifteen last night, and asked everybody to go back to the shop, to the store, to "your situation" and be reborn — "courteous, gracious, kind and loving your neighbor." If anyone would like to come forward and have "the personal encounter with Christ, we're not going to embarrass you; we're not going to ask you to say anything. You know you have to come back to God. Your friends will wait; we won't keep you more than a few minutes." Jacob had to wrestle with the angel, but the bus waits for Billy Graham's disciples.

They came shuffling down from the balconies, by way of the escalators. A few were crying, but none came close to any posture describable as possession. There were great numbers of young people among them; there were also a few of those old women whose faces reminded Baudelaire of old oranges. There was a terrible pathos about them; one thought of the daughter of Lane Adams who told her father, who is one of Billy Graham's team:

"The faces in New York remind me of people who played a game and lost."

They came in docile droves; you remembered the faces of those who had lined up for draft examinations at Governors Island. They seemed an enormous throng. Downstairs, when the heads of the reclaimed — the retreaded really, since an estimated 60 per cent of them already go to church — were tabulated, Lorne Sanney, Billy Graham's Director of Followup, estimated that 485 souls had been saved last night.

The rest of this great herd were counselors, advisers, team members, the camp followers commanded by the new science of human behavior to accompany Gideon's army. The counselors were in a permanent state of grace; the recruits had just been through a shattering religious experience; the horror was that you couldn't tell them apart without looking at the badges.

There were 18,500 persons in the Garden last night and 485 of them — less than 3 per cent — had affirmed the experience of the living presence. The figures are below those accounted satisfactory by a direct mail appeal. What was extraordinary was the fact that Billy Graham seemed to feel that this was a triumph of his ministry; he reported that he had never had a better opening, and the records bear him out.

He had stood up downstairs and looked down upon the reborn, looking in the fine condition of the boy whom Babe Ruth, of course, had told once he had the build of a first baseman, and said that his throat was very bad and that he could hardly talk, and that another evangelist would have to deliver the coup. I can only think of this ailment as psychosomatic; he had the letdown that comes to a man who has run his course better than he expected.

It is sad that Billy Graham preaches peace and that the Old Testament God has brought him so little peace. He said in his pre-opening messages all around town early this week that he feared most that God would turn his lips to clay. The sense was inescapable that he was afraid that God might get jealous of his press notices, and punish him for the sin of getting top billing. Last night, at the end, he sounded relieved, as though God had let him off.

He sat on the platform earlier in a terrible paroxysm of the jitters; when he got up to give his message, he went forth with four encouraging slaps on the back from Roger Hull, executive vice president of the Mutual Insurance Co. and chairman of the executive committee of the New York Billy Graham Crusade Inc.

He arose thus fortified and talked for an hour. You watch, because it is your business, for gestures and paces and rhythms and images, but you hope that you will be caught up in them and forget to count; the sad thing is that Billy Graham, as preacher, cannot make you stop counting and begin to inhabit his own world.

He has somehow sterilized the old shouting faith and made it polite, tamed and fit for broken people. The vengeful God is a stallion; in Graham's hands he is a gelding. The references to psychiatry, the call to put away one's tranquilizer pills and go down the escalators to Christ, the quotes from Nathan Pusey, all came out by rote; there was a moment of quiet; the choir began the soft song about going home to Jesus and the terrible interior question came beating forth:

"Is there no more than this, is there no more than this?"

[May 16, 1957]

The Inheritance

When they ask you what labor unions have meant to America, set down this:

In the Teens of this century, Philip Murray was fired for hitting the weighmaster who cheated him on his tonnage, and he walked back from the mine, up a hill, into the torches held against the night by the other miners, and listened to the speaker talking about the United Mine Workers of America.

In the Twenties of this century, the miners struck in West Virginia and were thrown into the state prison. They looked out their jail window at the state capitol and laughed and laughed every time a visiting intellectual translated the inscription on that edifice. It was: "The Men of the Mountains Are Free."

In the Thirties, the auto workers won their strike at General Motors, and streamed down the streets of Flint, their beards wild in the auto lights, the conquerors and the liberators of the earth.

And for the Fifties, set down this:

Last March 6, James G. Cross, president of the Bakery Workers Union, which is almost as old as the Knights of Labor, was put on trial before the executive board of his international union on charges of corruption. His accuser said that there was $29,000 missing from one local union fund and that some of it had gone for a Cadillac for Cross. In his own defense, Cross answered:

He had a Cadillac. It had been given to him under these perfectly reasonable circumstances: The Chicago Bakers locals had wanted to give him a Christmas party, but he couldn't come.

"Then a man who I figure is smart said, 'Jimmy, if we give you a party, half the money will go to a hotel, so why don't we present you with something that will be worthwhile and you won't have to split the money with a hotel?' "

That something, said James Cross, was a Cadillac. This version of events appears on the evidence to have been a lie; you can judge a man by the sort of lie he considers an account of justifiable conduct.

His accuser said that Jimmy Cross had wasted union funds on his expense account. Jimmy Cross replied that his duties had been heavy and the burden onerous:

"Almost every night we were in Miami Beach, from the Fontaine-bleau Hotel to the Eden Roc, the Americana, the Cotton Club, Dorio's restaurant."

His accuser said that Jimmy Cross had spent union funds to call his girl friend. Cross answered that the union was supposed to pay his phone bills, and it didn't make any real difference if they were $2 or $10,000. The general executive board heard these charges and this defense and it voted in a very few minutes to clear James Cross and continue him in his stewardship. It then moved unanimously to suspend Curtis Sims, the secretary-treasurer who had brought the charges.

The general executive board of the Bakers Union consists in the main of pie-cards, appointed and removed at the will of James G. Cross. No reasonable man could think of any cause, except simple economic necessity, which would make them look at this image of the labor leader of the Fifties and find it good. I think, in making this judgment, most of all of Herman E. Cooper, general counsel for the union, who took away $81,000 in legal fees last year.

Cooper told the Senate Committee on Improper Labor-Management Practices yesterday that it is impossible to measure the value of a lawyer's services. I certainly cannot measure it; I can only say that $81,000 is more than the lifetime income of Wolfgang Amadeus Mozart. By that standard, it may be enough to justify Cooper's sitting at that meeting, hearing Cross thus describe himself, and going out into the streets to fight with passion to help him keep his job.

It is not the cash or the skills it bought which disturbs me; it is rather the passion with which Herman Cooper accepted the assignment. He is, by the way, general counsel for my own union; to the extent to which I contribute to his retainer, I too am a sinner, and I apologize.

James Cross needed money for a house in Washington. The union was supposed to pay for it, but the money was slow in coming. So he borrowed the $56,000 from an employer with whom the union dealt. The evidence indicates that the employer had no reason to be dissatisfied with the investment. Cross then needed — or thought his status required — a house in Palm Springs, Florida, and he borrowed $40,000 from the same employer for that.

Cross was accused of cuffing around five persons who opposed him at the union's last convention. One of them was a grandmother. In this gallant exercise of his decision for democratic centralism, Cross is alleged to have employed the assistance of a vice president of the union who pulled a gun on one of the recalcitrants.

Cross is now before the Senate of the United States and charged with explaining himself. The horror of the condition into which circumstance has brought American labor in the year 1957 is that he will try to make the case for himself without either denying or apologizing for these facts: (1) An employer helped him buy his house. (2) His duties required a tab at the Americana. (3) He charged the union for his fights and his frolics.

He proposes to stand before us all and proclaim himself innocent of any sin except these inconsequential ones. Let us, when we judge him, remember that the leaders of his union knew everything we know now more than three months ago, and refused to act against him.

We should remember that last fact when anyone says that the unions can cleanse themselves as they are now constituted. We should also remember Philip Murray and the West Virginia miners and the Flint strikers and the dream to which they gave their lives, and the terrible, empty world in which James Cross is their heir.

[Washington, D.C., June 19, 1957]

The Party's Over

The crest of Mike Todd's gala was the afternoon before it began.

Then, the desperate emissaries of desperate account executives held their imploring hands across the railing of Mike Todd Enterprises and cried for tickets. A press agent at the last extremity came with a letter from Frank Sinatra asking that his tickets be given to a girl singer for whom he has an avuncular kindness.

"Frank can't come," the press agent said. "He asked if you couldn't give his tickets to ————. She needs them; she just got married."

The keeper of Mike Todd's gate was as kind as a higher power can be.

"Look," he explained. "There's fifty ambassadors who want that box. If Sinatra comes he gets it. We need Sinatra. But we don't need ———— this year; maybe we'll need her next year."

That afternoon Mike Todd's party was everything. His gatekeeper could describe his guest list in terms embodying the whole hierarchy of the Burke's *Peerage* of this our society: Frank Sinatra, then nothing, then fifty representatives of foreign powers, then nothing, then a girl singer.

At four o'clock in the afternoon, Mike Todd was assembling the spear carriers for final rehearsal in Madison Square Garden. He was called to the phone. The Mayor of New York wanted to know if he could get a walk-on part. All of a sudden, Mike Todd looked as though he was about to cry.

"Look," he said, "I built a whole sequence around New York. I'm making this town. I'll kill the whole sequence before I let him in." He could brush off the Mayor of New York.

And then the hours went by, and it was almost midnight, and it was near its end, and people dressed by Mike Todd's order in dinner jackets were kicking and scratching to steal free bingo sets off trucks. A man snatched and walked out with a hi-fidelity phonograph; a woman knelt down, the confetti sticking to her evening dress, and gathered up paper plates to take home; a woman with pearls in her ears stuffed her evening bag with Turkish taffies forcibly ravished from the person of the driver of the truck which bore them. The cameras were off, and Mike Todd was home in bed.

He had accomplished the most thorough expropriation of the capitalists since the Bolsheviks snatched the Kremlin. He gave nothing away that he had not cadged from its manufacturer. He had made the Columbia Broadcasting System give him premium time and pay him for stealing it for a vast trailer on *Don Quixote*, a movie he hasn't yet cast, let alone produced. The symbol of his triumph was a birthday cake provided by General Foods and bearing the strange device: HAPPY BIRTHDAY FROM SWANSDOWN.

The General Foods public relations man said in the morning that it weighed more than a ton, and came around later desperately apologizing that he had underrated this great pyramid and that, in point of fact, it encompassed 1,350 pounds of Swansdown cake products, 2,000 eggs, 63 gallons of water and 500 pounds of icing, especially tinted for television to a hue repellent to any sensitive eye.

As midnight came, the cake was in process of being sacked and pillaged by the embattled, frustrated freeloaders who were Mike Todd's guests. They fought tooth and claw as though going home with some piece of this blue-baby-colored mix would make them feel less cheated. Mike Todd had played Maecenas for 18,000 middle-class scavengers among garbage cans.

Mike Todd is hardly as bad as the sort of companies he bamboozles and the kind of guests he draws. He is a manipulator of proportions that make the floater of the South Sea Bubble look like the sort of banker who tells old ladies to stick to nothing but blue chip offerings. To the confidence man the build-up is all; the performance nothing. I could condemn Todd if he had spent his children's inheritance last night; since he conned the scratch from soulless corporations, I cheer him here, although I wish his talent for pillaging the rich would result in more pleasure for us poor.

The fact that his party was a dog is, after all, yesterday's news. It had to be a dog. When the word got around yesterday afternoon that

Sinatra wasn't coming, every adult in town knew it was a dog. Sinatra doesn't pass up good parties. So, only the squares came last night and, if they feel cheated this morning, I can't help them. Squares always get cheated.

It may in the end even have cost Mike Todd a little bit. The hit of his show was a wild fire-wagon smoking like Mount Etna and drawn by a team of crazy horses accompanied by a demented Dalmatian. On its side, it bore the label: VICTOR ADDING MACHINE COMPANY. Mike Todd sold space like that; and I think it says something for the great love he bears Elizabeth Taylor that he did not send her into the arena with a necklace of neon tubes certifying her gratitude to Hazel Bishop. Even so, it may have ended up costing him a little, since the vultures from the talent unions descended upon him at the last minute and extorted $67 apiece for the spear carriers.

There had been some wild surmise from the press agents that we would all dance till dawn. The guests were pilfering the gifts; Todd was announcing that 14,000 prizes would be drawn and that it would all be on the dead level, and, while our host was sneaking away, Duke Ellington brought his band on. It very plainly mattered to no one present that any guest had a good time. The members of Ellington's band looked at a crowd ripping out the furniture, and a few of them understood that they had been paid only to show up, and began walking away.

Duke Ellington looked at every one of them and said he wanted everyone to stay in his place and do his best. Duke Ellington gives value; he understands what Mike Todd will never know: That to be a gentleman is to be oneself, all of a seam, on camera and off. You cheat nobody, because you can only cheat yourself.

And so Mike Todd went home and went to bed and had put one more over. God pity him for wanting so little. How awful it must be to have scored a triumph and still to remember that you held a party for the kind of people who steal eight-month-old domestic champagne.

[October 18, 1957]

Joseph Puts a Nickel In

On Election Day, that time when all men are brothers, an East Harlem boy named Joseph Ernest Pereles sat down and wrote a letter to the Mayor of New York. Its text follows:

Honorable Mayor Wagner
City Hall
New York, New York
DEAR SIR:

I am in the 6th grade. I go to P.S. 121, Manhattan. I am writing to say that I hope you win the election. And also to say that I wish you do me a favor. I wish that you would do something about the housing problem. We are in great need for a housing apartment.

My smaller brother, who is only one has to sleep in my aunt's house. We sleep four in a bed. There are only two rooms in the house. My father wrote an application for an apartment, but it has been one year, and still we have no answer. Our church has written letters to them, the school, my mother's doctor, the social worker, and we haven't got the apartment yet. We have all the furniture and things, but we have no project.

Yours truly,
JOSEPH ERNEST PERELES

Three days later, he received the following answer:

DEAR MR. PERELES:

Mayor Wagner has asked me to acknowledge the receipt by him of your letter of November 5, 1957, concerning your need for housing.

The Mayor has forwarded your letter to the Hon. Philip J. Cruise, Chairman of the New York City Housing Authority, 299 Broadway, New York 7, N. Y., with instructions that your case be given every attention and consideration.

Sincerely yours,
HERMAN WEINKRANTZ

Now that letter, on the official stationery of the Mayor of New York, is quite simply a lie. According to any fair construction, it says that the Mayor of New York read little Joseph's appeal and passed it on to Herman Weinkrantz for prayerful consideration.

But, if either Wagner or Weinkrantz had read this letter, would Weinkrantz have addressed his reply to a "Mr. Pereles"? Of course he wouldn't. This is not an answer to a little boy's cry in the night. It is a form letter to a faceless inconvenience.

We shall not hear the heart of man call to man again. There will never again be an Abraham Lincoln watching through a night of sorrows and then taking down his pen and writing to Mrs. Bixby, a stranger with sorrows greater than his. If there were a Mrs. Bixby, the most that could happen would be that some press agent would find her and bring her to the White House on a deal with TWA, and then the President would be briefed on her, and say a few hollow words conceived in haste by an assistant, and she could go home with her medal and a mimeographed press release.

No politician will ever again sit up at night and read his mail and come up with a start and painfully write an answer full of his sense of government's failure and compassion. We have organized our society to avoid such freaks of human feeling. There is no Joseph Ernest Pereles; there is only this Puerto Rican problem, subject to some distant solution by a Mayor's Committee.

There is a majestic equality in the government of this, our particular people's democracy; for the young and the hopeful, for the old and the desperate, for the just and for the unjust, the appointed form is precisely the same. Sleep well, Joseph Ernest Pereles and three brothers all snug in your bed, and take comfort from the protection of a machine which recognizes all men as equals and returns the same empty piece of paper to any who presses its button.

I have been sitting a long while, struggling for some fine professional frenzy of irony and pity on Joseph's behalf, which wouldn't of course get him an apartment but might win me a plaque from some organization dedicated to the general good. But the conditions are lousy for concentrated passion. It's late at night; the charlady is here cleaning up. She is, I suppose, in her fifties, and not built for picking up cans full of the *Times* and other pieces of the discarded paper of my life. She makes a dreadfully distracting noise dragging them around. I know just how Wagner feels; why can't people like this leave us at peace to serve mankind?

[November 13, 1957]

Tell Your Face

The Migrant Ministry of the National Council of Churches held its annual luncheon yesterday "as a tribute to those who harvest our crops." This is a gentle phrase of love used to describe the families of pickers who wander the rural slums.

The guests at the Hotel Plaza were mostly ladies, and their toastmaster was Mrs. Norman Vincent Peale. Mrs. Peale apologized for starting the program of speeches "while many of you have not finished your ice cream or that delicious cup of coffee, but we know that many of you do not like to stay too long."

Mrs. Peale remembered the little story about the child who told her mother that, if she was happy, she should tell her face she was. "I can see," said Mrs. Peale, "that you have all told your faces that you are a happy group." "Reads her husband's books," said a visitor. "That's more than you could say for Mrs. Spinoza."

The cover of the menu was the jacket of a new book, *This Is the Migrant*, by Louise Rossiter Shotwell. It is a five-color wash drawing of pickers at work; only one of the three adult subjects appears to have told her face that she is happy. There was a packet describing the literature available to those who would learn more about the migrant's life: the book *Sandy and Mr. Jalopy*, by Edith J. Agnew, "The experiences of seven-year-old Sandy as he travels from 'crop to crop' with his migrant family and Mr. Jalopy [their car], make up the delightful story for this book." There is room for confident living everywhere and no proper pill is without its coating of sugar.

There was, as usual, very little fiscal gain from these events for the Migrant Mission, which spends $200,000 a year serving migratory workers in thirty-one states, and is, whatever its limitations, a unique and lonely expression of national conscience.

The $5.50 cost of yesterday's luncheon left very little for the work of the mission, since it barely covered the cost of the food, and the minimal fee of Peter Merivale, who did handsomely by "Homing" and "The Lord's Prayer," without both of which no luncheon of ladies is possible in New York City.

I have had occasion in the past for melancholy reflection on the addiction to numbing foods of Americans gathered to celebrate their part in the betterment of the unfortunate. Miss Elsie Farris, the main speaker, reminded us all of the "sacrifice attendant upon Christmas witness," according to what I can decipher of the notes on her message written across a menu consisting of "Supreme of Fresh Fruit; Stuffed Chicken Gatti; and Bombe Glace Cardinale."

It is distressing how humble the true Christian is, and how muted his message. The Migrant Mission, on occasions like these, can only express the wish that the brotherhood of man prevailed everywhere without blaming the condition of the migrants on anything more specific than the absence of universal Christian love.

Miss Edith M. Lowry, national director of the Migrant Ministry, has been at her labors since 1921, and, if anyone is entitled to screech like Jeremiah, I'm sure it is she. Even so, she remains a gentle lady with a child's blue eyes, although I have no cause to doubt that she has bawled out her share of peach growers who sleep their hands in tents in the mud.

Mrs. Peale told the audience: "I sometimes wonder how she does the many things she does, when I consider the tensions that are about us."

Miss Lowry reported that she wished she had more to report. "Some things are encouraging . . . others are complex." It was a happy choice of words in the presence of Mrs. Peale. Miss Lowry mentioned her charges as among the loneliest, the most inarticulate, the most forgotten group in our society. There was an expression on her face indicating she had forgotten to tell it how happy she was.

She told of the Migrant Mission's Harvesters, the station wagons in which its workers travel from camp to camp carrying "balls and bats and horseshoes, a folding altar, and Bibles and a portable organ." And of the teen-age boy who was caught stealing fruit from a farmer, and how, when he was carried before the judge, the Migrant Mission worker went with him and said, "Judge, Jimmy knows how wrong he did and, if you let him go, I'll be responsible."

The work of the Migrant Mission is much more than this, but Miss Lowry has learned not to trouble a luncheon at the Plaza with the passion which must sustain the long hours of her life.

We owe to the National Council of Churches, in large part, what little society has done for the migrant. Its local committees have lobbied incessantly for housing codes and social security and some measure of comfort for these poor people. Hundreds of church ladies in dozens of places have gone to camps and done their little bit, drawn there by a spirit far more important than anything drawing us to the Plaza.

One thinks of these women, and one thinks of Mrs. Peale, who is free of evil because she is innocent of its sight, and then it is difficult to think of her as really very important. It is only sad that hers is the face American Protestantism presents to the world, as though it were ashamed of any Christian woman who would tell her face that it felt pity, compassion and shock at the misery of mankind.

Whether for gangster's wedding or migrant's luncheon, the American menu must conclude with *bombe glace*. The books on a migrant child's life must be described as "delightful." These women should be locked in a bare room and have Dostoevski read to them by teams of rabid holy men for twenty-four hours. Without that, they can only go away and reflect on what interesting work Miss Lowry did take up.

[November 21, 1957]

Group Dynamics

"The Commission on Intergroup Relations (COIR) is an agency of the City of New York through which the city *officially* [italics theirs] may bring about mutual respect and understanding among the many racial, religious and ethnic groups living in the City of New York and eliminate prejudice, discrimination and segregation."

The commission's name, among its familiars, is COIR, pronounced "choir," as in harmony.

Sunday night and yesterday, COIR assembled 150 civil servants, sociologists, and neighborhood social workers to help it discover how to get down to the people or, as it so well said, reach that "basic unit of intergroup and interpersonal relations" which is "found at the local level."

We had best resign ourselves to living with this version of the English language until some Mau Mau of the hipsters can be organized to burn, raze or gut the New York School of Social Work and other local shrines of its propagation. It is the only narcotic for which the social workers have never tried to prescribe a cure, which may be because they understand that withdrawal from it to reality is far more unsettling than from heroin.

As COIR said in its summons, to ignite the pot one more time before I kick it: "It is the hope of the commission that the intense focus of a work-conference of experts shall provide us with an accurate picture of the ever-changing, dynamic urban neighborhood, so that we may chart our program course effectively, and disseminate this knowledge to groups working in the field."

COIR broke its one hundred fifty, uh, of course, resource people into panels of twenty. This is a technique known as group dynamics. COIR Chairman Alfred J. Marrow said that five months ago he had seen this in operation at an American Management Association session and that everything that was said had been fed into an IBM machine and they had made fifteen decisions in an hour.

The first panel had barely begun when a lady from one of the community councils reported that her own neighborhood had been decently integrated until the city projected one of those housing warrens with a prospect of 99 per cent Negro occupancy.

She and her associates worked heroically and with remarkable success to persuade whites to apply for places in the project and maintain something like integration there. But only twelve of the four hundred and fifty white applicants were accepted by the City Housing Authority. Reasons for rejection ranged from too high income to lack of a marriage license. The result was a project segregated in fact.

Couldn't we, she asked, get the City Housing Authority to show a little more understanding?

In which moment of crisis, a representative of the Youth Board intervened to suggest that we were moving too fast. You can't build anything until you say what your tools are first. Now what is a neighborhood? Group dynamics had cremated its first Jeanne d'Arc.

All over the Carnegie Endowment's lounge, there was the hum of voices trying to devise the methodology to describe a neighborhood. A lady said that it might be well to have a conference for lay people.

The morning ended and a group of visitors went looking for an Italian restaurant described in the conference's list of approved eateries. It had been torn down some years ago, the victim of the aggressive alliance of Robert Moses and the housewreckers union. A worker for the Puerto Rican Labor Office said his panel did not seem yet settled on a definition of a neighborhood. He had one, but it seemed useless to offer it.

"A neighborhood is where, when you go out of it, you get beat up," he said.

The agenda seemed infinitely distant. A visitor said he lived in Princeton. A youth worker said he lived in Massapequa. Dan Wakefield of the *Nation* remembered asking a dedicated young Puerto Rican why he didn't live in the neighborhood to which he was devoting his labors. "My God," was the answer, "I've got three children."

The conference's experts included six cops, dispatched there by Commissioner Kennedy. At least one was a distinct ornament to the proceedings. This cop suggested that it might help if the city told the citizens the truth every now and then. Wasn't COIR set up to come into areas and tell people the truth about the race rumors that occasionally stirred his neighborhood?

"No one," he said, "trusts the city. All they get is double talk and run-arounds. It's this business of being unable to pin anyone down. God help you, if you write to the Board of Education."

Over in the first panel, the lady who had wanted to discuss the City Housing Authority was dauntlessly fighting for a recommendation that COIR set up pilot projects in selected neighborhoods and see how they went. The Youth Board man said that there was great prejudice against pilot projects. Someone wondered whether they couldn't be called by another name.

The afternoon all but ended with an hour-long showing of a Reginald Rose film. It was a shocking piece about the near lynching of a Puerto Rican tenant. Its ugly echoes were all over the room when Chairman Marrow arose to express his regrets at the absence of an IBM machine and to say that, since it was late, he would send them all their findings by mail. They would agree, he was sure, that they were embarking on an exciting program.

These are people whose fingers are swollen at the dike, and I will not make fun of them. Frank S. Horne, COIR's executive director, is a tough, and not unbloodied, fighter for the Sharkey-Brown-Isaacs bill. I can only assume that they do what they do in spite of rituals of this sort and only because each goes home and laughs at the next one's capacity for talking all day without saying anything.

[December 3, 1957]

The Artisans

Remember, wherever you are and however you get there today, quiet men were your trouble. Quiet men without press agents. Quiet men forgotten by government. Blundering quiet men, the sort who smile pleasantly and pass all but a few quarrels by, patient men, amateurs at making nuisances of themselves.

And remember too that, on Sunday last, 560 of our free fellow citizens gathered for a union meeting at the Palm Gardens here, and that a detective employed by the son of the author of the National Labor Relations Act did hide on the premises in a closet and did bore a quarter-inch peephole to spy on their proceedings.

James Wesley, a Transit Authority detective, was assigned to this piece of espionage in order to catch Theodore Loos and the other officers of the Motormen's Benevolent Association fomenting yesterday's hemi-demi-semi subway strike. It was Wesley's evidence which sent Loos to jail two hours before the strike began. Municipal socialism has nothing to learn from Nate Shefferman.

The motormen were summoned to their strike meeting with a leaflet barren of anything hortatory except those grand old words of Abraham Lincoln's about this country and its institutions belonging to the people who inhabit it, and whenever they shall grow weary of the existing government it being their revolutionary right to overthrow it.

The motormen who gathered in their headquarters in a loft above Union Square yesterday were wonderfully patient and good-humored. The reporters among their visitors, who, thank God for the safety of the Republic, are generally less tolerant of anarchist disorder than I, were enchanted by them as by no other set of strikers in our experience.

As a human being, the motorman would appear to be the best of possible rebuttals to the doctrine of togetherness. He is unique in the transit system because he is uncontaminated by contact with the riding public: If you have any doubts as to the superiority of solitude over community, just spend five minutes with a subway motorman and cap it with five more in the company of a bus driver.

The motorman rides alone, sealed off from the customers in a cubicle in communion with his God and the remembered treasured wisdom of mankind. The most conspicuous sign in the hall was a carefully lettered quotation: JUSTICE IS THE CONSTANT DESIRE AND EFFORT TO RENDER EVERY MAN HIS DUE — JUSTINIAN. One looked at these men — at the moment one of them was clearing a table so a cop could have his lunch — and one conjured up the vision of the old artisans who read Martial and Catullus, and the issues, in a tired time, seemed between the new man as part of the mass and the old one as individual. The old one can hardly win so unequal a contest. In any case, the issues are much more complex, but at that time, with the rain outside, it all seemed that simple and that pure.

One of them came up the stairs, shook off the rain and reported on his trip to his shop to pull the motormen out. He had been chased away by the supervisors; he said, without bitterness, that he might have been able to stay longer if Mike Quill's men hadn't fingered him. He wasn't sure he was for the strike. "But, after all," he said, as if it were the most reasonable statement in the world, "they got our president in jail. It wouldn't be right to back down now."

Frank Zelano, the MBA's executive secretary, had been awake for forty-eight hours. He got up to give a reporter a seat. While he was talking, Michael Neil of the Conductors, and Julio Garcia of the Signalmen, came in as representatives of small craft unions which are watching the motormen with sympathy. Neil had on the black suit of his craft. They talked gently, and without much decision, about the chance that they might go out this morning too. Their visitors began drifting away with very little sense that it could come to much. One of them was saying he had been there since five in the morning and had yet to hear a bitter word.

The warden of the city jail on West 37th Street opened his little peep-out door and said that Theodore Loos couldn't have any visitors. There was no one else to go and see except Mike Quill.

A Daily News photographer was taking Mike Quill's picture. ("If the Daily News ever starts speaking well of me, I will resign.") He sat in his office under various signs of himself threatening the city with Armageddon, and said into the telephone that he would get a squad on it right away. Mike Quill was running a back-to-work movement.

He had shamrocks for cuff-links and a shamrock in his tie, and other insignia of his blazing revolutionary temperament. He said it was a mistake to arrest Theodore Loos. "He's been running around all over town trying to get somebody to arrest him all week. Nobody would pick him up even as a vagrant. He was begging the cops to book him at City Hall last week, but the city fathers are very charitable people; they always were."

It was Mike Quill's particular hope that the signalmen would not join the strike:

"I'm worried for the signalmen, they're not essential to the operation. The Transit Authority may find that out. We don't want that to happen, the same as we don't want the motormen to run the risk of losing their jobs."

Mr. Quill is president of the city CIO.

He passed around a leaflet: "Don't let a handful of bungling misleaders disgrace the excellent name of all TA employes." There was also a press release affirming that "IND service is steadily improving."

His visitors departed, leaving him alone among the portraits of his flaming youth. It had stopped raining. It does not rain on the enemies of irresponsibility. Down at the motormen's shack, the MBA's board was awaiting an important visitor, unidentified except for the fact that he was a powerful non-political figure bringing help. He never came. Afterwards, Frank Zelano said that he didn't know who the mysterious stranger was and that if he had come he would identify himself only as "Long Distance." It figured. He wouldn't come to the poor and humble. They never do.

[December 10, 1957]

The Substitute

Little after ten o'clock yesterday morning, an exhausted boredom had fallen upon the Senate Committee on Improper Labor-Management Practices and it agreed to go ahead with its investigation of Walter Reuther's conduct of the four-year-long strike at the Kohler Plumbing Co. on the terms dictated by Walter Reuther's enemies.

Reuther was a mechanically protestant scratch from the top of the list of his auto union's witnesses. Out in the hall, John McClellan was pouring his cold Methodist wrath upon Barry Goldwater.

And Alan Graskamp, president of Local 833 of the Kohler strikers, whose job it seems always to be to pick the rubble off the floor, walked into committee counsel Robert Kennedy's office and asked what he was supposed to do now.

"We'll start with the first witness in twenty minutes," said Bobby Kennedy, with his crooked smile, "and you're it."

Alan Graskamp, unknown to us all, was marked for comfort and opportunity perhaps once in his life when Kohler offered to make him a foreman in 1951. He turned the company down to stay an officer of Kohler's independent union, then to head Kohler's new UAW local, then to lead its first strike four years ago and remain, at $50-a-week strike benefits, so long as it lasts.

There is still, after three years, a pleasant little ceremony when a striker caves in and goes back to Kohler. The company loyalists meet him at the gate and follow him in, singing "Solidarity Forever," the UAW anthem, in the mocking tones of victory. Alan Graskamp has seen eight hundred men go back that way; most of the nearly two thousand he says have stood with him have gone off to other jobs. There is even a colony of Kohler strikers in California.

It is left to Alan Graskamp to carry on as best he can. He is proud that he was one of Kohler's best-paid production hands; staying on strike costs him $3,000 a year. He has been offered jobs in other plants, but he cannot take them, because, he says, "Someone has to stay there for these people."

When he sat down — he looks oddly like Walter Reuther — surrounded by the professionals who had had to yield their case to him, Bobby Kennedy told the committee that Mr. Graskamp had had only twenty minutes' notice and that it would be quite understandable if he did not sound too well prepared.

But Alan Graskamp will run you on any track. He apologized because he had no written statement. But he would like to say a few words before he began.

"This is a strike of the Kohler workers, the people who work at Kohler. They are continuing to strike until justice is won."

Carl Curtis and Barry Goldwater went at him and he told about the secret strike ballot, and the great surge of pickets, and the time his house was stoned. They pressed him again about the fights on picket lines, and then Alan Graskamp said:

"We may have made some mistakes. We did some things that I don't know whether we would do again. I can never get back what I have lost from this strike." He said he doubted if he could ever go back to Kohler; he stood and waited only in the hope for the kind of Kohler "for which my son will be able to go to work."

"They are fighting, Senator," he said, "for the wife and children. We have stood and watched people steal our jobs and take them away. And, in that case, I'm sure that tempers are not always what they should be."

John Kennedy asked him what the union's grievances were:

"The wages was never the number one question, Senator," he answered. "It was the dignity of the guys working there."

And then, all of a sudden, he was talking about what it was like to work in the enameling room, where the men wear asbestos gloves and winter underwear in summer to keep off the scorch, and the temperature of 180 degrees, and how during one squabble, the company turned off the fans, and about the silicosis in the pottery division, and how the company gave each man an X-ray twice a year, but would not tell them the results, because a management spokesman said, if a man has a spot on his lung, "They'll all worry themselves to death and become hypochondriacs."

This was not Walter Reuther, with his new-sharpened pencil and his charts and his paper. Suddenly the Senate, for the first time in the memory of Washington, was hearing a factory worker talking about what it is like to work in a factory. By brushing Reuther aside, Barry Goldwater had left nothing for Washington's eyes but the flesh of the client himself.

So there sat Alan Graskamp, with nothing to talk about except the whole meaning of life, about the loss and pain and suffering and glory of the illusion that the poor are equal to the great and powerful. He pronounced the word "dignity" as though the Lord would call him in the very next second, and he was content to stand judged on that word alone.

Then there was a recess, and Walter Reuther carried his brief case into the caucus room to tell the television cameras that Barry Goldwater is "a political hypocrite and a moral coward," that he had "been deprived of a basic opportunity." We had gone from Alan Graskamp back to Washington, with the beating of wooden swords on tin shields. The reporters struggled back there without much conviction or passion; there were few questions; on no other occasion has Walter Reuther seemed less a focus of interest. He seemed, as any man of great affairs had to seem after Alan Graskamp, like papier-mâché after flesh.

The substitute was standing on the sidelines. Somebody asked him what fixtures he had in his bathroom. "I got Kohler," said Alan Graskamp. "I was loyal to my company." He should be; he went to college there.

[Washington, D.C., February 27, 1958]

The Junkyard Off the Highway

The most important officer of United Auto Workers Local 7 just now is Mike Moresco, who is chairman of its Community Services Committee. It is to Mike Moresco that the Chrysler-Jefferson losers come with their doctors' bills, and their garnishments, and then with their problems with the unemployment insurance system and then with their threatened foreclosures and, at the very end, in the moment that they accept the fact that they are going on relief.

That last moment came yesterday for Martin Loftis, fifty, assembly hand.

The only date in his life that Martin Loftis remembers with absolute firmness is June 22, 1948, which is the date his seniority began with Chrysler.

He sat in Mike Moresco's office yesterday, a thick man in overalls who looked more like a farmer than a city factory worker.

"I was born," he said, "in Jackson County, Tennessee, but I have been in Detroit so long it's my home. I come up here with U. S. Rub-

ber in 1928 and then I got laid off and I went home for six months
and then I come back here and I started tightening fenders at the
Chrysler plant, you know with my head up there under the hood. I
went up and I went down and I got six years of seniority at Chrysler,
and then I went to California and they lost my address and I lost that
seniority and when I came back on June 20, 1948, they started me off
again, and I got laid off last August."

He bought a house on the fringes of Grosse Pointe three years ago;
and when his daughters got married he had so much room that he
built an apartment upstairs and took in a tenant and the $20 a week
he got that way covered his whole mortgage.

"I guess I got $6,000 in labor in that house. I found a fellow who
made me a deal to do the plumbing and this other fellow moved in
and I guess the word must have gotten around that I was renting, and
the city inspector came around and checked everything and then
came back and told me that my plumber wasn't licensed, that was a
violation, and I'd have to get a new plumbing job in thirty days or
move my tenant out.

"Well, I ain't got no money and I'm laid off and I'm not working
and I went to a bank to get a FHA loan, but of course they couldn't
give it to me. The fellow who was living with me had a steady job at
Cadillac Motors, and with that $20 a week I'd be all right. But he
moved and now I got this paper from the land contract woman and
they tell me I'm going to lose the house.

"Everything I had," he said, "was in that house, $6,000 cash
money. If it hadn't been for that plumbing violation, I'd a been all
set. I'd a kep' dragging along."

His unemployment insurance had all been used up, and Mike
Moresco told him that he would have to go on welfare. That may
have saved the house for a little while and every two weeks he gets
$17.84 all to himself just for food.

Martin Loftis sat and talked about these things absolutely without
rancor. "When they get here," said Mike Moresco, "they don't fight
any more. They are just beaten. We can get a little something for
Martin every now and then. People die and they need pallbearers;
you'd be surprised how many of our people just don't have pallbearers. We can use Martin for that. Of course, he's the kind of

fellow who would do it for nothing, but this way we give him $3 or so and it's not a handout."

Martin Loftis is, and he knows it, a piece of machinery in the boneyard. Chrysler-Jefferson, whatever happens, will never call the ten-year men back again. He is an auto worker who has never been able to afford to buy a new car. And yet how much of the history of the American automobile is bound up in him and the fenders he tightened since 1928 — a nation on wheels cluttering the great roads, free to wander as it pleases because Martin Loftis was on the line?

He sat there and laughed gently at "the way brother Williams took on that Republican at the unemployment conference." One of the stewards was saying that Martin had never in his memory filed a grievance against Chrysler. The $6,000 he put in the house almost gone, the years under the hood all gone, the life junk and the junk-yard its end. This is one of the men that people like myself were writing about just two years ago as members of some new middle class or other. It is no excuse to say that we did not know we were lying; if there is a God in heaven, He will pay us for that lie, and He will pay Martin Loftis for enduring it and all the other lies.

"I never know what you fellows want," said Mike Moresco to his visitor. "I got some figures here, but I never know what they mean. Are you looking for a real hardship case?"

And the visitor answered with a kind of vision very rare for him that he didn't want a hardship case; he wanted just the opposite; he wanted a Chrysler worker who hadn't been laid off.

"Why don't you talk to Otis?" said Mike Moresco. Otis P. is thirty-two years old, a Negro, with seniority that goes back to 1943. He came in and sat down; I would judge his IQ at about 140. His wife was a schoolteacher until she quit to raise the children.

"We've been working twenty-one hours a week since Christmas," he said. "That is $46 a week. I had a little bank account back then; now I guess I've got $5 in the credit union."

He would make more money if Chrysler laid him off. His unemployment benefits would be nearly $60 a week. But he is a very lucky man; his seniority goes back fifteen years and he is not laid off. His seniority date is his insurance policy; it is his only possession. Since Christmas it has cost him $18 a week to keep it.

"What can I do about somebody like Martin?" said Moresco. "Who is responsible for a group of people who just want to work?"

The top letter on his desk yesterday was from an auto worker who had been sick with asthma for two years. He had come to the point where he could not pay for his latest prescription.

"I hate to bother you with my troubles," he said, "but I am in a bad way." That, and not a roar and not a howl, is the voice of the people.

[Detroit, April 10, 1958]

Where Dreams Come True

The Chrysler Company sent a new Plymouth with a sticker on its bumper saying KEEP DETROIT DYNAMIC — BUY A PLYMOUTH, a uniformed driver in its front and in its back a young man from the public relations department to a hotel yesterday to pick up a visiting observer who had expressed a wish to see the interior of its Jefferson assembly plant.

The young man from public relations apologized for not really knowing very much about these things, and wondered if his guest would be satisfied with the regular public tour, which has a trained guide. His guest answered that Chrysler had already been too kind. So they sat in the lobby of the plant, while the children were assembled for the public tour; the guest studied the folders for the 1958 Chrysler — "Glamour Car of the Forward Look."

The wall of one hall near the lobby was covered with framed citations awarded Chrysler's advertising department in recognition of its craft by various professional societies dedicated to the proposition that the billboard is more lovely than the tree. We are a nation which honors not the men who build automobiles but the men who advertise them.

The party went past the purity of the lobby to stand in the alley just outside the assembly plant itself, while their guide explained that he would take them "down where the body meets the chassis." That is a phrase of wonderfully lyric cadence suitable for singing at boat parties on soft midsummer nights.

There was a quarter-mile trip back to that point through the new cars with their decorator colors. "The cushions are the last things to go in so the men won't get them dirty while they're working in there," the young man from public relations said. He had evidently been quite modest about his knowledge of the reality of an assembly plant. They passed by a Negro woman sitting on a box binding up the wires attaching the shiny red inspection card to the shiny blue one. She was dressed like those of her sisters you occasionally see in North Carolina sorting tobacco leaf by hand. That is the automatic factory — a country woman picking over not living matter but glossy cardboard.

Down where the body meets the chassis, there is an overhead crane which was, at the moment the tour arrived, dropping a fuschia body down on an uncoated naked metal chassis. Two members of the new middle class eased it into place. One of them was a Negro with a pipe in his mouth, a large man of middle years, balding a little. The expression on his face said absolutely nothing. The pipe had a broken shank; he had bound it with a piece of wire picked from the floor, the guest supposed; his work shirt was torn at the back. The line turned out to be a kind of treadmill set in the floor; its rhythms and the rhythms of its human machines almost dreamlike, the pace of the work not frantic, not passionate, but a kind of quiet, continuous flow like a dirty, half-stagnant river.

The floor where they make the glamour car is a kind of paste of grease and discarded screws and parts, thick enough now to be almost a carpet. The visitor started to take notes; and as he did so, the men in various places took notice of him and looked up, their hands still doing their duty because by now they do not always need their eyes. There was no rancor on their faces; they must have been resigning themselves to the presence of some sort of incompetent time study man.

Some of the children on the public tour had rather lost interest by now in anything so ugly and alien as this — ugliness brought about by indifference — and had gone back to look at the finished cars again — ugliness brought about by bad taste. The guest and the young man from public relations were left to wander alone, weaving in and out of the line, which is circular at Chrysler Jefferson and moves slowly enough to be crossed.

A handsome Negro with patches all over his dungarees was running the machine which puts the tire rims into the tires, and the guest and the young man from public relations stopped to ask him how the machine worked. He explained with great courtesy, but diverting his attention and breaking his rhythm was no special favor to him because, while he was talking, he cut his thumb on one of the tire rims. It wasn't a bad cut; he didn't even comment, but pulled out a dirty handkerchief, wiped a spot of blood off the new gray paint of the tire rim, and then wrapped his own hand and went on working.

It is strange how many dirty rags hold things together in the automatic factory, rags around men's thumbs, rags around the rubber air hoses of the power tools, the slow accretion of the mixture of oil and paint and sawdust on the floor. How much would it cost any of us if there were less chrome on the new Imperial; and we spent a little money to have it manufactured in a place fit for the stabling of a farm animal. The visitor was grateful to Chrysler for what must have been, counting the car, the driver, the young man from public relations, no less than $50 of its budget to gratify his idle curiosity.

How many of the men he left behind him will ever buy a brand-new Plymouth? To this question, fortunately, there exists an answer. Three years ago, the auto workers' union negotiated a 20 per cent discount for its members on new Chrysler cars. The company even put special men in the plant to assist in sales. At the end of the year, they gave it up; less — a good deal less — than 1,000 of the 100,000 eligible for the discount had bought a new car. That is not because they hate the company or its product; it is because they don't make enough money to buy what they produce.

The visitor was driven back to his hotel and, with his usual slack morality, let Chrysler waste more money better spent by buying him a drink. He then packed his bag, and in the process picked up a booklet issued by the UAW to describe its triumphs. Its title was: "We Dared Make Our Dreams Come True." Where dreams come true, down where the body meets the chassis.

[Detroit, April 11, 1958]

Daddy

Yesterday was one of those Mondays, crowning the centuries of the common law's slow progress upward, when Judge Samuel F. Leibowitz passes those sentences on the sinners of Brooklyn that are the distilled wisdom of the long nights he has sat up thinking about justice.

Judge Leibowitz's court was half-filled yesterday, as quite often happens, with school children, in this case a delegation of Princeton junior high school students. Their presence was a mark of the judge's cosmic syndication; he is the last institution left in Brooklyn for the sight of which buses are chartered.

They come because their teachers read the magazine pieces in which Judge Leibowitz explains how we fail with our children because there is insufficient dignity in our posture towards them.

The children arrived a little before eleven, and were installed for the rumination of the appointments of a Brooklyn courtroom. Judge Leibowitz showed up a little before eleven, put on his glasses and called the first loser.

A young man named Martin Miller was led forward and set beside his court-appointed attorney, who mumbled something about this being a first offense.

Judge Leibowitz pointed out that Miller and an associate had held up a taxicab with a toy pistol. Miller had also told his probation officer that, when the fancy moved him through the year previous, he enjoyed rolling drunks.

"A married man with two children rolling drunks," he said judiciously. "He's a no-good tramp; that's the kind of fellow he is." Under ordinary circumstances, that, said the judge, meant ten to thirty. As he poised his terrible swift sword, he was interrupted by a probation officer at his back with a hunk of paper. They conferred, and the judge announced to the populace that the defendant was now being investigated by the district attorney's office for attacks upon girls.

"Put off the sentence for two weeks," he told his clerk, "and expunge that record."

There followed Kenneth Coleman, sixteen, who with Gerard Woolridge, sixteen, had, in the judge's summary, "waylaid a fifteen-year-old newsboy and dragged him to the seventh floor and robbed him of a few dollars."

Coleman, the judge observed, had been before Children's Court three times in the last year — once for stealing candy from a candy store, once for breaking a parking meter — "when he was consorting with bad girls" — and once when charged with disorderly conduct for "being boisterous and breaking a lock."

The victim in the latter case had been permitted to withdraw the charges; Judge Leibowitz said he would have permitted no such thing. Then he ran down, and Kenneth Coleman went off to Elmira.

Then came Gerard Woolridge, and with him the flame of inspiration to Judge Leibowitz to display the proper deportment of secure maturity towards troublesome adolescence:

"What goes through the mind of a young fellow like you? That's of the greatest interest."

Gerard Woolridge mumbled, and the clerk shouted forth his answer, "I knew it wasn't right but I was with my friend."

"You were with that other young hooligan, you mean," Judge Leibowitz replied in his majesty. "You're just like an animal. Haven't you figured that out? You just don't care."

Gerard Woolridge mumbled that he did care. The judge turned to Gerard's court-appointed attorney: "You're a reputable lawyer; what is your answer to this?" The poor conscript mumbled something about not condoning this sort of thing in his conscience, but . . .

"Whadya gonna do with animals of this type?" said Sam Leibowitz. "They have no conscience. No sense in lecturing him; I don't think it would do any good. How would you like seven and a half to fifteen?"

Gerard Woolridge mumbled that "I guess I'll take what you give me." As he went out the door, Judge Leibowitz called after his prep-school-jacketed back: "Tell the hoodlums upstairs you got seven and a half to fifteen."

He turned to face one Adam Green, a thief of riper vintage, this being his second offense for burglary. Green assumed that practiced posture of humility which is a mature man's shrewdest defense against the state. It served him well.

"I'd like to give this fellow a break, because he was drunk," said the judge. "His trouble is liquor." The assistant district attorney said he would look up the law in this case.

"Never mind the law in this case," said the judge. "We're dealing with human beings here. The fellow was cock-eyed drunk." Adam Green was sent off with a postponement: "Adam Green, what is it?" said the judge. "I want to help you."

The love of man and child suffused the judge's face. "Bring back Woolridge," he said. Back came Woolridge. "Whadya gonna do after the fifteen years?" the judge asked him. "Get a job," said Woolridge. "You been doing a job on people," said the judge. "You got a troubled mind. I'm gonna vacate the sentence, and sentence you to three and a half to five at Elmira." Woolridge was led away again. "You got a break, didn't you?" the judge called after him.

Judge Leibowitz had cleared his calendar. He was free to visit with the Princeton teacher. Her charges watched them at the bench.

They had learned their lesson. The majesty of the law is just like Daddy, loud, without dignity, a showboat who doesn't really mean it.

[April 23, 1958]

The Meek in Babylon

One comes, let one confess, to the confrontation of Jehovah's Witnesses with a certain predisposition in their favor. By the mere act of converting Mickey Spillane to put aside his pen, they have on the record served their generation better than any of their competitors in the service of God.

They are with us today, bulging Yankee Stadium, overflowing into the Polo Grounds, a gentle herd lowing on the meadows where Mickey Mantle is wont to ramble. Dan Topping is their landlord and heaven is their destination.

They now have 770,000 members, and are the fastest-growing religious movement on earth. That fact is as irrelevant as the conclusion that their doctrine is probably nonsense. Their true beauty is not in their theology or in their statistics. It is in the presence of grace they bring to a hot dog line; we may not need them for our souls, but we desperately need their spirit on the shuttle; they are, this gentlest of all armies of occupation, a living reproach to a city which by custom runs to crowds which for mere malignity would disgrace Little Rock.

A visitor yesterday fought his way with elbow and kneecap towards the Yankee dugout and stepped on the toe of a Witness who looked up and said, "Excuse me, brother, can I help you?" Outside, under the lowering clouds, the Witnesses sat unconscious of the pagan symbols on the signs that preached Scotch whisky and male deodorants. In the dugout where Casey Stengel prowls on more serious and secular occasions, Hans Rasmussen, formerly of Denmark, explained his witness:

"I've been in truth about ten years," he said. "I had a photographic studio in Denmark and one of the brothers called on me and I asked him a few questions and he answered them. I publish about five hours a week."

Hans Rasmussen is in Vancouver now, and hopes the Witnesses will send him to Ecuador. He is in a lonely trade, but it has its rewards:

"One of our brothers met a man on the street last month who said, 'Brother, don't you remember me?'" He didn't, and the man said that he was the one who had thrown him downstairs when he came with the truth. 'I stopped to think after you got up and left, maybe you're a better Christian than I am. So, brother, I'm in the truth now.'"

"Satan came to Jesus Christ," said Leo Newell of Payette, Idaho, "and showed him the kingdoms of the earth and told him he could have them." He reported this event as though he had read it in the *Times* that morning. He went on to say that he had been born in the truth, and sells clothing part time to eat while he witnesses.

"I sell good clothing," he said, "but if I ever thought more of it than my ministry, I would quit."

Out in the infield a brother and a sister were standing under a yellow canopy over a retaining wall covered with linoleum masking as brick — the earthly paradise come to Yankee Stadium. She was saying that through the undeserved kindness of Jehovah she now had the supreme joy of going to Penang. Through the undeserved unkindness of Jehovah, it had commenced to rain; the Witnesses sat there; a little boy — wearing a souvenir hat saying JEHOVAH'S WITNESSES, DIVINE WILL ASSEMBLY, 1958 — slept on undisturbed. Next to him, with a pair of binoculars and a camera, sat Marina Berescosher of Tangier, the cloth of purdah covering her face up to her eyes.

"I was born in the truth," said Leo Newell. "My mother was a Methodist and my father a Presbyterian. They read the tracts."

Thus is a child's life changed; he has been to Italy and Nicaragua since, living as the birds do from the air, a clothing salesman in Idaho now, bearing the truth inside.

"Everyone here, as you can see, tries to dress as best he can, but these things are only a means to the end."

The full-time Witnesses are called pioneers. They get food and lodging and $14 a month allowance here and $5 abroad. Douglas Martin, a tall and solemn man, was a farmer in Canada in 1938 when a publisher of the Witnesses came by and took him from the Methodists. He is in Nicaragua now, riding horseback to native settlements where train and bus do not go.

Their endurance was massive and rather touching yesterday. It was the graduation ceremony of their Gilead Bible School, which trains full-time missionaries. It must be the only school on the continent of North America whose students are graduated in the burnoose of the Arab or the kente of the Nigerian.

As the rains came down upon them, their orators proceeded undampened; they marched in the mud of the Yankee infield to get their diplomas while Nathan H. Knorr, their president, introduced them.

"Here," he said in one case, "is Brother Hinkley from the Fiji Islands. His father and mother were cannibals. But you needn't worry about Brother Hinkley now."

Various of our resident juvenile delinquents were passing among them, selling GI surplus raincoats for $1 apiece. They bought them and put them on, felt them melt in the rain. They were sitting in the earthly paradise being bilked by teenage sharpies and they were beautifully uncomplaining.

"We are," said Wally Olmstead of Portland, Oregon, "the only people on earth who know the future and are untroubled by it. We get tired of course" — they were now in the fifth hour of the rain and the exhortations — "but we get happy tired, not mad tired."

There is obviously nothing wrong with the manners of The Bronx that the infusion of a little bad theology won't cure.

[July 28, 1958]

Lost Horizon

The Commissioner of Education of the United States was reported day before yesterday as saying that, since he had never heard of either *Brave New World* or *1984*, it would be quite improper for him to comment on the decision of the Miami School Board to drop them from the English curriculum for high school seniors.

Lawrence Derthick turns out on inspection to be a former president of the American Association of School Administrators, a Master of Arts from the University of Tennessee, a former student at Teachers College in Columbia, a member of the National Conference of Christians and Jews, the Chamber of Commerce and the Kiwanis Club. (There used to be a theory that teachers were under-appreciated in the United States because they were odd-balls and unlike everyone else.) He would seem, on that record, to represent the best available kind of professional training.

Last summer, Dr. Derthick was crowned with an honorary degree as a Doctor of Humane Letters by Yeshiva University. In his acceptance speech, he expressed the gratitude of all scholars that his country was beginning to regain again that "respect for the truly learned person that once so strongly characterized us as a nation." Fortunately, for Dr. Derthick, this renaissance does not seem to have gone far enough to endanger his job.

The point about the troubles of George Orwell and Aldous Huxley in Miami is that no one in that school system ever seems to have heard of them except the poor English teacher who had made the mistake of reading them in the first place. She had put *Brave New World* on the required and *1984* on the supplementary reading list for seniors at the North Miami High School.

Orwell and Huxley were first called to the attention of School Principal Wilfred E. Rice by a mother who called him one afternoon and said that she had discovered the word "erotic" in *Brave New World* and demanded to know how anyone could make children read such filth. It is the essence of our educational system that whatever part of the institution is not run by the inmates is reserved for the parents of the inmates.

Principal Rice hadn't read either Orwell or Huxley, so he took the matter to Joe Hall, the superintendent of schools. Hall hadn't read them either, so he did what the President of the United States does in cultural matters: he farmed them out to Robert Wilson, director of high schools. Wilson gave both books a fast brush, found them "trashy," showed Hall an "off-color" passage and they were dropped from the reading list.

There was so much stir about all this in Miami that later the chairman of the school board said that he was thinking seriously of reading the books himself to see what they were about. There is no record of whether this threat was ever consummated.

Superintendent of Schools Hall said yesterday that he had just read 1984, but couldn't report that he had anything "good or bad" to say about it.

"But I do think the book would be over the heads of many students at that level," he went on.

What level?

"The high school senior level.

"It's our feeling here that no child should be required to read a book to which any appreciable number of parents object. There certainly must be enough books in the world."

Dr. Hall said that he had earned his Ph.D. in education.

"I'm so involved in action," he said, "that I never get to read much. When I do, I read books on education, on social development and things like that. The last novel I read? I suppose it was James Hilton's *Lost Horizon*, but then, I'd read that before."

Just that far have we carried our distance for all conceptions of an intellectual elite. A man can be a doctor of philosophy in the United States and never have to read a novel or a poem.

The last word on this belongs to Orwell. In his book on the Spanish War, he had a long section on a friend who had been put in prison by the Communists. It was a horrible story. Orwell, a tired man and a sick one, finished it with this sentence:

"It is ridiculous to get angry, but there is a stupid malignity in these things which does try one's patience."

[March 31, 1960]

Social Notes

The American Sociological Association is convening this week at the Statler-Hilton. After fifty-five years, the sociologist is so much a part of normal society that today one of the stores is tendering a fashion show for his wife to indicate her status equal to the wife of the politician, the labor leader, the doctor or any other example of social adjustment to be found at a convention in New York.

He forms an increasing tribe. His association is twice as large as it was ten years ago; twice as many sociologists are teaching in colleges; and twice as many are working for private industry.

There are no areas of our civilization which escape their interest, and, I'm afraid, very few where their results arouse ours. The papers presented at their convention can only represent a tiny sample of all the chaff that is annually struck up by this vast communal threshing crew. Yet no one of them could physically hear 10 per cent of the papers delivered by their authors; they are ground through at thirty different section meetings a day. And no one could read them; there are close to five hundred different papers; the press room where they are set out for the enlightenment of the journalist looks like a warehouse for the storage of telephone books.

And yet what delights their titles promise: "Some Aspects of the Deployment of Symbols" (the case of Elvis Presley); "The Van Doren Syndrome: A Study in Student Reactions"; "Beyond Utopia: The Beat Generation as a Challenge for the Sociology of Knowledge"; "Passing and the Managed Achievement of Sex Statuses in a Series of Intersexed Persons"; "Command Decision-Making in the Far North."

In a minority of cases, there are press releases summarizing the findings. My personal favorite comes from the University of Michigan: "Negro family life is not 'happy-go-lucky,' two University of Michigan social scientists reported today." It should be noticed that this discovery took the serious research effort of two men plus an ant colony of graduate students.

A major characteristic of sociology as a discipline is its remorseless pursuit of proof of what everyone knew all along. We owe many of these papers to the broad tolerance of the American academic community which apparently approved and even financed them without one man in a supervisory position having the discourtesy to suggest that the matter under study was self-evident.

There is the paper of the young man from a Southern school who discovered through 453 hours of interviews that non-college graduate Massachusetts Catholics liked the late Senator McCarthy. These findings will shock Senator Kennedy.

The young man went on to learn, among other things, that people who liked Senator McCarthy tended to have authoritarian personalities. This comforts me, because my chief personal memory of the terror of that period was being assailed once at a cocktail party by the wife of a Princeton sociologist who had seen a picture of me talking to Roy Cohn.

There seems also to be developing a sociology within sociology which promises much. Its best sample is a paper which indicates that persons who fail to answer sociological questionnaires by mail come from homes where their parents habitually beat them.

A young man from one of the women's colleges has a content analysis of Elvis Presley's songs which indicates that 29.4 per cent are masochistic (the female has a mother role); 35.3 per cent are characterized by the "authoritarian love appeal and verging on the sadistic love threat"; and 41 per cent are a "playful, quasi-humorous invitation to love play." Presleyism, he says, is badly ridden by the Protestant ethic as delineated some time ago by Max Weber, but has the difficulty of "overcoming Protestant suspicion of entertainment and free-flowing sexuality."

This is done (see Nathanstein and Leites) through Fun Morality. The Presley façade is therefore adorned by assertions from his writers that "he has brought joy unlimited to god-fearing, good, clean-cut Americans, to wit, the Good Folks Back Home."

I do the young man an injustice, of course; the extract of selected passages from sociologists has become the lowest form of wit. He is an honest scholar not bucking to be sociologist for MCA. And somewhere in all these depersonalized piles of paper, there must be some residue of insight. But sociology is the most democratic of sciences; a man need only write to publish and join his voice to a common gabble. The overall effect is one of inferior journalism, or exposition of the perfectly obvious, or timidity about expressing what is not perfectly obvious or crocheting the irrelevant. But doesn't that figure? What is sociology if it is not a reflection of American society?

[August 31, 1960]

Let Me Off Uptown

Upon this note, let us cease all debates about the national purpose. It is simply this:

Love B. Woods was born in Columbia, South Carolina, ages ago. When he was young, he was so religious that he considered it a sin to read a newspaper. After graduation from the Negro college in Columbia, he took a job as a waiter, as a bridge to the higher life. He wanted to save enough money to go to Palestine and walk in the steps of Saint Paul.

After that pilgrimage, he went back to being a waiter; the vocation of Christ slipped away, but the faith remained. Love B. Woods became a Harlem real estate man.

He owned the old Woodside Hotel, which is engraved in the cultural history of the United States because it was there that Count Basie wrote "Jumping at the Woodside." Basie went downtown; the Woodside is forgotten; but Love B. Woods stayed on in Harlem.

He came to the peak of his life when he bought the Hotel Theresa at 125th Street and Seventh Avenue. The Theresa was where the Negro entertainers stayed in the Thirties; it was, like most Harlem property, owned by white people in those days. After the war, the downtown hotels began taking Negro guests; the Negro entertainers went downtown, and the Theresa drooped, victim of the first stages of integration. Then, since it was no longer a profitable property, the white people sold the Theresa to Love B. Woods.

It was a sign and symbol of pride with him. He is an old man, and he remembers a time when a Negro had as much chance to own the Theresa as he does now to be United States Senator from Mississippi. Since the Theresa was at last the property of Negroes, he wanted it to be a model of Christian conduct. He closed the bar because he did not like the class of girls who came there, and he caused to be put in the lobby a sign courteously requesting that the tenants not congregate at the door and inspect the sidewalks because women prefer not to be stared at when they are passing a hotel.

I should strongly doubt, having seen the manager of the Shelburne, that he operates an establishment morally superior to Love B. Woods's. But, as the manager of the Shelburne knows, the rewards of purity are not excessive; Sunday, as on most days, the Theresa was far from filled.

When Love B. Woods came home from church on Sunday, he had a call from a man asking if he might have forty rooms for Fidel Castro in case of an emergency. Love B. Woods answered that it was the policy of the house to take any guest who sought admittance.

The next day, shortly after noon, two Cubans came to see Love B. Woods.

"They had a conference with me for half an hour," the old man said. "I gave them the rates of the rooms, $20 a day. They offered me a check. I figured I better call the Police Department about them before I took their check, because it is not our policy here. So I went around to the precinct to ask the sergeant what he thought, and he said that I should use my own judgment, but if I had any trouble, call them. After that, I thought I better ask for cash.

"So they went downtown and got me the cash for one day, and I told them that today at two o'clock, I had to have the rest of the cash for ten days' worth of rent. But you know, I've never had a more orderly group of people. And they're such good tippers that I don't think I'll press my point about the cash this afternoon."

So the Theresa yesterday was the capital of the revolutionary tide. Outside on the sidewalk the black nationalists walked around and argued respectfully with Jackie Robinson, who explained that he was an American and that whenever Castro attacked America, he attacked all of us.

America had suddenly absorbed Fidel Castro; we were in a Southern town standing on the corner, quietly intimate, human again. No pickets, no wild cries. Jackie Robinson was saying that he was devoted to Love B. Woods, but even so, he waved at the heap of the Theresa — and asked the group: "Would Castro stay in a place like that except for purposes of propaganda?"

And then there was scream of siren and gang-shag of cops, and a black Cadillac and Nikita Khrushchev in a blue suit and the Order of Lenin embracing a barbudo on the sidewalk.

Love B. Woods stayed in the kitchen instructing the waitresses not to forget to hand the guests in his Gold Room the menu.

Khrushchev was forty minutes with the maximum leader of the revolution — the conjunction of the unlikely with the impossible and, of course, in Harlem. In our time, the field of the cloth of gold is 125th Street and Seventh Avenue.

Knock our country, tear it down, call it what you will — and I shall call it worse — but name me one other piece of real estate under the eye of God where a man can be born a Negro in South Carolina and grow up to possess the summit where Fidel Castro and Nikita Khrushchev, after so long a climb, finally pause and wrap their arms around one another.

[September 21, 1960]

A Time for Greatness

The Newark Democracy held its quadrennial assembly to alert the citizens to the imminent peril of Wall Street within and communism abroad at the Armory last night.

Governor Meyner was invited as guest of honor at these alarums and excursions and Adlai E. Stevenson as chief speaker. To fill any pauses in the wailing and gnashing of teeth, the Democrats asked along a singer once rather familiar to patrons of the old Adams Theater, who had not been back to Newark for twenty years and who promised to bring a few friends.

The invitations to the Armory read, "Speakers: Governor Robert Meyner and Adlai E. Stevenson" and at the bottom, in diminished type, "Entertainment: Frank Sinatra." They must be getting that message about greatness in the Sixties in Newark; by five in the afternoon, the police barricades were up; two hours before the rites were scheduled, there were 15,000 serious thinkers — the most conspicuous of them girls in their high school graduation dresses — inside the armory and another 10,000 thirsting to be talked sense to in the streets outside. The police had thrown a wooden bar and their bosoms in front of each entrance.

One consequence of these siege measures was that the flower of Newark civilization, which had gold invitations and name cards waiting on the podium, was left largely wandering in the urban blight in the chill night outside. The Governor and Adlai Stevenson did manage to break through, and the Governor to bawl an introduction to Stevenson, who spoke a half hour.

It was his customary graceful performance, played against the noise of distant drums. Mobs were beating at the iron doors.

It was the general atmosphere of a poor and distinctly raunchy high school whose principal, in desperation, had decided that the only way to get the inmates to graduation was to give the diplomas out at the Dick Clark show. Yet Stevenson was attentively listened to and respectfully applauded. Then he finished, and Frank Sinatra and Tony Curtis and Janet Leigh and Peter Lawford were propelled upon the dais.

Women lay across the tables and screamed. Adlai Stevenson turned and looked at the scene with an expression which conveyed his arrival at the ultimate indignity in a political career whose consequences have so seldom been worthy of him. Frank Sinatra, who can be a graceful man too, said he was sorry.

Someone threw Janet Leigh an ice cream bar and she gave it to Tony Curtis. "Don't," she said, prettily, "let any vote get away." Assembly candidates were lining up to get their pictures taken with Peter Lawford. The chairman introduced Tony Curtis.

"This is my first political speech," Curtis said. "Vote for Schwartz. I hope we all go out and vote for a man who will be a great President. I can't stand pat either. And now I give you the next ambassador to Italy."

Sinatra quieted them with one imperial hand and sang "You're Just Too Marvelous" and "Take It Easy" and ended with "The Lady Is a Tramp," turning around on the platform while wails and screeches followed the revelation of that wise and troubled face. He stopped, while they were still beseeching, and lifted the hand in a blessing again, and said very quietly:

"I'm terribly honored to have been invited here. If you care for the future of your children, I hope you will be aware of the fact, as I am aware of the fact, that there is greatness in John Kennedy."

Then he was swept out and disappeared, while, behind him, the cry of "I love you, darling" died in a woman's throat. Adlai Stevenson had gone away a while before. I do not think men of Adlai Stevenson's and Frank Sinatra's class should play joints like the Newark Armory.

[October 27, 1960]

In the Rock Pool

All the civilized world rejoiced today in our Cuban adventure.

The French, for instance, rejoiced that we now have an Algeria. The British were glad to know we had found a Kenya. Only Mr. Tshombe, a representative of civilization by *grace belgique*, must as Tuesday wore on have felt a certain aesthetic contempt; they do these things more tidily in Katanga.

The debate in the United States followed the lines customary in our debate: (1) it did not exist; (2) what faint quivers there were appear to have been resolved by the reflection that Castro had betrayed the revolution. Ask no more why we do not give BARs to people attempting to overthrow Trujillo; Trujillo never betrayed a revolution.

We live in the year 1961 and America has made much progress since the 1850s. In the 1850s, Abraham Lincoln damaged his political future and Henry David Thoreau went to jail because they opposed the Mexican War. I do not propose to go to jail over this matter — assuming that the rulers of the earth would condescend to send me — and thus our grandchildren will miss the catch in the throat which would otherwise dampen their eyes at the news that a man I revere had said to me, "What are you doing in jail, uh, Murray?" and I firmly and bravely gave reply: "And what are you doing out there, Arthur Schlesinger, Jr., and what would your father think if he could see you?"

Poor Thoreau! He lived in a world before the invention of the Americans for Democratic Action and the syndicated columnist; he was thus pathetically uninformed. But, if Thoreau could stand and say a word for such as Santa Ana, can anyone do less for Castro?

The reports yesterday were not encouraging to those who invoked the ancient, queasy prayer that if it were done when 'tis done then 'twere well it were done quickly. The Latin Americans, none of whom had the loins to speak out for Castro in public, were somewhat derisive toward us liberators in the corridors. They were as usual wrong; we will, I fear, get the business done, sloppily but on the record.

One thought all day of Adlai Stevenson and of Raul Roa, Castro's Foreign Minister.

There was the feeling that the administration had handed Stevenson that cup and that he would drink it like the gentleman he is. There was also the feeling that he knew no more than the rest of us precisely what had happened.

Roa was something else, a free and happy man. "Today," he said, "I am fifty-four years old. It is the spring. With the revolution, it is always the spring."

It cannot always have been the spring. Roa knows the Cuban revolution. He knows the lies Castro has told himself and through himself the people. But yesterday it was spring again; he was only a Cuban patriot, standing against the alien.

We had a bad day in this rock pool. It left us only with the consolation that no truly great power can ever be called to book for its sins in the UN. But it was a day that belonged to the Poles, the Czechs, and the Rumanians — the enslaved given the floor, to cry out at slavery elsewhere.

In all I have to say about this dirty business, I hope that I would speak nothing harsh about those Cubans we sent on this errand. I would not be caught speaking against a soldier lying on his stomach on swampy ground being shot at. Under ordinary circumstances, being no Fidelista, I should wish them well; as it is, I could not wish them ill. There is every excuse for them; but there is no excuse for Allen Dulles or John F. Kennedy. If you think there is, you are, believe me, wrong.

[United Nations, April 19, 1961]

Albany Humanists

The woes of the lower social orders occasionally touch the Legislature of the State of New York but in rigid levels of priority. The last four rungs on its ladder of sympathy are, in order, dogs, migratory apple pickers, cats and, at the very bottom, boxers.

The boxer is an animal and not even a domestic one. Still, Benny Paret was dying and Albany had a dim sense that something should be done for the species. The Governor had asked for a full, fair report on the Paret-Griffith fight. The Boxing Commission weighed in with a finding that it was nobody's fault; the affair had been supervised by men of sensitivity so humane that any reader had to be surprised to find them associated with ruffians like Benny Paret. There was even an appendage by Dr. Mal Stevens to the effect that boxing is less dangerous than skiing; the beast Paret is apparently lucky that he didn't spend last weekend on the slopes at Stowe.

The Legislature set up a joint committee to investigate the manly art; we may assume that it will spend $40,000 and produce something like yesterday's report on migratory labor — otherwise known as "Outdoor Recreation (1957-1960)" — and tell us that Benny Paret found his visit to the metropolitan area "profitable and for the most part enjoyable."

Assemblyman Satriale of the Bronx had worked out a bill for the relief and assistance of boxers. It was debated and passed by the Assembly yesterday; even the opposition took time out to announce that Satriale's program was one more proof of his abiding concern for the unfortunate.

The law was a magnificent example of what respectable society conceives to be the rights of a boxer. Assemblyman Satriale proposed first of all to help the boxer out of the boxer's own pocket. This indicates the creature's position below dogs, farm laborers and cats. As an instance, if the Assembly should decide to help the apple picker by giving him a Bible, it would be above billing him for the Bible. (No dog has ever been charged for a rabies shot either.) The boxer's relief would come from a fund supported from 1 per cent of the boxer's purse and 1 per cent of the gate receipts; since he is paid from a percentage of the gate receipts, he would be paying for his relief twice. And then, to get it, he would have to prove himself indigent. The benevolent Mr. Satriale won't let the boxer get his own money back unless he can prove he is broke.

Then the boxer has to prove that he is a resident of New York State. If he's a resident of New York State and gets killed in action, his heirs get funeral expenses. If he's not a resident of New York State, the Satriale fund puts up $75 to ship the body home. Paret is not a resident of New York State; his purse for being beaten insensible Saturday night was $50,000, which would have meant that he put $500 into the fund, from which his wife, should he die, would get back $75, which is ample, because they can put the body on the night flight to Puerto Rico for $47.50 and have $27.50 left over to pay a fisherman to smuggle it back to Cuba.

Yesterday, everyone attacked the fighters and the public, but almost no one mentioned the promoters, who, being businessmen, are contributing to the growth of the state's economy. Mark Lane suggested that whenever a fighter dies in New York, the promoter should be required to pay $100,000 to his heirs, a marvelously simple suggestion that would probably cut fatalities in half since it would inhibit the promoters from taking chances with other people's lives. But then we all know what a demagogue Lane is.

There was as usual a moment of laughter. Assemblyman Plumadore, a Republican, said he used to be a wrestler too. "Tell me," Assemblyman Capanegro, a Democrat and another ex-wrestler, challenged across the aisle "Did you ever throw a match?" Plumadore answered that he never had to throw one ("They always told me who was going to win before I started"). The great thing about the Assembly is its preinduction training program.

[Albany, March 28, 1962]

Loyalty Day

This city's elaborately refurbished Convention Hall seemed oddly like a church yesterday, with the organ playing dreary threnodies and Walter Reuther's Auto Workers sitting hushed waiting for the President of the United States.

The Auto Workers are themselves elaborately furbished as against their old standards; the necktie seems as much their uniform now as the open shirt used to in the days of romantic illusion.

At the end of each session of this convention there is a queue lined up for Walter Reuther's autograph. A picture of John F. Kennedy, the signature of Walter Reuther, a box, one supposes, of salt water taffy — these are the souvenirs a delegate takes home from the four-teenth constitutional convention of what is remembered as the most disorderly and creative union in this disorderly and creative nation.

The President's reception was the more heartful for being so muted. It would have been disrespectful in this atmosphere for anyone to emit a partisan whoop. The tone was reverence occasionally profaned by the clapping of hands.

John F. Kennedy's head cherishes order in the population; but there is enough Irish in him to enjoy conflict and challenge. Placid devotion is the most tedious gift any man can receive; after twenty-five minutes of it, the President's oppression was noticeable. His posture seemed suddenly flaccid, as though the mind had for a moment let slack its continual preoccupation with purpose and destiny and was merely re-peating over and over the horrid question: if there are no kicks in the Auto Workers, then where can a combat soldier look for kicks?

The UAW had run up the suggestion of a flag of challenge last weekend with a resolution declaring it an "imperative necessity" for wages to increase faster than productivity. The President, of course, is committed to hold all wages within the limit of productivity improve-ment; this seemed the language at least of disagreement. But, on Monday night, Reuther issued an interpretation of the resolution, which declared the UAW's commitment to the President's policy. Even the shadow of dissent had been lifted.

When the President had refocused his lagging attention and found some passion for the peroration about asking the UAW to help move the country forward again, and had departed, Walter Reuther stood up to express his confidence that the President will "prove equal to history's great challenge of greatness.

"Mr. President, I should like to say that you have our support and prayers in your effort to seek a meaningful beginning to disarmament so that peace and freedom can be made secure in our troubled world."

It is sad how the critical and creative energies of this great institution have been covered over by its compulsion to trust the President in all things. Today, as an instance, the convention will pass a resolution accepting the President's decision to resume nuclear testing and blaming this renewed competition in terror entirely on Nikita Khrushchev. Walter Reuther, as president of the AFL-CIO industrial union department, had previously opposed American nuclear testing. The policy, one supposes, is to disagree with President Kennedy's decisions only before they are made.

The historic high point of the UAW convention had been thus one long Loyalty Day. The audience had been wonderfully dutiful and anxious to serve. It is a sad circumstance that the only people who will sit still and accept a sermon on the need to sacrifice private profit to the national welfare are people who have never in their lives had a chance at private profit. But can a man who supports a family on $100 a week in an auto plant really believe that he would be a selfish pig to strike for $110? Apparently he can. Just as his leaders can believe that their highest duty to their country and their President is almost uncritical acceptance.

[Atlantic City, May 9, 1962]

The New Diem

Since the export of American ideals and business methods to the backward peoples is a national aspiration, we should all be pleased at the *Wall Street Journal*'s report on Kastor, Hilton, Chesley, Crawford and Atherton, the firm which handles public relations for President Ngo Dinh Diem of South Vietnam.

Kastor-Hilton gets $100,000 a year and expenses for its efforts to improve the Diem government's image here. The U.S. is estimated to have spent $2,500,000,000 on South Vietnam; and the chances are that we are paying most of Diem's public relations bill. In America, the customer is used to paying for messages designed to convince him to buy more of the product.

The product which Kastor-Hilton peddles is Diem himself. His Consumers Union rating is not impressive, and a certain discouragement of journalistic curiosity seems required to protect his image. In this security assignment, Kastor-Hilton seems to have worked out a neat mixture of our own more subtle techniques with those traditional in dictatorships.

"Uruguayan-born Jorge Ortiz, the firm's chief in South Vietnam," the *Journal* says, "on occasion has confronted newsmen on the streets of Saigon with copies of their stories with 'unfavorable' passages heavily underlined; though the U.S. is heavily backing South Vietnam's fight against Communist guerrillas, President Diem's regime has been criticized for its authoritarian tendencies."

Of course any goon is capable of doing this sort of thing for his boss; we can only hope that Kastor-Hilton will be able to instruct Diem in the infinite refinements of our own system for protecting public officials from embarrassment. Any assignment to a foreign dictatorship is a pushover for an American newspaperman of reasonable training because its representatives, once they decide to answer questions, are entirely unskilled at avoiding dangerous ones.

Every American cop at a precinct desk, for example, is so used to our feeble devices that he will close the door gently but impregnably as soon as the questions start down a line which might lead to some revelation. Diem, being without experience in free exchange with newspapermen, appears to reveal the worst about himself whenever he opens his mouth.

Kastor-Hilton has a training problem; but, if the free world survives in Diem's person for a few more years, the old man, in the right hands, may become as good at evasion as Robert Wagner and might even bemuse the South Vietnamese into voting for him in an honest election.

I have to confess a certain sympathy for Diem, since the liberals call him a fascist, according to their custom of describing ordinary men as saints and bad ones as monsters. Official liberalism always exaggerates the evils of the regimes propped up by American policy, and then goes on to support the policy, the libel of its beneficiaries being a method for appeasement of conscience by rhetoric.

We cannot, as good Americans, object to Diem's using our money to advertise for more of our money. This is a sound and tested business practice. The real objection is that Diem does not understand that Madison Avenue is entirely deficient in the techniques of political propaganda. It sold Eisenhower, but anybody can sell a glittering product; the test came with poor Nixon and the results were appalling. The liberals are the people who can sell a lemon.

The proper method to rehabilitate Diem is to let a selected group of his political opponents out of the clink. If possible they should be liberals affiliated with downtown Saigon law firms. They should then be encouraged to form a Committee of Democratic Voters of South Vietnam. Diem will run against his sister-in-law on a campaign to clean up the mess created by his family.

He will tour the villages, in the company of his new Commissioner of Buildings, reeling with indignation at the sight of any leaking thatch. He can promise a rent control law, a Fair Employment Practices Act, and an unbossed South Vietnam. The peasants will rally to him; and when it is over, their lives will be precisely the same but they will have the laws; if they don't he can always blame the reactionaries in Washington.

And, after this performance, best of all, he is guaranteed a raise.

[May 10, 1962]

TIME and *Nixon*

Richard Nixon's defeat in California has removed him to that small place in history which belongs to national disasters which did not quite happen.

We hear now, after the horrid self-exposure of his farewell, from those people who had told us that this poor man was the candidate best qualified to be President of the United States. The *Detroit News*, as an instance, bravely and handsomely apologized to its readers for that mistake.

But *Time* merely remembered that Mr. Nixon's enemies had insisted that his character was flawed. "As of last week, his admirers could only agree." Those admirers are unidentified; *Time,* of course, was never there. Henry Luce did not sit on a stage in October, 1960, and look at Richard Nixon the way a nanny might at Prince Charles.

Time did not do a series of cover stories on Richard Nixon, the chief artistic discipline of which was the care that excised every suggestion of a flaw in his character.

It is unkind to disturb Nixon in the shadows, but one last word should be said, a word more about Henry Luce than Nixon.

Richard Nixon was the pathetic hero of one of those lower-middle-class tragedies to which the American muse so often directs her servants. He was one of those bellboys or salesmen who are victims of Darwinian forces they do not understand. And Henry Luce, among others, almost made him our national image.

No other politician ever rose so steadily through a succession of personal humiliations. He was stoned in Caracas; he was treated with contempt by Khrushchev; and *Time* explained these indignities as triumphs. President Eisenhower tormented Nixon with doubts of his favor for the succession; he was treated like a footman. He ended the 1960 campaign wandering limply and wetly about the American heartland begging votes on the excuse that he had been too poor to have a pony when he was a boy.

He moved towards the majesty of the Presidency with a loser's face, desperate to please, pretending to be bold when he was only daring to insinuate. A man needed no research service; he had only to use his eyes to see that here was a loser, who, if he were not beaten by the voters, would be beaten by Nikita Khrushchev.

And the Fifties were not the Eisenhower years but the Nixon years. That was the decade when the American lower middle class in the person of this man moved to engrave into the history of the United States, as the voice of America, its own faltering spirit, its self-pity and its envy, its continual anxiety about what the wrong people might think, its whole peevish, resentful whine. The Nixon years belonged to all the young men who had been to the schools which instructed them that they could not be too careful, to the graduates of those courses in how to influence people since it was no longer of value to win friends, assistants to chairmen of boards, former captains in the service of supply, clerks who call themselves junior executives, young men ashamed of their origins and of themselves. In a word, the sort of people who write most of the letters to *Time*.

They were the saddest because they were the most abject years in the history of the United States. And *Time* did not find out about them until they were over. That is because *Time* was a part of them. Richard Nixon was the man who believed that it was enough to read a weekly news magazine to know all about the complexities of life. Henry Luce was prostrating himself before the face of his market.

Then it was over, and Richard Nixon blamed everyone but himself for the Nixon years. *Time* was shocked. It blamed Nixon.

[November 13, 1962]

Dubinsky's Critics

Harper's magazine this month publishes a pained and censorious evaluation of David Dubinsky by Paul Jacobs. It cannot be described as premature. Still, it is one of those certain signs of public climate. The first sign came last summer when the *Times* published a headline reflecting discredit on the ILGWU. *Harper's* likes to do studiedly unconventional things, but it does not do unsafe ones. It would not, as an instance, make public that private boredom which most of us have to feel about Robert Frost. Its commission to Jacobs — like the *Times* headline — merely indicates that Dubinsky is no longer a sacred object.

Jacobs's piece cannot really be answered and probably won't be except for hire. My own experience is that you can criticize almost any labor leader alive these days and never get a protest from a union member. That is not because union members dislike their leaders but because the average member has never heard of his leaders.

The American labor leader is just not that consequential. This reflection is the only one which might trouble a reader of Jacobs's critique. He fails only in detachment. The exhaustion, the cynicism, the sense of failure which permeate the ILGWU seem to him a betrayal of what he remembers of his youth as one of its organizers. The truth is that the ILGWU was probably never all that much, and by 1939 its atmosphere was not perceptibly different from what it is today.

Many of Dubinsky's new critics complain because there is no place in the ILGWU's leadership for the Negroes and Puerto Ricans who form so impressive a numerical proportion of its membership. But the overwhelming majority of the ILGWU's members in this century have been women, and no woman has ever had more than a token place in its leadership. I doubt if the women cared very much about their exclusion; I would be surprised if the Negroes and Puerto Ricans are terribly exercised either. When people are cast into ghettos, cheated by landlords, confined to menial labor, cast away on these terrible streets, it is possible that they have larger resentments than the condition of being unacceptable as business agents.

But I cannot imagine a time when the leaders of the ILGWU did not consider their members somewhat inferior to other citizens. This sense may explain why, when the ILGWU reviews its achievements, it concentrates not on the wages it has gained for its members but on the stability it has brought to its industry and on its cooperation, rather than its conflict, with the employer.

A union which cannot look back on one outrageously selfish act on behalf of its members may have a respectable history but it can hardly claim an important one. I can conceive of even a teamster's being embarrassed at having to say that he pays dues to Jimmy Hoffa, and certainly no one could be ashamed to pay dues to David Dubinsky. But, at the same time, it is hardly inconsequential that an ILGWU member driving a truck in the garment district makes less money than he would if he were a member of the Teamsters driving a truck somewhere else in town. One reason why the garment unions have so sedulously promoted the slogan that man cannot live by bread alone may be that they would prefer not to limit judgment of their worth to their success at providing bread alone. It is rather a pity that Dubinsky, who has extraordinary human qualities, has always been so dependent on the kindness of the papers. They, like him, are not that important. We are not always wrong, but there are usually better judges.

He might reflect that few of us are important and that almost none of us are remembered. This is particularly true of labor leaders; John L. Lewis is the only one who can seriously be thought to have left any real imprint on his time. Who, as Richard Rovere once noticed, remembers Sidney Hillman? The labor leader's stature is almost always illusory; it is a mixture of hope and fear based on a misconception of his real power to affect history. He does not, after all, own property and therefore began with a strictly limited potential for changing its disposition. Most labor leaders live up to their potential; the disappointment in their careers comes from the illusion that their potential was larger than it really was. When they have impact, it is largely poetic and comes in moments when they stand for us as moving embodiments of their class and their kind, as Lewis did for the vengeful side and Philip Murray for the gentle side of the miner. Those are personal moments; I'm afraid Jacobs rather skimps them in his disapproval of Dubinsky; for myself, it has been a solace to know a man at whom you could yell as loud as he yelled at you.

[December 4, 1962]

IV

Among School Children

And has it been only seven years that I have been going South —
less time than Mr. Eisenhower was our President?

There are few things to say about those years except that the Southern Negro began them as victim and ended them as healer.

In *Free Fall*, William Golding has Sammy Mountjoy, grown, remembering the hospital ward where he had been ill as a child:

> I have searched like all men for a coherent picture of life and the
> world, but I cannot write the last word on that ward without giving
> it my adult testimony. The walls were held up by sheer, careful
> human compassion. I was on the receiving end and I know. When I
> make my black pictures, when I inspect chaos, I must remember that
> such places are as real as Belsen. They too exist, they are part of this
> enigma, this living. They are brick walls like any others, people like
> any others. But remembered, they shine.

There is nothing else to say about these journeys. There we were
and are a great people.

He Went All the Way

Mose Wright, making a formation no white man in his county really believed he would dare to make, stood on his tiptoes to the full limit of his sixty-four years and his five feet three inches yesterday, pointed his black, workworn finger straight at the huge and stormy head of J. W. Milam and swore that this was the man who dragged fourteen-year-old Emmett Louis Till out of his cottonfield cabin the night the boy was murdered.

"There he is," said Mose Wright. He was a black pigmy standing up to a white ox. J. W. Milam leaned forward, crooking a cigaret in a hand that seemed as large as Mose Wright's whole chest, and his eyes were coals of hatred.

Mose Wright took all their blast straight in his face, and then, for good measure, turned and pointed that still unshaking finger at Roy Bryant, the man he says joined Milam on the night-ride to seize young Till for the crime of whistling suggestively at Bryant's wife in a store three miles away and three nights before.

"And there's Mr. Bryant," said Mose Wright and sat down hard against the chair-back with a lurch which told better than anything else the cost in strength to him of the thing he had done. He was a field Negro who had dared try to send two white men to the gas chamber for murdering a Negro.

He sat in a court where District Attorney Gerald Chatham, who is on his side, steadily addressed him as Uncle Mose and conversed with him in a kind of pidgin cotton-picker's dialect, saying "axed" for "asked" as Mose Wright did and talking about the "undertaker man."

Once Chatham called him "Old Man Mose," but this was the kindly, contemptuous tolerance of the genteel; after twenty-one minutes of this, Mose Wright was turned over to Defense Counsel Sidney Carlton and now the manner was that of an overseer with a field hand.

Sidney Carlton roared at Mose Wright as though he were the defendant, and every time Carlton raised his voice like the lash of a whip, J. W. Milam would permit himself a cold smile.

And then Mose Wright did the bravest thing a Delta Negro can do; he stopped saying "sir." Every time Carlton came back to the attack, Mose Wright pushed himself back against his chair and said "That's right" and the absence of the "sir" was almost like a spit in the eye.

When he had come to the end of the hardest half hour in the hardest life possible for a human being in these United States, Mose Wright's story was shaken; yet he still clutched its foundations. Against Carlton's voice and Milam's eyes and the incredulity of an all-white jury, he sat alone and refused to bow.

If it had not been for him, we would not have had this trial. It will be a miracle if he wins his case; yet it is a kind of miracle that, all on account of Mose Wright, the State of Mississippi is earnestly striving here in this courtroom to convict two white men for murdering a Negro boy so obscure that they do not appear to have even known his name.

He testified yesterday that, as Milam left his house with Emmett Till on the night of August 28, he asked Mose Wright whether he knew anyone in the raiding party. "No, sir, I said I don't know nobody."

Then Milam asked him how old he was, and Mose Wright said sixty-four and Milam said, "If you knew any of us, you won't live to be sixty-five."

And, after the darkened car drove off, with his great-nephew, Mose Wright drove his hysterical wife over to Sumner and put her on the train to Chicago, from which she has written him every day since to cut and run and get out of town. The next day, all by himself, Mose Wright drove into nearby Greenwood and told his story in the sheriff's office.

It was a pathetic errand; it seems a sort of marvel that anything was done at all. Sheriff George Smith drove out to Money around 2 P.M. that afternoon and found Roy Bryant sleeping behind his store. They were good friends and they talked as friends about this little boy whose name Smith himself had not bothered to find out.

Smith reported that Roy had said that he had gone down the road and taken the little boy out of "Preacher's" cabin, and brought him back to the store and, when his wife said it wasn't the right boy, told him to go home.

Sheriff Smith didn't even take Bryant's statement down. When he testified to it yesterday, the defense interposed the straight-faced objection that this was after all the conversation of two friends and that the state shouldn't embarrass the sheriff by making him repeat it in court. Yet, just the same, Sheriff Smith arrested Roy Bryant for kidnaping that night.

When the body supposed to be Emmett Till's was found in the river, a deputy sheriff drove Mose Wright up to identify it. There was no inquest. Night before last, the prosecution fished up a picture of the body which had been in the Greenwood police files since the night it was brought in, but there was no sign the sheriff knew anything about it, and its discovery was announced as a coup for the state. But, with that apathy and incompetence, Mose Wright almost alone has brought the kidnapers of his nephew to trial.

The country in which he toiled and which he is now resigned to leaving will never be the same for what he has done. Today the state will put on the stand three other field Negroes to tell how they saw Milam and Bryant near the murder scene. They came in scared; one disappeared while the sheriff's deputies were looking for him. They, like Mose Wright, are reluctant heroes; unlike him, they have to be dragged to the test.

They will be belted and flayed as he was yesterday, but they will walk out with the memory of having been human beings for just a little while. Whatever the result, there is a kind of majesty in the spectacle of the State of Mississippi honestly trying to convict two white men on the word of four Negroes.

And we owe that sight to Mose Wright, who was condemned to bow all his life, and had enough left to raise his head and look the enemy in those terrible eyes when he was sixty-four.

[Sumner, Mississippi, September 22, 1958]

An Intruder in the Ashes . . .

The Delta Cooperative is not twenty years old, yet it seems as far back in the past as Natchez. Dr. Sherwood Eddy began it in 1936, in Bolivar County at first, to rescue tenant farmers from the plantation system. They were to share their property and their tools and any profits from their cotton.

There were thirty families in the beginning; at the end of a year, each got a little less than $300 in cash and the missionaries thought themselves a success.

"When I came up here," says Gene Cox, one of the last survivors, "we had thirteen staff members. We had to give up Bolivar; it was buckshot land, mostly clay. We closed it and moved over here."

They called their 2,700 acres, sixteen miles into the plantation country around Tchula, New Providence Farm. Most of the tenants left New Providence with the war; only seven still live there; Gene Cox, once their accountant, and David Minter, their doctor, are the only outsiders left. The cooperative vision has passed, but Cox and Minter still do what they can, which is no small thing.

David Minter, who first came to the co-op from medical school, returned from the South Pacific to convert one farm building into a clinic with Mrs. Cox as his nurse. Cox's little store is a non-profit institution but no longer a cooperative. He runs a small credit union for tenants; it has always seemed a peculiar institution to his planter neighbors who say that any tenant who wants a loan need only come to them.

White Holmes County has never understood what moves Cox and Minter. One resident said yesterday that he can't understand how a qualified physician would bury himself out there when he could make real money in the city. But David Minter's freak has brought its advantages to his white neighbors; J. P. Love, president of the White Citizens Councils of the delta, until recently sent his children to the New Providence clinic.

What made Cox and Minter different was an unchanged Christian impulse. Minter was a minister's son and the brother of two medical missionaries; he seems to have conceived his clinic as itself a sort of mission.

Gene Cox, his cooperative dream passed, went on doing what he could with what was at hand. Until last year, Cox and a group of Negro teachers ran a summer camp, its emphasis heaviest on crafts and Bible studies. He borrowed sanitation films from the Agricultural Extension Service in Jackson and religious films from churches and showed them in the schools. Every fourth Sunday he held a Bible meeting at his campsite.

He had a private distaste for segregation; but he lives by the rules, and, when his troubles came, no one could offer any real evidence that he had ever broken the Holmes County pattern.

Minter and he were always outsiders and subject to gossip; but, even after the pattern hardened and the White Citizens Councils came, they were free of any overt public distemper. County Attorney Pat Barrett was at once Lexington chairman of the Citizens Councils and Gene Cox's lawyer. They acquired with time just one open enemy, Holmes County Sheriff Richard F. Byrd.

The cause in both cases was a specific affront: Cox intervened for a Negro in a bootlegging case, and Minter, as attendant physician, was a witness for a Negro shot in the leg for the sheriff's sport. Afterwards, the sheriff swore he would run Minter out of the country before his term ended.

The real trouble began on September 23, during the fever about Emmett Till. A white girl waiting for a bus near Tchula heard someone in a group of four young Negroes say, "Hi, Sugar, you look good to me." The offender afterwards attempted to explain that he was calling to a Negro girl named "Sugar." In any case his putative victim screamed, and the four Negroes were borne off to Sheriff Byrd.

All four, otherwise inconsequential, were neighbors of Cox and Minter. The sheriff caught the connection. He called in County Attorney Barrett; Edwin White, legal adviser to the Citizens Councils; and William Moses, their Holmes County chairman — Byrd and Barrett for the law in theory and Moses and White for the law in fact.

They questioned the defendants for two hours and a half, setting it all down on Moses's wire recorder. The resultant tape has been "lost." Those who heard it describe something that sounds thoroughly trivial and designed, if anything, to fortify the Citizens Councils' general theory that no Negro witness is worth credence. The boys knew Minter as a doctor and Cox hardly at all; they had never heard either discuss segregation. One of the boys believed that he might once have seen a Negro with white children in Minter's swimming pond. There were no questions about the white girl at the bus stop; Sheriff Byrd already had his confession and one boy got six months.

The investigators went home to call a meeting of five hundred citizens at Tchula School the night of September 23. J. P. Love, as state representative-elect and Citizens Council chairman, was presiding officer. He opened by saying that he would play the tape and let the citizens hear the charges, and then Minter and Cox could defend themselves.

Then the Reverend Marsh Calloway, a Durant Presbyterian minister, arose to ask whether Love had any legal or moral right to play this tape in public. Love looked at County Attorney Barrett and Barrett looked at Edwin White and the counsel for the Citizens Council rendered the opinion that this sort of thing was done often.

The record ran through that steaming room, a two-and-a-half-hour pattern of long, leading questions and inconclusive stumbling answers; at its end, Minter and Cox stood up to defend themselves. A voice in the crowd asked Cox whether he believed in segregation and he answered, "I think segregation is un-Christian, but . . ." And the howl came back, "No buts — you're convicted already."

When quiet was restored, Cox went on that he obeyed the law, and no man can say that he has never preached or practiced integration. Then Edwin White made a speech about following the Communist line, Marsh Calloway came back to say that he had known Dave Minter since boyhood and that he was a fine Christian gentleman. When the torrent of abuse died, Minter and Cox were formally asked to leave Holmes County.

Three days later, the story filtered down to Jackson and some of Holmes County began re-examining itself. J. P. Love said, "I wish Dr. Minter wasn't inclined the way some people say he is. He is a real fine doctor."

County Attorney Barrett went out to see Gene Cox. Couldn't they have another meeting to talk this thing over; he could promise it wouldn't be like the last one. Cox said that his daughter had come back from school that morning and asked, "Daddy, do we have to leave here?" Barrett looked at the floor and left to call back later to say that he had been sitting with his own daughter on his knee and he just couldn't make Gene leave.

But Ed White would not be appeased. "Some people believe what they want to believe. But what those nigger boys said was enough for us people who have suspected what was going on for twenty years."

Then Ed White got in copies of Sherwood Eddy's autobiography, and called a Citizens Council meeting and read, as Deputy Sheriff Coy Farmer reported, "where this Eddy is a Russian Communist that's been sending them money and he goes in and out of Russia every year. It says right there in that book that they're out there whipping the niggers to vote and go to our schools and they get word from Russia."

There was no appeal from that writ and Pat Barrett has no further comment either way. This week, David Minter went off to a University of Pennsylvania Medical School reunion. The clinic's traffic was down 50 per cent and it was hard not to believe that he was looking around.

Gene Cox asked his wife to go down to the empty store and get any visitor a Coke. His troubles do not seem to him a subject of much interest; he says few Negroes were coming to the store any more, the credit union has lost most of its members and the fourth Sunday worship meetings are suspended. He looked over his barren hills and laughed at the thought there might be any violence. The implication was that Christians have no need to go armed. Still, he couldn't say he'll stay. "I don't know how we can afford to make it go."

He is gray now and looks like any other delta farmer; it is hard to think what he must have been like when he was a student at Texas Christian and went to hear Sherwood Eddy at the YMCA and first felt the call to the Delta Cooperative. For seventeen years, he has seen that dream wither and shrink and now the little that was left is expiring too.

[Tchula, Mississippi, November 17, 1955]

The Southern Gentlemen

The come-on flyers for the Southern Gentlemen's organization of Louisiana are tricked out rather drearily with a stock drawing of an ante-bellum colonel, goateed and string-tied. Their living expression, as in most of the South, is thicker of blood and closer to the earth.

J. B. Easterly, Southern Gentleman No. 1, is a spike-haired, square-bifocalled, heavy-necked man of sixty-one, alternating explosions of laughter and indignation. His grandchildren call him "Pop-Pop" and he's totally impossible to dislike.

The Southern Gentlemen are Louisiana's militant symbol of the counter-attack against racial integration. As such, they maintain warm fraternal relations with a brotherhood of resistance ranging from the Citizens Councils of Mississippi to the Apartheid Bund of South Africa.

Its Mississippi and Capetown brothers are, of course, the government; in Baton Rouge at least, J. B. Easterly commands a ragged outpost in the shed next to his bungalow which serves both as home office of the Southern Gentlemen and his own modest, pre-fabricated concrete step business.

As tycoon and opinion-maker, J. B. Easterly is his own secretary, turning from time to time to assault the typewriter with his thick fingers and render his accounts. As opinion-maker, J. B. Easterly's expression is somewhat inhibited by his two youngest grandchildren who toddle around the office step and have to be shooed out of hearing whenever he wants to advert to the prime subject of miscegenation.

"I'm a very illiterate man," says J. B. Easterly. "My daddy went broke when I was in college. I was raised on a cotton and cane plantation; when I was a boy, I hardly knew what a white child was.

"We have no secrets here; all we want to do is maintain segregation by legal means. We're definitely opposed to rough stuff. We believe the Negro race should advance. Look, boy, it's an accident you're a white man. We think the Negro should be proud to be a Negro and be just as good as God gave him the brainpower to be. If we got rough on them, we feel we'd be doing an injustice to 95 per cent of the race.

"But we're definitely goin' to apply economic pressure to white people who contribute to the white Communist NAACP. There's a lot of 'em. They don't come out openly — these rotten politicians slip 'em cash, no checks. We got them people down here. Look at this."

He fished among his papers and came up with a leaflet headed "The White Sentinel — official organ of the National Citizens Protective Association" and pointed to a picture of shadows purporting to be the vice president of the Falstaff Brewing Co. presenting a $500 check to the NAACP.

"See that. We're putting that all over East Baton Rouge. We're not gonna buy their beer. Let the niggers buy it."

The finger poked around and found another paper. It was the *South African Observer*, a magazine for realists, featuring the news that the message had reached the States and, for spiritual comfort on the lonely veldt, an article called "A Christian View of Segregation" by a Mississippi college president emeritus.

It costs 10 shillings a year. Realist Easterly asked his visitor how much that was in dollars so he could subscribe, and the visitor thought it might be $1.60.

"You know there's a lot of science in this. They've found out that there's a difference in the blood. There's no one smarter than a little nigger kid. But, when they get to be sixteen, they just stop. You don't see the AP, the UP and the NAACP printing that.

"That northern press is still fighting the Civil War. We forgot it down here. But our sentiment is gonna be all over the United States. There's Citizens Councils in twenty-three states. I get letters from up there saying that, if we lose, the North is lost. A woman from Illinois told me" — he looked to see if his grandchildren were out of hearing — "that in her child's school, the little nigger boys were always pulling up the little white girls' dresses."

W. L. Lawrence, secretary of the Southern Gentlemen, came into the office carrying membership applications decorated with the stars and bars. (This, like the Southern colonel, is stock for mimeograph stencils and turned out in some commercial art saltmine on our own West Side.) This was fortunate, because just after Lawrence, there came a recruit.

He was R. B. Davidson who said he had reached the shotgun stage. "We don't want none of that," said J. B. Easterly. R. B. Davidson wanted to know what we were gonna do about our parks and playgrounds now that the niggers were coming in. "Turn 'em over to the weeds and dogs," said J. B. Easterly.

R. B. Davidson said he liked a nigger if he stayed a nigger.

"It's all in the Bible. The Lord said of the children of Cain that he'd put a mark on 'em and all their children would be the servants of servants. We're God's servants and they're our servants."

"Sign this," said J. B. Easterly. "It says you never were a Communist. You couldn't be a Communist; you talk too much.

"And don't forget our big parade. We're going to drive up to L.S.U.

and let 'em see how we feel about those nigger graduate students they have. We gonna roll this thing back. Put any sign you want on your car, so long as it's not obscene or anything."

The militant Mr. Davidson said that he didn't know about no parades; he had to worry about civil service. "But, civil service or no civil service, I'm with you in the showdown."

Secretary Lawrence said, no, he couldn't say how many members he had. "That's one of the strengths of our organization," said J. B. Easterly, "we have ministers; we have school superintendents."

There would be dangers in making membership public, Lawrence pointed out. "If a member was known, these agitating Negroes might do something to him.

"They do put economic pressure on our boys." But the Southern Gentlemen exact no reprisals. "When a Negro signs a school petition, we just try to persuade him he's wrong. Sometimes, we get his employer to talk to him just to encourage him to take his name off."

Lawrence handed over a mimeographed letter. "I just got this up; do you think it will work?" It was a protest to Philco against a recent television play about a Negro married to a white woman. "I have a number of appliances in my home manufactured by your company." The visitor said it had worked in Queens.

"The worst thing was," said J. B. Easterly, "the girl was from New Orleans." He was looking through the yellow pages for a cab. "I got a lot of right talking about niggers," he said, "I can't even read." He found a number and called a cab, and stuck his huge hand out to the invader. "I'm glad you came; this sort of thing is real educational."

[Baton Rouge, November 14, 1955]

"What Have They Got to Live For?"

Richard F. Byrd was a Chevrolet salesman before Holmes County made him its sheriff three and a half years ago. He promised what candidates usually promise — to end cattle-rustling, gambling, and traffic in whisky. And, if there was any voter who needed further certification of his good deeds: "Just ask the Boy Scouts about me."

Scoutmaster-Sheriff Byrd began by closing down every gin mill in the county. A little while later, a fresh cluster opened under new management; now Holmes County's approved bootleggers all buy their produce from Bluford Taylor, Sheriff Byrd's good friend. The slot machines came back a little later; now nearly every country gas station, though its proprietor be so pinched and parsimonious as to keep the beer-can opener on a chain, has its place for one or more quarter slot machines.

This was a new flowering of an old weed, and what indignation any segment of Holmes County might have felt was soon dissolved in the larger outrage of the Supreme Court's integration decision. Richard Byrd seems thereafter to have had very little time to enforce morals; he would rather ride the county with his deputies, stopping at whim, hobbling on his gimpy, gun-shot knee to a Negro's car and buffeting its occupant with a blackjack or his cane or his flashlight or whatever happened to be in his hand.

It was not a hobby calculated to offend many voters; there are no voters among that 75 per cent of Holmes County residents who are Negroes. Their status under the law is best described by the experience of a Negro woman schoolteacher who was shot in the leg by one of the county's first citizens after an argument a year or so ago. While she lay in the hospital, the school fired her and the gas station laid off her husband. Her father came over to get her; there was a suggestion that he go into court and he answered, "There's not enough blood or money in my family to do that," and took her off to Chicago.

Some of the victims of Richard Byrd's evening bouts of mayhem went to lawyers, but no one would take their case. By now, white Holmes County was united behind the worst; and Sheriff Byrd had only one open enemy left.

Hazel Brannon Smith came here from Alabama in 1936 to take over the county's weekly newspaper. She remains a saucy, pretty woman. When the gin mills reopened, she went to Byrd's office and said, "Richard, you're not keeping your promises," and, after watching the sheriff dodge and bluster, she went back and began needling him in her columns.

But no one talked about Scoutmaster Byrd's afterdark sport. Then, on July 3, 1954, he had his gaudiest night of all. Around twilight the sheriff's car passed a group of Negroes near a rail spur at Tchula. He got out of the car and told them to "get goin'," beating one example along the way. And, as they ran, Richard Byrd picked him a target and fired one shot, and, as his quarry fell, got back in his car and rode forth for more sport.

The fallen rabbit's friends took him to the clinic near Tchula where Dr. David Minter treated him for a gunshot wound. Hazel Smith heard about it the next day and went to Tchula to find out.

"He turned out to be a boy named Henry Randle who had never been in any trouble and was in town to buy food. I was born and raised in this country, and I wouldn't defend a troublemaker. But it seemed to me the whole future of race relations down here depends on our protecting our good citizens. If we don't work for them, then what have they got to live for? I thought a long time and then decided that, if I didn't print this story, I was just as guilty of shooting that Negro as Richard was."

And, while she waited, seven other Negroes came to her with the scars and rubble of Richard Byrd's great night — the broken glasses of a thin young Negro teacher and the pieces of the sheriff's flashlight which he had shattered when he used it on a bystander at a crossroads filling station.

Then Hazel Smith ran a front-page editorial:

> The laws in America are for everyone — rich and poor, strong and weak, white and black and all the other races that dwell in our land . . . Laws were made to protect the weak from the strong.
>
> This man was shot in the back. He was running only because he had been told to "get going" by the sheriff. He had not violated any law . . . He just made the one mistake of being around when the sheriff drove up.

She signed her name, Hazel Brannon Smith. She had, of course, hoped for too much from Holmes County; such hope is a natural weakness in places where everyone calls you by your first name. She says that almost all Lexington said afterwards that it was too bad what Richard had done, but Hazel hadn't ought to have put it in the paper because it was bad for the county.

Her visitor left and walked across the square to visit the sheriff. The sun was out in all its terrible majesty; the clock on top of Lexington's fading brick courthouse — its hands stopped how long at 6:10 — looked down on a dusty square barren of human passion or human form. Deputy Sheriff Coy Farmer was in Byrd's narrow office and made mechanical conversation about the Russian Communists and stirring up the niggers.

And then there was a shoving of the door, and its jamb was filled by Richard F. Byrd, himself, angling his shoulders to get through, a great, stubby, pearl-handled pistol cradled flat in his right hand as though he were carrying an ice-cream cone starting to melt.

Coy Farmer backed off to a corner, and the sheriff of Holmes County — the strong right arm of the bootleggers and the Citizens Council — his pale hat drawn down to his steel glasses, a thick vein beating in his neck, pulled open the desk drawer and laid his weapon beside all its pretty sisters, another revolver, two blackjacks and a sap. He was like a collector savoring his treasures, and then he turned the eye of a basilisk upon his visitor.

The visitor said he was in town looking over the sheriff's troubles. "What troubles?" said the sheriff. "This is a law enforcement agency; do you know any law enforcement problem?

"What's yer name," he said. "You've been around here before, haven't ye?" The visitor said no, and gave his name and the sheriff wrote it down as slowly as though the pencil were a blunt knife and he were cutting flesh. There was a slow recognition beginning at the ankles and rising to the knee-hinges that the sheriff of Holmes County was sitting there balancing the pleasure and the peril involved in working over his visitor right there in the office.

What need is there here for the sheriff to carry a gun in the daylight? Of course, the need is interior; Richard F. Byrd needs the feel of a weapon by daylight as some of us need whisky for breakfast; the only lawless, violent man in sight in Lexington at high noon is the appointed guardian of its law.

The visitor went back to say good-by to Hazel Smith, and said that he calculated his supply of adrenalin was good for just three minutes more in town. Hazel Smith rolled back her curly head and laughed; it was the laugh of a debutante. It will take a braver man than I to look Richard Byrd in the eye again; but, praise God, it takes a braver man than he to look Hazel in the eye.

[Lexington, Mississippi, November 16, 1955]

The Alabama Story

Dennis Holt, of Birmingham, is stringy and skinny and wears glasses and is the national debating champion of the United States. He is also president of the student body of the College of Arts and Sciences of the University of Alabama, and, oddly enough for a tall, thin boy, who does not play basketball, is something of a hero on his campus.

Night before last the holy war against one poor, lonely Negro woman (Autherine Lucy) settled down near midnight outside the home of O. C. Carmichael, the beset president of Alabama University. What was left of the rioteers hollered for the head of their president, and Mrs. Carmichael came out to beg them to leave. Dennis Holt stood by the steps of the presidential mansion and watched what happened.

"Somebody called out, 'Let's go get 'em,' " said Dennis Holt last night.

"And three people — two high school boys and a man so drunk he could barely lurch — walked up those steps. And some of us stepped in front of them, and one of us said, 'You're not going anywhere.' You know, they fell back.

"That's all it took — just a little resistance."

But there was no other resistance; the grownups had already capitulated in giving the mob what it wanted. All yesterday Dennis Holt and the rest of the student leaders of Alabama University worked to save their school's honor. They are better than us, their elders, and last night they met and calmly and unanimously resolved that the law must be upheld and justice done and wrong redressed.

All the leaders of Alabama's Student Government Association are Alabama boys and girls. They are, above all other candidates, the elected conscience of their college. Last night, with not one dissenting vote, they voted to accept a Negro as a fellow student rather than bow to the rule of a mob.

Thomas Thigpen, of Greensboro, Alabama, the presiding officer, called them to order and announced that Dennis Holt had a resolution to read. Let us remember these kids who will excite the passion of no headline writer, because, more than sheriffs who do not enforce laws and attorneys-general who do not listen and college presidents who cannot lift their heads, they are the light of the world and whatever hope this sad and tortured territory has.

Dennis Holt stood up to read his resolution. America, he said, has been called to greatness and we, too, have been called. Great segments of the world are watching the student government of the University of Alabama on this seventh day of February, nineteen hundred and fifty-six.

We have a chance, he reminded them, to tell the world that this, our student government, is not run by vandals, goons or thugs. And then they began, these children of the South, to applaud.

Let us say here this evening, said Dennis Holt, that we live by democratic means and democratic methods and that we're opposed to mob violence and mob rule. And then very slowly he recited the terrible events of the last three days:

"An ink bottle — remember that — was thrown at the American flag. An Episcopal minister, a man of God — remember that — was hit in the back with an egg."

Every one of us, said Dennis Holt, has been dealt a blow. The question is not what we may think of integration but what we think of law and order.

And then he looked at these, these students most trusted by the other students of the University of Alabama, and said that he had a thing to tell them. That was his own theory and not necessarily theirs.

"Our university and its trustees may well be famous for all time for running away from a fight. They have acquiesced to the mob. Let us face it: The mob is king on the campus today. We must all think a little bit about the fact that the mob won. Let us remember that high school boys were able to sway the board of trustees of a great university."

Let us, he was saying, let us accept our shame and our responsibility.

Dennis Holt's resolution affirmed that the student government hereby resolves that mob violence be denounced at the University of Alabama and that means be found to protect the future personal safety of the students — white or Negro — and the faculty and the reputation of the university.

And then he was finished, and they applauded him for thirty-five seconds, which is too long to be quite proper for sixty people. They seemed to keep it going out of some need to affirm what they had waited so long to hear someone say loud and clear. And when they had shouted their approval, Hartwell Lutz, of Huntsville, Alabama, arose to ask what his resolution meant and how it could help the situation.

"It means," said Dennis Holt, "that we are saying to certain responsible officials of this state that when mob violence occurs, it's time for the law to break it up. We have to convince the state officials that they have the responsibility, not just the students."

Last night, the Student's Christian Association and the International Relations Club passed resolutions like Dennis Holt's; today the law students will follow. Every responsible representative of the opinion of these Deep South students is coming forth to speak for government of law and order. They are better than their elders; we would be lost if they weren't.

All day yesterday, their elders paltered and fumbled. O. C. Carmichael sat in his office and twice announced and twice deferred sessions at which he would be compelled to show his beaten and shamed face to the invading press.

At the end, poor Carmichael could defer no more; and yesterday afternoon he went before a meeting of the university faculty to explain to them why the board of trustees had capitulated and, in Dennis Holt's words, made the mob king of their campus.

He looked with his frightened eyes and his pleading hands — everything about him seemed to cry out, please, no questions — and told them that, if any of them had been confronted with the problem facing the trustees, he was sure that he would have surrendered, too.

Then he said that the hour was growing late and there were many problems to which sensitive troubled men must give their most serious attention, and so didn't they think it was time to adjourn? They thought that it was, most of them. But up stood a very few and spoke with the voice of Dennis Holt.

Charles Farris, of Florida and the Political Science Department, said he thought somebody should ask why the Tuscaloosa police had been so inept in handling the riot. President Carmichael could only answer that he agreed that things might have been done better, but that reality was reality.

Then Charles Farris went to the platform and offered a resolution urging that the university take its Negro students if the law says it has to and ride through any future riots and, if they cannot be quelled, that the university suspend its operations until peace is restored.

At this President Carmichael shrank back with his fluttering hand against the red plush curtain and asked for the ayes and nays. With eyes cast down and heads averted, the majority of the Alabama faculty voted to adjourn and support surrender.

As they walked out, some of them were heard to say that they wished people like Farris wouldn't rock the boat. A few hours later the student leaders met and, without a vote dissenting or a head averted, cast their future behind Dennis Holt.

It is perhaps too much to hope that any of us are as good as our children; we can only thank God that they are better.

[Tuscaloosa, Alabama, February 8, 1956]

The Way It's Got to Be

Autherine Juanita Lucy is not really Autherine Lucy — except to strangers to whom she is a symbol. To her family and to her friends, she has always been Juanita Lucy.

She appears to have been less afraid than most persons in authority were on Monday when a mob seized the campus of the University of Alabama and stoned not just her but, deplorable as it is, two white people as well. The mob was shouting, "Autherine's got to go!" They were shouting about a stranger and not about Juanita Lucy. She may owe some of the glory of her posture to a sense that, when they howled at Autherine, they were howling at a symbol and not the name of a real woman who is Juanita.

She started on the road which brought her to where she and all the South stand today very casually in the summer of 1952. Polly Myers Hudson, who was her classmate at Alabama's Miles College, called her up and said:

"Juanita, how would you like to go to the University of Alabama?"

"I said I'd like to very much, and we got all the forms and filled them out and went to the university and applied in person — me for library science and her for journalism. We were refused and then we went to court."

In the beginning, she did not tell her family: "They would have opposed it to the nth degree." They believed — who can find a Negro in Alabama who doesn't? — that Negroes should go to State University.

"But they would say and did, 'Why does it have to be you, Juanita?'" Why should she go through this? "My sister still says that. If she were Juanita, she wouldn't be in the University of Alabama."

When she began, Ruby Hurley, the Southern field secretary of the National Association for the Advancement of Colored People, wondered whether she was really a good choice. She seemed, as she seems still, so quiet and reserved that Ruby Hurley was inclined to doubt that she could run her appointed course.

Polly Myers Hudson had been NAACP president at Miles and seemed of stronger cast. Now Polly Myers Hudson has been shunted aside; it was Juanita who went into the bearpit; it was Juanita who was stoned; and it is Juanita — why Juanita of all people? — who has run the course.

She was admitted after the courts gave the university no other choice. The first two days at the school were the lonely days that every new student has, but they were calmer than she expected.

"In the history of education class, I asked a young lady what the name of our professor was and she told me. As I was coming out, a young lady said 'How do you do?' and I answered 'How do you do?'"

The name of the girl who spoke to a lonely student on her first day in school is not known to any human record, but it must be written somewhere.

"I saw a boy in the bookstore make a funny face at me, but that was all." The first two days were more normal than she could have hoped. Her instructors were especially courteous; there was only one who paid no attention to her at all. He was Charles Farris, who taught her American Government. "He didn't notice me."

She wondered at the time if this was a snub and only found out yesterday that Charles Farris, more than any man on the university faculty, had risen in public to speak for her rights as a student. ("I went to bed," he told his class the next day, "as an employe of the trustees of the University of Alabama and I awake today the employe of a mob.") When she read that, she understood the special courtesy he had shown in simply taking her for granted.

"I guess that is the way it should be." The name of Autherine yesterday brought reporters from London and offers of scholarships from the University of Copenhagen; but the heart of Juanita understood that the only victory would come on that day when she walks unnoticed and taken for granted on the campus of the University of Alabama.

She sat yesterday in Birmingham's colored Masonic building — this is a town where everything is black or white — in a powder blue suit, a mystery to all who came to talk to her. Someone desperately seeking asked her how she would feel if she got into the women's dormitory and was coldly treated. She answered:

"If I go into a dormitory and there are people I cannot reach, I'll just have to remain what you call nonchalant."

He asked her if she was just a young woman who wanted the best education available in the state of Alabama or whether she considered herself a pioneer for her people. And was she proud of her glory, or did she sometimes wonder too why it had to be Juanita?

"I guess," she said almost in apology, "that I do consider myself something of a pioneer. I wish these cameras would go away. I can't be haughty or proud just because everybody seems to know me now." She opened a sheaf of roses from the New York Dress Pressers Union, and rendered by request of the photographer a pose which conveyed with infinite subtlety how ridiculous this all was. "It just seems that it was put in my lap."

There were scareheads in the papers outside Birmingham that she had fled her home in fear of her life. But she spent Tuesday night in her house as she always has; all night the telephone rang with obscenities and every time it rang it was answered.

"Perhaps," she said, "I need a gun but I carry none."

She is the daughter of an Alabama farmer, at twenty-six the baby of nine children. Her family has dispersed all over America; she has brothers in Detroit and Chicago. She lived a while in Detroit, and she was very happy there, because it is easier than Alabama.

"But this is my home and I must stay here. The Negro must stay in the South because he's needed here. If he must do something new and different, he must do it here."

And what does she want?

"I have a combination of desires," she said. "I would like to go to the university in peace and quiet and have friends there."

And when that is over, she would like to be a librarian at the high school two blocks from her house. That is the wild dream for which Juanita Lucy reaches: peace with dignity.

When the riots came, she had not felt their terror directly; and she had been frightened first because the university officials who came to her geography class to protect her had been so frightened. "I kept asking them what was happening."

The university officials asked afterwards where she could have found her calm; they assumed that she must have had training somewhere, and must be paid a great deal; as one of the girls said, where could she have found those lovely shoes?

Why you of all persons, Juanita? What is this extraordinary resource of this otherwise unhappy country that it breeds such dignity in its victims? Why is it, in every great tragedy there is some poor Negro you can prod and push and never hear say the wrong thing? Where, as a matter of fact, did those white students come from who were elected as leaders of their university and, in their test for which no one could have trained them, stood up as no grownup did for the dignity of the human person?

This is what William Faulkner was talking about when he said of the Delta Negro that he endured. Through poverty, shame and degradation he endured.

You push and drive Juanita Lucy, tired and holding, so terribly tired and so totally contained, about why of all people she runs her course the way she has and neither of you can answer. This side of God, every observer can only wonder at the resources of the human spirit.

[Birmingham, Alabama, February 9, 1956]

The Victors

Fifty years from now the only present resident of Clarendon County whose name is likely to be known to such of our children's children as study the Constitutional history of these United States is

Harry Briggs, Jr., son of a displaced Negro sharecropper and an unemployed mother, who lives in a shack on a dusty road just out of town.

Harry Briggs was an eight-year-old boy in 1949, when his parents and fifty-nine other Negro families in Clarendon County petitioned the Federal courts for better schools. By the coincidence of the alphabet, Harry Briggs, alone from Clarendon, got to the Supreme Court, and he was the victor of record when the nine justices ordered South Carolina to integrate its schools.

He is fifteen years old now — this monument of the future — and a freshman in the Negro high school. Yesterday afternoon, he was off on his paper route (he is the only employed member of his family living at home); and his mother said he could be found talking to the teachers at his school. When he grows up, his mother says, Harry Briggs wants to be a teacher or a preacher, and he enjoys hanging around school.

The victor may own the future of Clarendon County, but he is dispossessed in its present. Harry Briggs's father was fired from the St. Clair filling station here just as his integration appeal reached the Supreme Court, and he went to sharecropping. He had a hard go of it: he searched Clarendon County with a full wagonload of his cotton and three operators refused to gin it because his name was Briggs and he was one of those NAACP Negroes. Denny Grayson, the seed man in Summerton, finally let in the father of the victor. "I'm in business to make money," said Grayson. "I don't care about no NAACP. If the NAACP was cotton, I'd gin it for money." In Clarendon County, this is the parable of the good Samaritan.

But the bank would give Harry Briggs no credit; this winter he gave up and went to Florida to work as a trucker. His wife went on working as a chambermaid at the Summerton Motel.

"They kept telling me they was gonna fire me, so I tole 'em to keep me on as long as they could," she said. "Comin' up near Christmas, they called me in and said this yere City Council had started on me again, and would I go down to this lawyer and tell him I wanted my name taken off the school petition.

"I said my name is not on that petition, and they said my husband's was and that I was responsible for him, and I said I couldn't see where I was responsible for him if he's grown. They axed me what I wanted and I said we only wanted for our children what every child in America was getting. So I said you want for me to go today and they said yes unless I wanted to go down to that lawyer and make a statement taking my name off and I said, no, I didn't and I haven't worked since.

"Heck," said Harry Briggs's mother. "We been on that petition for seven years." She says she can get no credit in the Summerton stores: that "City Council" did that good. Harry Briggs, Jr., monument in our Constitutional history, a pudgy little boy, came home and talked about basketball and looked with his mother out across a dusty yard landscaped with cinder blocks.

I do not think that when he grows up and becomes the new Negro, he would mind a literal transcription of his mother's grammar, or the memory that she said "axe" for "ask" and called the Citizens Council the "City Council," which is not after all inaccurate in substance. For it was his mother who made him possible; she might not have known the gloss, but she knew and was ready to endure for the fundamental, which was that she wanted for Harry Briggs, Jr. what other children in America were getting.

Elder Dash has nine children and farms his own twelve acres — its main cash crop cotton — with mules and hand plows a few miles outside Elloree. The small farmer lives by credit from year to year. Just before Christmas, the Bank of Elloree turned down Elder Dash's customary $700 loan.

"Two weeks before last Christmas" (it's always near Christmas) "I went into the bank to get $50 and the man there said, Elder, we got your name on a petition and you got to take it off before we give you any loan. I said I didn't sign my name to nothing, but that, if it's there, I ain't sorry to see it; I guess it belongs on there and I ain't gonna go and have it took off. I been dealing with that bank for thirty years, and this year they wouldn't give me nothing."

His nephew, Lowman Dash, who is a sharecropper, had his name on a school integration petition and lost his loan, too. "I never had no trouble 'fore. I put in for the usual amount I been gettin' each year since '45; they didn't say nothin' about no NAACP; they just turned it down."

Over the last few weeks, the Dashes have gotten loans from the

Victor National Bank of Columbia, a Negro institution; they're putting fertilizer into the ground now. Yesterday, the sun was burning, and Lowman Dash was driving his hand plow and his scarred-side mule through the dust of his field. The rhythm of a life which goes on as though Cyrus Hall McCormick had never lived had been restored and his name was still on the integration petition.

But he was not quite what he had been. The Negro farmers around Elloree, their relations with the white jobbers cut off, have set up their own cooperative and buy their fertilizer direct from Savannah at $8 a ton below the old price.

"I didn't buy all mine through the co-op," said Lowman Dash. "Mr. Hock, one of the feed men up here, said he wasn't gonna hurt none of us, that the colored made him what he is today. He said he'd take my cash whether I was on the petition or not. So he helped me, and I'm gonna help him by buying his fertilizer."

It takes just that little help — selling him fertilizer at a profit — for a white man to retain the trust of a Negro farmer out here. Lowman Dash turned towards his mule, and a visitor asked when he'd be ready to take his name off the petition. "I ain't never gonna be ready," said Lowman Dash.

They live back in the dust; they are cut off from you and me and all the outside world for help or harm; time has not changed their methods of farming; they will live out their lives in a changeless cycle of debt. Somewhere in that life — the hardest $1,000-annual-cash income to be wrung from the American earth — they have learned to endure and to hope for more for their children.

The Citizens Councils began last August to destroy the menace of integration by destroying the petitioners for integration. They have put into that all their passions for nine months: the petitioners are still there, taking off their hats and leaving their plows for a white visitor.

Harry Briggs, Jr. and his father and his mother and less than two hundred poor Negro families, in the three counties in this area, will live in histories that most of them will never read, histories that will not say very accurately who they really were, because they are only field Negroes and it will be necessary for history to gild them and give them a polish they could never afford.

They are, let history remember, and the parents among them will remain, poor farmers following mules. And the news of the last ten months is not the Citizens Council boycott, or the speeches in the Legislature, or the redoubled harshness of their lives, but the fact that they endure. The one crop they take from their dusty land which is not for sale to the profit of some white middleman is their endurance.

[Summerton, South Carolina, March 28, 1956]

A Wild Man

Tolliver Cleveland Callison, Attorney General of the State of South Carolina, addressed the Junior Chamber of Commerce of this city Wednesday on what the local press described as "the battle to preserve segregation."

The National Association for the Advancement of Colored People, said the Attorney General, "has been able to brainwash millions of Negroes as well as public officials in high places in this government court, and the leaders in the two national political parties must be conscious of the fact that they have an ally just as determined to disrupt the South in the form of the Communist Party . . . Some of the leaders in the organization [the NAACP] responsible for the conditions we are facing today are Communists and members of an active and subversive organization."

This presumably was the voice of the armed and aroused South, and an invading visitor in the Attorney General's office could assume with safety that here he would find hard, solid conviction and the face of violent resistance.

T. C. Callison turned out to be a neat old man, with white hair parted in the middle and a blue bow tie and an expression of tolerance for all conflicting opinions, fussing with his law books alone in his old-fashioned office. The South Carolina Legislature had wound up passing a parcel of new segregation laws or rather resolutions, and this kind old gentleman — impossible to confuse with the roar in yesterday morning's prints — plainly regarded them as inanities.

The visitor asked how he proposed to enforce, say, the new state law decreeing that any member of the NAACP be dismissed from the public payroll. The Attorney General said that this was the legislature's child; it would be enforced by the legislature.

"I hope," he said, "I don't have anything to do with them." There sat a man roaring for blood.

Nothing depresses a man who has to deal with reality so much as the things that happen in the final throes of legislative assemblages from here to Maine.

"I couldn't comment on this bill," said T. C. Callison. "I couldn't tell the legislature what will happen when it gets to court, any more than I could tell you.

"We get a lot of calls this time of the year," he said; the voice was that of the sane and civilized warden of an institution for the feeble-minded. "A superintendent called me and asked me what he should do about the new law. I said that he shouldn't ask too many questions of his Negro teachers. Of course, if some fellow insists on shouting that he's an NAACP member, I don't know what the superintendent would have to do. You've got the state after all."

The telephone rang. The caller was a merchant who wanted to know what he should do about a new law passed by the legislature to protect South Carolina textiles. The law says that every establishment which features imported (enemy) Japanese textiles must henceforth post a sign in its window saying "Japanese textiles sold here."

T. C. Callison smiled and said not to worry. "These fellows who think they're saving our industries will probably find out that it pays to advertise. You put the sign about Japanese textiles in the window and people will just rush in to buy them."

The Attorney General put down the phone, and said this sort of thing — "all these radicals talking" — had done the state irreparable harm. All these people shouting; "It makes the North think they are our voice." There was a sudden, shocking sense that the Attorney General of South Carolina was not talking about the NAACP; he was complaining about white people.

The visitor said that to him the great tragedy of the South was not segregation, which is a way of life that can pass, but the fact that there is no communication, that Negroes and whites cannot sit down together and work out some solution.

Attorney General Callison nodded his head. "It's political fear," he said. "Personally I'd welcome it if the legislature would pass a bill to set up a committee to talk things over with the NAACP and find out what they want. But, right now, I don't believe you'd find anybody who would agree to serve on it. It's just political fear."

The voice of the warden had lost some of its amused tolerance; there had entered into it the recognition that the inmates after all do run the institution. Callison began to talk about the danger of violence; make no mistake, there are counties in South Carolina where there'll never be a Negro in a white school; "they" won't allow it. "They," presumably are the wild ones, like that fellow who worked on the Jaycees day before yesterday.

He said he hoped the visitor would go out and look at the new Negro schools around the state. The visitor said he had and as real estate they were irresistible. "Of course, people will say we built them because we had to and that's true," said the Attorney General, "but they are good schools. We've spent a hundred million dollars on Negro schools, and I think that's something."

He asked whether the visitor had been to Montgomery, Alabama. The visitor said he had. "Those people down there are wrong," said the Attorney General of South Carolina. "A man's got a right to refuse to ride a bus if he don't want to."

The visitor said that he had had a conversation in Montgomery which summed up the whole thing for him. He had been talking to a Citizens Council member who had complained that his cook just wouldn't ride the bus. The visitor had asked, in the cause of logic, if not of freedom, why the complainer didn't just fire her, and the complainer had answered, "God, how could I fire her? She's been in my family twenty years."

The Attorney General of South Carolina smiled and said that was how it is. He said he wished he had a house in his backyard he would let out to some Negroes. Of course, the visitor must understand that they'd have to come in the back door. He said again that he wished the white radicals would be quiet and give us all the blessing of peace. Then his time was up and he walked the visitor to the door.

"I hope you can do something," he said, "to tell the North how we really feel down here." Who did he think his visitor was, Fyodor Dostoevski?

[Columbia, South Carolina, March 30, 1956]

"If You Got the Guts . . ."

On the Wednesday after Labor Day, the Kentucky National Guard lumbered into Sturgis to bring peace to nine Negro children who had entered their hometown high school.

The guard brought the clatter and the tumult of history, and ten-year-old James Gordon sat on the floor of his white house back in the hills of the worn-out mine four miles from here and thirteen miles from Sturgis and heard the radio talking about it.

He listened all the way through, and then he looked up at his mother and said:

"Mommy, if they can go to the school in Sturgis, why can't we go to the school in Clay?"

Louise Gordon said she began then to really think about it for the first time. And then she answered:

"D'you got the guts to go, I got the guts to take ye."

"Every summer for the last three years there's rumors back here that the children are going to school in Clay in the fall. Of course there's nobody you could ask about it. And then the bus comes back here in September and picks up the children and takes them down the road to Providence and the school they've always gone to.

"And then James asks me this question, and him a little boy and me twenty-eight years old and I'd never even thought of it."

She drove down to Clay on Thurdsay and up the hill to the white school and talked to Mrs. Irene Powell, its principal. Irene Powell said Clay Consolidated was terribly crowded and Louise Gordon answered that it wasn't as crowded as the school in Providence. Irene Powell said that James and his little sister Theresa couldn't meet the school standards and would probably have to be put back a year. Louise Gordon said that she and they could bear that.

"So I went back and called the principal at Providence. She said, 'Mrs. Gordon, your children are qualified to go into the grade they're in here in any school in the United States.' "

William Lloyd Garrison said, "I am in earnest and I will not equivocate and I will be heard." Ulysses S. Grant said he would fight it out on this line if it took all summer. A Marine sergeant whose name no one remembers said, "Come on, you bastards, do you want to live forever?" Those are the lines of the American legend; they are in the books and engraved on the plaques.

Set beside them Louise Gordon saying to her little boy in her house on a coal bed: "If you got the guts to go, I got the guts to take ye."

The words that will make up the American legend of our lifetime are not spoken by generals or by candidates for the Presidency of the United States. They are spoken in a bedroom by a woman who is a stranger to us all, a thin, wonderfully sassy woman named Louise Gordon.

Last Friday, she got in her car with James and Theresa and drove to the Clay Consolidated School to take them in and a group of citizens met her at the entrance and told her to go home. They knew her only, they still know her only, as Louise who used to work in the kitchen of their short-order café. That night the Reverend Minvill Clark, as representative of the Anglo-Saxon God of Clay, came out to persuade her not to come back.

"He asked me, 'Louise, could you promise that one of your children wouldn't end up marrying one of our children?'

"I said I couldn't promise anything. My kids will come home with somebody, and I got a son and a daughter and I can't help it. But I must say I wouldn't mind seeing it legal for a change."

She was obviously a hard case.

Her sister, Mattie Smith, cooked for Herman Clark, the Mayor of Clay. On the morning Louise Gordon was turned back first, Mayor Clark led the defending army. Mattie Smith was standing on his porch and watched him, and then went back to the kitchen and hung up her apron and went home for good.

But, by now, Louise Gordon was almost done. Most of the Negroes who lived around her in the patch began to fall away; they were not hostile, but they were confused and frightened. The Reverend Mr. Clark's missionaries went to see her husband, James, over at the garage where he works in Sturgis; James stopped talking about how he felt. "I don't know about James," she said, "I can't seem to get through to him. I don't know what he really thinks." And there came into her voice the edge of sadness at thinking about somebody who had to bear the load she carries so casually without understanding why he bears it.

She talked a long time to two visitors yesterday morning, lying on the bed at the house of one of her neighbors, casual talk most of it, leading nowhere much, wondering as her visitors wondered what were the roots of her lonely pilgrimage.

"What are the roots, do you suppose?" she said. "I wish somebody would ask me that, instead of this stuff about my long-range plans and all this silly publicity, because where the roots are is really the thing I'd like to think about."

She'd given up reading the papers and she does not seem more than politely interested in her television schedule, because the Louise Gordon she sees and reads about obviously does not seem to her the Louise Gordon she knows.

She was sitting up on the bed when she began talking about her loneliness.

"I think of my people working over there" — she waved her hand at Clay — "Somebody ought to beat their butts for them. God knows, I need a job" — her feet came down on the floor — "but to go over there to work and cook and scrub" — she was on her knees now, her face down to the floor in a pantomime of the ancient posture of subjection — "and prostrate myself and humble myself for three dollars a day? That Mayor didn't even know my sister Mattie's last name."

And then, as she got up, Louis Lomax, a Hearst reporter who happens to be a Negro, said with the infinite, tolerant wisdom of his Southern childhood:

"Oh, heck, Louise, next fall all your neighbors will have their kids in that school and they'll be sitting here telling you how they won the fight." And Louise Gordon smiled and said she supposed they would.

"And now I think everybody ought to go home; the National Guard, you all, yes, me too, and leave those kids in school to make their way. My children will make their way; the white children will make their way too. Let them work it out together."

She smiled and thanked her visitors for passing the time with her.

There's no running water back on the patch; one man who delivers her water bottled from Clay refused to go on selling it to her three days ago. She found a new supply, but it did not seem to her a very important issue.

"The way things go, if I can't buy water any more, I figure God will make it rain for four days. There's springs back in those hills. What's water, anyway?"

It seemed, walking away down the road that will probably not be paved in Louise Gordon's lifetime, somehow silly to believe in cause and effect; history is a series of divine and beautiful accidents like the moment of truth that happened at the same time to a little boy and his mother when she looked at him and said that together they would charge the guns. It is a little hard to think that now I am coming home and I am condemned before the week is out to have some smug party who has never seen Clay or Louise Gordon explain to me exactly what made her do what she did.

The story of the South is the most beautiful and important story on earth today, because it is the frontier of an old, heroic American tradition. These are great people — great Americans — and they are the heritage, not of some race or other, but of all Americans. Each is different, but, with all of them, the mystery of someone like Louise Gordon, who can live in the shadows all her life and then be ready with precisely the right word abides to taunt and tease us and touch our sense of awe. The story is quite simply that a terrible beauty sleeps and waits down here.

[Clay, Kentucky, September 14, 1956]

Two Ballpoint Pens

The Reverend Martin Luther King is only twenty-eight, and it is not impossible that he may have to live the rest of his life in the shadow of the miracle he helped bring about in Montgomery, Alabama, last year.

Whites and Negroes are intermixed in Montgomery's buses now, although a few of the Negroes who walked for miles every day rather than ride a segregated bus still edge to the rear from ancient habit. Montgomery is the only victory in the long war in the South, and Martin King is that victory's embodiment as a personality.

He remains the minister of a Negro Baptist church within sight of the first capitol of the Confederacy, and he expects to remain with his people.

Occasionally he leaves his ghetto as ambassador plenipotentiary to the great world: last spring to Ghana, next January to see Nehru in India, yesterday to present his congregation's petition for redress to the Vice President of the United States.

This voyaging to the world of temporal power leaves Martin King with mixed feelings. He is supposed to have said recently that he hadn't read a new book or thought a new thought or made a new speech in the last year, and that he was in terror of losing his amateur standing.

But then, if he had not gone to Ghana, he would never have met Richard Nixon. The Nixons were coming from some ceremony last March 16, and the Vice President stuck out his hand and said he had read all about Martin King in *Time* — King, John Sparkman and Willie Mays are Alabama's only three cover subjects, which is two out of three for the race whose members cannot get their hair cut in a hotel in Montgomery. Mrs. Nixon told Mrs. King that she had been deeply moved by her love story. The Vice President asked King please to drop in when he got back to the States.

This amateur symbol of non-violent resistance came to the Senate cloakroom yesterday afternoon to meet that professional exemplar of non-violent reconciliation. The Reverend Dr. King came accompanied by the Reverend Ralph Abernathy, an associate in the Montgomery bus boycott; the Vice President waited with Labor Secretary Mitchell.

When their business was done, the Reverend Messrs. King and Abernathy — who not much more than a year ago were being hauled in handcuffs into a Montgomery police court — returned to the Raleigh Hotel in an air-conditioned Secret Service sedan.

The Vice President had told them that he could, due to pressures of state, see them only an hour; their talk ran closer to two hours, and Nixon's administrative assistant said later that he had never known the Vice President to get caught up so long with any visitors. There are techniques of hospitality untaught in the hotel schools.

Martin King came most of all to ask the Vice President to go South to give the moral support of the national government to the achievement of integration. He pointed out, of course, a fact which the Vice President is the first man in America to confess; that Richard Nixon is no full substitute for Dwight Eisenhower. Mr. Nixon appears to have plenipotentiary powers only as the President's representative in

Ghana, not Alabama. Still, he is chairman of the President's committee to enforce fair employment practices on government contracts, and he would hold public hearings of the committee in any one Southern city the Reverend Dr. King might suggest. The Reverend Dr. King suggested Atlanta, and the Vice President said Atlanta it would be.

The visitors recalled the long roll of crimes of violence against Negroes, and asked at the end whether the President might speak out against this sort of thing. Mr. Nixon made a note of it.

Irving Ives, with the scent for libertarian symbols which is granted to Senators whose terms expire in 1958, came by to have his picture taken with the group, but there were no other efforts at entrapment. The Vice President gave Martin Luther King and Ralph Abernathy ballpoint pens with his name imprinted upon them, and autographed calling cards for their children.

Near the end, Mr. Nixon wondered aloud whether the Reverend Dr. King, when announcing the approaching march on Atlanta, might point out how close the President and the Vice President stood together in their devotion to the common cause. Martin King was too gracious to reply, but he did not allude to the subject when he met the papers.

Over in the House, the debate on civil rights went on; Martin Dies of Texas pleaded with his colleagues not to pass laws which "would check the tide of tolerance which is sweeping America." Bigotry is unfashionable in Washington; Richard Nixon is not the worst representative of an America which treats the embodiments of our most beautiful aspirations to the tasteless, unnourishing but pipe-hot broth of good will.

Richard M. Nixon departed — the poorer by two ballpoint pens — and Martin Luther King went back to the Raleigh to meet the press. The hotel electrician held up matters to change the fixtures to accommodate the television lights. Our Gandhis come to us through a screen of harsh and artificial light.

The Reverend Dr. King is a very young man, and almost a diffident one. He is also the doctor of theology who had great promise in Boston University, an intellectual of the first class who lives in a ghetto and would not look incongruous as a side-man in one of Dizzy Gillespie's big bands. He is hip in the word's deepest and finest sense;

the night his house was bombed by the Citizens Council, he came out and told his neighbors to remember that their one, great unconquerable shield was the whole armor of love.

He looked at the television cameras and read his statement and prepared to endure the kind of questions natural to a city whose inhabitants are trained to see not the image of the man but only the mask of the politician.

[Washington, D.C., June 14, 1957]

The Wrong Man

Claud Cruell and Sherwood Turner did not know each other very well, even as a Negro knows a white man. Claud Cruell was old enough, for one thing, to be Sherwood Turner's father. He had, in fact, known Sherwood Turner's father; they had grown up together in these hills near the North Carolina border.

No one prospers to excess in that country. Claud Cruell was thirty-three years old twenty-five years ago when he got the $500 it cost him to buy the fifty-two acres which form the basis of his one-hundred-acre farm tract.

"They gave it to me," he says, "because nobody else wanted it." He and his brothers farmed it and worked it over mostly for corn; they were Negroes surrounded by white neighbors. The size of his acreage is no measure of wealth; he and his wife, Fanny, made most of their cash income taking in laundry from ten white families in their neighborhood, carrying it down the hill to a stream below their house and beating it clean on rocks with sticks.

Six years ago, Claud Cruell began building his house. It took him five years; when he had finished he and his wife moved from their old cabin into this brick house with its wide porch and its square columns which has almost too much room for a couple in their late fifties without children. Still life had been kinder and more peaceful for Claud Cruell, an old Negro, than for Sherwood Turner, a young white man. Sherwood Turner had stomach trouble; he worked on the rarest of occasions; he was on what passes for public relief in Greenville County. The children kept coming; about a year ago, there were seven when the landlord told Sherwood Turner he would have to move out. That afternoon he met Claud Cruell and asked if he could rent the old cabin.

"I told him," says Claud Cruell, "that it wasn't worth living in. But he said he had to have something, so I let him have it for $5 a month, which wasn't too little for what it was worth."

"I think," says Sherwood Turner still, "that he's as good a colored man as I've ever seen in my life. I hate to say this, but he's holped [sic] me when none of my brothers would holp me.

"I remember once I came out of the hospital and we didn't have food in the house, and Claud put me and Goldie and the children in his car and took us down to the store and bought us $15 worth of groceries."

It may have been putting them in the car and carrying them down to buy them groceries which started the rumors about Claud Cruell. That, and the Turner children playing on the Cruells' large and empty porch. "Claud thought the world of the kids, and they think the world of him," says Sherwood Turner now.

The Klan is far away from the hills, at least thirteen miles away to the south in Greenville. There are perhaps twenty active Klansmen, truck drivers most of them, with Elvis Presley haircuts. On Saturday night, July 20, they met and elected young Marshall Rochester, a sash-and-door factory hand, as their president. Rochester said that something had to be done. Someone present had a dim recollection that there was something about a Negro man and a white woman having an affair in Travelers Rest.

Two Klansmen with their wives and their children went berry-picking to look the terrain over the following afternoon. Sherwood Turner passed them as he was driving Goldie down the hill to the Greenville Hospital for a kidney operation. He left the children alone in their cabin, in the care of Marie, the oldest of them, who is eleven. As the sun went down, Marie grew lonely, and went to the Cruells' house to ask if they could sleep there. They were asleep when there was a rattling at the door, and Claud Cruell looked up to see the avenging army of the Klan around him.

They put a chain around his arm and beat him. He kept saying that he was the wrong one, and they went on beating him. At last they left him and took his wife and put her in the car and rode her around, cursing her and telling her to stop mixing with white people, and dumped her out. While they were hitting Claud Cruell, little Marie got up with the gun her father had left her, and they took it away, and wanted to know why she had so few clothes on around these niggers. In her statement to the police, Marie Turner referred over and over to Daddy Claud.

Fannie Cruell walked home to find her husband sitting outside in the car, bowed over. He had sent the children home. He says he didn't see much sense in calling the police. But Sherwood Turner called Sheriff Bob Martin and the deputies came out and took the depositions. Sheriff Martin talked to the neighbors and satisfied himself that the Klan had picked the wrong man.

A visitor drove by Marshall Rochester's dirty red house on a rutty dirt road; it was dark at 9:30. He and the Klan seemed somehow irrelevant; what was relevant and unanswerable was the question of the dark passion that moves a man to use up his weekend avenging a rumor in a strange county thirteen miles away.

The Cruells have suspended their laundry business until they get their morale back. The Turners, upon the sheriff's advice, moved away last week. Claud Cruell sat on his porch in the dark glasses his eye doctor has prescribed. "Yes, sir," he said, "I miss the children. A fellow can't help but miss children for a while."

Goldie Turner, returned from the hospital, was away from her new home. "She went out to see if she could pick a few beans and get us some money," said her husband. "I didn't want to move out of there, but if a bunch would get up there and start shooting these kids, it would be terrible." He said again that Claud Cruell had been kind when nobody else was. There was about the children the awful stale smell of unwiped, unwashed vomit. Little Marie, her shoulder pulled up against the weight, was carrying a huge pail of water into the house.

It cannot be counted among the least of the South's sorrows that she and her brothers and sisters have been parted from the best and kindest friends not of their blood that they have ever had.

[Travelers Rest, South Carolina, August 15, 1957]

Upon Such a Day

7:55 A.M., SEPTEMBER 9 — The ladies of North Nashville were on parade, in sweat socks one, in formless cotton sacking others, with signs saying, "Keep Our White Schools White"; "Keep Your Kids Home"; and "KKKK," which stands for Knights of the Ku Klux Klan. Their husbands, the knights, stood protected behind them, on the grass around Glenn School. One knight held up a sign saying: "What God Has Put Asunder [sic], Let No Man Put Together." A little girl pointed to him and said, "Gee, there's Carol Sue's daddy," and, with her mother and her little brother, joined the little clump of indecisive who milled not in or out but on the rim.

8:15 A.M., SAME DAY — A convertible came by; the ladies of North Nashville set up their tribal cries. The police told its driver to park down the road. He came out, at last, a large man, holding by the hand his daughter, a small Negro child named Lajuanda Street, and followed by a woman with her child, Sinclair Lee, Jr., and a man with glasses and his daughter Jacqueline Faye Griffith. The children were all first-graders. "If that don't make my blood boil," said a woman. The children passed through the crowd; they were out of sight; nothing of this historic parade could be seen except Harold Street, who was bulkier than anyone there. One of the knights looked at Harold Street and thought better of pushing him, and pushed M. J. Griffith, who is smaller, instead.

"You'll come out of there feet up," one of the Valkyries shrieked. City Detective C. E. Burris, a fat man in a Panama hat, shoved the knight halfway across the walkway. The menace collapsed. The cry came up safely from the back: "You see what they do to the white people. Who's gonna take up for the white people?"

9 A.M. — Some thirty-odd mothers, dragging their children, had come out, each one to be greeted by wild cries. Three or four of the children were crying. Their mother comforted two of them by giving them signs saying "Keep Our White Schools White." They were not quite large enough to carry this burden; the sign kept bowing and falling away. But a white woman walked the gantlet escorting her two children late to school. One of the Valkyries called her a tedious ob-

scenity. She answered: "You tend to your business and I'll tend to mine."

10 A.M. — John Kasper, taller than all his flock, with his felt hat sweated through, was telling the crowd that the jails weren't big enough for all of them. "The niggers are in there now; we're gonna continue the boycott." A cop said everyone should get up on the sidewalk, "because we don't want nobody to get run over." "We're gonna stand and stand and stand," said John Kasper.

10:15 A.M. — Edna Jean Moore, arrested at Fehr School for throwing a stick of wood at a Negro mother, was bailed out for $10 and brought back to the scene of the resistance in a KKK car. A mother whispered in a little girl's ear, and having learned that lesson, her child, a blond, marched the sidewalk, chanting, "Go home, niggers, go home, niggers."

11 A.M. — The intervening minutes had been occupied with Kasper on the need to keep on, keep on. Jones School was very peaceful. Inside, a visitor looked into room 105, and saw first-grader Charlie Battles, with the smile all children have at peace, playing blind man's buff with the white kids. It seemed a pleasant place to watch and wait; Charlie Battles sat down and began working earnestly with another child on his drawings, and before long the first day of school was over.

Mrs. Pauline Brommer, Charlie Battles's new teacher, said that the children had been bothered a little by the clatter outside, and that they had asked what it was. "I told them," she said: "Those were mommies and daddies; they're just waiting for us to finish school.

"It was," she said, "a delightful day. I wasn't sure at the beginning just how it would be, but we began to play the game of sharing, and right away Charlie said he had a song to share with us, and he gave the most wonderful imitation of Elvis Presley singing 'Hound Dog' and the children just loved it." Her visitor left walking past a sign which said: "God is the author of segregation."

There were very few of them really, these criers against the daylight, and, once school was out, Nashville was as it always had been. They met at seven fifteen, 400 or so of them, on the steps of its War Memorial, and, with the city going about its shopping hours unheeding, listened to John Kasper. It was a date-night audience.

"We've started from nothin'," cried John Kasper. "They said it couldn't be done but we did it. Let's start hating the nigger until we get him out of our schools. Let's say we want him either to be a dead nigger or back to Africa." The audience laughed. "We say no peace," said John Kasper. "We say attack, attack, attack. There ain't any jails big enough." A high school boy, who preferred not to give his name, bawled he would die before he'd let yer little brother grow up to marry one of them black et ceteras, et ceteras. The crowd went trooping up the steps of Nashville's State Capitol to better affront Governor Frank Clement.

John Kasper held up a rope, and everybody laughed and cheered. This is Dixie, he said, the best and most bloodthirsty people under God's skies. "Let's for one time show what a white man can do." He announced that ten men would pass through the crowd soliciting funds. The crowd began to flee, while the high school boy, still anonymous in his red sweater, said: "It's like a football game; we're not out for love; we're out for blood and victory."

It was horribly ugly, and it was about nothing. Upon such a day, Charles.Battles played blind man's buff with the white children on his first day in school.

[Nashville, September 10, 1957]

Next Day

The gathering place of the Klans of Nashville had been moved yesterday from the streets to the City Court where Judge Andrew Doyle adjusts the passions of the disorderly poor.

In Judge Doyle's court, by tradition, Negro and white, although united in trouble, sit segregated as spectators. As defendants, they are intermixed in the bullpen where they await trial. A man was saying yesterday that the quickest way to get integrated in Nashville is to resist a cop in the cause of segregation.

The judge was gentle enough with most of the rioters who were before him for loitering. Glowering and disturbing, they are a thin-blooded crowd, most of them; the passion which had flared in them Monday was down to soggy mush. G. H. Akins, who had been calling the cops to come and fight him in front of Caldwell School Tuesday, broke down and blubbered, with his two little girls clutching his knees before the judge. To such as these Andrew Doyle gave $5 fines; he knew they would not trouble him again.

He saved his moral indignation for people worthy of it. Marvin Sullins, a farmer in his fifties, was before him for hitting a thirteen-year-old Negro boy in front of Caldwell School Tuesday. William Jackson had been running from an assaulting corps of white children when Marvin Sullins got him. The police had found a pair of brass knuckles on Marvin Sullins when they brought him in.

William Jackson told his story and looked up at Marvin Sullins's eyes. Marvin Sullins had not the moral force to brag about his moment of struggle for the purity of the white South; he mumbled that he couldn't have hit this boy: "He's too little." Judge Doyle said "Yer a coward," and fined him $200 and told him he could never again be a free patient at the county hospital, and Marvin Sullins shuffled off to the county workhouse to render his payment to the God which watches over little children.

Then John Kasper came in on the counts of vagrancy, loitering and disorderly conduct. Andrew Doyle looked at him and saw only William Jackson who was chased on the street by white boys and was caught and hit by a fifty-five-year-old man. The point to him was not about fascism or racism or other abstract things; it was that John Kasper makes his war on little boys.

Floyd Peek, a county constable, told of Kasper's standing on the steps of the State Capitol and waving a rope and telling the poor that blood should run in the streets. John Kasper, dream-walking, stumbling in his speech, kept asking if he had said that, like the man who had blacked out on whisky the night before and was asking around town what had he done? He is an apprentice demagogue in a section whose politicians can summon up passion as Horowitz plays the piano. It is extraordinary the passion this essentially passionless man can arouse. Assistant City Attorney Robert Jennings cried out for a punishment that would degrade John Kasper and bring him to his knees in atonement:

"I hope your Honor fines him so much that he will be unable to pay and have to go to our workhouse where they'll put him behind a clean broom and send him back to those schools to clean up the debris he's left behind in our streets."

I would swear that John Kasper winced. And then Andrew Doyle raised his eyes from the docket and stared straight at John Kasper, and the back of John Kasper's neck went red with the blush that small boys cannot hold back and his eyes had no sight in them. Andrew Doyle spoke without a note and he drew the line where it belonged:

"I only wish," he said, "we had enough policemen to take you by the seat of yer britches and the nape of yer neck and throw you outside the city limits of Nashville as far as possible.

"Yer purpose was to cause trouble and fatten yer pocketbook with the dimes and dollars of irresponsible and uneducated people. You go into homes and take food from their mouths when they can hardly feed their own children. You pass the hat to nobody but people who can't afford to give the money you take from them. I wish I could do more on the vagrancy charge, but the only thing that I can do is to fine you $50 and that is what I will do, because you are the worst vagrant ever to hit the city of Nashville and the state of Tennessee, and I hope we never see another like you."

And then Andrew Doyle fairly cried out from the scar that the sight of little Willie Jackson had left upon what should by now be a calloused memory:

"We tried this white man just now for something that happened as a direct result of what you have agitated. He had no more sense than to attack an itty bitty kid. Only a coward would take after an innocent child rather than pick on somebody his own size."

And having said this, Andrew Doyle fined John Kasper $200 on four counts. There was an indecisive floundering about for a bondsman; none was found, and John Kasper went back to the workhouse. At midnight last night, he remained unbailed; it seemed impossible that this shaker of the earth could not raise $200. It may be that he has been left, as so much of his battleground is, morally exhausted, and will go stumbling tomorrow as a city prisoner cleaning the streets in the company of some defaulting Saturday night drunk who might be white or might be colored, because only accident and pauperism brought him here.

The point of it, I think, was moral exhaustion. The schools were emptier than they had been the day before; some of the Negro children even stayed home. The father of one of them said yesterday that he was tired and that he just didn't think he would mess with it today. So long had it been since Monday. The sidewalks in front of the schools were barren of disturbers of the peace; the cops lounged in the sun before Jones School, and Cecil Ray, a little Negro boy who has come here every day, was by now quite the pet of the policemen. Nashville will pick itself up and begin again today. Yesterday it was used up. The moment of purgation was, for John Kasper and everyone else, the moment of exhaustion.

[Nashville, September 12, 1957]

The Soul's Cry

John Kasper was cleaning the bars of the city jail yesterday. It was just the latest of the waiting rooms in which he tarries, this permanent vagrant, between his wanderings across the face of the South between the gutter and the sewer. John Kasper lives nowhere except in the backs of old cars with a pile of leaflets as his pillow.

But, if John Kasper is of the air, the Reverend Fred Stroud is of the earth. Fred Stroud — "Call me Brother Stroud; that's what my people call me" — is pastor of the Bible Presbyterian Church. He is twenty-four years out of Georgia's Columbia Theological Seminary; he is twenty years out of the Southern Presbyterian Church, which he declared "officially apostate" in 1938, and seceded, carrying some 400 members of his congregation with him.

Fred Stroud is chaplain of the ragged, temporarily routed army which went into the streets here Monday to fight integration of Nashville's schools. He roamed from school to school that day, a short, lantern-jawed man carrying a sign proclaiming: "God is the author of segregation: Sixth Corinthians."

Fred Stroud is immobilized now. Mayor Ben West has moved to enjoin him from preaching in the streets. He sat yesterday in his study looking out over the shabby streets of "this receding neighborhood" he holds as a fortress of the fundamental creed. He looks at an indifferent city, a city of people who are unlike him because they do not really care. His verse in the Bible is the verse of the truly committed, the verse in Revelations which says — be thou hot or cold; if thou art lukewarm I will spew you out of my mouth. It is, I confess, my verse too.

"I wouldn't say John Kasper is a failure," he told one caller yesterday. "Not everybody who gets in jail is a failure. Just keep looking up, boy. That's all I know to do, just keep looking up. The Lord will take care of us; he always has."

He hung up, and told his two visitors of "my soul's cry for Nashville."

"John Kasper found me here and I will be here if he has to leave. I have been standing alone here since 1938 against all the modernist preachers." He riffled the Bible: "There's not one word of compromise in this. Christ set his face steadfastly to go to Jerusalem."

He waved his hand in the direction of the comfortable churches across the river. "They preach the false philosophy that it is un-Christian to fight. They're teaching the fatherhood of God and the brotherhood of all mankind. But, unless a man has been born again, he cannot claim to be a child of God.

"Christ hated mixing. God has always been a segrationist."

One of his visitors asked Brother Stroud what he had thought of his flock boiling in the streets last Monday.

"It just shows a sincerity," he said. "They have convictions. They don't want to be pushed around."

Is John Kasper saved, the visitor wondered?

"Of course, John knows no more about theology than you do. He went to Columbia. But he tells me now that he is a believer in the Lord Jesus Christ."

Fred Stroud is a wandering holy man, an eater of locusts. He preaches in the market and in the streets.

It is odd what forms of witness God chooses for his ministers. While Fred Stroud stalked the streets on Tuesday, Robert Kelly, rector of a Negro Methodist Church, visited the homes of the parents who had enrolled their children and were, most of them, afraid to go back.

"I told them," Robert Kelly said yesterday, "that, if they were afraid to go and take them in, that I would take them in." Fred Stroud is not alone among the committed.

But, if this is Armageddon, one of Fred Stroud's visitors asked, are you not lonely and weary among the few who battle for the Lord in this city of neutrals?

The light of the message came to Fred Stroud's eyes under their jutting, tangled brows:

"What do you know about Armageddon?" he said. "Are you saved?"

The visitor said that he was not. "Boy," said Mr. Stroud, "can you face the lake of fire?"

It was time for the sinner to flee the tender of grace. "Before you go," said Fred Stroud, "could we stop for a moment for prayer?"

He put one hand on his New York visitor's hand, and another on the shoulder of William Emerson, of *Newsweek*, a Georgian of charming mien and traditional outlook.

"Oh, Lord," cried Fred Stroud on his knees, "watch over this good boy from Georgia and save this poor boy from New York. He is alone and suffering; come to him, save him, and perhaps he will grow up to preach Thy gospel."

Then, "Oh, Lord," he cried, alone with his vision, "You know that I don't hate anyone. I just feel sorry for ole Ben West, I just feel sorry for these niggers."

In my job we travel, wayfarers as rootless as — if less vandalic than — John Kasper, and our moments of reward are our moments of engagement. They are moments when tragedy and comedy are all mixed up, and God and the devil contend like scorpions in a bottle inside the soul of a man before us. Oh, Lord, Fred Stroud cries, You know I don't hate anybody. Fred Stroud has sacrificed life and comfort, and he does yet not know inside himself whether God or the devil sends him into the streets, and makes him happy when a mob chases a Negro away from a school.

What I have said about him probably makes very little sense. He is my brother. We are bound together, he and Emerson and I, through all eternity by that horrible, desperate prayer.

[Nashville, September 13, 1957]

The Book

There is a picture of Ernest Green in its proper order as a member of the class of 1958 in *Tix*, the yearbook of Central High School, and the notation that jazz is his hobby and that he was a transfer from Horace Mann, the Negro school.

There is in addition a panel of pictures of soldiers, but no other suggestion of the events for which this year at Central High is unlikely to be forgotten. *Tix* is otherwise what every high school yearbook, however increased by substance and imagination, ends up being, the portraits of the homecoming queen and the football players and the reserve cheerleaders and the members of the societies in this particularly complex civilization.

But Ernest Green's yearbook is different from all others, because in it are written the good-bys of fourteen of his 601 fellow graduates to this boy, a Negro, younger than the average among them, whose name has engraved their class in history.

"You know how it is in high school," said Ernest Green yesterday. "Kids ask you to write in their books and then they ask to write something back in yours."

Some of them began, unconscious of any need to celebrate this moment with rhetoric: "Man, this English is rough" . . . or "Enjoyed having you in solid" . . . or "This government course is for the birds" and like expressions of solidarity against the oppressor. But they all ended up expressing some of the same soul's cry:

"I have found you a real nice fellow."

"I want to take the opportunity to tell you that I think you have displayed remarkable courage in your struggle to prove your rights as an American."

"I have admired your courage this year, and I'm glad you made it through all right."

"I have enjoyed having home room with you this year. Your friendship has meant a lot to me. I want to wish you all the luck possible in the future, for you deserve it. May God bless you richly."

"May you always have the best during the future. Things have turned out for the best no matter how one feels personally. You've stood the test and passed it. May you always have this much courage."

"I know it has been a hard year for you."

"I have really admired you for your courage through all the year. I hope you can always remain so."

"I know you're a real nice guy and best wishes."

"I know it has been real tough for you over here. But now that it is all over, I know that you and I are happy."

"It has been a sincere pleasure to have been your friend. May God always guide you and keep you safe."

"I really admire you, Ernest. I doubt if I could have done half so well had the circumstances been reversed. May you achieve all your goals, and they be the best."

The last was written across the portrait of a girl especially marked by her classmates for honor for her qualities. And most of them had been written by those seniors most admired by the rest of the class, by Student Council members and by belles, which, of course, figures, because pretty girls feel no need to assert their place in a master race. They were, these fourteen souvenirs of Ernest Green's, from the leaders of the school.

No one who has ever tried to do his best and failed could read them without taking note of their uniform sense of envy of Ernest Green for having done what they doubted they could have done. This sense seems to have occurred to Ernest Green, who, having done what he did, of course does not find it especially brave.

"I don't know what it would do, if you ran their names," he said. They are that hope out of all our troubles, the historic best of the white South, the silent South.

Ernest Green closed the book and talked about how it felt to be graduated.

"You know for me," he said, "there'll never be a graduation like this again. I've been looking forward to it for twelve years."

It may seem odd, but he was not talking about being the first Negro to be graduated with white children from a high school in Arkansas. He was talking only about what it was like just to be graduated from high school.

He sat among his records, Errol Garner, Art Blakey, the Modern Jazz Quartet; there is a marvelous process of cultural diffusion among those who know, wherever they are.

"I got a record," he said, "one of my friends borrowed. I like it more than anything the Modern Jazz Quartet has ever done. It's that Variation Number 1 on 'God Rest Ye Merry, Gentlemen.' That John Lewis . . ."

It seemed a little beside the point, looking at the jacket of the MJQ record, those four familiars of Padua bearded like pards, three of them Southerners, to ask of this Southerner how it had felt to walk across the grass carrying his diploma. For this, at the end, is simply a kid who owes money at the record store and hasn't had much time this year for the tenor saxophone.

"I don't know," he said, about the moment he walked under the lights and waited for the boos that never came. "It was kind of like a bomb that was a dud."

There remains the book with its notes of homage; there remain the crowd in the stands and the wonder that lay behind its silence, a silence of respect and envy. That silence seemed to say that this is a Southerner, this is our child and this our product; we made him and we salute him. He is better than we are; he has done something we would not have the guts to do, and we salute him with our silence. The South made him, and he is its better, most of all because he does not boast or brag or in any way indicate he knows it.

[Little Rock, May 29, 1958]

Tear Gas and Hymns

"Bless those cowards outside and our stupid Governor."

Montgomery is a legend written by cooks, janitors and country preachers. They came last night, as they have come so often to their First Baptist Church, this time to greet their children, twelve of the Nashville students whose test of segregated bus facilities had ignited their city the day before.

They came through unaccustomed attention, past clusters of white teenagers, standing in couples in the park across the street, silent, untrustworthy. John F. Kennedy's United States marshals, looking as if their hands were already blistering from the tense and unfamiliar grip of the billy, seemed a home guard of family men suddenly called up for an invasion.

A GUARD OF MARSHALS

In moments involving urgency, the average marshal was puffing after he had lumbered so much as ten feet. There were seventy of these gallant but unskilled conscripts; and going up the steps no wise man would have bet on them to hold off a minority of dedicated hoods — no more than fifty — who dared to aggress against them.

The national honor was being defended by men who looked over-matched even wearing six-shooters. The mob was pushing them back and back until the pavement before the church had become a postage stamp beachhead. The marshals experimented with tear gas and it floated back up the steps. The Negroes came out through the church doors coughing and wiping their eyes.

Inside, little pockets of tear gas floated about the rear of the church. The cooks and janitors and country preachers had every reason to believe — knowing themselves under siege — that the mob outside was bombarding them. They sat waving the fans donated by the Ross Clayton Funeral Home and they sang "Love Lifted Me." The chorus was thin, the melody sad and without pulse.

THE VOICES GROW LOUDER

Somehow they seemed to have come not to lift themselves and those fortunate strangers privileged to watch them, but only to sit together and endure what might fall upon them.

The Reverend S. S. Seay, their chairman, stopped them from the rostrum. "Nobody is singing as if he believes," he said, "I want everybody to believe."

They began again louder and with more effort and spirit. It still seemed as if the years have brought them, more than any other sadness, a terrible loss of hope in a white South.

The bus riders, looking like children, were lined up in the second row of steel chairs. None of them sang and half of them held their hands over their eyes in the prayer gesture. The Attorney General of Alabama had haggled over them all afternoon; they are subject to arrest for contempt of a state injunction. There are restraints on arresting sinners like these in church, but they had no reason to believe that they would not be taken away some time that night. They are the best kind of protestants, the ones who will go to jail if they have to but do not exult at the prospect.

Downstairs before the meeting they'd quite suddenly put their hands together and one of them had said, "We've gone this far through hell; we can go a little farther."

The windows had been closed one by one against the gas and the high old room had begun to stifle, and the thunder outside was silent. The Reverend B. D. Lambert, who has a dancer's soul in a short clumsy body, began the prayer chant: "This is a great moment in history. We thank Thee, Lord, for the protection Thou hast given us. You have blessed us in so many ways that we have not the words to describe them. You are too wise to make a mistake and too powerful to fail. Bless our enemy and we thank Our Father for these fine young people."

A REPORT FROM THE OUTSIDE

One of the children in the second row felt the white bandage on the back of his head and looked embarrassed at this compliment from a grownup. "You, God, have been with us since 1955."

An outrider came back to whisper a report of a car burned and rocks hurled and even the fire trucks called out to hold the patch of pavement, and then stopped in mid-passage as the cadence of the Reverend Mr. Lambert began to move the church into a world of hope and prayer somewhere beyond battles' menaces.

"Bless all those cowards standin' outside that can't fight unless they have a mob to come with them. Bless that stupid Governor of ours."

The riot car went by outside screaming through the windows. "He holds us in the hollow of His hand." The Reverend Mr. Lambert beat on. "We don't know whether we will get home or not. But we are with Him in His house."

Somewhere in those few moments in the house when all pain and menace were forgotten, the police and the marshals and the sheriff's men cleared the streets outside.

MARTIN LUTHER KING SPEAKS

By now there was not a breath of air in the room. The Reverend Ralph Abernathy arose to say: "We don't have to sweat here. The United States marshals are supposed to be out there to protect us." And then, in his shirt sleeves, Martin Luther King walked onto the platform and said: "We aren't going to become panicky. We're going to stand up for what we know is right.

"I just talked to Attorney General Kennedy."

His tone was matter of fact; the fans went on futilely beating before faces unsurprised. A Montgomery cook takes it for granted that while she sits under siege, Martin King can call the Attorney General of the United States on a Princess phone in the basement downstairs.

"He says he will stay in his office all night. He had been promised that no mob would be allowed to assemble. But they are at that door. Fear not. We have gone too far to turn back."

King and Abernathy went outside to talk to the marshals. They were met by a state trooper who said, "All right, are you going in or out?" In Montgomery, whatever the freaks of circumstance, a Negro minister is to be yelled at, a white thug to be cajoled.

The various choirs sang; the room settled down to a quiet where the sounds of the fans struggling through the air was loudest of all. There had fallen the long silence of endurance. There was a collection. The Reverend Fred Shuttlesworth, the merriest agitator of them all, had won them back to laughing at the Governor when he stopped in the middle to listen to a whisper in his ear and announced:

"The city is now under martial law and troops are on their way here."

There was a sudden great cheer. These people ask so little. The windows began to open to an unexpectedly quiet outside world; the damp, cool air came in; the fans slowed down; the cooks and janitors seemed to feel themselves solid protected citizens, waiting for the United States Army. They got John Patterson's National Guard, blinking against the television camera lights, lining up with jittery bayonets at the ready, perhaps one hundred scrawny boys who looked like the kids who had been standing in the park earlier and perhaps were those kids and thus to be commended for getting home and into their uniforms so quickly after their dispersal.

A Birmingham girl who had driven downtown for Coca-Colas came back with her car windows smashed by a rock. The First Baptist Church seemed to be the only place of peace in town. In the church, Martin King was speaking. On the pavement outside, Police Commissioner L. L. Sullivan was arguing that the meeting should break up now and the congregation go home. He was soft and soothing and without a note in his voice a stranger would trust.

By now, they had been there more than three hours. Little children were sleeping on the red plush back of the altar, like Italian paintings of the little St. John drowsing at the Last Supper. By now, the lights from their windows shone only on the bayonets of the National Guard in otherwise empty streets.

They began singing the "Battle Hymn of the Republic." The face of Fred Shuttlesworth seemed suddenly gray with weariness. At twenty of twelve there appeared on the rostrum State Adjutant General Henry V. Graham and State Public Safety Director Floyd Mann. Mann, almost by himself, had broken up the Greyhound mob the day before.

The Reverend Mr. Seay said that he had been asked to introduce the Adjutant General but first he would like to introduce a friend. "I choose my words when I talk about white folks, but there is a Christian soul in Mr. Mann. I think we ought to stand on our feet and thank him."

A WORD OF THANKS

And everyone in the room stood up, and the mother in front awoke her child so he could stand up too and thank a white public servant who had done his duty.

And then arose the Adjutant General, a tall straight man, and said, "Fellow citizens of Alabama," and then read Governor Patterson's proclamation of martial law, a horrid, pompus mash blaming the victims for the crime.

General Graham read this affront through right down to the words "so that the great seal of Alabama" and said that for their safety, the well-being of the city and the good of the state he was ordering them to stay there until morning.

And they rose, these gracious patient people, having again been insulted according to the habit of their state, and applauded General Graham too.

The Reverend Mr. Seay's misty glasses were heavy with reproach, "I don't think," he said, "that was a document for cheering. I want to be respectful to our leaders and to the government of Alabama but if John Patterson hadn't been playing cheap politics we wouldn't be here now. I think you ought to take those cheers back."

The repentant heads nodded and they began singing that they would overcome and sat down for the dawn watch. Out on the pavement, hemmed in by the National Guard, a woman was wondering how she would be able to call her boss. These are proud, brave and faithful people and some of them even found time to worry about the wives of pillars of the White Citizens Councils who were in danger of having to cook their own breakfasts this morning.

That danger was lifted three and a half hours later, when this message was transmitted over the Montgomery police radio:

"We understand that at 3 A.M. the National Guard turned those niggers loose from that church. Look for them, and if you find any see them safely home."

[Montgomery, May 22, 1961]

A Seat on the Bus

Three country boys with tickets for Meridian, Mississippi, stood ringed round by bayonets and waited for the 7 A.M. Trailways bus out of Montgomery.

"I don't care," said Jack L. Kelly, of Orangeburg, Mississippi, "I immigrated with 'em in the Army; I don't care if I immigrate with 'em on a bus."

The line of Guardsmen opened a passage by the terminal, and six cars led by a proud People's Cab and filled with Negroes came through and stopped by the white waiting room. Martin Luther King, Jr., pushed open the door and the Negroes filled that sacred precinct. The clerk began stamping the tickets.

Six Freedom Riders sat down at the lunch counter, ordered coffee and were served. All the customs for whose sake Montgomery had come close to murder were suspended yesterday for the higher purpose of getting the plague out of town.

By now the three country boys had been swept away, to get to Meridian who knows when. The National Guard of Alabama had commandeered the 7 A.M. bus to Jackson. There climbed aboard, in mixed and irregular array, eight Jim Crow college students, two of them girls, three Nashville Negro ministers, and a white companion, Paul Deitrich, a Washington office worker. Also sixteen communications specialists, three out of Luce, and six Alabama National Guardsmen and last of all, Major General Henry Graham, Adjutant General of the state of Alabama.

"We wish you sincerely a good trip," he said, and sent on its way the bus and its forty-two-car escort with the three search planes sweeping back and forth over its head.

A reporter told Paul Deitrich that he had guts. "I hope I have them tonight," Deitrich answered in a soft voice.

The children were tired, no one had slept much the night before. They began singing their calypso song, which cries brightly out: "Come on Mr. Kenn-ee-dee, Take Me Out of my Miseree."

THE PASSING SCENE

Then they began to drowse, looking out the windows at the flat country of their great-grandfathers' childhood. Every now and then, they would pass a car with silent white men lined up at a crossroad, once or twice a Negro cabin with its tenants standing expressionless on the porch, only watching, most of the time; occasionally, in places safely isolated, managing a sudden, momentary wave.

Past Selma, where the Alabama Citizens Councils were born; past a road gang whose white-jacketed Negro prisoners stood lined up, wondering; past Femopolis, where a truck driver threw some unknown object and slapped the side of the bus loud enough to wake a sleeping student.

The Reverend James Lawson, of Nashville, teacher-in-charge of this field trip, was sadly reading his Methodist prayer book. He said that they had hoped to come here as ordinary Negroes must, testing and meeting all the hazards. Now they were extraordinary Negroes sealed off from the reality of the sullen, watching clumps of whites, and the occasional expressionless Negroes on their way.

These laden hours might not shine, but they should not pass un-improved. He called his students back, and began once more to go over with them the endless questions and judgments about specific incidents of the test.

He asked the reporters and cameramen to move up front; the students sat in the back, cut off, by coincidence. Except for Deitrich, the Freedom Ride was segregated.

The reporters talked about other times and other places. Once or twice a voice came up from the back. "We should stand," the voice said, "and wait for the violence and, if the violence breaks our ranks, we should join our hands and hold together as long as we can."

After three hours and a half, General Graham ordered a rest stop. These were captured invaders being carried out of Alabama; they could not disembark within sight of an Alabama citizen. They stopped by an empty field. Lawson stood behind the bus — the Guardsmen lined up, their backs to him, their bayonets fixed against some invisible hazard — and Lawson explained that this was not the normal course he and the students were committed to run.

"We are a non-violent force and we are protected by the instruments of violence. We would prefer not having this protection. We are not seeking violence, but, if it is coming, we must accept it as other Negroes have to."

The prisoners went back to their internment. They rode on to Scratch Hill; it was the border of Mississippi. One of Governor Ross Barnett's helicopters came down in a field beside the road. It had come up rain. The Guardsmen with their bayonets stood at the ready, the rain soaking their fatigues.

Julia Aaron of New Orleans, who is just twenty, looked out from the bus at them, and said: "That's terrible. Those poor men having to stand there and getting wet."

STATE LINE

The ear listened for the note of mockery. It did not come; Julia Aaron's voice was all concern.

The thought of Mississippi, dark and swarm-haunted, worked its mysterious chemistry. General Graham was scouting ahead. The reporters were once more in front; the students in the back. A white man catching himself sitting automatically next to a white man thought of all the acceptances the name and memory and custom of Mississippi had laid upon him, and he began talking to another white man about all the little nonsenses and silences one must endure — petty but hardly prideful — and suddenly they both understood at just the same time how wonderful these students are — bravely and casually walking straight through everything as far as their bodies will take them.

It rained on, Julia Aaron was saying that she had heard that Mississippi is a beautiful state. The tensions of the prospect otherwise sat even on those who had no sensible reason to feel tension. Most of all, perhaps, only on those. All over the bus softly, slowly, oddly sweet, the voices of the students began to sing "Go Down, Moses, Away Down in Egypt Land."

After an infinity, General Graham came back and the convoy rolled to the rendezvous with the Mississippi National Guard — a garage at a crossroad — and Alabama got off with a cursory farewell and Mississippi got on without a greeting.

Mississippi turned out to be Lieutenant Colonel "Sunny" Montgomery, a State Senator from Meridian, a captain and six Guardsmen, with bayonets; two fat sergeants stood in the aisles (to sit would be to integrate), the hard faces like the heavy clouds above.

Mississippi's orders were to scuttle westward, the colonel said he knew not where. A student started a question; another student said "play it cool," and they sang awhile, "Black and White Together We Shall Not Be Moved," and Colonel Montgomery squared the shoulders of his back.

There were two hours and a half left. The silence of imprisonment fell. The students looked out windows through streets dotted with clumps of white citizens, offering a silent, obscene gesture of derision.

A REQUEST

Thus came Khrushchev to Iowa, or candidate Kennedy to Indiana. But they represented great physical forces tolerating unfriendly lands; they had other places to go. This rolling, shuddering paddy wagon was alone in the world.

There had passed six-and-a-half hours without food or respite. The Reverend Corty T. Vivian, a Nashville minister, got up and asked the colonel to stop the bus and let some of the passengers off to go to the

bathroom. He was suffering a condition thought of as comic and certainly not dignified, but still the most painful known to a man of good
conscience. The poor man fought for his dignity until his hands were
gray around the rail in front of him and his face was the face of a
deep interior wound.

He went to "Sunny" Montgomery again and "Sunny" Montgomery
told him to get back in the bus. The Reverend Mr. Vivian stood arguing and the colonel said to the trooper, "Put him back; there'll be a
stop before long," and the Rerevend Mr. Vivian sat back down again
and through his teeth and in the agony of his body said, "May you
come to the point when you can ask His forgiveness for these animal
acts. Not to allow a man a common decency. What do you tell your
children when we go home? What do you say to tell God when you
pray in church, or do you pray?"

The colonel looked out on the road, his back to that voice, his
shoulders stiffening, but with a neck that never reddened. Thus, in
military glory, Colonel Montgomery brought the inmates in to Jackson.

DESTINATION: JAIL

Jackson was ready, the Trailways station surrounded by policemen,
the crowds sparse and at a distance, a path cleared to the colored waiting room. The Reverend Mr. Vivian sat and fought the needs of his
body until he could get off with the other Freedom Riders.

They came in silence and were met in silence, and walked in silence
into the white waiting room. The two girls and Paul Deitrich and
Matthew Walker, a thin Fisk boy, stood in front of the white restaurant. A policeman said in flat tones that they would have to move on;
then he took out his book and wrote their names and they marched
to the police wagon already installed and off to the new, model, separate and equal city jail. They were guarded from the strangers on the
sidewalk by Jackson's famous separate and equal police dogs.

Paul Deitrich and Matthew Walker walked to the wagon together;
Matthew Walker put an arm around Paul Deitrich's back. It had all
been done correctly. It was done correctly with the second bus from
Montgomery sealed and guarded by air and land like the first (altogether, there were twenty-seven riders arrested) in a total of six silent
minutes, a record for tidy dispatch.

Later on, Chief of Detectives Meade Pierce met the reporters, and reminded them that "We haven't mentioned segregation; the charge is not moving on."

The students, he said, are just as polite as they can be. He hoped they would be comfortable; Jackson is proud of its jail. It has its customs, of course. He had asked them not to sing. He closed by extending the visiting press all possible courtesies and hoped it would respond by telling the North how cordial Jackson's response had been.

A small section of the North is hereby informed that Jackson at least defends itself against the future under the auspices of its Chamber of Commerce.

[Jackson, May 25, 1961]

"Go Home, Freedom"

This puzzled city, after three days of decorous attention to adult matters like courts and motions and counter-motions, is once again at the unpredictable mercy of teenagers.

There are still more than two hundred Albany Negroes scattered in jails from here to Americus for prayers, pilgrimages and other disturbances of the peace and the number grew yesterday. The most conspicuous is Martin Luther King, but the most consequential may be the children.

Albany let ten teenagers out last night on their simple promise to picket no longer. But fifteen more went to jail for congregating on the steps of the city library, to the disappointment of a community that opened a new colored library just three weeks ago. Six adults were arrested praying in front of City Hall in the afternoon and a little before nine last night Alice Porter led seventeen other persons in prayer before the Albany police force, all of them bowed on their knees on the sidewalks with the police looking down upon them with expressions mixing embarrassment and wonder. "All right, now," said the officer in charge, "you've had your prayer. Now will you move on?" They stood singing that they would overcome and, having finished one chorus, marched off to be booked. One of them said he was twelve; he was just tall enough to peek over the booking window.

The other night, Police Chief Laurie Pritchett was arresting a group in prayer. One of the demonstrators was no more than three feet tall. "How old are you, son?" said the chief. "Nine," said the boy. "What's your name?" said the chief. "Freedom, Freedom," said the boy. Chief Pritchett put his hand on the criminal's head. "Go home, Freedom," he said. The rule by now is that you throw back Albany Movement soldiers when they're younger than twelve.

In sum, the jails of southwest Georgia had gotten rid of ten of these unexpected and unwanted tenants and picked up thirty-nine more. One of those released was Willie C. Lovett, who is sixteen, and had been in the Americus jail for seven days. His mother had asked him to come out. "I promised the chief I wouldn't picket, so I'll just march for a week," he said. He spoke from what was plainly a sense of honor, and he will keep his promise. But he will be back before long in any case, because by day he spends his time escorting country Negroes into voters' registrar offices to try and qualify them for the rolls.

He has been in jail seven times.

"I think jail's easier," he reported. "In jail they just try to scare you. In communities, they beat you up."

He was on his way back to Mount Zion Church, where the cooks and maids of the Albany Movement were singing that "All God's children got a race to run" and waiting to hear a message from the Reverend Martin Luther King, Sr., who follows his son to spare little churches like this one, less than two years after the political scientists credited him with carrying two states for President Kennedy.

Other kids came up in the light outside the church and asked Willie Lovett and his three friends when they had gotten out. They stood talking in the yard of one of the houses and its mistress came to the door and smiled at these children and said, "Welcome home, gentlemen."

Roosevelt Matthews, who is thirteen, is still in jail in Americus.

His mother, Annie Pearl Matthews, is a maid. Roosevelt went in two weeks ago for picketing City Hall after the arrest of Martin Luther King. The police sent word the other day that Roosevelt wanted to get out, and she went to talk to him and was about to give her word for his bond when she was struck with mistrust. "How do I know he wants to get out?" she asked. "If he did, one of the boys there would have brought me a message when he came out. I don't think it's fair to bond him out if he don't want to come. He's strong; as long as he gets a little something to eat and a little water, he'll be all right."

Annie Pearl Matthews spent a week in jail as a demonstrator last December.

"The people I worked for never mentioned it until yesterday. She paid me my $15 a week right along while I was in jail. She mentioned it the first time yesterday. She said she didn't understand why we listened to that Martin Luther King. I said, 'Miss Allison, you don't know how mean some of these white people are. You all are nice; you pay me $15 a week. But I got neighbors who work from seven to seven and get only $12 a week.'"

In the Post Office, Judge J. Roland Elliott listened sympathetically most of the day while the City of Albany and the State of Georgia tried to enjoin Annie Pearl Matthews and her son Roosevelt from continued mischief. It is not a case with much future; the Court of Appeals seems likely to throw out any order Judge Elliott writes. The South spends most of its time these days getting decisions in its favor from new Kennedy judges which are promptly reversed by old Eisenhower ones.

The court was full of Negroes who had the pleasure of watching Donald Holloway, an Atlanta Negro lawyer, brashly cross-examining their police chief. It was not an unmixed pleasure; they have a certain affection for Laurie Pritchett. He is a large man, proud, as he deserves to be, of his city's record in maintaining order. He was especially gratified yesterday at being able to tell the court that he had kept what he called the "Kluckers" in hand. He spoke, perhaps from policy, perhaps from a certain respect, of the difficulties of dealing with "the Reverend Mister Martin Luther King and these other Nee-gro leaders" who kept telling him that the city laws affronted their consciences. "Go back," he had kept saying to the demonstrators, "to your, uh, way of life."

King, as a defendant in the suit, was out of jail to sit in the courtroom, in short-sleeved shirt, his eyes patient, a mysterious mixture of indifference and endurance on his face. To counsel for Albany, he represented the incalculable force of the humble which has laid their city under siege. They made him sound like an awful presence indeed. His real strength, however, may be simply that he is led by children.

[Albany, Georgia, August 1, 1962]

The New South

The City of Albany seemed to spend most of yesterday morning offering evidence to show that Martin Luther King and others had failed to obey traffic signals while walking through its streets praying publicly unto God for justice. Albany was down to demanding that the federal government move in all its majesty against jaywalkers.

Martin King on his side could not, of course, seriously demand a federal injunction against sheriffs who hit Negro lawyers. The American Gandhi has been confined to the endurance of a country lawsuit.

He stayed in his chair through the morning recess, which is the only chance itinerant journalists have to talk to him. "Did the mayor make any reply to President Kennedy's suggestion that he negotiate?" he asked. There was the vaguest impression of forlorn hope still not abandoned. A visitor said that Mayor Asa Kelley had spoken well of the President and expressed himself ready to go to Hyannis Port for the weekend but otherwise adamant against any negotiations while Martin Luther King was in Albany.

"Oh," King said, with terrible sadness, "there's never been any issue of negotiating with me. I've never asked to be in on the negotiations." He looked about him, as though measuring the great breadth of a wall. "But they use me. They have worked out the subtlest, the smoothest, the best-designed way of maintaining segregation that we have seen yet."

He is absolutely right. The kids who are in part his followers and in another part his leaders have fooled us and him before but, unless they think of something, the power structure of the South has Martin Luther King in a cleft stick. The South has begun to understand that the ordinary Negro is poor and unlettered and unprotected, and that, with patience and care and abstention from violence, all the outsiders who ask the nasty questions will someday go away and things will be as they have always been.

The North has never really cared, and the Justice Department cares even less than the North. The North, as an instance, is disturbed by quotable sheriffs. But suppose sheriffs are no longer quotable; suppose, as an instance, sheriffs are instructed merely to say "Negrow" when they used to say "Nigger." What can the Justice Department do then?

Sheriff Zeke Matthews sits in his cave at the bottom of the tower of the Terrell County Courthouse, a wonderful brick imitation of Venice or Milan. "We don't keep it up as well as we should. The taxes are too low. You don't see buildings like this any more." There is a sign over the ash tray in the lobby. It says "White."

"I'm not giving no articles no more, Cap'n," he says. "I opened my mouth once and the *Atlanta Constitution* said I was the czar of the county. I'm not giving no articles any more.

"This voting by Negroes is very simple," he went on. "We're under a federal court order. And we're gonna follow the federal law."

His visitor reached for his note pad. "Now, Cap'n, don't put that down," said Zeke Matthews. "I said I didn't want no articles."

Zeke Matthews was called last week to a meeting in the Mount Olive Church to encourage Negroes to register. He walked into the church and asked those present why they were dissatisfied and it was all over the papers.

"Cap'n, I want to tell you, I walked into that church and the leader was praying and I bowed my head while he was praying. I'd do that anywhere. Then they got to the political part and I asked to speak. That's all that happened. Oh, they said my deputies were smoking in the back of the church, but I didn't see no minister. It was a political meeting. I only explained to them how simple voting was.

"But it was a meeting of Negroes and white people. That's not against the law in this country. Now, Cap'n, don't reach for that book. But it is [long silence] unusual. To a citizen. A citizen called me and I just went to see if the law was being violated. All I do here is serve writs and take calls. I'm the humblest man in the country. I didn't see the law violated and I left.

"Cap'n, I don't know why these Nigras can't improve themselves. We have this public school law and we spend most of our time trying to find out why their children aren't going. I look at the voting thing like this. You need a license to drive a car. The hearings are on Wednesday afternoon. Suppose you had a bunch of people bringing people in and giving them all the answers. Would we have qualified drivers? It's the same with voting. We've got to raise our standards.

"You know, Cap'n, they left us here after the War Between the States with nuthin', not even food, and all these Negroes. Between us and the niggers we've built a pretty good economy."

The instructions were wearing off a little in the give and take of the dialogue. Sheriff Matthews is a model of the peace officer constructed in a hurry by the new South. In his vocabulary, a "Negrow" is a nonresident of the county who comes in spreading discontent, followed by journalists, who are fleas on the dog. A "Nigra" is a native who listens to the Negro agitator. A nigger is my good friend whom I can still trust.

It is doubtful that the Justice Department can deal with a man who has been instructed in these subtleties. There are very few unreconstructed sheriffs left; one finds them as archaeologists unearth artifacts, but, like artifacts, they are useless to the new civilization. One such is D. C. Matthews of Dougherty County, whose seat is Albany, but whose law enforcement is in the hands of Police Chief Laurie Pritchett.

Last weekend C. B. King, a local lawyer, who is a "Nigra," came in to visit a client imprisoned for a demonstration, that is a Negro who was in Sheriff Campbell's custody.

"I told him," said Sheriff Campbell comfortably, "to leave twice. And then I had to remove him. He's walking around with a bandage all around his head. That's the way they are. A little patch that big would have covered it. I just hit him with a little stick once or twice. I would have done it to a white man. One of those little sticks out there."

"Out there" identified a stand of soft pine canes fabricated by the blind, which Sheriff Campbell, as a charitable man, retails for 50 cents apiece. The sheriff had broken a cane he borrowed on King's head. It was a poor enough piece of wood; he would have been ashamed to do less with it.

Out in reconstructed Terrell County, the official enemy of Sheriff Matthews is Lucius Hollaway, a Nigra who lives in Dawson and is leading the Negro registration drive.

He was found down the clay road outside his house.

"You see what I'm doing?" he said, hosing down the road. "That's to keep the dust from the house. That's what this is about. Pavements.

If I were a politician I wouldn't even meet with a delegation of Dawson colored. We're not even voters. Why should they listen to us? They won't listen to us until we can vote.

"Segregation? Can I afford to go to those places downtown? They don't have to worry about a colored kid around here trying to get into the University of Georgia. They have a tough enough time trying to get into a colored college. In the class of '60 at the high school some of the boys tried to enlist in the Army, and they hadn't been taught enough to pass the Army test."

That is how far behind a Negro starts in Terrell County. Then what can the Justice Department do? That must be what Martin Luther King thinks about in his long hours in court and that must be why he is discouraged. But, then, he might be encouraged if he talked to Lucius Hollaway, who has lived all his life in Terrell County and knows all these things and who was taught somewhere — and where else? — that it was his task to do what he could about them.

[Albany, Georgia, August 3, 1962]

The Hostile Witness

The City of Albany wound up its case Friday against Martin Luther King and dozens of unknown Southern children for littering the streets and praying in places of public passage and otherwise disturbing its way of life.

The final witness for the city was Charles Jones, field secretary of the Southern Non-Violent Coordinating Committee, who is in jail for disturbing the peace and who was therefore a hostile witness. Charles Jones is twenty-three and of Charlotte, North Carolina, and that state's colored college. He has been in jail ten times or more, the longest on the Rock Hill, South Carolina, chain gang.

It was the assignment of Grady Rawls, Albany's City Attorney, to set Charles Jones before Federal Judge Robert Elliott, who wants very obviously to hate and fear him as a vagrant, a disturber and an enemy of concord.

Grady Rawls is a fat man, and an unexpected embodiment of the tense and disturbed white South, because he almost falls asleep on his feet and frequently falls asleep in his chair. Charles Jones is young and thin, his hands and feet moving all the time, a live one with a body going places. Grady Rawls confronted Charles Jones with the assurance that no Negro could do anything but make a fool of himself when confronted by a distinguished white attorney. And Charley Jones was scared; he wanted terribly not to make a mistake. He sat on the stand, and in the long intervals between the questions, he shook almost with the ague. But when he came to answer, he went very fast.

"Are you paid a salary?" Grady Rawls asked. "How do you subsist?"

Charles Jones rubbed his hands and smiled, "At times I wonder."

Grady Rawls asked him if there were Communists in the movement. Charles Jones answered, "No." Grady Rawls handed up a leaflet labeled "Remember This Week" and asked Charles Jones whether he had had a part in preparing it.

"I didn't," said Charley Jones, "have a part in preparing it. But I do remember that week. I remember Martin Luther King being arrested, and Bill Hanson being arrested, and C. B. King being struck by the sheriff."

Grady Rawls rocked back and forth, almost asleep, his belly brushing now and again against the counsel's table, and put the next question:

"Have you encouraged juveniles to sit-in?"

Charley Jones looked at his hands. "I don't check ages," he answered. "I have informed people what I intended to do, and that anything they did was their personal commitment. If they felt they should, they should make up their minds."

Charles Jones is an anarchist and a proud one.

"Do you," asked Grady Rawls, "regard the city ordinance to regulate parades and mass demonstrations as illegal?"

Charles Jones looked up straight in Grady Rawls's eye.

"I don't think there's an ordinance against a mass meeting yet. And I've never considered what I've done a parade. On the legality of the legislation, I am not qualified to judge. But in its application, I have definitely felt that it has been unjustly used to deny Negroes the right of assembly to redress grievances."

"And why," Grady Rawls asked, "don't you exercise your legal right to resort to the courts?"

Charles Jones shook a little and framed his answer.

"I don't know any legal proceedings that would require the City

Commissioners to sit down on our grievances. Many grievances cannot be settled by legal proceedings. I think that is why the Constitution provides for freedom of assembly so that people can bring their grievances before government and bring them to a peaceful, democratic result."

And those, by one of those accidents which make the South enchanting, were the last words spoken for the plaintiff in this case. They were, of course, the point. Albany now has to go to the Court of Appeals and try to prove that the exercise of free assembly is a nuisance. And Charley Jones had closed the question. Grady Rawls, still unconscious — he had only been cross-examining a colored boy, after all — turned and began putting irrelevant documents into the record.

I don't think anyone understands what has happened to the South in the last ten years. Negroes have come up who sit on the stand and confound white lawyers.

Charley Jones was so weary when he finished that he left the courtroom and shook by himself for a terribly long while. Then he came back to the recess. A visitor said to him that it was too bad that the South knew at last what it was doing and, without violence, is containing him and the children who listen to him. This, of course, seems to be defeat; to Charley Jones, who has been to Southern jails, it seems like victory.

He looked at the wall across the way. "And, you don't think," he wondered, "that we have come a long way when they don't hit us any more?"

[Albany, Georgia, August 5, 1962]

V

Powers—Foreign and Infernal

One of his juniors is said to have asked Ignazio Silone why he had never thought of his long time as an exile as matter for a novel.

"No one," he is supposed to have answered, "can ever write about anything that happened to him after he was twelve years old."

It isn't easy. I had a year in Italy, but nothing I did there seems to me to have much life and relevance now. There is nothing here from that experience except a report on the Modigliani retrospective show in Rome, 1959; it seems to come closer than anything I ever did to saying why I, always an alien, came to love the Italians who are a sad people always searching for the secret of how to live.

I also had a little time with Castro and with Trujillo, but those fruits are dried up too. It is not work of which I am ashamed, but it was terribly damaged by the anxiety to be correct. In the end, the only usable matter was a collection of disparate remarks by Cubans. It might serve to give some detached sense of what Cuba was like in the first winter after the revolution, as a stone tells us about a lost time. Somehow or other, we are always wrong a little about other countries; we never quite get them right; a myth in another language is not our myth and the children to whom it will someday be told are not our children.

Mr. Khrushchev's trip to the United States was my single entirely fulfilling experience as an alien. It is odd that no one of my fellow voyagers has thought to do a book; it has to have been the most profoundly entertaining public experience in our lives. Perhaps no one believes it.

Near the end, and past exhaustion, we were in Pittsburgh at night, having been in Des Moines in the morning, and one of us said: "Do you know, six months from now, somebody will ask me if I was with Khrushchev in Iowa and I will answer 'Khrushchev in Iowa? Are you crazy?'" He was right; there could never have been those ten days which began with Nikita Khrushchev in a helicopter flying over the Burning Tree. We dreamed it all, but in that dream we were Martians.

Still and all, the wildest comic scenes in my life in this comic country have always belonged to Nikita Khrushchev. I have, in this spirit, left in my recollection of the evening Sylvanus Olympio, president of Togo, innocently invited Mr. Khrushchev to a small reception at the Plaza and watched with wide-eyed delight the consequent destruction of the premises by a great buffalo herd of American cameramen. Mr. Olympio died horridly at the hands of assassins in the winter of 1963; I have never felt so intimate a sense of loss in the death of a foreign statesman. In Mr. Olympio, we have lost a man who truly enjoyed the spectacle of that insane America which Nikita Khrushchev more than anyone else has the trick of touching off.

The Ghetto

The superficial fact about Harry Belafonte is that he is returning home, heavy with the triumphs of his first European tour, and that, when he gets home, he will have no place to live.

He wound up in Rome last week, and the U. S. Information Service was very proud to sponsor a reception in his honor for the Italian press. The State Department met his plane. As a great corporate entity, when he comes home, he can get office space where he chooses. As a Negro, he can't find an apartment in New York.

His wife, who does not happen to be a Negro, has gone around looking at apartments and, until she says that she is Mrs. Harry Belafonte, she is welcome. His agents have the same experience; it has been suggested he find a "dummy" of acceptable pigmentation.

"But I will not," says Harry Belafonte, who has reason to be a proud man, "take a place in any name but my own.

"With the office and my job, I've got to be in midtown. We had two rooms in the Seventies, but it's too small with a baby. I don't want anything very heavy, just something comfortable and middle-class. We tried all those new places in the Village; Mrs. Roosevelt even offered to take one in her name."

But Belafonte explains that he could not even use that name in place of his own.

"I guess, with just a word or so, we could get a suite in a hotel as long as we want. But how can you live all your life in a hotel?"

He and Mrs. Belafonte have come down to those little jokes without much mirth in them. They were asked this season to be on "Person to Person."

"We talked a long time about saying yes to Ed Murrow and then setting up on a bench in Central Park and saying this was our home."

But the important fact about Harry Belafonte is something much more complicated than that. He went to the Brussels World's Fair at the request of the State Department. Ever since then, in England and France and West Germany and last of all Italy, an Embassy representative has sat beside him at his press conferences and every time, after a wandering sequence about music and the movies, the question about Orval Faubus has finally come.

He was asked it in Rome, in the baroque splendors of its Grand Hotel, and he answered, as he has answered all over Europe: "These troubles represent progress and not retrogression."

He can't find an apartment and Faubus's name and face follow him wherever he goes: "He has never seemed so close, and I, like a dope, can only say that this represents progress and not regression. This is the thing I really believe. I can say 'God damn New York,' but I still feel the same way. It is true; this is progress."

He was eating in Old Rome, in what used to be the ghetto — the only Jim Crow district Rome ever had, next to the gate Augustus dedicated to his poor, deserted sister — in a *trattoria* called Giggetto's. He could not eat outdoors as the Romans do, because it was obvious that the children of the ghetto would swarm upon him. But the telegraph of the Roman streets had done its work and there were children at the window yelling "Eh Harry, 'Banana Boat.' "

The waiter came up and closed the shutters on the window and they began to cry louder and to beat at the slats, and Harry Belafonte said: "You cannot close doors on children; if you do, before long they will knock them down and come in by themselves."

The waiter seemed to get the message, as Archie Moore used to say, and he opened the shutter again. By now there was a great cluster of children. For a little while they were quiet, pressing their noses against the grate, and then they began to yell and push again. A grownup on the roof began throwing water down to drive them off, and two or three of them ran away and got umbrellas.

Finally he gave up and went out into the street in the Roman sun and, standing there in his jacket and his sport shirt, in the oldest center of man's vanity and inhumanity in all the old world, he sang the song of the Jamaica fruit-handlers by himself, accompanied only by a chorus of children who knew all the responses.

That may seem odd in this foreign country, and yet it is not strange at all if you remember that there are no foreign countries; and that this is a song about work and waiting, as Harry Belafonte waits, as these children wait.

And that, by the old gate, is the important fact about Harry Belafonte. It is not the great crowds and dinner with Anna Magnani and the burgeoning of the corporation on the one side or the New York real estate agents on the other. It is not even that with all these things he is glad to be going home, and that he is ready to bear Orval Faubus and still glad to be an American.

It is, rather, something that he said in his press conference here when he was asked one of those idiotic questions about who was the greatest figure in jazz. He ran through various names: "Louis Armstrong and . . . the Modern Jazz Quartet . . . and Count Basie and, a man who died not long ago, Big Bill Broonzy."

And who, my masters, was Big Bill Broonzy? He was a Mississippi Negro, who once got as far as Chicago and scuffled all his life, and died, as he had lived, on the race label. No Persian Room, no Rome premiere; also no apartment in Robert Moses's Fifth Avenue South. What he was summoning up then was the whole community of man; he was reminding and remembering that, when you take him, you take Big Bill Broonzy or you don't get him.

For the blues are Harry Belafonte's cargo and they go where he goes. Standing and singing to the children, he was saying that the world belonged to them and to all children, and it was almost as though he said that he and Big Bill Broonzy could never know that world when all the daylight came but the children were young and they might. There is a community of all who wait, and so long as there is one who waits, Harry Belafonte will live there.

[Rome, October, 1958]

These Unquiet Americans

Every forward thinker knows that foreign movies are better than our own, and I have so long been neglecting my duty to this art form that I was very glad to get a summons from United Artists for the press preview of a new American film called *Non Voglio Morire*, or, since we cosmopolites prefer the name of origin, *I Want to Live*.

The foreign movie is particularly valuable because its directors give us an unsparing portrait of what life is like in their own odd civilizations; every American knows as an instance that there are only two kinds of Italian women, Sophia Loren and Anna Magnani.

We Italians rather spoil this effect of total reality, because we dub our films, using a very limited troupe of actors, so that the voice of Jean Gabin and Rock Hudson come to us from the same Tuscan tongue, and when Marilyn Monroe and Susan Strasberg open their mouths on the screen, the same voice comes out.

When I see Susan Hayward playing a San Francisco hustler, and her lips form the phrase "Okay," it is a shade unsettling to have her say "Va bene." But even with that limitation, *Non Voglio Morire* told me much about America.

The thing opened in a cavernous dive where Art Farmer and Gerry Mulligan were blowing some sort of nervous music which I found rather gloomy and disturbing because we Italians, who every American knows are true connoisseurs of jazz, are entirely faithful to the New Orleans tradition and a group of us in Milan last month were so unsettled by Miss Billie Holiday that we hissed her. We are, if nothing else, a happy people.

The camera then mounted upstairs to a *pensione* of the sort that would not even be listed in one of our tourist guides and into a room where Miss Susan Hayward was revealed in her slip in the company of a man very plainly not her husband. A policeman came in and threw her out.

She was next seen at a party for sailors: there was a consistent impression throughout this film that American girls do this sort of thing for free. She kissed a boy because he was lonely, agreed to provide an alibi for two friends because they were "buoni ragazzi," and then ended up shaking wildly for the assembled company.

We next see Miss Hayward in prison for her good deed of perjury. She comes out, attempts an honest living as a "B" girl, and is so harried by the cops that she has to go to work as steerer for two hoodlums and she is shown assisting in the mulcting of a drunken Texan at a poker game; fortunately, even if Sicily may not be safe for Sicilians, it is safe for tourists.

As soon as she got a stake, she broke with these unpleasant fellows and married a young lawyer who of course drank, and beat her. America is a nation of sexual freedom; I get the impression from its films, to paraphrase Hemingway, that this has produced Miss Hayward as a magnificent representative of the largest American class, the woman who is abused by four-letter men, as Frank Sinatra so well represents the second largest class, the man who is abused by five-letter women.

Her latest bum cuts out, the baby is crying — Italian babies never seem to cry — the landlord comes around, and there is no way out for her but to seek her bad old companions. They have not improved morally in her absence; they have in fact just murdered an old lady. She takes them food in the walkup where they are hiding; and there follows a brutal exposition of the American science of pursuing the weak. She rides a bus, and almost everyone else aboard seems to be a policeman, equipped with Dick Tracy radio and assigned to her trail.

The police follow her to the lair of her colleagues; they know they are caught when the great lights come into their room and they hear the public address system announce that they have sixty seconds to come out. A crowd waits to watch their capture, eating hot dogs.

Nothing could be less like the charming faces in the Italian realist film than the monsters of the American crowd which thereafter pursues Miss Hayward, the fish-eyed harpies at her trial, the adolescents piling on the car which is carrying her to the deathhouse; the papers calling her "The Tiger Girl," the television announcers greasily prejudging her.

The end of the affair is a remorseless half hour of the preparations for her execution. Miss Hayward performs all this to the gas chamber with the delicate mixture of wit and terror which I must now think of as the American image; she plays her deadly serious moment, as Americans seem to, for laughs.

Roberto Rossellini would never have been that remorseless even in the days before he diverted his social conscience to the liberation of imprisoned Swedes and Indians. When the lights went on, Miss Hayward arrived wearing lavender gloves and a pastel mink, and looking altogether a different girl; but even so we could not hide our discontent.

Didn't she get tired playing such tragic characters and didn't the thought of them keep her awake at night?

"Good heavens, no," Miss Hayward said brightly, "I love it. It's not pretty but it's true. And I just do it from nine to five and sleep very well, thank you."

I do not think we Italians liked *Non Voglio Morire* very much. Alberto Moravia, our prime realistic novelist, wrote a lukewarm review, but he did commend the producers for showing the "usual atrocities" attendant upon American justice, dependent as it is on ambitious cops and sadistic newspapers.

It is a fine thing to be a realist, but you shouldn't be uncomfortable about it. The Americans disturb me. They are so troubled, so unquiet. They seem to think somehow that the wrong things in their society may be their fault.

[Rome, December 29, 1958]

Modigliani Comes Home

So Rome has had its Modigliani show, as Milan had its, although not the same show, because these affairs have to be accompanied by the loeal rancors to be expected in Italy, which is a nation in all save fact.

Milanese collectors refused to send their Modiglianis to Rome because they would be too close to the *banditti* of Naples, but then Roman collectors took out the few Modiglianis they had, which they would not under any circumstances have trusted to Milan.

The true excitement of Modigliani's homecoming has been not these ambient disputes but the great crowds of Italians he has drawn. I have never before seen so many Italians in a museum, an institution largely for foreigners. They are young, mostly, and they walk about and look at these portraits and talk about how sad they are and how modern. So many Italians are sad and they would dearly love to be modern.

The Commission of Fine Arts has doubled all prices, suspended all but the most sacred of free passes and extended the hours into the night, but the Modigliani gallery seems still as crowded as the Piazza Colonna. It is something more, I think, than the pride of the recognition of an Italian who succeeded in Paris. I do not know Paris, but there are apparently ways in which Romans think of Paris as residents of Jackson, Mississippi, would think of New Orleans.

And yet one goes back again and again to look at these chaste nudes and these Madonnas *perdues* as one would not in Paris or New York. Modigliani is, of course, one of those painters who cannot but be fashionable and topical. He has subjects, for instance, out of the

Lacaze case. They will, on the surface, always be Parisian subjects; yet theirs is an Italian painter, and to see him here is like seeing him nowhere else.

There is, of course, the legend of the alcohol and the opium and the destruction of himself, the early death brought on by all this; and what is less Italian than the image of an alcoholic? Modigliani is almost the only Italian I can think of with a legend like Baudelaire's or Rimbaud's or Verlaine's. And yet he is not like them because, although the work of Baudelaire is certainly morally affected, I should not think it the work of a clean man and the paintings of Modigliani have a purity of absolute innocence until the very end, as though all the sin of legend were surface.

There are here the photographs with the fatal Italian beauty which should have warned the heroines of E. M. Forster not to extend the acquaintance. There was, in fact, even an English mistress, whom he drew from memory at the end with the face of a slattern and the body, essentially unviolated, of a girl.

Yes, Modigliani was an Italian, a provincial in Paris, as any Italian except a Papal nuncio has to be a provincial in Paris. When he was drunk — Picasso says that he only got drunk in public — he always waved Dante, that flag of the Italian abroad. It is, I think, because he was an Italian that the paintings were innocent to the very last, that they are of children we can only love until the end of time and of women washed clean every morning. They are Parisians; yet somehow, gravely serious, they are the women of Fra Angelico.

One afternoon, it is told of him, he did a drawing for a friend. It had been a dreadful day, a hot afternoon in August. There had been the usual fight with the concierge, and the interruption of his painting by a visitor and so many more of the necessary inconveniences of Italian life, and Modigliani had been in a bad mood all day. Then he finished his drawing and wrote a few words on the bottom:

"Life is a gift from the few to the many, from those who know and have to those who know and do not have."

Modigliani died crying out that he wanted to go back to his dear Italy. It had, of course, driven him out, but that fact is not relevant to his homecoming. He could not, quite simply, have been a painter in Italy in 1900. There is a picture of him in the *atelier* of his master in Leghorn; the master has a goatee and his palette is at the ready.

The room seems stale and stuffy and nineteenth-century; the master is a man who teaches art to *contessas*. And Cézanne was already an old man in Paris.

Lionel Venturi, the critic, discovered Modigliani in Paris in 1928 and brought him home to Venice for a show in 1930. It was the first sign to young artists that there could be an Italian who did not paint in the Fascist style and, after he displayed these portraits, Venturi went proudly into exile.

"He could not have been what he was in the Italy of 1900," Venturi says still. "There are the letters he wrote from Rome in 1903. They are full of a kind of revolutionary sense. But it was a literary sense; he had no way of knowing in Italy that the revolution had anything to do with art."

Venturi does not believe entirely the legend of self-destruction. "When he was first in Paris," he says, "his mother supported him; then, with the war, she could send no more money." That was five years before he died. "Then he tried to sell his paintings and he destroyed too many that did not satisfy him for me to believe that he was not painting seriously. And the last year of his life he sold quite a lot."

Modigliani left behind a family in Leghorn that loved without understanding his course. Venturi knew his brother, a Socialist deputy; they were exiles together. "He was," said Venturi, "the best kind of anti-Fascist, but he did not understand his brother's painting."

And as for poor Modigliani, who had been wasting his time and troubling his family, there was nothing but this squalid end and such personal effects as a portrait of a little girl in a Catholic school uniform, the eyes — formally unseeing black — proclaiming all by themselves what Fascism would violate and what would come home intact to Rome.

[Rome, March 4, 1959]

Castro's Cuba Today

There should be, at the end of any journey, I suppose, a closing of its log-book with a final, balanced page about the lessons it taught. I'm afraid, casting the balance, that no such discipline is possible after a journey to Fidel Castro's Cuba. What is friendly in me says that it is as yet unformed, while something hostile keeps insisting that it is by nature formless.

There are only, at the end, a few disparate fragments of conversations:

The last Americans, a half dozen so, were fired the other day from the Hotel Riviera, the newest of the glass monuments left behind by Fulgencio Batista. One of them was aroused from sleep and told to get out. "Humanism," he said the next day. "Firing a man at three o'clock in the morning."

Most of the evictees were gamblers, if that is the proper word to use for the supervisors of gambling houses, and they spent the next day sitting in the American Embassy waiting for an airlift to Las Vegas. Cuba's casinos will be run from now on by Cubans.

Some of us sat the next night in the empty bar of the Riviera. There were three customers and six waiters. The saloon of a luxury liner might feel like this when the passengers had taken to the lifeboats.

Cuba's last American gambler came in.

"Go to the casino," he said. "It's open night. I just played a hand of blackjack. I had a jack and a seven; the dealer had three sixes. I looked at him and I said: 'Pay me; I got seventeen and you got fifteen.' He looked at the cards and he counted with his lips and he paid me. Sure, it'll be lonely, but I'm living next to a casino where the dealer can't count.

"This is the place for me: the shills have taken over for the bosses."

ANYONE CAN PLAY

The dealers, of course, will learn to add before long; I should hope that the capacity to afflict the eye of God with a well-managed card game is not a skill confined to citizens of the United States alone in the Western Hemisphere.

It is strange, though, that the most fiercely moral of revolutions should feel this compulsion to keep open the casinos that were part of pre-Castro Havana's status as the most vicious capital in the world.

The reason is rooted somewhere in a Latin economics older than the new Socialist concept. There are seven hundred Cubans working in the Riviera, and only fifty guests. Those employes cannot be fired. And, for their sakes, the revolution keeps the Riviera going, at who can say what cost, an empty luxury hotel in a society of workers and peasants.

In an all-night cafeteria we met a young poet, a Communist. He was gentle (in Cuba only the rhetoric is really fierce and hostile) and he asked our help in correcting three lines in English he had inserted in his new poem. They began: "Do you hearing me, Mr. North American . . ." We agreed that their innocence was artful enough to make tampering a violation and cast our eyes over the Spanish text. It began: "I am a new man" and, as to be expected from a new man, was indistinguishable from the work of Allen Ginsberg.

We asked him how a new man spent his day in the revolution's service. He acted in radio serials, he said; and between times prepared three propaganda scripts of fourteen pages apiece for broadcast each day on Radio Rebelde.

THE NEO-BEAT

Didn't he think, one auditor wondered gently, that this was a nonsensical pursuit — "The revolution is to build" — wouldn't it be more sensible to go out into the provinces and manage one of the new cooperatives? "Oh," he said, still gentle, "I do real things. Look at this." He took out his wallet and showed a picture of himself in the cap of a member of the people's militia.

What could be sadder than to think of yourself as a new man when the first words you write are a Spanish translation of Jack Kerouac, whom you have never read and yet to whom you are bound by a sort of telepathy of the demi-talented?

"We are new," a Chilean who was present explained, "because we have no complicity with the past."

But what a terrible thing it is to have no past. What is there native to Cuba? There are not even handicrafts, except a few botched imitations of Africa.

There is a cathedral in old Havana which is the purest seventeenth-century Sicily; it is not even a bequest of Spanish power; the architect, as I had suspected, turned out to be Italian.

This poor people, for centuries under foreigners, now struggling to express themselves, must begin without one structure that is native to themselves. From the Morro Castle (Spanish) to the Riviera (Miami), they are surrounded by alien monuments. Demi-literate, demi-cultured, demi-Spanish, demi-North American, nothing their own. The most popular native drink among revolutionaries is still rum and Coca-Cola, once the Cuba Libre and now, in the Riviera at least, the "Fidel Castro."

I have no hope of understanding Cuba. The only way to understand a country is to read its novels; I should not suppose there is such a thing as a Cuban novel. José Martí, its revolutionary martyr, was at least a remarkable journalist; he was the New York correspondent for a number of Latin American papers. Cubans are entirely satisfied to pass up his perceptive passages and put little cards in their store windows saying things like: "The future of a people is in its children — José Martí." The culture seems to ask nothing better than such stuff.

I found this paragraph in a new textbook of geography, compulsory in all high schools under the revolution, written by Antonio Nunez Jiminez, Director of Agrarian Reform, and sometime professor of geography at the University of Las Villas:

"Forty-one point seven per cent of the rural population and 11.6 per cent of the urban population is illiterate. In total that is for the country a 53.3 per cent of illiteracy."

Now, this cannot be a typographical error. It is not even a mistake in statistics. It is a simple violation of common sense. The professor has added figures a child would have divided; he could as well find by his technique that Cuba is 130.7 per cent literate. And this is a document prepared by a full professor and approved by a Minister of Education.

It cannot be wondered that, in a country where even to the literate the novel and the statistics are alien, all ideas are alien, seized from the vagrant air. It is no wonder that the air seems to be infected by the crude echo of the Marxist idea. To the new man, there are no lessons from the experience of the old.

And yet how, with all this, can one return without some hope from a conversation with a twenty-five-year-old boy running a cooperative?

Martí said seventy years ago: "The frock coat is still French, but thought begins to be Latin American. The youth of America roll up their sleeves and plunge their hands into the dough. 'Create' is the password of this generation. The wine is from bananas, and, if it proves sour, it is our wine."

One comes home to find Washington debating whether to cut off the sugar subsidy. We kept sending Batista the sugar subsidy when his soldiers were shooting Cuban children in the streets; now, from injured pride, we think of taking it from Fidel Castro. Could any nation that used it ever assert again the right to such power over adventurous children?

No, the experiment with banana wine is unpromising, but if Cuba is ever to have anything of its own, it must be played out at least without interference from us.

A JOURNEY IN TIME

The man in Cuba most like ourselves is Rufo Lopez Fresquette, Minister of the Treasury. He is a Columbia-trained economist with an American wife; the course of the economic revolution must be an affront to all his training, but he says loyally, "Every time I have questioned Fidel I have been wrong.

"This," he said, "is the most important revolution in the history of the world."

A revolution in a backward island, with an economy based on rum and sugar, in a country of six million people, is the most important in the world? And yet it is, I suppose. How many revolutions do we have left? Each of the great powers, the Soviet Union and the United States, has failed and stopped; if there is a new idea to come, it must come from those peoples who have never yet produced one.

And yet what to say when Fidel Castro begins by acting as though there were no experience prior to his and then walks step-by-step down all the old roads, his revolution destined to repeat all the mistakes until an end like all the revolutions of this century before it? One feels in Paris in 1791 talking to a Girondist, in Russian in 1917 talking to a Social Democrat. He is the last moderate; if he is wrong who can hope for another one after him?

Conversation with a young revolutionary official:

The visitor: "What political figure do you like?"

She: "Fidel."

The visitor: "But who else, anywhere in the world? Do you like Khrushchev?"

She: "I don't very much like Khrushchev." He is, I suppose, with all his other sins, too old.

The visitor: "Do you like Tito?"

She: "No, I don't suppose I much like Tito."

The visitor: "Well, who then? Isn't there anyone anywhere in the world except Fidel?"

She, after a while: "Nasser."

A whole broad, huge world and no hope in it except Fidel and Nasser.

There is a sign in the lunchroom of what used to be the Hershey sugar refinery near Havana, now taken over by the revolution. It has two lines. One says: "*La reforma agraria va.*" The next is in English: "The agrarian reform goes forward."

The counterman said that it was translated into English so the Americans would be sure to know what it said. For fifty years, everything in Havana was put up for North American eyes. Abject then, spiteful now. The new man.

Francisco Santana is thirty-four years old and has four children. He cannot read. His identification card lists his job still as "peon"; there are words a revolution does not change. He is a watchman in a sisal plant closed by its owner and reopened by the government as a worker's cooperative. Someday he expects the government will build new houses for everyone and set up a school to teach him how to read.

"I am," he said, "a leader in the people's militia and a leader in the people's militia should know how to read."

It's a lousy reason, but a man has to begin somewhere.

[February 21, 1960]

The Chairman

Nikita Khrushchev is an authentic, the real thing. He alighted on Andrews Field yesterday as a vice-president of the International Ladies Garment Workers Union might descend upon Unity House. He even bore along in his wake his son-in-law, the editor of *Izvestia.* You could almost hear the echo: "Alexei is a bright boy, so I made him educational director of the local."

It is a type widely beloved, unless you happen to work for it, and engraved in the American mythology of the Sunday night television plays. And, given free play, it is engaging enough to be irresistible. And Khrushchev enjoys, by our option, free play.

Khrushchev was nearly an hour late, and the President of the United States had to endure twenty minutes of scuffing about the red carpet in attendance. There was a dreadful, almost Middle Eastern, Washington sun, and it worked squint furrows in Dwight Eisenhower's forehead. The President had the expression of the good soldier wondering just what the chief might be up to. He had, as he always will have, the face of the people who voted for him.

Riding out to Andrews, one watched what would be the first corner of his beloved land that Nikita Khrushchev would see and one looked at houses still habitable but unoccupied and with their windows broken and at tractors with nothing better to do than to pull lawnmowers along the sides of the Sutland Drive. It was a picture of wealth, which best defines itself by conspicuous waste. But coming back, one saw only the faces of the roadside, the soldiers with their personal cameras, the women in slacks, the men in shirtsleeves; Nikita Khrushchev's Italian tailor had dressed him better than anyone on the road.

There was a collective impression of a broad line of fatuous smiles. One remembered only teeth. We rode through fifteen miles of the audience at Don McNeill's Breakfast Club on that unthought-of day when the master of ceremonies hadn't come to warm them up and tell them how to respond.

Afterwards, there was great speculation on this strange and silent crowd, neither hostile nor friendly, but only emptily waiting. But the answer was quite simple: no one had held up an idiot card and we are no longer a spontaneous people.

The one quality everyone else present lacked was the open, crude assurance which sits on Nikita Khrushchev. There had been, as an instance, various procedural flutters in advance of his coming; technically, he is not the head of the Soviet state but only the chairman of its Council of Ministers, which means in terms of protocol that the Grace Kellys rate twenty-one guns and Khrushchev only nineteen. According to the Soviet constitution, Klementy Voroshilov is the head of the Soviet state, so Nikita Khrushchev simply declared Voroshilov vacant and himself chief of state for the occasion and here he was looking upon the honor guard and listening to the twenty-one guns.

He remained, of course, the chairman of the Council of Soviets, which meant that, when General Eisenhower addressed him, the President had no salutation at his disposal but "Mr. Chairman," as though he were a South Dakota delegate to the Democratic convention imploring the mercy of Sam Rayburn. Nothing incommoded him; the President invited him on a helicopter ride, which I would think a trap for a fat man of sixty-five. But he climbed into this frightful object, and as it creaked and groaned aloft, he was comfortably waving a stubby paw from its window; the President had simply disappeared somewhere in the shadow.

There was a state dinner at the White House last night. The guest list was officially drawn from a cross section of American culture, and a slice of life it was, with two Negroes and a Japanese Senator from our autonomous republic of Hawaii and Perle Mesta walking in with J. Edgar Hoover. It was prescribed that all masculine specimens in this mixed bag would wear white tie and tails; Nikita Khrushchev showed up in an all-purpose suit like the one he had worn all day. He writes his own rules.

We are, because spontaneity has died within us, for the occasion at his mercy. It does not even matter that our manners are better than his, because our manners are only correct without ever being quite right. The foreign press corps struggled all day yesterday for the proper word for our reception of him; it seems generally to have settled for "grim." "Edgy" would have been better. Poor Dwight Eisenhower stood waiting outside for Khrushchev's plane door to open yesterday as though he were waiting for some White House attendant to come in with a package that ticked. The Chairman came down the special stairway built for him; he was so small that the President of the United States had almost to bow down to shake his hand. He waddled like some duck on a purposeful expedition through the honor guard ceremony. This dispatched, he endured the President's official words of welcome with his hands clasped across his stomach, his eyes aware that the cameras were working only on him, his rudeness not quite definably rudeness because it could not with certainty be described as conscious.

He is that sort of force; we do not know with certainty what he will do. It will be two weeks of horribly anxious waiting. What we will do is certain, because we are predictable, but Nikita Khrushchev is not. We are at the mercy of an adventurer.

[Washington, D.C., September 16, 1959]

Notes from Underground

I suppose we are, this early, all quite simply exhausted. We are also in another country. The numbers on the timetable come from the Trans-Siberian Railway and are in a language foreign to us. But no matter; we no longer count time by clocks; for us, there is no day or night. On the Khrushchev tour, it is always three o'clock in the morning.

Last night Nikita Khrushchev addressed the Economic Club of New York in the Grand Ballroom of the Waldorf. The bindle stiffs of the press party had to take his voice, depersonalized and disembodied, on a loudspeaker remoted into the press room, which had begun rather elegant by Hilton standards but had become in a few hours as horrible as the waiting room of a Greyhound station in Vincennes after the bars are closed; we all looked, I'm afraid, like persons who have nothing in common but that they were all condemned to wait three hours for the connection to Fort Wayne.

The mechanized voice of Nikita Khrushchev grunted and squealed, presumably holding David Sarnoff and Alfred P. Sloan in thrall. And then, as it always does, that voice enforced a change of locale; listening we had become villagers in Ulyanovsk, standing around that communal loudspeaker which is the major instrument of our education listening to a broadcast of the Supreme Council of Soviets meeting in Moscow at the other end of the world. We were just that far away. It did not matter that Khrushchev was addressing an audience of American businessmen and telling them to stick with him and they'd all be buried in gold caskets. From where we drooped, David Sarnoff and Alfred P. Sloan were simply distant members of "our" Presidium, and Nikita Khrushchev the Comrade Secretary delivering his report.

I have never been to the Soviet Union, and am therefore baffled by the repeated experience of feeling as though I am there every time I hear the voice of Nikita Khrushchev. For this is so peculiarly a Russian trip — not, if you please, a Communist trip, but a Russian trip.

I think I know the reason. The debate, or perhaps better the presentation of conflicting formulas — least of all can it be called a dialogue — with Khrushchev is, begging his pardon and Cabot Lodge's, not a debate between communism and capitalism. It is, in its simplest terms, a debate between Thomas Jefferson and Peter the Great. Our difficulty is that Thomas Jefferson is not precisely a live current figure in the United States and Peter the Great is very much in business in the Soviets. Thus we talk of a memory, and Nikita Khrushchev bespeaks a living, continuous presence.

He came into New York from Washington on a silver Pennsylvania Railroad train. I would swear that the windows had been washed. There was not one of yesternight's orange peels on the floor. The wheels were almost round. In his honor, the Pennsylvania had even painted a portion of its New York station, the Lubyanka of us commuters. Is there anyone alive who has ever traveled the Pennsylvania Railroad and who can remember conditions of such comparative decency? Of course not; the Pennsylvania had faked it, and the image which came to mind was Russian; this train was one of those villages Potemkin used to build to satisfy the eyes of Catherine the Great.

I have come to think that Khrushchev is barely describable in Communist terms. He is simply a Russian. Before the press club and television Tuesday he presented an exposition of the Marxist analysis of the inevitable collapse of capitalism. (Elizabeth Gurley Flynn was sent to jail in America for three years for presenting these ideas more intelligently and coherently than Khrushchev did, and Khrushchev was permitted all major networks, but then I am aware that in America we have one standard for those who own real estate and another for the poor.) It was a terrible performance, and it was obvious that Khrushchev had studied this stuff for no higher purpose than to get promoted in the Ukraine Soviet twenty-six years ago and then had properly forgotten it.

Benjamin Stolberg said once that David Dubinsky talked about his socialism the way a Wall Street banker talks about his Iowa farm childhood. I would put Nikita Khrushchev's bolshevism in the same class. He goes back farther than Lenin; he is the peasant who said that he would cut down the cherry orchard. That peasant had, of course, a vast sense of inferior origin, and there were those in the waiting room last night who drew some comfort from the recognition that Khrushchev's arrogance covered a massive inferiority complex; but then so did that of Chekhov's peasant, and I would remind you that he cut down the cherry orchard.

But, most of all, he comes from the world of Fyodor Dostoevski. This trip is like one of those tea parties in Dostoevski when everyone meets in apparent comity and then, after three or four minutes, Niko- lai Nikolaevich for no discernible reason overturns the boiling samo- var on the head of Alexander Alexandrovich. The Khrushchev tour is fascinating only for the presence of Khrushchev; what we do at the tea party is irrelevant; it is a Russian party, elevated only by the pos- sibility that the guest of honor may blow his stack. It is both awe- some and deplorable how suddenly Nikita Khrushchev can blow his stack. Yesterday afternoon there was a moment when one thought he was about to take offense at Robert F. Wagner, a man whose entire life I had previously thought dedicated to the single-minded purpose of avoiding offense.

Of course. We are entertaining the father Karamazov. Lenin was only transient; Dostoevski endured. In heightened reality, we are in the presence of that horrible old man, not Communist but Pan-Slav, infecting each of us with his madness, making Russians of us all, forcing us to think only on Russian terms and in Russian imagery. Thomas Jefferson is gone; we have forgotten him; we droop here in this waiting room only languidly, to watch Tolstoi release his dele- gates and, resignedly, to cry Dostoevski, Dostoevski, who would have thought it? They have nominated your candidate.

[September 18, 1959]

The Interruption

When the report first came yesterday morning that Nikita Khru- shchev proposed to walk towards the head of the train carrying him from Los Angeles to San Francisco and inspect the press, the reac- tions were those to be expected from artisans humble but not without pride.

We had just stopped at Santa Barbara and Khrushchev had been welcomed by a crowd which, at a minimum, had been kinder to him than Santa Barbara had been to Harry Truman in 1952. It would be too much to report that most of us really responded to this signal development; we were in the press room at the typewriters trying to make sense out of yesterday and here he came today.

I think that by next Wednesday, if I try hard, I may be able to make sense out of last Tuesday. This is an interstellar voyage.

The difference between yesterday and today on the Khrushchev trip is measured as by the time sequence of a whole lifetime. The difference between today and the day before yesterday is the span of the record of all civilized man. Sitting here on Sunday night, Thursday is lost somewhere in pre-history.

Still, when it was announced that Khrushchev intended to walk through and greet the working press, we reacted as though we still lived in the past we left behind. The original idea was for all reporters to sit in their places and promise not to stop him with any questions. I doubt if even the fight writers in the old days would have sat still to such a proposition from Jim Norris. It was reported first that one American had said that it would be a violation of his sacred duty to let Khrushchev walk by without stopping him to ask a question. There were reports that a Russian had said the same thing; presumably the international principle that the first duty of journalism is to invade the privacy of any target rash enough to show himself had in this case triumphed over Leninist precept and Stalinist habit. After these vetoes, it was announced — or rather there was allowed to drift forth the probability — that Khrushchev would not come at all.

So we all went back then to our typewriters and wrestled with yesterday; then, suddenly, there was an announcement over the loudspeaker that Khrushchev was coming through the train and that it would be a courtesy and a concession if we would keep our seats and not block the aisles.

He came into the press work car preceded by a Southern Pacific Railroad cop of the bearing, manner, social conscience and type Joe Hill must have died cursing. Then a State Department man, and then Khrushchev and then his interpreter and then Cabot Lodge. We were working, or rather floundering, in a press room that was simply a converted bar car. We were struggling with the historical record of the day before, of which the most precious artifact was a Los Angeles Hearst paper with the headline: "Khrushchev, angry, interrupts Skouras." Tattered fragments of the bourgeois prints were on the floor, paper coffee cups were melting on the tables, the Western Union men were ordering their papers, and on such a stage there entered, if you please, the great Khan of the advancing proletaire.

It was one of those dreadful moments which can only be described in the tone of Dorothy Kilgallen or those British journalists who begin their stories, "Today, I walked up one hundred yards of the base of Everest to meet Hillary and Tenzing coming back." I mean the tone which regards oneself as more important than the historic occasion. I have to confess in this tone that the whole thing seemed to me rather as an intrusion. After all, I was trying to do yesterday's story, and that was quite impossible enough without this sort of distraction.

The Russian-speaking correspondent of a French newspaper caught Khrushchev's eye and then went over and pushed him against the train window, more to embrace than to aggress. There ensued a scene which called back to mind nothing quite so much as one of those *Life* shots of the district leaders huddling at conventions. It was most distracting; one absolutely had to stop typing. The Frenchman would ask a question and then listen and then kindly translate the answer. Khrushchev was saying that he was certainly glad to get a look at the people, "the real people." "They've finally," he said, "let me out from house arrest."

He seemed to be saying that he had suddenly found himself, ordinarily a free man, in a police state.

His questioners asked him whether he had managed to forgive Mayor Poulson of Los Angeles who had baited him to his face on television the night before and had provoked a storm which I can describe as barely this side of apocalyptic.

Khrushchev said he had discovered since that the father of the mayor or in any case the father of his assistant had come from Rostov and that he therefore had some grievance "against us." I had not thought to hear from the Chairman of the Soviets that the mere experience of having lived in Rostov constituted by itself an understandable grievance; the place must be to a Russian what Birmingham, Alabama, is to an American. So much for the un-Marxist analysis of the motives of bourgeois politicians.

They broke up — why do people always yack in press rooms? And I tried to go back to work on yesterday, but it seemed only proper to quit when the Chairman came by and incline my head to him; the man was after all our guest. He stopped and looked; I have to admit that I had rather let the State Department down and that he had finally found an indisputably exploited American toiler. There was one of those silences which Cabot Lodge and I were brought up to fill, and I said, for want of something better, "Mr. Chairman, when you were down in that coal mine, did you ever look as tired and dirty as we do?" I confess I said it with a certain envy; the man is twenty-three years my senior and he looked as fit as the entire left side of the Baltimore Colts' line and I cannot say that these events confuse him less than they do me, and he is certainly more harassed, because, in these conditions, I would not certify my sanity if I had successively to engage Spyros Skouras and Norris Poulson on the same day.

Those eyes, executioner's eyes I should think on the record, were as soft as those of Sam Leibowitz forgiving a delinquent and he made a two-minute speech, presumably Stakhanovite, in Russian which the interpreter translated as: "When I was in that coal mine, even there I always sang."

He went on for two more minutes and this was translated as: "The secret of my health is that I never let my nose get down."

We were passing through the John Steinbeck country and I let my nose down into the typewriter and he smiled and was gone. Then he was stopped by the *Daily News* table, which as usual asked the relevant question, in this case whether he had enjoyed the buttocks display put forth for him by the *Can-Can* dances at Twentieth Century-Fox.

"A man with normal morals cannot be interested by such a dance. This is a mild form of pornography. The dancing was better than the backsides — but then the man's face is better than his backside. The thing is immoral; we do not want that sort of things for the Russians." I hope Twentieth Century-Fox is happy; by American standards it is an indorsement of cosmic commercial worth.

He moved on and someone stopped him to ask if it was true he might go home in disgust. His answer was translated as: "I feel that they have me under house arrest. I think I should go home. Maybe I'm a burden." Cabot Lodge intervened that he was not a burden and that we certainly wanted him to stay.

He had passed, in the time it took to get the length of one train car, from expressing relief at being free from house arrest to expressing regret at being under house arrest. Every stop this stranger takes seems the distance of the moon.

We were close to San Luis Obispo by now and the walk stopped so the guest could get off and fraternize with the crowd. Cabot Lodge and Soviet Ambassador Menshikov held hands to form a protective cordon; Nikita Khrushchev stood in the middle trying to talk to a little girl. She seemed about to cry and he was saying that it was commendable of her mother and father to let her talk to a Communist. There was also a little boy and the visitor picked him up, but the crowd was pushing so hard that he immediately had to put the child down in the dust, where, as the train went off, he appeared in process of being trampled to death.

While these tender scenes were playing out, word filtered back of another conversation on the train walk. Khrushchev had been stopped by Harry Schwartz, the *New York Times* Russian expert, who came up to say that, while the Russian people may not be rehearsed to cheer his work, Schwartz's nine-year-old son had asked him to get Khrushchev's autograph, and that after all it wasn't the boy's fault that his father sinned against the Soviet state.

And Khrushchev answered: "Stalin said that the children are not responsible for the sins of the fathers but we must not forget the sins of the fathers," and then stalked away, refusing the autograph. Kissing babies and quoting Stalin he makes his way across our land. And I had thought the most extraordinary thing I should ever see in life would be something quite simple.

[San Francisco, September 21, 1959]

That Day in Hollywood

Nikita Khrushchev spent a Saturday in Hollywood. He was being introduced to the America outside of Washington and New York.

His day began with a luncheon at the commissary of Twentieth Century-Fox. It was solemnly pointed out by the television commentators that as many stars came to see him as go to the average Academy Award dinner. We are all provincials, including the guest of honor, and the television announcers went on to say that Madame Khrushchev was like a schoolgirl in the presence of the gods and goddesses of the silver screen.

But the first reaction of me, as a schoolboy, is that our gods and goddesses bloom on film and wither in flesh. It is as though the camera had sucked their blood. I speak in general, always excepting in particular Mrs. Arthur Miller and Frank Sinatra. And then Madame Khrushchev is no schoolgirl. Let's pull ourselves together and face the terrible truth that she doesn't go to the movies on an average Saturday night.

She knew Gary Cooper, but, with all due respect, that is like knowing Grandma Moses. Sinatra reported back that she had never heard of him, he being my age and one of the younger actors. The Khrushchevs did not come to this country to go to Hollywood; what is terrible is that Hollywood could accept this cultural lag less gracefully than it could accept, say, Hungary.

At the luncheon, Spyros Skouras, president of Twentieth Century-Fox and thus the proprietor of this particular plantation, asked the guests of honor where in the world but in America a poor Greek boy could become president of Twentieth Century-Fox. (I could describe the limitation of this outlook only by asking where in the world but Italy could a little peasant boy become Pope.)

There ensued a wild hassle between Skouras and Khrushchev, which was like television night at Sunnyside Gardens when the Russian Angel is on a tag team against the Greek Angel. If I were being my customary professionally facetious self, I would sum the occasion up by saying that the sight of Skouras was a comfort since it held forth the hope that Hollywood intended to offer Moscow a bold challenge in the monster race.

But I can't fault Skouras; at least, he tried to talk to Khrushchev, rather than to the audience, which puts him rather ahead of the average guide we have offered Khrushchev, this being otherwise — and I except Henry Cabot Lodge — the first time anyone ever offered an idiot-to-idiot, as against coast-to-coast tour of America.

Khrushchev replied that he began as a poor boy and was the head of the Supreme Council of Soviets. This being Hollywood, Skouras accepted this response as though the guest of honor had boasted that he was head of Monogram Pictures. The luncheon ended, and it was now time for the Khrushchevs to see the American working man at his craft — in this case the shooting set of *Can-Can*.

Someone asked, after this particular disaster, just why they chose *Can-Can*, which is an especially dishonest bit of goods of the type that sneaks past the Breen office, since it offers smut without precisely delivering it, and cries out for a Fair Trade Commission to enforce the rule that no one should advertise dirty pictures unless he has them in his pocket. The reason they chose *Can-Can* was quite simple: this is a pluralist society and it was Twentieth Century's turn to buy a plug.

They had persuaded Sinatra to be master of ceremonies, and even though it meant that he had been nominated keeper of the Gate of Hell I was glad to have him, because he is a professional and there weren't many such on this itinerary. As keeper of the Gate of Hell, Sinatra is more appetizing than the Mayor of Los Angeles as guardian angel of the Gold Bar of Heaven.

The schedule broke down at this point because, as Gary Cooper explained afterward, he thought it his duty to go over to the departing guest and explain that he was glad to hear Khrushchev promise to surpass us because "that's a capitalist idea — I mean competition — and I'm glad to see that you are a capitalist." (All right, it sounds crazy, but it was.) Khrushchev replied at length and the interpreter went to work, but, of course, Gary Cooper walked away.

"The fellow Khrushchev didn't seem to understand that this wasn't a working day and that he was overtime," Cooper explained later. "I wasn't going to stand there and listen to that stuff."

While this held up the schedule, Sinatra was on the shooting set pacing in his elevator shoes like a damned soul in Hell. I would have sworn that he was about to walk off. He said afterward that he judged Khrushchev to be something of an actor but, more than that, a man of impulse. He was suggesting, however unconsciously, that they were brothers; Sinatra must be the only man we have equipped to meet the Martians when they come.

Sinatra didn't walk away and at last the Khrushchevs were brought in and sat in a balcony overlooking the set. The girls came on to do the Can-Can, 1895 France and fraudulent at that, and Hollywood's available version of American folk culture.

Sinatra stood up and said, "Mr. Chairman, we're going to run this number through, but I don't think we can synchronize with the playback, because we haven't rehearsed and we were all up late last night." At last and for once, Khrushchev was meeting an American craftsman — a professional who confessed the possibility of failure and knew too much to suggest that this is a perfect society.

The girls came out, the music began and they fought their weariness to render the Can-Can. It began as a simple expression of the folk joy of living. Then the girls began to show their behinds through black silk. A chorus boy ran his head under Shirley MacLaine's petticoat and, after too long a delay, came out with her pants. I cannot otherwise describe the moment when the acceptance of healthy animal passion passed to rejection of capitalist decadence; I can only say it happened to me at just the moment it happened to Nikita Khrushchev.

What has happened to us Americans that we could conceive such a scene without immediately rejecting it as inherently disgusting — not for showing to Communists but for seeing ourselves?

I have to concede the contrast to Madame Khrushchev. She never once looked at Nikita, as an American wife might, to see if he was about to defect.

Khrushchev posed with the dancing girls and left shaking Sinatra's hand. Then he went off to dinner, where he was greeted by Mayor Poulson.

In the interim he was the guest of the Ambassador Hotel, G. David Schine, president. While we waited, David's mother, who looks like his sister, took me up to see David's new daughter, who is a treasure.

I asked David's mother on the way whether she had met the Khrushchevs.

She answered: "There were only two tickets for the family, and David and Meyer took them so we had to stay home. But after dinner I called Mrs. Skouras — you know we're very good friends — and asked her what the K's were like. She said I would really like them. 'You know,' she said, 'they're very natural people. K says the first thing that comes into his mind — just like Spyros.' "

There is the moment when the mind ceases to judge; it simply records.

Before the dinner, Henry Cabot Lodge asked Mayor Poulson please to take it easy. It was a boyish hope. You cannot expect someone who could not stand up to his own wife, let alone Walter O'Malley, to pass by the chance to let the world know that he could at least defy Nikita Khrushchev. So Poulson turned to Khrushchev and said that Khrushchev — the tone, I think was jocular — was rather well known in America as the man who had promised to bury us.

Then up rose Nikita Khrushchev to say that this was a deadly serious business and couldn't we stop meeting him with pleasantries. "I come here with serious intentions," he said, "and you try to reduce the matter to a simple joke. It is a question of the life and death of the people . . . One should not play on words. We hold positions of too much responsibility and the consequences of a play on words can be too sad for our people."

It was a terrible moment. And the audience applauded, as though this were a fight and Khrushchev the underdog. Lodge was in the wings waving his hands at Poulson, as close as a gentleman could come to screeching in fear. We had permitted — we had almost invoked — Khrushchev to make make us look like bums.

Is there nothing more at stake, can we ask for nothing more in this tragic hour than that Norris Poulson be re-elected and *Can-Can* break even?

[Los Angeles, September 28, 1959]

No Room at the Inn

This rocket of ours, nearly spent, has alighted in Des Moines. By now we are, all of us, Martians. The measure of our voyage is in light years. Those fellow Martians, Nikita Khrushchev and I, are, I think, still mourning for San Francisco.

San Francisco is beautiful even in its aggressions.

But it was Iowa that the State Department had really expected most to please us Martians, and we arrived at Des Moines to look upon a cartoon of measureless perspective in the *Register and Tribune,* its caption: "Khrushchev's Best View of the Typical American Way of Life Will Be an Iowa Cornfield." One grows self-centered in one's old age; after one day in Des Moines, I cannot speak for my leader, because I am too inner-directed on the subject of the Iowa which the Department of State has chosen to show me, a minor Martian.

We alighted at an airfield and were told to wait at its rim for the arrival of our Chairman. In the interim, advance member Richard Rovere of the *New Yorker* and party arrived to report there were no hotel rooms in town. He had not reserved a room in San Francisco; when word got around about this crisis in San Francisco's cultural history, the governor of the state had offered him his suite in the Fairmont Hotel. Rovere reported that in Des Moines, he had finally been able to find a room in the YMCA. He had defined the difference to the smallest caliber. Meanwhile, the National Guard of Iowa was defining it in front of us by lining up in order so serried that it was impossible to see anything.

Miss Mary McGrory of the *Washington Star* beat me to the last seat in the press car, which would only be fifty yards behind Khrushchev, so I had to go to the general press bus, which, if all went well, wouldn't be more than 500 yards out of sight of the subject. In Iowa, where inhospitality knows no bounds, the press buses carried signs announcing the price as a dollar to carry us into town. It was a disgusting but small sacrifice of the publisher's hoard.

The only problem was that the driver — he was the sort of fellow who uses a holster as his change purse — refused to take any passenger's dollar until all were seated. Then he walked back and collected the fare and then sat and counted it — moving his lips — for five minutes. Then he waited until a twin brother of Grandma Moses came into the bus, counted the money again and gave him a receipt. I should think that a busload of Negro convicts in Alabama, treated in such fashion, would have an immediate certiorari to the Supreme Court.

At the end of this bureaucratic process the press bus was approximately six years, as us Martians count these things, behind the Chairman's blue convertible.

There was a sign saying restaurant, and there came back the memory of my last meal, which I ate during the Grant Administration. The waitress said I couldn't have steak; it was soup and pink salmon or nothing. I sat down and ordered it. Days passed, and she brought forth a greasy mess of tomato soup soggily fortified with macaroni, but suddenly behind me there was a shaking of pressed flesh; Khru-

shchev was leaving the hotel to go on his tour. I stood up. The waitress, a Medusa with every snake dyed red, screamed: "If you don't sit
down and eat, I will take away the soup," presumably to poison the
cat. This is why I love Iowa: every waitress is your own wife as avenging angel.

There remained the fantasy that, if one kept moving, one might
fool the cops, so I commandeered a car, which I suppose was otherwise reserved for Ambassador Menshikov. Two net gains: I had
tripped Miss McGrory on the way, and I had jumped the check, which
is as close as you can get to a principled position in Iowa. The am-
bassadorless ambassador's car was so crowded that I had to sit up on
the back of the seat and was thus exposed to the adoration of the
peasantry on the sidelines. I gave them the old back of the hand
gesture. To co-exist is not to accept.

Khrushchev had booked a slaughterhouse. We disembarked to
meet the smell of ill-disposed intestines, and an attendant handed me
a butcher's coat. I put it on; there was an illusion that, thus disguised,
I might make it. I walked up the steps, and was pushed down them
by a State Department security officer. I was finished off by an Iowa
cop.

Beaten, in fact darkling, I sneaked into a CBS mobile unit where I
had the consolation of looking at what the television boys were finding inside. They found mostly the backs of Nikita Khrushchev's hosts;
with all the general acceptance of the new Leninist dictum that man's
face is better than his backside, I particularly except the population
of Iowa.

We were to try again at a farm equipment factory; so I commandeered the car of Governor Loveless. Upon my arrival, in this
improbable disguise, an attendant gave me a pair of safety glasses.
They didn't work either; the State Department bouncer threw me
back downstairs.

Once again an Iowa cop finished me off; he said, breathing a little
from the effort of working at the back of the victim's head — as God
is my judge, he really said: "If you don't like Iowa, why don't you go
back where you came from?" Just as though anyone who had ever
been anywhere else would ever be in Iowa.

So much for the experience of the welcome us Martians got in Des
Moines. I commandeered Mrs. Lodge's car, and was borne back to

the hotel. On the way upstairs, I asked the bellhop where a man could find a little restorative. He answered — once again I am forced to swear this, because it is otherwise unbelievable — that there were two liquor stores in Des Moines and they were both closed for remodeling. Even so, the Bellhops Union, out of its abounding cornball heart, would find me something for $10 a pint. If Nikita Khrushchev can find it in his heart to forgive us Iowa, then my differences with him are more irreconcilable than I had before imagined.

[Des Moines, September 23, 1959]

Ten Days That Shook

This was the night and this the place where they closed the show. The wagons trail home to Pittsburgh and then to Washington. But no one day will ever again be the length of a man's life. The future can only be unlikely; the impossible belongs to the past. There is a little madness to come, but it will be a madness henceforth controlled by James C. Hagerty.

The white lights of the million rockets are going out in the night of the Iowa sky. The sound of the million voices singing a dozen different Handel oratorios at once is dying, although no one can say how long the memory of those lights will blind our eyes and the echo of those noises will deafen our ears.

But they are only memory and echo. We shall not ever see again the scenes of a single yesterday; in a week, we shall have begun to doubt we ever saw them:

Nikita Khrushchev, heir of Lenin, Stalin and Peter the Great, standing, his ventilated shoes encased in silage, in a field of beheaded sorghum, watching his host, Bob Garst, go down to the earth to pick up handfuls of the infinite essence of the droppings of generations of prize cattle and throw them in the face of a banzai charge of cameramen.

Henry Cabot Lodge, American Ambassador to the United Nations, Brahmin-born and schooled for command, bending over to ask the Chairman of the Council of Soviets if he hadn't seen enough. "See," said the Chairman, "the capitalist is trying to hide things from me." "This will be a jovial day," said Lodge. He spent it handling the microphone for the interpreters, a grand duke become overnight a Paris doorman.

Khrushchev and Lodge walking through the Department of Swine Nutrition of Iowa State University. Khrushchev observed with satisfaction that the sows were standing up in their lying-in rooms "at attentior. for me." The air was filled with the bursting smells of excess animal vitamin. "In all his life," said Khrushchev, "Mr. Lodge didn't take in as many smells as he did today." Their trip completed, the Chairman of the Soviets said: "It's too late for me to enroll here in your school. But, if you have a Chair of Pork Chop, Mr. Lodge and I may be useful there."

Khrushchev looking at a machine which is a pride of Bob Garst's farm, although it seemed at the moment to exercise no visible function except to pick up two hundred pounds of chopped sorghum and dump it- on the heads of the photographers. A television man stuck a microphone next to the Chairman to catch his reactions. There was a pregnant silence; it was ended for national consumption by the voice of a State Department security man reaching for the intruder: "Throw the SOB out on his head."

Now they are over, those ten days of voyaging into astral reaches beyond prior limit of the imagination. How can we measure the distance we have traveled or the time we need to recover from it? Will life ever be the same for any of us again? And will not Moscow seem just as gray to Nikita Khrushchev as Pittsburgh or Washington or New York to us his fellow travelers?

Adlai Stevenson had lunch with Khrushchev and Bob Garst yesterday. (It is the measure of this epic that even Adlai Stevenson becomes a parenthesis in it, although it is the measure of Adlai Stevenson that he offered the presence of a shining and honorable parenthesis.) Stevenson was saying afterwards that he found Khrushchev a man changed since he saw him in Moscow a year ago; he could not define the change very well, except to say that it seemed to be a matter of education. I think we have changed him, although I can define it no better than Stevenson could.

The memory he takes home is not just of the color of the country, or the richness of its earth, or of the luxury of its appointments. For the gaudiest image he has seen is of our fools, our vast national surplus of the comic and the excessive. We tend to think of our country as having become gray and characterless; but Nikita Khrushchev comes here and who does he meet in quick succession but Spyros Skouras, a drunken CIO vice-president, Bob Garst and the American photographer, all abounding with idiot delight?

It was a trip which might have been planned by a committee of trained Bolsheviks to show him America in its least respectable aspects.

Yet has anybody on earth ever had as much fun as Nikita Khrushchev has had for the last ten days? We can never put mankind back into its old sober mold again. Nikita Khrushchev may very well go home and be his old self in a few days, but he will miss us as long as he lives. He knows now that no place on earth is as much fun as America.

What will happen — and I am quite serious — to the Soviet state when Nikita Khrushchev wakes up back in a country where all day long nobody laughs but him?

[Coon Rapids, Iowa, September 24, 1959]

The Fitful Light

Our Chairman spent his last night on the Columbia burlesque wheel as guest of the Carlton House's $75-a-day V.I.P. suite.

"His excellency," reports the Royal Gazette's Carlton House stringer, "will be the first guest of the V.I.P. suite to use a newly installed $500 television set . . . Former guests of the Carlton House V.I.P. suite include Perry Como, Sir Thomas Beecham, Jerry Lewis, Casey Stengel, Sammy Davis, Jr., and Thomas E. Dewey . . . During a recent visit, Vice President Nixon utilized a smaller suite on the hotel's fifteenth floor." Even in heaven not all angels are equal.

The next morning offered Nikita Khrushchev little prospect for those sorties into fantasyland which delight him; the only opportunity for free play was a one-hour inspection trip of the Mesta Machine Co. in West Homestead.

It is Mesta's boast that it is the only installation on earth where copper and iron ore are poured in at one end and a whole steel mill can come out the other. A walk through this dingy fantasy, peopled by grimed gnomes, is two miles; it takes an hour and the temperature was high noon in Iraq. At the core of production, everywhere, there is always a slum.

The Chairman opened the meeting in form. He stopped at a cutting saw. "We don't make them that way. That's an old one, an old workhorse. We had saws like that when I was a young steel worker. I am surprised at you American capitalists. There was a time when you were bold. Now you're riding these old brutes."

"That's a relic," said his guide, Mesta vice president M. K. Powell, cheerfully. "We're keeping it for a souvenir." "Relics will empty your pockets," said Khrushchev. An engineer in the background estimated the poor saw to be no more than eight years old. It is discouraging to think how far we have to go to close Nicholas III's lead over us.

The Chairman walked along, shaking hands with dirty workers and looking at clean machines; then, out of the blue, he stopped and said, "This is a good plant."

The earth shook for what has to be the last time on the voyage. "I'm sure," said M. K. Powell gracefully, "that you have better ones in your country."

"Don't be so sure," said Nikita Khrushchev. "We have better ones; we have the same kind; we even have worse. I don't say that all you have is bad and all we have is good. We can learn from you."

It is very difficult to remember that long ago, but somehow I cannot conceive of the Chairman of the Soviets who flew into Los Angeles Saturday making any such concession as that. We have changed him somehow; I do not know how much he has changed or how long that little will last, but, of all the fantasies of this last week, the one I should have thought most unlikely at the beginning was the smallest sign of change in Nikita Khrushchev.

Ken Jackey, a storeroom clerk, came out to give him a cigar; the Chairman took off his wristwatch and gave it to Jackey. No detail of history goes unrecorded; an attendant Western observer noted that the greatest emperor on earth wears a $5 watch.

He stopped beside the frame of a cold rolling machine. It looked five times his height.

"Now that is good," he said to Powell. "Let's start trading."

Powell smiled: "Sure." And Nikita Khrushchev answered in the longest speech he has made in English since he landed: "Yass, yass, shure, shure," then in Russian, "but you never do it."

And back he swung then to what had been for so long the normal. He looked around to find something unlovely and found a machine drill and said: "We wouldn't buy that machine even if you offered it. It's too slow. You'd have to get an operator who knew a lot of good long songs or he'd fall asleep from boredom."

But it was not a mood he could sustain long that morning.

Without warning, he stopped and said almost to himself a meditation which was translated as: "You have good cadres of engineers and skilled workers. You can make use of all that science can give you."

A mill hand shouted something to him across the cordon; it must have been Ukrainian, the Chairman's platoon went rumbling over and Khrushchev was rolling back on his heels and bubbling: "Rushky? Bialystok, Pinsk? Eh, Minsk?" He fairly ran away from his guards to bring back Soviet Foreign Minister Gromyko to shake the hand, jerking back his thumb to indicate, "Gromyko . . . Minsk."

And he was off to the cathedral of learning at the University of Pittsburgh without a single further attempt at one-upmanship. He had reached, here in this steaming pit, the mellowest point of the last ten days.

It is a small change since it leaves largely intact his faith in terror and dictatorship. But it is as much as I think we could hope to gain from this wild odyssey. But I do not think it is a tactical change, because Nikita Khrushchev's repeated refusal to be graceful about American achievements is an almost obsessive habit rather than a tactic. And it is most probably an impermanent change. But, to have extorted it at all, even temporarily, we must have performed last week better than we looked.

[Pittsburgh, September 25, 1959]

Fellow Rulers

The honorable Sylvanus Olympio, president of the new Republic of Togoland, invited his fellow rulers of the earth to a small reception at the Hotel Plaza yesterday afternoon.

President Olympio is a man with all the higher graces, and speaks French, German and English with cosmopolitan ease, this being a necessary facility for any Togolese gentleman, since his little country has, in the course of his lifetime, been successively controlled by the Germans, the British and the French.

There is, I am sure, a Togoland anthropological society for the study of primitive cultures around the world, and Sylvanus Olympio would naturally be its honorary president. In such case, when the society meets next, President Olympio's little monograph on the domestic habits of the Americans should certainly be the high point of the proceedings.

For his own modest contribution to the UN social calendar, the president of Togoland invited all delegations. The Americans sent no guest of more elevated station than an information officer. Nikita Khrushchev sent himself on behalf of the Union of Soviet Socialist Republics.

He was, of course, a whale in a bathtub. President Olympio's other guests had not begun to drink when the battalions of New York police set up their encampment outside the Plaza. Khrushchev arrived, was booed soundly by three thousand persons around the fountain where Zelda Fitzgerald once bathed, and booed not much more decorously by the ladies in the lobby who henceforth will be able to tell their grandchildren that they stood up to Nikita Khrushchev. I can't see how much more mileage Nixon can expect to get out of having stood up to Khrushchev; in another week Henry Cabot Lodge and I will be the only two Americans who haven't.

"Savages," said Khrushchev and went upstairs to join the gentry from Africa.

An advance party of some thirty journalists and bearers of television equipment and cameras were already staked out in the Crystal Room across the hall from President Olympio's reception, and the quarters were soon bulging with fifty or so more of their kind who had come with Khrushchev. President Olympio had personally invited six journalists who had done some service to the state of Togo. The first invasion of his privacy came when a squad of State Department security officers, an alumni association of Mafia sergeants-at-arms, entered the gold-and-white room with a view to throwing the journalist guests out into Central Park.

President Olympio managed to divert this particular marauding tribe and his guests were then permitted peacefully to engage Nikita

Khrushchev in conversation while Khrushchev toasted his host in orange juice.

By all reports it was a pleasant interlude which might have gone unspoiled were it not for the high civility of the innocent Togolanders. They thought of the non-invited tribe of pressmen confined across the hall; it seemed only simple courtesy to invite them to share these genteel revels.

The doors were opened, the press came in. Wild elephants have done less to native compounds. Heads of state in parti-colored kentes were knocked against the walls like so many rag dolls; waiters were trampled to the floor, as the herd swept towards its object, Nikita Khrushchev talking to Elaine Sheppard. "Goodness," said President Olympio, neatly balanced between shock and laughter, "we have been invaded."

Nikita Khrushchev was swept up in the herd, and carried towards the exits and the stampede went God knows where, although one cherishes the hope that it cost the lives of at least three of those colonial dames in the Palm Garden. When it had gone and the wounded picked themselves up and limped away, the guests seemed to have been carried off too, leaving nothing but President Olympio and his staff and a few stray members of the herd who had been cut off at the pass.

President Olympio found them drinks and made them welcome with the grace which allows a gentleman to pass without strain even among wild savages. One of them fingered the President's kente — the tribal toga — and he explained its varieties and their general lack of symbolic significance; polite as he was, he sounded as though he were being asked about the difference between a gray flannel suit and a blue serge. He endured a few rather-too-searching questions about Togo culture, and let us drift away. He did not ask any of us about our own tribal customs. For the moment it was understandable if he would rather not.

[September 23, 1960]

VI

Politicians—Seekers and Finders

It is hard for a man who has enjoyed both the taste of our beer and the flavor of our politics to say which of these national glories has gone flatter in his lifetime.

Both, I think, were the victims of modern merchandising, and the need to adjust to the taste of women, who are serious about serious things and trivial about trivial ones.

The politics I miss ended in 1952, although we did not know it then.

The 1952 political conventions were the last to which a man could come with any real cause to doubt the outcome or to hope for excitement. The delegates to a modern convention have become mere members of a studio audience; this change, which is important to aesthetics if not to history, seems to dominate most of the essays I have collected here, and it is a depressing one. The Democrats had one last fling with the Stevenson demonstration in 1960; the Republicans obliterated the Goldwater people — their own faction of commitment — in Chicago two weeks later, proving again that, in this case at least, they are the party of the future. No faction of commitment will ever be permitted to embarrass any major party by intruding its passions into an American living room again.

The campaigns are like that, too, great leaps by plane for brief stops to serve as studio audience. By all accounts, the 1960 election was decided in the empty television studios; that also is the future. Yet the flavor of politics was not in the candidate but the atmosphere he carried with him, the smell of the train, the smell of the local politicians, the smell of the crowd, the play of the man against the crowd, the dance and not the dancer.

Most of what is printed here was written by a man who does not vote. There is one piece about how I felt when Eisenhower beat Stevenson which I have kept because I feel the same way even now. I quit voting after 1956, the second time Stevenson lost; I could not think of a better time to stop. We lost in Adlai Stevenson a truly great President; General Eisenhower was his inferior not because he would have or did damage the country — the gift of command was his in any great emergency — but because he had no sense of style or tone and because he had no sense of sin.

I do not argue that political reporters do better work if they do not vote but rather that a man with as little emotional self-control as I have should either give up voting or give up political commentary. Otherwise he cannot judge events. Mr. Nixon rather strained this policy, and I confess that I only abstained because it seemed to me impossible that he could be elected. I had, of course, underappreciated the blanket which President Eisenhower had thrown over the judgment of the American People.

It was Mr. Eisenhower's sloth and irresponsibility which brought this poor man to within 100,000 votes of the White House, and he should thank his guardian angel for the narrow margin by which there was preserved the gratitude which, on balance, American history is likely to feel for him.

I do not think, in sum, that I much like politicians, especially successful ones, since they need for success a high quotient of the selfish and a rather unattractive contempt for anyone who dares run against them. Strange then, that, with the art in decline, these pages should so celebrate a man who has both these qualities to the required degree and who yet remains one of the most engaging I have ever seen. In an age when so much of the flavor has gone out of his trade, John F. Kennedy, just as horse, is something to watch run.

Jenner Grabs a Ride

General Marshall is not only willing; he is eager to play the role of a front man for traitors . . . The truth is that this is no new role for him, for General George C. Marshall is a living lie . . . Everything he has been a party to for the past ten years has helped to betray his solemn trust and to set the stage for the staggering Soviet victory that is sweeping across the earth. — Senator Jenner (R-Ind.), September 15, 1950.

George Marshall is one of the patriots of this country . . . If he was not a perfect example of patriotism and loyal service to the United States, I never saw one . . . I have no patience with anyone who can find in his record of service to this country anything to criticize. — Dwight Eisenhower, August 22, 1952.

Let me assure the Indiana . . . Senators, that when you meet with me, there shall be only one point on which we all agree . . . Are we trying to do something for the good of the United States? . . . I shall never lose patience with anyone who is firmly convinced he is working for that. — Dwight Eisenhower, September 9, 1952.

I agree with the General 100%—100%. — Senator Jenner, September 9, 1952.

In this campaign, I am requesting voters to support the entire Republican ticket from top to bottom in every state I visit. — Dwight Eisenhower, September 9, 1952.

When Dwight Eisenhower landed at Indianapolis, Bill Jenner was the first man up the ramp. The General came down, shuddered a trifle and extended his hand to Jenner. The girl who ran second for Miss America this year handed him a bunch of roses, and the General seemed glad of a chance to look away.

Bill Jenner put his arm around Eisenhower's shoulder; the cameras clicked; the General scuttled his head down a little as if to duck behind the roses. Jenner said, "You have lovely weather here, don't you, General?" and Eisenhower said he had.

When the ceremony was over, Jenner and Eisenhower climbed onto the back seat of a convertible and rode through the streets of

Indianapolis together, Eisenhower working the right side of the street and Jenner the left.

Through the streets Bill Jenner's friends were passing out a leaflet calling for his re-election to protect America. His, the leaflet said, had been a "brilliantly patriotic career." Among his shining deeds had been a vote to reject George Marshall as Defense Secretary, and "think how many would oppose him now." Jenner had not changed; only Eisenhower had.

But Bill Jenner had other fish than George Marshall to fry. The polls were running badly for him; he was hanging on Eisenhower's coattails; and all day he never left him.

They went to lunch for 1,100 people and Bill Jenner rose to speak. He turned to the General, dimpling, and said that Indiana would give him a 200,000-vote majority. The General applauded.

Then Bill Jenner went on proclaiming that he and Dwight Eisenhower were on a great crusade. The General applauded.

Jenner said that the people were tired of "crisis, war, inflation, high taxes, mink coats" et al., and each time the General roared with the rest.

After which Jenner, whose taste is never totally beyond reproach, ended with a gag about bed-wetting and the Fair Deal. Eisenhower and all the audience broke down in applause and laughter.

The luncheon was ended, and Eisenhower walked off the platform, stopping a minute to catch his breath and raising his ring hand to lean on a friendly shoulder. He reached for Bill Jenner's shoulder, then he saw who it was, and he let his hand drop. Let it be said for Dwight Eisenhower that he did the thing he did not utterly without shame.

No one else can really say what George Marshall meant to Dwight Eisenhower; he himself said it three weeks ago in choked and angry terms. The man who said that must know better than anyone what it means to pass the gates to glory by kicking your father in the stomach.

Bill Jenner had the high honor last night of introducing General Eisenhower to 16,000 Hoosiers at Butler University. When Eisenhower arrived, the audience stormed before him and Bill Jenner reached out and raised the General's right hand. The ears of the world, Bill Jenner said, were on Indianapolis and this truly great American.

The General's ovation lasted a minute and he had time to shake Bill Jenner's hand. He went on to make a speech centered around the verse from Ecclesiastes which says, "There is . . . a time to keep and a time to cast away."

There is another verse in Ecclesiastes and it says, "There is a time to embrace and a time to refrain from embracing."

[September 10, 1952]

The Sorehead

The sun was shining, just as it always does, yesterday morning; the elevator operators, the charwomen and the waiters went about their business at the Hotel Commodore with no visible signs of enchainment.

Downstairs at Eisenhower's headquarters, they moved in silence and slow time, still prisoners of the dream. The mimeograph machine ground forth the itinerary of the General's newest flight; reading it, there was a moment when you were hearing again the marching orders of the crusade, but this was only the winner going off to play golf on a ten-day pass.

The sun was shining, and it was the same 42d Street; the taxi drivers growled the old fraternal obscenities at one another. Nothing had changed; nothing ever will, I suppose. There was no surface sign that this was the end of the world. But for my money, it was the end of the world; and neither sun nor the amenities is going to trap me into saying something pleasant about it.

The knuckleheads have beaten the egg-heads. You're not going to catch this baby jumping over the net and extending his hand to the winner. Would Colonel McCormick extend his hand to me?

The difference between me and the General is that I may be just and I may be fair, but I sure ain't friendly. David Dubinsky can go ahead and call up Winthrop Aldrich any time he chooses.

The Republicans were sitting in the Commodore celebrating their deliverance Tuesday night. One of the attendants came in and asked whether a Dr. Hartman was in the house. "Oh, Harry needs a doctor tonight, oh, Harry needs a doctor," some wit sang out again and again in one long croon of hate. The man sitting at my right hand said in tones of the philosopher that, after all, these people had been losing for twenty years and they deserve a chance to win.

What is this, Ebbets Field? The Republicans haven't deserved to win since Lincoln and they don't deserve to win this one. The only justification for their quadrennial assault on truth and reason was the kind of excuse people used to give for holding debutante parties during the depression; it gave employment to a lot of people. But it was one thing to put up with a campaign pretested by B.B.D. and O. and something else again to have it win.

I suppose the woman with the diamond lattice work who was pointed out to me as Mrs. Alfred Gwynne Vanderbilt has been losing for twenty years, and I've been winning. Man and boy, I've been losing since birth, and the only time I've ever won has been with the Democrats. Couldn't George Sokolsky and Fred Waring at least leave me that?

I've been a Giant fan since 1930 — four miserable pennants. When a ball player breaks his ankle, it has to be Monte Irvin. When a pitcher shows up with a back ailment defying medical science, it has to be Sal Maglie. Why does it always have to be my team?

During the war, I had a brief, tenuous relationship with an outfit called the 38th Division. Its nickname was the Cyclone Division. Do you think they called it the Cyclone Division because it had swept through the enemies of freedom? Of course not. They called it the Cyclone Division because all its tents got blown down on maneuvers. That's how it is with my team every time. I can't even persuade my kids to be Republicans and escape the family curse.

There are those who say that at least Adlai Stevenson was right, and we have the satisfaction of knowing we lost in a good cause. I think it would be a little better to know you'd lost in a bad cause. The notion that you deserved to win and didn't may bring some lonely gratification to the noble of spirit; for me, it makes the whole thing twice as bad.

I should have spent election night with Tallulah Bankhead croaking curses upon the electorate, with Joe Bushkin playing a little blues through the smoke behind. That would have been the way to go out

— not watching some idiot girl with a dress imprinted with her affection for Ike in five different languages waving a megaphone around the Commodore. The sun yesterday may have shined on the just and the unjust. It didn't shine on me, Mac; it didn't shine on me.

[November 6, 1952]

The Millennium

The Republican army of liberation, gingerly juggling the awesome fact of the millennium and blinking at what passes around here for sunlight, descended on Harry Truman's citadel today to celebrate as best it could the first respectable event in these precincts since the inauguration of Herbert Clark Hoover twenty-four years ago come March.

It arrived, as must all armies of liberation, to confront a mess rampant.

The Democrats, whatever their other sins of malfeasance, have the Inaugural ceremony down to a routine by now; the Republicans are fumbling, bumbling amateurs at it.

All night the Inaugural Ball Committee fended with the demands of variant victims of creeping socialism anxious to pay $8 for tickets to the Inaugural Ball, which among other delights, offers Mrs. Martin P. Durkin, wife of the incoming Secretary of Labor, in a bouffant gown of toast-brown chantilly lace combined with plaited silk set in a ten-yard sweep of skirt, designed by the Countess Alexander, presumably one of David Dubinsky's pensioners.

The "standing room only" sign has been posted since early morning yesterday, but stubborn stragglers from the Crusade kept queueing up for tickets, presumably driven past caution by the promised enchantment of Mrs. John Foster Dulles in a strapless model of heavy silk in deep blue designed by Oldric Royce, winner of the Chicago Tribune American Fashions Prize. Mrs. Durkin is the only cabinet wife to rate a designer of the blood royal.

The Inaugural committee had also run out of press releases, credentials, and schedules of impending festivities, the latter not an unmixed blessing since the Republicans had celebrated the return to businesslike methods in Washington by listing Monday's events for Sunday.

Far from this madding scene of frustration, the liberators hustled through scenes of unbridled revelry all over town.

For example, the North Dakota Society held a reception in the Senate caucus room under the chandeliers and ever so careful of the red carpet. It was an occasion not utterly without peril for passing strangers; the Crusade has not yet solved the Washington manpower shortage and there were at least five ladies for every gentleman.

It was also not an occasion unfraught for innocent fellows with a reputation for the President-elect's ear; Senator Young (R-N.D.) hadn't been there two minutes before he was fairly drowned in importunities.

One visitor clutched poor Young's lapel and explained that he was a man of substance in soil conservation down here to discover what the new administration had in mind. Young replied that if the visitor knew what the new administration had in mind, the visitor was a better man than the Senator.

"I don't know about this new Secretary of Agriculture," said the visitor, "him a Mormon and all. What do you know about his new Assistant Secretary from Minnesota?" All he knew, said Young in the tone of a high churchman describing a Holy Roller, was that he was a dairyman.

"When are we going to get a grain man?" asked the visitor. "That's what I keep worrying about. A lot of farmers are starving. If we don't watch out, a lot of good Republicans are going to get beaten."

The starveling farmers ate their cookies and sat down again, the girls on one side, the boys on the other. Mrs. John B. Cooley, North Dakota's Republican National Committeewoman, was talking about all the letters from ladies who wanted to be postmistresses. Mrs. Cooley said that she had never known before how serious it was to be a National Committeewoman.

Outside a beet-faced man in a white Stetson was bewailing the myth of the millennium.

"They told me I had the nomination for the job," he said, "but did I get it? No. I told that fellow last summer that crowd of New Dealers was going to crucify his boss. They will, too."

Around the corner, Richard Nixon, never a man to leave an hour unshining, was holding open house in his old Senate office. He wasn't there, but the visitors trooped in and his secretary did her best to leave them all with the sense that they had been vouchsafed the ultimate presence.

At the inaugural Committee headquarters the only printed matter left was a list of the boxholders for the Inaugural Ball ($300 a box). Martin Durkin's name was next to that of Eugene duPont III. The AFL's George Meany and James Petrillo had boxes, as did those men of steel, Ernest T. Weir, Ben Fairless and Tom Girdler. Also Robert Alphonso Taft, four box seats only.

National unity suffused all except Nebraska, where Dwight Eisenhower had appointed former Governor Val Peterson, Republican, as Ambassador to India and both the state's Republican Senators promptly indicated that he was personally obnoxious to them. The Nebraska society foregathered for cocktails at the naval gun factory and Val Peterson stayed away. Senator Butler arrived, snorted at the suggestion of Peterson's name and said he would have a drink before commenting.

But Republicans of greater substance were gathering three thousand strong at the Governors' reception in the Statler. Robert A. Taft stayed home, but Tom Dewey showed up for something approaching a debutante's reception. A vast outpouring of common folk turned out for this particular display; they were pushed back to the sidewalk by Washington cops anxious to create an aisle for the departing Republican ladies, not more than half of whom wore mink and half of whom carried it as though they had just been elected queen for a day.

For aficionados of genuine substance, the Republican National Finance Committee was meeting in the Mayflower. Its sessions were closed, but their tone was established by the "Of course I know him — Republic Steel" introductions in the washroom.

Outside, little groups clustered to discuss the challenge of power. The talk turned to Charles E. Wilson and whether he could continue to run both General Motors and the Defense Department.

"I don't care what they say," said a woman with a mink stole. "I wouldn't give up any of my stock to take any government job."

"But you have to understand," said her companion, "it's like Dick Nixon says. A man shouldn't have a government job and an outside income too."

They sat there regurgitating their bliss. There is a Washington mess, and it's theirs, all theirs.

[Washington, D.C., January 19, 1953]

The Kittens

Early this week, students of representative government could have looked down on the Senate chamber and seen the Honorable Bill Jenner, swaying like a blacksnake and screaming like an eagle that Dean Acheson still rules the White House. "We are told we can't go it alone," shrieked the Honorable Bill, "but why can't we?"

Anyone resisting the impulse to go it absolutely alone after that would be rewarded a little later by a ninety-minute parade of Senators paying tribute to "the integrity — above all the integrity" — of Minority Leader Lyndon Johnson, who does not beat his wife or forge checks, but is after all reasonably safe from being carried off to heaven before his time by impatient angels.

But, on Tuesday, Congress was gone and nowhere here was there an opportunity to witness the awe and majesty of the legislative process. Nowhere, except in an odd assembly called Girls Nation.

Each summer the American Legion Auxiliary picks two girl high school student leaders from each state and brings them to Washington to learn citizenship. Girls Nation rates high enough on the protocol list for four Cabinet officers to take time out to meet the students and answer questions.

In these affairs, the party in power of course gets to run the show. Last summer, the Girls Nation students were confronted mostly with Democrats; this year they dealt mostly with Republicans. This, of course, is a very bad system; if you are looking for the answers to a question of high government policy, you should ask the outs. Last summer, the Republicans knew all the answers; this year the Democrats do.

One afternoon, the girls went to the Agriculture Department to meet Undersecretary Morse. Morse beamed at his pretty auditors, spoke favorably of integrity and asked for questions, presumably on home economics.

So this chick put up her hand and said shyly: "Mr. Morse, what do you think of 90 per cent parity." Morse blushed and said for five minutes that he had no opinion on the subject because we are here to serve and not to dictate. "Are you going to sell the TVA to the private utilities?" Question of high policy, said Morse for another five minutes, but believe me nobody will suffer under us.

These ninety-six Lucrezia Borgias sat there and threw curve balls like that until poor Morse said with a sickly grin that he would love to answer questions all day but, how about a movie?

As a climax the girls split into two parties and ran an election for president and vice president of Girls Nation. Both parties campaigned on a platform of aid to Europe and more immigration. The Legion would appear to have so much to teach them.

That same night, Miss Bertha Adkins, Republican Women's Director, came out to explain politics to the girls. Woman's chief contribution to any cause, said Sister Bertha, is "vocal." Women yell and men don't. In politics there are rewards — service, integrity, and maybe even a job although warped people call that a spoils system.

Just before Sister Bertha clanked these hollow changes, a Danish girl named Annette Bogelund talked for half an hour about what it had meant to her to spend a year in a California high school. "There's something greater than nationalism," she said, "that's universalism . . . I speak for a beaten country . . . you are creating a new spirit in us; do you realize that? . . . we have got to humiliate ourselves, all of us . . . please realize that."

When she finished, they sang "America the Beautiful," and Annette started crying and so did everyone else there below the age of twenty-one. They weren't crying for Bill Jenner or Lyndon Johnson or 90 per cent parity. They were weeping from the sudden sense that there is a sisterhood of women all over the world. Washington really does have so much to teach these girls. It's going to have Sister Bertha around to explain that kittens do have to grow up and be cats.

[Washington, D.C., August 7, 1953]

The Last Hurrah

The reporters sat outside Harry Truman's suite on the fifth floor of
the Sheraton-Blackstone just as though his actions were still of consequence, and there remained all day the brave but hollow illusion that
here sat the center of power of the Democratic Party.

The old man was down to haggling for the votes of single delegates
from Montana and one such came, went in under two-by-two Harriman dragoons and came out saying it was an honor to meet one of the
great men of American history, but, no, he guessed he hadn't quite
yet made up his mind.

The Democratic Party was disposing of its own Taft wing, and the
saddest thing of all in the Presidential suite was that no young men
came to ask the old man's advice. An anonymous fellow in a seer-
sucker suit who looked like a pig kept coming in and out and Frank
McKinney, who used to be chairman of the Democratic National
Committee, kept dodging into side exits with an air of transcendent
purpose, and those of us who had never been anywhere else all day
caught a little bit of his illusion that big doings were afoot.

But no doings at all were afoot in the Presidential suite; the old
man was wheeling and dealing with nothing but his old guard; it was
dying yesterday, and it makes very little difference whether it sur-
renders Thursday.

All day there were rumors of breaks in important delegations — at
3 P.M. there was a great flourish about South Dakota, but even that
was only rumor. Harry Truman, who is a stand-up guy, had done what
he could and Adlai Stevenson seemed unharmed. The past was passing; the father was yielding grudgingly and the sons were taking over.
The Democratic Party had decided that it would run no more against
Herbert Hoover and that this was the year 1956.

A half hour after Harry Truman declared for Averell Harriman the
notion was irresistible that, in this one act, he had buried the past and
himself with it. The Stevenson group had been handed the Democratic Party: this mild, troubled, dumpy man was now the boss. All
afternoon the word rolled in from the Kennedys, the ADAers and

the Monroneys — all the names of the future in the Democratic Party — and every one said that he was still for Stevenson.

Stevenson laughed that we Democrats do have fun, and worked at polishing his acceptance speech. With Stevenson there were always crowds; even with Truman, the house seemed always slightly papered. After Truman announced, Stevenson walked in to say a few words to the television men. He was in a room absolutely full, and they gave him, when he came in, a great cry of warmth. It was remarkable because there was absolutely no bitterness in it.

It is the one great quality of Adlai Stevenson that he brings out the best in those who follow him. It would be refreshing after all these years if our politics suddenly brought out the best in people. An odd and extremely sophisticated labor skate stood and looked at the crowd and said, "Aren't they the most beautiful people you ever saw in your life?"

Stevenson never quite rises to these occasions, and what he says is always just a little bit flat. But, watching Frank McKinney dodge around corridors in the obscene blotting-paper suit he affects on business of consequence, it is a wonderful thing to look at Stevenson. To write him off is somehow to say that you have surrendered hope.

All the old men departed this weekend. Former Governor John Battle of Virginia said that Harry Byrd had been on the phone for two hours trying to swing the delegation to Lyndon Johnson and that the delegation wouldn't budge. Even Harry Byrd has become part of the past. I do not think that John Battle takes Stevenson because he believes that Stevenson is soft on civil rights: I think it is more than he understands that Adlai Stevenson might make a better man of John Battle. There are occasions when it is almost enough to look like a conscience.

And last night, quite late, Harry Truman broke on the strangest rock of all, Michigan, wild and crazy Michigan, was suddenly 80 per cent for Stevenson. This is the delegation which is the great fruit of the social revolution of the Thirties; there are people in it who were arrested on sitdown strikes twenty years ago. The old CIO is stronger there than anywhere else at this convention; and Michigan is important because, in Michigan, the Democrats win elections.

And last night Walter P. Reuther told the Auto Workers' delegates in a private conference why he is for Stevenson. He said to them that what is good for America is good for the Auto Workers. What does Harry Truman have to do with anything when Walter Reuther is a moderate and Frank McKinney is a symbol of the unreconciled New Deal?

Half of the Michigan delegation comes from the United Automobile Workers of America; and, let the worst come to the worst, Walter Reuther, who says he's non-partisan, will persuade that half to go to Stevenson. Michigan caucused last night and Harriman came and Stevenson came to ask its support. Harriman came with all the rag, tag and bobtail of the clichés of the time that is past; it was a horribly empty parade of entirely correct and prefabricated opinions on all subjects. And Stevenson came — this was the unkindest cut of all — with a smile, a few jokes and Mrs. Eleanor Roosevelt.

Mrs. Roosevelt walked in and had her picture taken by Sammy Schulman of INS, who was her husband's favorite photographer. "Hello, Sammy," she laughed. "Still going around?" Still going around, Mrs. Roosevelt? She told the Michigan delegates that there are some things more important than winning; there is, I assume, one's image of one's possibilities. They cheered Stevenson and Mrs. Roosevelt three times longer than they cheered poor Harriman. Afterwards, Gus Scholle, president of the Michigan CIO and the most immoderate moderate alive, said that he was particularly pained because Harriman was so bitter and nasty.

Moderation, after all, is only the belief that you will be a better man tomorrow than you were yesterday.

[Chicago, August 13, 1956]

New Faces of '56

Richard M. Nixon and wife Patricia arrived at the Cow Palace to pick up the marbles a little after four yesterday afternoon, alone together in the back of a car the color of banker's ink and at least twice the size of the store where he was born in Whittier, California.

A room had been set aside for their seclusion in the twenty-odd minutes while they awaited the call from the wings. Nixon debarked, somber as he always is in repose, lighting up as he always does when the cameras light up; it was possible at once to feel the burden of a son with a sick father and to admire a man who can throw everything off and assume the ageless glassy glow of the campaigner who sees only endless horizons of joy and beauty ahead.

The door opened; three or four outriders welcomed them; the door closed and a California cop took his station in front of it. From behind the door came no sound of conversation; a twenty-seven-inch television set had been provided but there was no clangor indicating that Richard Nixon had tuned in on the convention and the wisdom of the Honorable Dan Thornton.

They were there, five of them, a half-hour or so, and were then escorted to the platform. A curious bystander looked in at the room they left behind to see if it contained a prayer rug. It contained nothing at all but a picture of President Eisenhower, the big television set, and some slogans urging a Republican Congress. There was not one cigaret butt in an ash tray; there was no sign that anyone had sat in the chairs; there was no sign indeed of any human habitation. Richard Nixon leaves no fingerprints. You looked at that room and wondered whether it really had been Richard Nixon or whether there ever was a Richard Nixon anyway.

Great care has gone into the construction of the shadow which declares itself to be Richard Nixon. He had on a suit of shoddy which only the most expensive tailor could have cut to fit so badly, and his shirt was a wonderful facsimile of the one he wore when he was in the ground forces of the U. S. Navy. The ends of its collar kept coming out over the lapels of his jacket; it was an effect achievable only after consultation with the board of directors of the Master Tailors Association of America.

And then he stepped out on the platform, turned once to wave to Herbert Hoover to establish the true pedigree, and raised his eyes to heaven, which at the moment was full of balloons scheduled for release upon the entrance of President Eisenhower, and, looking like a blue-jawed YMCA secretary wearing a seminary issue suit, intoned a speech which was distinguishable from the 1948 platform of the Americans for Democratic Action only by the absence of assaults on the Communists.

"We will not rest secure," he said, "until every Negro, etc. . . . The triumph of aggression in any part of the world is a cloud of war over the entire world . . . We will not rest content until . . ."

I do not think it fair to Herbert Hoover to live eighty-two years and then have to sit and hear his great-grandson fruitily chant fugitive passages from Henry Wallace's "New Frontiers" in your own house.

It is the great quality of Richard Nixon that he can bury his own image, and then spit on its grave, and still be so marvelous a craftsman all the while. This is a convention which has been run three days by amateurs; then the ghost of Richard Nixon came trailing in and the pros had taken over. For the first time all week George Murphy sat down.

Nixon is going a bit in the jowls; but then he always did give the effect of having a great wad of unmelting butter stuffed next to his lower jawbone. He looked otherwise like the White Rock Girl staring with wild surmise at the new freedom. At last he ceased his looting of the collected works of Jane Addams; and fell back to the shadows, and the real pro came on.

Dwight Eisenhower has somewhere learned to play the nonsense of our political carnival the way Ben Hogan plays Pebble Beach. The President was on the platform crooking his finger at Dick Nixon to get him and Pat in front of the cameras, snapping like a drill instructor at his daughter-in-law Barbara to get out there under the light on the double.

He had been given a speech carpentered by Arthur Larsen, the house intellectual, which contained various recondite references to great thinkers of the past. This is not quite the old man's track; at one point he was assigned a quote from Henrik Ibsen, whom he identified as Henry Ibsen. If the trend continues, the Republican campaign speeches will be written by the board of editors of the *Partisan Review* and they're going to be dreadfully pained when the President starts quoting from Andrew Gide and Ignatz Silone.

But he is a man who knows by instinct that no election was ever won by relevant quotations from the Hundred Great Books; and from time to time he threw away Larson's lacy script and began barking out to the troops to get in there with the Boy Scouts and get out the vote. Dick Nixon watched the while, the way Eddie Stanky used to look at Willie Mays. Nothing touches the conscious craftsman like a spectacle of unconscious genius.

Between times, he widened his social horizons by asking Mrs. Eisenhower about the children. Then the President led us all in singing "God Bless America" and the angels came down and he and Mrs. Eisenhower were transported off in a cloud of dreamdust.

Dick Nixon went about his homework. He shook hands with Herbert Hoover, and Herbert Hoover, Jr., and a little girl who obviously loves dogs, and the whole Cabinet. Harold Stassen was observed working his way down with the expression of the man who conducts you to view the body upstairs, but Dick Nixon couldn't wait.

Back at the Mark Hopkins they were packing his bags to put him on the plane back to Whittier. The bellhop looked at the luggage; there was one piece gleaming like a jewel.

"That's samsonite," said the bellhop. "It's a synthetic, but it sure is pretty when it's treated and polished." Let's face it; you got to give talent its due.

[San Francisco, August 24, 1956]

Production Number

The 20,000 free Americans who entered Madison Square Garden last night to celebrate Dwight Eisenhower's four-year struggle to restore individual initiative to our society were handed a twelve-page vest-pocket-size folder.

The first eleven pages listed the President's accomplishments. The back was a series of eight hints on: "How to make the most of your television appearances" (wear a dark-colored suit, either gray or blue; remember, mastery of the television medium is a political must, etc.). The time is not far distant when the right of free assembly will be limited to persons wearing blue shirts.

There were other duties. The old anarchist spirit depends on discipline. C. Langhorne Washburn, director of the assemblage, passed out to subsidiary agitprop directors a sheet labeled: "Action Plan."

Poverty of poetic invention being your agent's habitual condition, what follows are gleanings from the action plan, which matters went according to anyhow:

The assault craft were to land at 2 P.M. when "the Eisenhower Bandwagon takes position on 49th Street side of Garden.

2:45 — Audience interview reporters Wendell Corey and Walter Winchell report to control desk, main stage, Madison Square Garden.

3:00 — Audience interviewers report to control desk for briefing, timing and introduction to their reports.

4:00 — High school bands report . . . preliminary to seat briefing.

5:30 — Doors open.

5:45 — Prominent sports people . . . report to control desk for briefing.

6:00 — All card section personnel to be in their seats ready for instruction, entering through 50th and Eighth Avenue.

6:25–6:45 — Organ and bands alternate in providing musical entertainment. Also during this period, John Casey will conduct initial card exercises with independent public address system.

6:45 — Jinx McCrary and William Gaxton will be introduced as floor interviewers and will conduct a variety of interviews and acts to include: Irving Fisher (Truman); Victor Moore, prominent sports people.

Two five-minute periods for Congressmen's spotlight introduction in audience. Congressmen will assist spotlight in locating them by signaling with white card.

(Around this time your agent entered the studio to find a vast popular front ranging from grandmothers with lorgnettes to grandmothers with beanies topped by dyspeptic-looking little celluloid elephants. Fred Waring was rehearsing them in "We Like Ike." The tune is a two-beat version of "Three Blind Mice." Johnny Casey, of the University of Southern California, who does this sort of thing in the Rose Bowl, was drilling the rear balcony in mass card-display techniques. They spelled successively "We Like Ike," "We Want Ike," "We Need Ike" and "Thanks Ike," the last in script.)

"We need three hundred volunteers," Fred Waring cried out. "Be sure you know how to count." The audience cheered the card display, and Fred Waring rehearsed us again in the song. "Write down the words while you have a chance."

(The next two hours were a feast of reason. Jinx Falkenberg knocked tennis balls into the throng. Two seven-year-old girls wearing lipstick sang "We Like Ike." Rube Goldberg was introduced with a message; it was a cartoon. More rehearsals of the song. William Gaxton, a hoofer, predicted a storm of the people. Victor Moore, dressed as Throttlebottom, dragged a coonskin cap across the stage. Fred Waring told the second balcony to be sure to look at the instructions on their cards. A college girl spoke on democracy — "Peppermint Candy." There was a movie. There was also a political speech, allotted time, five minutes, by Jacob Javits.)

The climax swells through every line of Washburn's action plan:

8:40 — Waring glee club sings "Thanks, Mr. President."

8:41 — Frank Davis against Glee Club background sings "He's Got the Whole World in His Hands" — fades to blackness and glee club and orchestra swell to "This Is My Country."

8:46 — Audience interview. Walter Winchell dramatically introduces Sergeant Leonard Funk, who speaks for sixty seconds and then calls on members of the 82d Airborne to sound off . . . During this address by the 82d there will be very soft background music.

8:55 — Fred will instruct the audience on cues regarding the President's entrance.

8:57 — Mrs. Eisenhower may enter alone; if not, a Waring production number will be done between the instructions and air time when Roosevelt, on cue, introduces the President and first lady.

9:00 — The three bands will play the first thirty-two bars of the "Stars and Forever" (sic) in unison and will continue this through the card salute.

9:01½ — Washburn on control desk will receive cue from NBC to give signal which will start card display, which will be cued by voice. This signal will be in conjunction with the musical direction of Mr. Waring. Once this is under way they will run through their repertoire, which will take twenty seconds.

Upon signal from John Roosevelt off camera, audience subsides and President Eisenhower takes over. Washburn cue will silence bands at proper moment before Roosevelt signal."

While this ordered frenzy was going on, the television announcer was instructed to remind his audience that Henry Wallace is for Ike.

This is a party which appeals to reason and to persons of tested judgment.

[October 26, 1956]

The Return

The old, half-forgotten stern realities returned to Dwight Eisenhower a little before 3:30 P.M yesterday, as he was standing on the apron beside the Columbine, with his Mamie in her blue Sally Victor hat preparing to depart Jacksonville, Florida.

His press secretary, James Hagerty, came down the ramp to him. They settled into the posture they have learned long ago to use for private consultations in crowded places. Hagerty stands beside the President — his eyes at the President's chin level, his mouth talking at the President's neck. Hagerty was holding a sheet from the AP ticker and a few notes. And, as Hagerty talked, the President looked at the horizon, and for just a minute his lips drew up above and below his teeth in a moment's trace of surprise and trouble.

The sheet James Hagerty held was the first, scrappy bulletin announcing that the Israelis had entered Egypt. The President said a very few words, and then went back to his farewells. General James Van Fleet, the West Point classmate who is his Florida campaign chairman, shook his hand and said, "Good luck, boy"; Mrs. Eisenhower said, "Thanks so much, Van."

The Eisenhowers were at the top of the ramp, and he turned and his face worked its old plastic magic and he threw up his hands, the symbol of triumph over care. The last sounds he could have heard were the shouts of school children and of one small boy, who was crying.

That must be how his campaign for re-election ended; he can hardly go a-roving to Dallas and to Oklahoma City as originally expected tomorrow; the chance for pleasure, if that sort of thing can be described as pleasure, has been pushed aside. He had gone to his meeting with Hagerty after shaking his way down a line of what pass for dignitaries in the Florida Republican Party, and then the fragile police lines had broken and the children were upon him. They began shouting "Mr. Eisenhower," and he did not seem to hear them; they switched to "Ike" and he turned and laughed at them.

Someone held up the little boy and the President laughed again and held out his arms; there was a moment of indecision and the

President started back towards the Columbine. A cop picked up the little boy and trotted after the Eisenhower party. By the time he caught up, Hagerty had the President's ear, or more precisely his neck; and the little boy was set down unattended and yawping.

The President had had his last chance to present his untroubled vision of the world at Jacksonville before three thousand persons, spread out on the open flats of the airport. It was the second stop on his one-day aerial invasion of Florida and Virginia; Miami was the first and Richmond was to be the last. Airport-hopping may have its promise for the future, but its present is dreary indeed; all in all, no more than 15,000 persons saw the President in these three cities, which is a lonely display by his standards.

But they were, however, in miniature, typical of his crowds; in Jacksonville at the fringes, where clouds lowered and his voice was barely audible, a drunk passed out; a child was sick on the pavement, a young girl fainted, and the onlookers gave as much attention to these diversified phenomena as they did to the President calling earnestly down to them from the bunting on the platform. All through his speech, they were drifting back to their cars or taking places behind the platform, so as to catch him on the way to the plane. It was a crowd of watchers, not seekers.

Mee-a-mee, as he calls it, had been glittering hot; Jacksonville had been cloudy; the reports were of wind and rain in Richmond. In Miami, he had walked carefully by the harsher realities, speaking some twenty feet from an airport drinking fountain labeled "Colored" and saying that the condition it represented was more amenable to solution by the hearts of men than by laws, and complimenting Florida as "typical today of what is best in America," a verdict which might seem to some contingent on finding out what happened to the Negro snatched from the Wildwood jail Sunday.

Coming from Jacksonville, the Columbine was observed briefly pulling ahead of its lead press plane, and there was a moment's surmise that the news from Egypt was so grim that the President might be hastening to Washington to come to meet it. But he landed in Richmond, an hour and twenty minutes late; the Chesapeake & Potomac Telephone Co. met him with a special line over which he could talk to Secretary of State Dulles. Something slightly over 3,000 people also met him, standing patiently in the dark drizzle. He had come to do his duty of praising Harry Flood Byrd, that strong, still silent guardian of the Old Dominion's tradition.

The President stood up, an unfriendly wind blowing his thin hair, coatless and his smile for once not without effort. He mentioned the concepts of Jefferson and Harry Flood Byrd, and then, in a sudden foray into the jungle of syntax which improvisation is for him, said: "Now such concepts, my friends, is what I intended to speak to you of tonight, however briefly. They have been in my thoughts since the campaign began. But let me say this:

"All that concerns us today in our homes, in our jobs, in our country is, as nothing compared to the awesome choice now awaiting the decision of mankind. For the race of man, if there is no peace, there is no hope. The building of that peace is my all-embracing goal . . . (In the Mideast) by dedication and patience we will continue as I remain your President to work for this simple — this single — this all-embracing goal."

It was solemn and eloquent. When he finished, a stranger plucked at him and he returned to another form of reality. He had forgotten, he apologized, to mention his indorsement of Mr. Cabell for Congress. Then he could go back to Washington, and the larger reality.

The reporters sat about the lobby of the executive offices of the President, and arose together at the call for photographers to the front porch of the White House. The President and the Dulles brothers and Sherman Adams and Herbert Hoover, Jr. and C. E. Wilson were standing on the steps in the great white light. Wilson smiled and Allen Dulles waved at a friend. The President suggested that the photographers get on with it. His face looked like a face on a coin. There was no question of his weariness; there was no suggestion of triumph. It could be argued that he didn't have to run again; but it remained terribly sad somehow that it was so much more fun to run for the job yesterday than to hold it last night. Then he led them back to their deliberations, and the Negro attendants in their white ties and tailcoats closed the door behind him. His day, which had begun in the warm sun, had ended in cold, dark night.

[Washington, D.C., October 30, 1956]

De Profundis

On Wednesday, the *Times* published a two-thousand-word memorandum by Robert A. Taft on the reasons why he had come to the autumn of 1952 cheated by life.

Because he was a tidy man, I rather think this a memorandum addressed primarily to himself. But because he was a gentleman, he opened it by saying that it was for those who had bled with him and who might think that the defeat was in some part their fault when he knew that it was only the gods.

The wounds were by no means healed when he sat down to write, and he did not arise with the achievement of entire poetic reconciliation of the experience. There are sentences not without bitterness; the word "smear" appears several times.

There is the assertion, if only by omission, that the *Times* itself was almost a campaign sheet for Eisenhower, and there is the irony of the conviction by the greatest conservative figure of this century that the Republican Party had been stolen from him by Wall Street. But, with these few flaws, the effect is one of genuine dignity of expression; Harry Truman seems more unforgiving of a defeated enemy than Robert Taft was of a victorious one.

What makes this document important is not these subsidiary rancors but its absolutely pitiless analysis of the America which was then barely beginning the decade which it is now closing. The pessimism which underlies it is almost radical in its cast; one comes up out of these depths with conclusions that are more aesthetic than political; it is a long time since I have read a document which so well conveys the absolute squalor with which history is made.

The core of this memorandum is its reflection of that awful weekend before the 1952 convention began when Taft was struggling to hold the line. He was one candidate with no pretense of staying above this battle.

One gets the impression that he had to do his own haggling, that he sat in that hotel room counting delegates and writing down each delegate's name and commitment, knowing personally every promise and betrayal, and that even afterwards he took all his notes to Canada with him and chewed on them until he could write that, on one critical vote, he had lost four expected delegates in New Jersey and three in Nebraska.

He says at one point that he had a commitment from Harold Stassen to adjourn the convention after the first ballot to give him a chance to breathe and haggle on another day. It was a commitment which does not appear to have been honored, but Taft was beaten anyway, and it would have made small difference if it had been. What remains is the sense of what Robert Taft must have thought of Harold Stassen and the terrible sacrifice of dignity involved in merely sitting down with him.

But dignity in that hour was something to be thrown away and sought again in tranquility. Stassen was a giant beside some of the men with whom poor Taft was reduced to suing.

For what was left of his hope came down at the end of Governors Fine of Pennsylvania and McKeldin of Maryland and Republican State Chairman Arthur Summerfield of Michigan. Now, even by the standards of political life in America, have there ever been three more incredible characters than these?

McKeldin and Fine have mercifully departed; but they are images burned in the memory; Karl Mundt could not erase them. Summerfield lives on, affronting any illusion that this is a nation dedicated to the freedom of the intellect. He is below the level of the sort of mail-carrier who reads postcards; and now we are reminded that he sat with all the delegates of a great sovereign state in his pocket and it was with the likes of him that Robert Taft had to treat. The thought that history is made by such as Summerfield can produce nothing but a compulsion to abandon politics.

And that is the terrible, inescapable final lesson of this testament of Robert Taft's. He was — even according to the testimony of his enemies — a man of great personal morality. Yet he never seems to have thought that morality had any connection with the business of a great national convention, and before you dismiss him, grant him the credentials of an experienced witness.

He was entirely suspicious of Presidential primaries, and assumed that he won the primaries where his side controlled the state machine and Eisenhower won the primaries where he was similarly fortunate. He remained righteously shocked that anyone could challenge his ownership of those Southern Republicans who had been bought and paid for; and he had reason to be, because the credentials of this hired flesh have not been challenged since 1912 and won't be challenged for the next forty years.

There is only one expression of moral disturbance in all these two thousand words.

It is this single sentence: "(Our Texas) people had a sound moral claim that the Democrats had taken over the Texas primaries."

The bones of how many reformers lie bleaching on this desert. And this was a man universally respected for his personal qualities. He took them into a trade where they are of smaller use than they would be for a bookie. So colleges run courses in political science and the vice squad worries about marijuana.

[November 27, 1959]

The Ninth Life

Harold E. Stassen, fighting through what the professionals think has to be his ninth political life, stood in the morning sun in front of the Wynnewood shopping center yesterday and gazed upon the unpeopled vista of marked-down John Wanamaker outdoor furniture and said he was glad to be among his neighbors and fellow-citizens.

A couple in their autumn years walking with their backs to him along the sidewalk in front of his sound truck stopped at that, and turned and looked at him briefly and turned away. A few women stopped in the driveway; a salesman sat down on the merchandise. Far, far away, a haze in the distance, a woman stood waiting for her bus, the sound of his amplifier beating at her back. He spoke of the big issues —the need to back President Eisenhower and Vice President Nixon in their fight for peace; then the amplifier died in a silence altered only by the passing of cars.

Harold Stassen came down. A station wagon drove up with its chauffeur in front and the lady of the house in the back. The chauffeur got out and said, "Gosh, that's Staysen." His mistress cast a cold eye upon the enemy of the Pennsylvania Manufacturers Association and, true to her class and her kind, waddled into John Wanamaker's. Harold Stassen leaned over to shake hands with the chauffeur and with a mother and her moppet and raised his head and looked about and there was nobody there. The first public meeting of his Main Line tour was over.

Here is almost the last serious political figure who was a factor in the 1940 Republican convention. Harold Stassen has fought and lost to all the giants whose names are a catalogue of our afflictions since — Dewey and Eisenhower and Nixon. Now he is running for the Republican nomination for governor of Pennsylvania next Tuesday, and the chances are that he will lose to someone named McGonigle.

Yesterday morning he had scheduled public meetings at Bala Cynwyd shopping center and at Narberth. They were abandoned, because nobody came. At Narberth, he walked from his car, along an empty sidewalk to his sound truck by the railway station and talked to its driver a while — gravely courteous, undefeated — and walked back, alone with no sign of grievance. This is a primary; in a primary, after so many years, without the organization you expect these things.

He is that much alone. It is even said that, when some brave soul from the organization sends an overture, Harold Stassen himself must conduct the negotiations; there is no one else. He is only fifty-two, but a time that began too soon for him has worn him badly around the eyes; there is something oddly old-fashioned about the sweep of the hair back over his neck, the pockets bulging with papers; the Homburg with the patch at the back of its fold. He has missed too many boats. Yet there is nothing pathetic about him; Harold Stassen is a gallant man. If he must go, he will not sneak off to some law firm; he will go down in an uneven fight with his head up.

Life went on around him in these towns no sun could warm yesterday, indifferent, unremarking — the thinnest lines of the curious on the streets, and far larger clumps of the incurious in the Ardmore drugstore sealed off from the sound of his voice.

Yesterday Harold Stassen, who has won Presidential primaries, was visiting the editors of weekly newspapers. He explained very gravely that this could mean stories in four papers before the primary. He knows that the organization will vote; he has no chance unless somebody comes out in a state which hasn't had a Republican gubernatorial primary in twenty years. His enemies in the Pennsylvania Republican Party would rather beat him than the Democrats, although the bitterness with which they began has ebbed a little in the terrible indifference which is all the surface of this campaign.

He is not, of course, an insurgent by choice; his is a gallantry enforced by circumstances. Yesterday, Bernard Kramer, editor of the *Main Line Chronicle*, observed that he had the organization scared and Harold Stassen said very quickly: "We'd like to get 'em to join us." He is, after all, no longer a young man.

He made his speeches in Pottstown, and Ardmore, and Phoenixville as the cars went by and then he went back to the television station for the last of the Tuesday night talks on which he has staked most of the hopes he may be casting into the empty air.

He sat there and made a very few notes; he no longer needs to write a speech. The paragraphs come now to his mind in blocks; he can finish on the second, conceiving and framing a respectable sentence which sounds like a peroration with just eight or nine seconds left.

He had brought a few props, and he sat there and explained, to the cameramen how they should treat a still picture of self and running mates and wives; "Can you close in and pan down the line from left to right?"

There were about three minutes left and Frank Chirkinian, his director — does Lynn Fontanne need a director? — went to the control room. The tube showed Harold Stassen running through his pockets. He looked strangely like President Eisenhower, which is the tonic which his trade even in this dull market works upon him. When he is just working at a job these days, Harold Stassen looks a little like Herbert Hoover; when he is running for an office, even against these odds, he looks like Dwight D. Eisenhower. "Look at the pockets," said Frank Chirkinian with real affection. "I never saw a man with such bulgy pockets." When you've been this long on the road, you travel alone without baggage.

[Philadelphia, May 14, 1958]

The Trophy

Nicely, nicely, poor Richard Nixon was pushed and shoved — the only victim forbidden by protocol to complain — about the New York World Trade Fair in the Coliseum yesterday.

He shook the extended palms of all the world — from Bulgaria to South Korea — with the firm, non-partisan grip of salesman to salesman. He took home an Indian tea kettle — his wife is a collector; a stuffed black dog from West Germany — his daughter is about to be a collector; a large Benelux bowl of blue transparent glass; a volume of Israeli photographs of Biblical landscapes; a thing that looked like a lute with hangman's ropes attached from South Korea; and a cluster of flags from the European common market.

He told an Indian that the new agricultural program was a "stabilizing, ahhh"; he told a Brazilian that his new capital was like Washington, D.C., and built from the ground up and the President agrees; he told the European common market that it was a great stride forward; he told Israel that it too was a great stride forward; he told the Austrians that it was a thorn in his flesh that only five per cent of the tourists who went to Paris went on to Vienna; he told the Sicilians that there would have been no California without the Di Giorgio farms; he didn't mention the Di Giorgios to the Mexicans but he told them that they were friendly and had pyramids older than Egypt's and also the shrine at Guadalupe; he told the Poles that his grandmother had a feather bed; he told the Bulgarians that theirs was one country where he and his wife had never been but that, by all evidence, it had pretty girls; he told the Aubusson tapestry industry — behind its back — that its designs were a little over his head but certainly striking; and he told the South Koreans that he had gone to school with a Korean boy and that he and Pat would never forget, etc.

And through it all he was steamed and baked and crushed by the animal flesh of scribes from the prints and the Pharisees from the Coliseum management — "I started to hit one of those reporters, but I figured he was too important" — and tripped by television wires, and pushed into artificial flowers — "Clear out Israel; we're taking him there"—and through it all he remained pleasant, informing, and anxious to please, a single agreeable island in a sea raging with the unpleasant.

He ended his journey inspecting a detailed relief map of New York and environs provided by the New York Port Authority, with light-ups of its installations and a battery of telephones which the intellectually curious might pick up to hear a recorded description of the tentacles of that octopus. The Vice President of the United States picked up the phone and nodded his head and heard the description all the way through. When it was finished he hung up. Thank heaven, there is one limitation to Richard Nixon's manners: he does not say "Thank you" to a recorded announcement.

"This is the way you teach people," he told the Port Authority's attendant. "They see the phone and they pick it up because they're curious and then they listen because they're interested." He tried to heist the telephone. It was anchored to its place, an example of the abiding faith his servants have in the common man. "I see," he said, "you have them all nailed down."

A policeman was following him carrying his presents. The Vice President asked his bearer how long he had been on the force. Three months, the policeman answered. "That's what it is to be a recruit," said Mr. Nixon. "You have to carry the loot."

He was through it all a mine of information. He has been everywhere except Bulgaria. He knows the population of the European common market; he knows the percentage of tourists who go on from Paris to Vienna; he knows that in other Asiatic nations besides India you greet a voter by putting your hands together and inclining the forehead forward; he appreciates Polish hams.

He could even ask the Mexicans about a friend of his named Sierra. "We used to go to parties together. Does he still do those dances? No, I guess he doesn't. He has to be dignified, I guess."

How dreary it is to be Richard Nixon. There must have been a little fun in Mexico — however ceremonial and hollow — and now the man's been promoted and is only a memory as jackanapes. There are left just the maps and the figures on the Indian five-year plan. What must it be like to be an American tourist and never get to see the *Folies Bergères,* which you would have had the taste not to like, of course, but could at least have talked about as though you liked it as any other tourist can? There is left only the world in the form of small talk.

God, how Nixon must envy Khrushchev, who can drink Pepsi-Cola and spit it out in public disgust. What a terrible curse it is to embody America as a constant apology to the world.

But then there is the expense account and there are the trophies. I think of the Nixons in their golden years, the Vice Presidential family emeritus of the United States, with Mr. Nixon saying in the long winter evenings in San Luis Obispo, "Pat, show me that thing the South Koreans gave us before the night fell." He spoke last night at the Dutch Treat Club.

[May 5, 1960]

The Last Scene

All afternoon yesterday the Democrats played the damp and stagnant last pages of a novella called "The Young Man and the Sea."

It had begun on Sunday when Jack Kennedy lashed a big fish to the side of his boat and started to take it home. The sharks were around the boat by Monday, by Tuesday they were tearing the flesh off the fish and Jack Kennedy came home to port at midnight last night with only the bare bones lashed to the boat.

He was nominated by a tired and apathetic and resigned convention. He had all its votes but his enemies had all its style.

The Democrats always do it that way. There is something in their chemistry which makes it necessary for a majority of the delegates to dislike and distrust the man they nominate. That was by all reports the mood of the Democrats who nominated Franklin D. Roosevelt in 1932; it was certainly the mood of those who nominated Harry Truman in 1948. It seems in fact that a Democrat cannot win a national election unless he opens his campaign with the ill wishes of a majority of the delegates.

It took some doing in Kennedy's case because he is an engaging fellow; and certainly on Sunday he had the general good will, as well as the votes, of the delegates. But the Democratic chemistry worked in its mysterious way; on Monday Mrs. Eleanor Roosevelt slapped his wrist and on Tuesday Lyndon Johnson savaged him, and by Wednesday the galleries were packed with persons who coldly denied him their cheers and gave them all to a non-candidate who got less than eighty votes. It will pass; in a few days the flesh will all be back on the bones — by another mystery of Democratic chemistry.

But this a saddened moment of triumph in a sports palast which at three yesterday afternoon was the most septic mixture of chromium and pure air in this hemisphere and now, a little after midnight, is a charnel house of trampled posters, and limp confetti, and handkerchiefs dropped still wet with the tears of girls who broke their hearts for Adlai Stevenson.

It was three-thirty before Leroy Collins made the announcement that he hoped there would be a little decorum for the sake of the unprotected children in the living rooms and recognized Alabama, which yielded to Texas. The sports palast was under siege; there were reports that three thousand Stevensonians were walking around it chanting for their leader. Los Angeles is a city of faith healers. There is a tradition of belief in the arrival of the hero a little ahead of the buzz saw.

Sam Rayburn, almost a gnome from the great reaches in the back, told of all the great men he had known and decided that the greatest was Lyndon Johnson. The battle flags and locker-room shouts of the Confederacy went up. All demonstrations, by general agreement of the contenders, are limited to ten minutes. The favorite sons have to sweat to keep them going that long. The candidates with manpower will cheat a little. The Texans cheated by four minutes — the Democrats are the party of disorder even in apathy — before Collins shooed them out.

The Johnson posters were carried from the hall and stacked for ultimate incineration. A saving soul from the New Jersey delegation picked up one, saying "Louisiana Wants Johnson," and stapled the name of his governor underneath to read "Louisiana Wants Robert Meyner" and it served for one more processional.

Down on the floor, the Kennedy professionals were cold, the Kennedy amateurs edgy. The word was that Loveless, Iowa's favorite son, wanted to bow out and switch to Kennedy, but his enemies in the delegation were insisting he permit himself to be voted for. A favorite son at this stage of a Democratic convention is a man who wants out but who is enchained by the will of men who loathe him and insist on the right to humiliate him by voting for him as their favorite son.

Symington was seconded by Emanuel Celler and a Nisei Congressman from Hawaii. The Kennedy people were already bringing up their troops and their banners. They were at the ready before Celler finished; he exhorted aisles choked with Kennedy demonstrators. Alaska yielded to Minnesota.

Hubert Humphrey, who had stood his ground like a Marshal of France that morning and announced for Stevenson, arose to say that Governor Freeman would place the name of John F. Kennedy in nomination. Orville Freeman had lost his delegation to Stevenson after he had agreed to nominate Kennedy. He put on his horn-rimmed glasses, a hollow-cheeked and unhappy young man.

"My heart is full as I rise tonight," he commenced to read from the TelePrompTer; and then the TelePrompTer stopped. Even the mechanical instruments which our times substitute for true style failed John Kennedy last night. Orville Freeman looked at that one sentence and thought of the rest of his speech, locked beyond hope of rescue in that jammed box, and gravely but pathetically began to improvise. He had to settle by presenting the name of a great American.

The Kennedy parade was dream-borne and dutiful. A lonely horn would sound now and then. The candidate is young and slender; but those who marched for him turned out unexpectedly and unattractively splat; they were obviously unused to ambulation; I could not guess what was the last time any one of them so much as walked to the corner to place a bet. Someone had conceived the idea of casting papier-mâché heads of the candidate to be borne aloft in the procession. They bore no resemblance to Jack Kennedy, a fact to his credit; they might have been parts of displays for Wildroot Cream Oil from South Boston drugstores. Their effect in the flesh was horrid — as though their bearers were holding aloft dead babies.

There was a procession of representatives of the unfolding future of the Democratic Party to the podium to deliver the seconds; they are worthy persons but a little faceless; the next governor of North Carolina wound it up; we might have been at a mock convention at Wake Forest. The impression was inescapable that, if at any moment, Sam Rayburn had muttered into a sound system, "Hey, boy, come over here," the speaker would have paused, bowed his head and trotted at the command.

Florida inflicted George Smathers on a free people. In the Minnesota delegation they were reading the telegrams that had come in to Orville Freeman. Ten congratulated him. One hundred and fifty suggested in one fashion or other that he was the foulest traitor to the dream of a better world since Henry Cabot Lodge the Elder. Governor Blair of Missouri was saying that Stuart Symington was the answer to the nation's prayer for leadership. In Michigan, Soapy Williams knelt to inspect a delegate count; a man said, behind him, in a voice of awe, have you been outside, have you seen those people?

By now, everyone was waiting for Stevenson. Two hours and a half had dribbled away; a mumble for Loveless was concluded from Iowa; the name of Docking was languidly injected by the Kansans. The galleries were silent as they had been for three hours. There was only one explanation; they were Stevenson galleries. Henry Fonda stood in the back of the hall with a Stevenson button. Someone said Docking was a man of genius.

It came up Kentucky. A bald little man stood up and said "I am Wilson Wyatt and Kentucky would like to ask that Senator Eugene McCarthy of Minnesota be recognized to place a name in nomination." The sleeping galleries awoke, posters began to dance.

Eugene McCarthy came, a solemn young man in a blue suit. The galleries went up with one wild cry; in the moment when he was waiting for silence, Eugene McCarthy bit his teeth and a movement of muscle started at the chin and ran up the jaw line. For the first time since this convention began, there had appeared a face with bones in it.

The speech he made does not exist, I suppose, except in the heart of those who heard it. McCarthy works off the top of his head. The Stevenson people taped and mimeographed it, but of course it was lost somewhere on the floor just after the nomination by acclamation of Jack Kennedy. Anyone out there got the text of the speech Savonarola made the day he proclaimed the Florentine Republic?

That crowd in those galleries would have applauded anyone who so much as mentioned Adlai Stevenson. Eugene McCarthy understood that his duty was something more than that. He had to do more than merely mumble the litany.

He had to say: "Do not reject this man who made us all proud to be called Democrats."

He had the decibels, and Jack Kennedy had the delegates, but neither of these things is relevant. Still one thought of Kennedy sitting there, owning it, and looking at television and suddenly realizing that this is the kind of speech you do not buy.

I could not conceive myself being proud to be called a Democrat under ordinary circumstances let alone under those involving association with the New York delegation; but, quite seriously — with all this week's comparisons with Albert Schweitzer and Frank Sinatra — could you imagine anyone saying that Jack Kennedy, as he is now, makes you proud to be called a Democrat?

Eugene McCarthy stopped; he pronounced the name "Adlai Stevenson of Illinois" and evoked a lonely man stalking among the dawn stars in Springfield. There was a sudden wild beating of butterfly wings at the fringes; the young began swarming over the old. It went on past the agreed-upon time. LeRoy Collins looked down upon them and said this demonstration has far exceeded the rules of decency.

The bounds of decency were found again. Mississippi, in order to prove this a free convention proposed the name of the prime minister of South Africa.

After such moments of grace, there was naught to do but vote. Your agent stood between Massachusetts and Minnesota. Eugene McCarthy had gone home. Hubert Humphrey sat in his place to take his licking. Massachusetts licked its lips. Be it recorded, in this moment of truth, that Wyoming put Jack Kennedy over.

The roar from Massachusetts went up — the tone of lions after raw beef — and Hubert Humphrey sat there remembering the custom of disaster. People stood up, and we waited a half hour or so for Jack Kennedy to come out. As we waited the galleries began to thin out; the pickets outside went home; the conqueror could come to claim the spoils, but tonight we weren't giving away our hearts, thank you.

[Los Angeles, July 14, 1960]

A Farewell to the Troops

A Republican senator who is an ornament to civilization was standing in the reeking, smoking stable outside the Stockyards arena around eight last night and contemplating with a shudder the mimeographed program for the evening.

The Republicans were already twenty minutes behind schedule. "My God," he said, "Eisenhower won't be here until ten-thirty."

He read gamely on. He came to a name. He looked up.

"Goodness," he said, "Ev Dirksen is going to introduce the President. That will be extreme unction."

That was ages ago. This lonely man of taste has gone and gone with him are the Hallecks and the Dirksens, and the delegate from Iowa with the rampant facsimile of a piece of corn upon her breast, and the lights are going slowly out all over the Stockyards arena.

It is not yet quite dark; the chin of Richard Nixon shines on; the face of Abraham Lincoln is in shadows next to it.

The act of love was executed two hours ago. The last words on the TelePrompTer are: "Esteem, admiration and sincere appreciation." One feels as one might feel in Calumet City when the last B-girl has gone to the ladies' room and one knows that she is not coming back.

The killing-floor wallows in Goldwater leaflets and hate letters from the Texas delegation and a red-white-and-blue rag which a page gave Bill Jenner to wave when the battle monument made its entrance and with which he seems to have wiped his nose. A group of young Democrats have invaded the premises and are systematically pillaging them for holy relics.

"Look," one of them says, "I've got Ike's water glass." He began setting to work to dislodge the Lincoln plaque at the foot of the platform.

ONLY THE LONELY

A two-beat group calling themselves "The Steamboat Stompers" are playing "A Closer Walk With Thee." They had offered themselves for the sake of exposure to the Eisenhower demonstration and had been barred; they are sitting around now in this empty pit hoping to get on the "Today" show. They play for only the lonely.

The girls are gone; there are only three left, and those have gone as pilgrims to sit in the seats where Mrs. Nixon and her two daughters had sat and poor little Julie had dozed through the Eisenhower speech, rousing at moments of applause to blow a sullen, dreary tin horn.

The visit of the President of the United States to Chicago was an assignment welcomed by any journalist with a decent instinct for cheating his publisher, because he could take a three-hour nap in the afternoon with the reasonable assurance that the President was doing the same thing.

The President arrived at Meigs Airport two hours late by Army helicopter. Those present waved at him with the languid, loving gesture of the surfeited throwing roses. He entered his car. It was a triumph only faintly stained by small boys crying that they wanted Kennedy.

He stood up and bathed in the America he loves most of all, a long line of vacant smiles waving at him and him waving at them.

The crowd between the Blackstone and the Hilton was a tender, melted mass; one fought one's way through loving flesh and found that the object of all this affection had gone into his hotel. At the center, there was nothing; the crowd turned all together and began waving at the television cameras.

VOICES AND SONG

There was nothing to do save sleep through the afternoon. One awoke in the arena where Roberta Linn, in a red sheath dress, sang "Are You Having Any Fun" and followed it with "The Star-Spangled Banner."

Old Joe Martin was carted on and croaked a few sad words about how tough life had been after the 1940 election. Philip Willkie was circulating among the delegates with an attack on Rockefeller stolen without credit from a John O'Donnell column on Wendell Willkie; in the back of the hall, you could not hear poor old Joe for the gabble.

Sister Bertha Adkins was put on to remind those present that, when Eisenhower took office, he had given America "a voice to speak for human needs."

Mrs. Nixon and children came in. Nelson Rockefeller came in. Around nine, Dwight Eisenhower came in and waited among cheese-cloth blue curtains behind the dais. On the platform, a Negro delegate was thanking the President; behind him the ravaged face of Charles Halleck came together with the wreck of Everett Dirksen.

Little children with Ike placards waited outside in the stable; inside, the pages were giving each free delegate the red-white-and-blue rags he was to wave on signal to affirm his participation in the democratic will.

Charles Halleck introduced that grand guy Everett Dirksen of Illinois. He began to croon; a Michigan lady leaned back as though under a mudpack and said "Oh, the language he uses; isn't it wonderful?"

THE MOMENT OF MOMENTS

The President and Mrs. Eisenhower came in; the children rushed down the aisles; the rags waved. The act of love was rationed; after eight minutes, the sergeants at arms began brutally shoving the children and saying "All right, get along."

And while one guest was being thus thrown into the street he looked back to see a pink Dwight Eisenhower, fighting to choke back the tears at the spectacle of so much love so unbridled.

It would have been too much to ask them to listen. An Iowa lady observed that "this is a long speech; I've read it." He read aloud the prescription of Miltown for forty minutes.

Mrs. Peter T. Gibson of the Federation of Republican Women presented a box to Mrs. Eisenhower as a token of our esteem, admiration and sincere appreciation. Mrs. Eisenhower fiddled with the box; it was a bracelet; she said, "Oh, how lovely," and winked at Charlie Halleck.

The band played "Let Me Call You Sweetheart"; the President helped sing it. Charlie Halleck presented a Methodist bishop named Kennedy for the benediction. He asked the Lord to bless Richard Nixon, and went on so long that the President began looking at him from the corner of an eye not without bale; it was plainly time for the troops to be dismissed.

BACK TO BUSINESS

Then these monuments were gone, the flowers laid upon them and love went with them, and the delegates could return to the main business of delegates to a national convention, which is hating each other.

Within an hour, the hall was empty; the Steamboat Stompers had gone home; a cop sat alone on the speakers' platform and looked through smoked glasses at the gathering darkness, and there was no sound except that of one unattended television monitor set which was grunting the kicks and curses of "The Late Show."

[Chicago, July 27, 1960]

All in Favor Say Aye

Richard Nixon was nominated by delegates drugged and stationary. The convention demonstration is by now a tribal rite as empty as the voodoo ceremonies arranged by taxi drivers for tourists in Haiti. Authentic cases of possession will never again be recorded.

The only proper measure of passion in these affairs is to take a place in the aisle — preferably behind the South Carolina delegation where juices boil — and wait to be trampled to death by whatever peasants are unleashed against the infidel by whatever Peter the Hermit is working the rostrum.

A sociologist who made the test last night stood for thirty-seven seconds after Mark Hatfield had given the call without once feeling the pressure of human flesh.

Every delegate had merely stood up on the seat of his chair, the minimum physical effort imaginable, and looked upon the demonstrations prepared by the Young Republicans. It could not even be described as an audience-participation show.

One could wander for the next seventeen minutes through aisles free of any knees except those of poor old Joe Martin who was sitting alone, one's progress inhibited only once, when Harold Stassen, out of the pressure of dozens of prior moments of humiliation, wandered sightlessly into one's path, the Nixon straw hat dangling from his right hand.

One could walk without any other barrier all the way to where Nelson Rockefeller was standing, winking and smiling and tipping his Nixon hat, his linen jacket hung with a Nixon sash. One thought of Dartmouth reunions and wondered whether the nation loses much when it loses the services of a Dartmouth man.

ON THE BRIDGE

On the platform there were only two gestures. Thruston Morton looked at his watch every ten seconds, and old Charlie Halleck stood there for nine minutes and shifted his inhaler from nostril to nostril. Out of such transports is history made.

It must be said in fairness that this atmosphere is no portent of electoral disaster. If it were, neither candidate could win.

The demonstration for Jack Kennedy two weeks ago, fleshed as it was by publicans and sinners from Steubenville, Ohio, and Gary, Indiana, looked like nothing less ugly than a tattoo of Teamsters' business agents for Jimmy Hoffa. Nixon's demonstrators were more respectable, less ambulatory, and equally undedicated.

The love which these people bear Dwight Eisenhower has at best always been difficult for me to appreciate; but that it could have been demonstrated as it was night before last by persons existing under the conditions of a modern political convention simply passes understanding.

About a third of the alternate delegates here sit behind a pipe scaffold dedicated to the television cameramen and effectively impenetrable by vision. If they arise and try to catch a glimpse of the platform they are immediately jumped by sergeants-at-arms who have been wandering vengefully about this pit since the 1952 convention denied Robert Taft his just due.

It is in such positions that they sit and listen to speeches about the captive nations; and to expect them to roar with any true feeling for the voice that comes to them filtered through the pipes is to ask prisoners to bless their chains.

A LADY IN THE DARK

They had trooped the colors and darkened the lights for the platform movie last night when a party of adventurers made contact in the black behind the television stand with a sister who seemed still faintly breathing. She was an alternate from Minnesota.

"I wish," she said, "some of those people would kneel down. Then, if I crick my neck, I can see the monitor."

Had she seen the President last night?

"Oh yes," she said, "one of our delegates came back and said they were going to sing 'Let Me Call You Sweetheart' to Mamie, and he gave me his badge for five minutes so I could go up and see it."

They ask little and get less. A young Republican came in and gave her a Nixon straw hat, made of paper, and a Nixon sash and told her to put them on. She did her best in the dark.

"The other thing is," she said, "that you can't hear."

This is not entirely true, but the experience is a little ghostly. The words come through, but somehow garbled so that they sound like a series of honest admissions, which I could hardly believe. One reporter, a man known, respected and I might almost say beloved for the purity of his notes, came up from the back of the room with this version of Thomas E. Dewey's peroration: "If any man has credentials, it is Richard Nixon. He is deeply qualified to lead us into trouble."

Patricia Morison was singing "Some Enchanted Evening" and the South Carolina delegation was tearing Nixon's picture off the Nixon hats and wrapping them in Goldwater placards. The word came through that the Goldwater Komsomol squads had been barred from the hall and were writhing, pleading with Andy Frain's ushers outside.

A public relations man for the South Carolina delegation distributed the biography of Gregory Day Shorey, Jr., who would make the seconding speech for Goldwater.

"He is," he said, "the first man ever to receive a degree in public relations awarded by a college in the United States." And no one ever taught him to bribe an usher to walk away.

THE ROLL IS CALLED

Charles Halleck arose to say that if everyone would take his seat and get out of the way, the Young Republicans had arranged several spectacular demonstrations for Nixon.

But first the secretary would have to call the roll. It got by fits and starts to Oregon where Mark Hatfield used a decent four minutes to nominate Richard Nixon; the band began to play "Buckle Down, Winsocki," balloons ascended towards heaven, four young men carried a cannon around, firing it at random, and a girl from Bucks County who had made a special Nixon hat for the occasion with elephants all over it put it on her head.

Nelson Rockefeller arose and brought his hands silently together; he was wearing a red tie with gold embroidered elephants on it, which will go back to the hope chest.

It took some minutes to clear the hall, not of unauthorized bodies but of material junk, the cannon, the bells, the placards, the paper. Every placard costs $6, which makes two of them more expensive than a CARE package. There followed seconding speeches by Robert Taft, Jr., John Roosevelt, and Jacob Javits; some day this will be over; the Republicans will simply do the business by playing over transcripts of "Abie's Irish Rose."

The Governor of Arizona then nominated Barry Goldwater. For a moment there was a certain passion on the floor. A Goldwater delegate was pushed by an usher and said don't you push me and he was about to swing, and all the while his leader was behind the curtains on the platform waiting to dump.

After seven minutes, Charley Halleck drove this ragged, desperate cohort from the floor, and Barry Goldwater came on pink and smiling and blew a kiss to his wife and requested that his delegates give their votes to Richard Nixon. Any man who believes in a politician knows what it was to have bet on the White Sox in 1919.

The business was then snaffled; there were ten votes for Goldwater from Louisiana and 1321 for Nixon from everywhere else, because there are ten Louisiana delegates who hate State Chairman George Reece so much that they would vote for Khrushchev if Reece recommended General de Gaulle.

Chairman Halleck appointed a committee of eight trusted persons to go to the Blackstone at 10:30 A.M. today and tell Richard Nixon that he had been nominated. A man who has Nixon's interests at heart thought of calling and telling him please to be sure and be there because he would have visitors with a pleasant surprise for him.

But, after all, Charlie Halleck had given us a release date, and even a broad hint of that sort seemed unethical. But then, we all got to the office to look at television and NBC had gone and violated the privacy of the Vice President's family life and the plain wishes of Chairman Halleck.

They burst right in and found the Nixons playing cats' cradle all together at the children's hour of eleven-thirty and they told 'em and captured their sudden and most intimate, sudden and spontaneous reactions.

A political convention is just not a place from which you can come away with any trace of faith in human nature.

[Chicago, July 28, 1960]

The Prize Boy

Neutral observers of Jack Kennedy's safari through Texas, men not normally shaken by spectacles of mass delirium, wandered around the Waldorf yesterday still dazed by the memory that he had left Texarkana smoking in the night, that he had burned and sacked even the city of Dallas and sent the Baptist Council and the Minute women of America shuddering into the cellars.

On Tuesday, as Joe Turner used to say, Jack Kennedy was rolling like a big wheel.

He did not leave our topless towers burning yesterday; but this was not his purpose. He was here to spend the day closing the Stevenson gap.

His most important audiences were reformist and unorthodox — the state dinner of the Liberal Party and an afternoon rally of Democratic activists overwhelmingly anti-organization. They were reconciled but not ecstatic; Jack Kennedy, who has no false pride, cheerfully endured auditors who cheered the past in Herbert Lehman louder than they cheered the future in him, and cheered Adlai Stevenson louder still. The parallel was 1952 when Dwight Eisenhower traveled to Chicago to make his peace with a Chicago organization still wearing its Taft buttons.

Kennedy shared the Liberal Party rostrum with Adlai Stevenson. The total effect was that of a college commencement at which an extraordinary piece of bravura from the well-loved dean of men is followed by a perfectly proper valedictory oration by the outstanding senior. The audience left with a comfortable sense that the college had done its job well if this fine young man was any example of this year's class and that the country was safe with its younger generation, but it certainly took them back every time they heard dear old Dean Stevenson.

And as was proper for the prize boy looking around these hallowed halls for the last time, Jack Kennedy even quoted Dean Stevenson once and it was the sharpest phrase in his speech. But the Dean's farewell address was carpentry of a sort no one could ask from a prize boy. It began with the grace notes of the wit — the clean sharp image of "Nixon moving under cover of darkness — so the President won't know he is out — to rendezvous with Rockefeller" — and then it passed to the balanced measures of the peroration: "The future has waited long enough; if we do not grasp it, other hands, grasping hard and bloody, will."

The prize boys are all alike and encouraging, but the Dean endures ever refreshing, ever renewing.

That Kennedy's speeches should always remind us that the class of 1960 is standing on the threshold is no special handicap; it is, in point of fact, a general asset. It is the assurance that he represents something fresh, something innocent of all the sins and mistakes of his parents; the prize boy is our hope for the future; we are not bothered that his promise is greater than his performance.

The candidate also brought along Mrs. Kennedy, who is precisely the sort of a wife a prize boy should have. There has been some incredible nonsense from the motivation research people that she is too attractive to be an asset; a certain muting of her style seems to have preceded her reappearance. She had her hair long, and was wearing a white hat which accomplished the required miracle of being at once high style and slightly dowdy. From an entirely professional point of view, I find this a net gain; she was so ravishing a creature in her original state that I came out of a meeting in Boston once with the remorseful realization that I hadn't looked at any of the speakers, the witness of whose ravaged faces and misshaped forms I was being paid to convey. The effect she used to convey at a public meeting on her husband's behalf was of a Florentine madonna dropped into a Jack Levine painting.

Her husband said nothing especially memorable on what was a day of comparative rest for him, since it included only four public speeches and two private ones and was confined to a one-mile area, but then there is a certain peril in saying too many memorable things in politics. Even so, his speeches are improving, and their curiously tone-deaf quality is giving way to a very faint music. At the women's lunch he was eloquent for roughly five seconds. He said: "Our purpose is not to buy friends or win allies; our purpose is to defeat poverty." The audience, which had been relaxed in friendly torpor, stirred at a sudden presence of rhythm and began to applaud. "Our purpose is to influence history," he went on, "instead of merely observing it." Surprised again, they applauded again.

He was crushed by ordinary citizens whenever he ran into them on his rounds, which was not his primary aim yesterday. We will know his measure as a campaigner when he comes from New England to the Garden late in October. The suspicion off yesterday's performance is that the legend will be rolling by then and the congregation in a state of wild possession.

[September 15, 1960]

Mommy, May I?

John F. Kennedy treated southern Ohio yesterday as Don Giovanni used to treat Seville.

His progress, as ever, was an epic in the history of the sexual instinct of the American female. But yesterday field workers could detect small bumps, not yet roadblocks, in his progress. There were, as an instance, more Nixon signs in the huge crowds than a week ago.

Part of this display reflected the increasing unease of the Republican organization at the sight of crowds that would have made Cecil B. deMille weep for the dear dead days before the screen extras joined the union.

But the bulk of the resistance was plainly the offended males fighting back. We are not a strong set but we do have our resentments. A corps of devoted field workers checking this phenomenon visited the Dayton Nixon-Lodge trailer while Golden Boy was at lunch. They found therein seven pimpled adolescents, all male, plus a scout leader.

The scout leader said that this was the biggest day in the history of the trailer; he had given out 250 Nixon-Lodge hats.

The field workers asked him for a sex breakdown. He answered, with that instinct for cooperation with sociological inquiry which is to be expected of the well adjusted American, that he would judge that 80 per cent were high school boys. He went on to say that this restored his faith in the dedication of the American boy to God and country. But the authors of The Dayton Study, as it will indefinitely be known to the quarterlies, look beyond simplistic judgments. They know this as the moment of vengeance.

For these, quite plainly, are the very boys who gird up the kidneys for a week and then call the cutest girl in the class and she says she has a date for tomorrow and tomorrow and tomorrow. I was such a boy when I was young, and probably am, for all I know, such a man now, and there remain scars upon me which make me believe that, were I young again, I should stand with a Nixon sign in a Kennedy crowd. Richard Nixon is the candidate of all those who had pimples when they were young and have television make-up problems in middle age.

It is, I say, a cloud no bigger than a man's hand. Otherwise, Jack Kennedy rode the streets like Blazes Boylan. Outside Dayton, a woman of advanced years but intact instinct sat with her dog. Kennedy passed; she waved; he waved back; she waved back; in that moment of truth she clasped her dog and kissed his wet muzzle.

Jack Kennedy is starting to enjoy these moments, and he is starting to enjoy them as a man of taste. He turns back now and goes on waving; the lingering hand gestures and the eye follows; its object is always a quietly pretty girl and the hand says that, if he did not have miles to go and promises to keep, he would like to walk with her where the Mad river meets the Still water.

The Dayton field staff was otherwise occupied in questioning those of the sex who, apparently normal in every other way, kept their Nixon-Lodge buttons on their bosoms throughout the tribal rites. One high school girl kept her binoculars fixed and put them down, the face contained, the hands shaking under firm control and said, "I came because I admire the man. No, I have to say I don't think he's attractive, but then" — the smile was a mixture of pride and self-abasement — "I don't understand about Frank Sinatra."

Another was a woman with three small girls at Wittenberg College. She said, as the crowd was leaving, that she too admired the man. This is the problem for Nixon; in the last three weeks, he has to cut down an enemy who seems, even to Republicans, lean and vital and clean of limb. "But," she said, "it's a matter of party principle — all this spending." She stood proud in her Nixon button. Her little girl kept pulling at her jacket. "Mommy, Mommy," she said, "may I please, may I? May I go try and touch him?"

[Miami, Ohio, October 12, 1960]

Death of a Salesman

Richard Nixon and I came to New York yesterday afternoon like thieves in the night. There was not a soul at Butler Terminal — nor Javits, nor Rockefeller — save one man from headquarters, estimable but hardly puissant. The first words we heard were from the lips of a dazed witness who had seen secretaries running and squealing from the House of Morgan to look upon John F. Kennedy.

I cannot believe what my eyes are now seeing. What we watch is like the collapse of some great temple constructed with all the ingenuity of the set designers union for some historical spectacular when the rains come; and the paper columns begin to melt and the whole structure begins wetly to sink into the mud from which it came.

He is not a man I cherish, but there is in the sight of him the painful recognition that something human somewhere is being cruelly violated and humiliated. The gestures are the gestures of someone trapped five fathoms deep; when he stands on a platform and makes a fist, it is a piece of mush; the forearm no longer jabs for emphasis; it merely flounders. These are the movements of a drowning man. He appears to be going out, as John F. Kennedy would say, "not with a bang but a whimpah."

He cannot be entirely without resource; he cannot be entirely without courage; it is conceiveable that he can right himself and arrest this terrible slide. But he seems defeated in his interior. A reporter who has observed with friendliness his progress over the years said yesterday that he had never seen Nixon so limp and soggily desperate.

"I think they're staking everything on the last three minutes of the debate. You know Nixon has the last word." Three minutes to midnight.

They moved him Tuesday over a route essentially of comfort stations, St. Petersburg, Florida, at dark and the Wilmington of the du-Ponts at midnight. St. Petersburg is a Republican enclave; his audience was a Goldwater Golden Years Club of ten-thousand-odd. He told them that he was going to take the gloves off at last, and then he fogged and flubbed and reached for applause he did not get. It was his usual dishonest performance, but it was also pathetic.

The crowd was pathetic too — stout old parties holding signs saying "Nixon, Good to the Last Drop of Blood," and an old lady who had drawn a picture of a smiling dwarf's head — rather like Khrushchev — and labeled "I Wear a Smile Because I am a Nixon Man." A whole myth seems to be going with him, the golden years of white Protestant America; we seem to be witnessing the final entombment of William McKinley.

He told an airport crowd at Tampa that he thanked them for their, "frankly, loyalty." In Wilmington, yesterday morning, he seemed to be riding the coattails of a local Congressional candidate. When seven hundred people came to the airport at Wilmington to meet him, he held them in mush for half an hour saying that he had told Pat that no one would be here at this time of night, and that it was a miracle. He is embarrassingly grateful for any small attention.

It does not seem credible. Nixon is the candidate of an immensely rich party; he has the indorsement of an enormously popular President; he cannot go out quite so drearily as this, the way poor Harold Stassen and poor old Joe Martin and poor Bill Knowland went. But at least those men — some of them, at least — had dignity at the end; this is merely squalid.

Of course, he clings to the hope that Eisenhower may save him. The bleached bones of the Stassens and the Martins lie witness to the vanity of such hopes. Generals die in bed. Richard Nixon, a combat soldier, seems to be dying horribly on a public platform, an object of public humiliation. It cannot be true, but it is the evidence of the eye.

[October 20, 1960]

The Iron

The most golden hour of these final golden days of John F. Kennedy was in San Jose at little after three o'clock yesterday afternoon.

San Jose was once a sleepy town; it still has no square large enough for the proper assemblage of persons; Kennedy's crowd stretched for blocks along narrow streets; it pushed through its city's placable cops; and one four-block stretch took thirty-two minutes to traverse.

The phenomenon is no longer sex; men, young men, run and dance on the street to touch his hand as swiftly as the girls now; what emerges is the image of youth, the phenomenon of the new.

The loudest applause Jack Kennedy gets in these golden days is when he says that, when this election is over, Nikita Khrushchev will know that a new generation of Americans has taken over.

When he climbed to his platform in San Jose, the sound system was blotchy; the crowd kept crying for him and crying that it could not see or hear him; it was a moment when none but the most serious of men would have tried to communicate or to do anything else but radiate.

And yet fight to communicate he did. In this holiday atmosphere his voice was deadly serious. It was the voice of a teacher. "When 35 per cent of our brightest boys and girls cannot go to college, what kind of country do they think can preserve freedom? When we fade, freedom fades."

"I desperately," he went on, "desperately want to see the United States move forward."

Suddenly this is no longer an election campaign to John Kennedy. It is the blowing of bugles.

These long and passionate weeks have brought a great change in John Kennedy. Our campaign method tends to be nuisance when it is not nonsense; to Adlai Stevenson, as an instance, it was an unrelieved ordeal, but to John Kennedy the campaign is a tonic, an education, and a resource.

He has been captured by an urgency which is not political but national. A great part of it comes from the contempt for Richard Nixon which he has developed over the last few weeks and the assurance he feels that the election of this feeble, fumbling, hollow man would be a national disaster. Some of it comes from the faces he sees in his crowds; he believes at last that the country can be awakened, that the last eight flaccid years are finally over.

He is beginning here at the end to talk about ideas. He made a speech on education yesterday morning that was really about how to get more children into college. Last night, before a roaring, hungry crowd in the Cow Palace, he lifted up the sober, moving and revolutionary idea of telling the young that they could serve for three years as voluntary technical assistants in the underdeveloped nations rather than as soldiers in the peacetime Army.

"The generation for which I speak," he said, "has seen enough of warmongers — let our great role in history be that of peacemakers."

I stand on the sidelines of this election; but it would be a sad thing for this country if it chose against a man who draws the line this way.

The campaign remains gay. Yesterday the reporters transmitted word to John F. Kennedy that President Eisenhower had said that to elect him meant a risk of war. "I guess he's using Nixon's old speech writers," laughed Jack Kennedy. Last night in the Cow Palace, Ella Fitzgerald sang "Mack the Knife": "Someone's sneaking 'round the corner; could it be, could it be Jack Kennedy?" But, beneath all the laughter and the easy confidence, an iron has entered into John F. Kennedy.

[En route with Kennedy, November 3, 1960]

Slow Track

The American Legion today listened to Richard M. Nixon, John F. Kennedy and J. Edgar Hoover, the last of whom, in any honest count, would have been its nominee for President of the United States and existing satellites.

The applause count on these three characters was: outbursts, Nixon, twenty-one; Hoover, nineteen; Kennedy, seventeen. Nixon milked his audience with reference to wife and child. "America," he said at one point, "can't stand pat." Hoover, who has neither chick nor child but merely God and country and was therefore handicapped four outbursts in advance, won easily under the lighter impost.

The lord Hoover arose first; the audience arose with him. It must be said in simple fairness they pushed the pornography bit a shade too far; the Legion is embarrassingly lecherous in its response to attacks on pornography. At one point, the director of the Federal Bureau of Investigation turned his attention to the state of whatever screens are not showing *The FBI Story* and consequently indorsing mayhem and blood lust. He commenced to decry abnormality, adultery and other interesting deviations.

At this moment of truth one of those extraordinarily endowed waifs who make a habit of being cast ashore on Miami Beach stood up and walked slowly and sinuously across the line of vision of these old parties and all eyes followed her and the beat of applause came until no witness present could say whether it was for God's Hoover or the devil's left buttock. The stewards afterwards credited her to Hoover: at Legion conventions, he who brings the better props draws the larger claque.

Hoover took his dirty books and left and was followed by John F. Kennedy.

I am an old man and I propose to live at least sixty more years and never, during any four of them, will I vote for any candidate for President of the United States who dignifies the American Legion by appearing on its platform without at once purifying his trouser cuffs by denouncing it. There was no one in the building that I personally would trust with a garbage detail. John F. Kennedy flunked this test of decency and wore his Legion cap and apologized for having said in 1949 that the Legion hadn't had a respectable idea for fifteen years.

But I shall say one thing for Kennedy. He may not have had that peculiar dignity which was Adlai Stevenson's when he suggested eight years ago that interest in civil liberties might be one aspect of the Legion's Americanism program. But he does know how to pull rank. The tone was simply: "All right, you bastards, line for calisthenics at three o'clock this morning." His audience applauded as often as it could during intervals of falling out; any man who can get seventeen intervals of applause while horsewhipping his audience deserves, if not love, respect.

And then came, last of all, as climax, Richard Nixon, the man they would like most to love. He also wore the Legion cap and the odor of morbidity. The applause was dutiful, longer than Kennedy's by just a shade as though the participants had worked themselves to produce it.

He gave them his best in response. If not here, then where? "Opinion leaders in this nation . . . I am coming back to a convention of the American Legion next year . . . it is time to speak up for America . . . an enemy, ruthless, fanatical . . . a great lack of understanding as to why the United States has . . . I know Mr. Khrushchev . . ."

Yet they did not applaud him as much as he deserved; the response was only a hair warmer than the response to Kennedy. Even here, on his own track, he does not run as fast as he has a right to expect. Even the Legion is united only on Edgar Hoover. Jack Kennedy has pulled even this last rug from under Richard Nixon's humble feet.

[Miami, Florida, October 19, 1960]

Live and on Tape

Comes now Public Document 75452, from the Subcommittee of the Subcommittee of the Senate Committee on Commerce, the sober record of the fall of 1960 when America was deciding whether to move again:

> Vice President Nixon: Could I ask you one favor, Jack?
> Jack Paar: Yes, sir; you can ask any favor you'd like.
> Vice President Nixon: Could we have your autograph for our girls?

The notes on that particular meeting at the summit (Paar: I can't tell you how much this means to our show. It gives us "class.") are the opening exhibit in a Senate report labeled, "The Joint Appearances of Senator John F. Kennedy and Vice President Richard M. Nixon and other 1960 Campaign Presentations."

That was Sept. 11, 1960, and Nixon had packed. The Kennedys rallied two weeks later.

> Charles Collingwood: Hello, Caroline.
> Mrs. Kennedy: Can you say hello?
> Caroline: Hello.
> Mrs. Kennedy: Here, do you want to sit up in bed with me?

Mr. Collingwood: Oh, isn't she a darling?
Mrs. Kennedy: Now, look at the three bears.
Caroline: What is the dolly's name?
Mrs. Kennedy: All right, what is the dolly's name?
Caroline: I didn't name her yet.

The issues were, of course, sometimes met more decisively, so decisively in fact that both her elder campaigners may sometimes wish they had adopted Caroline's law.

For example, on the Paar show:

Question: Well, Mr. Vice President, I was wondering if the Congolese Premier sends his troops in Katanga . . . would the United States back up the United Nations in this . . . ?
Vice President Nixon: The United States does support the United Nations and must support the United Nations in the Congo . . .

Or:

Mr. Cronkite: Would you feel any restriction against naming a member of the family to the Cabinet, for instance.
Senator Kennedy: I think it would be unwise.

This has to be an incomplete record of all the wonderful nonsense we were embracing in that lost time of crisis, but it is still a delectable sample. Where else could we have the text of the fifth campaign broadcast of the International Ladies Garment Workers Union, that citadel of adult education ("During the series, we've heard from Adlai Stevenson, Mrs. Eleanor Roosevelt, George Meany, Tony Curtis, Janet Leigh . . . telling you why they, too, are voting for Kennedy and Johnson.")?

Tallulah Bankhead: I am here to introduce John F. Kennedy . . . who as of January 20 will be a resident of 1600 Pennsylvania Avenue, Washington, D.C. That's the White House, darlings.

Here are the debates and here are all the joint statements of Kennedy and Nixon to the American Bar Association (judges should be qualified lawyers), to the American Jewish Committee (there is no Jewish vote), to the Oklahoma Oil Producers (the depletion allowance is a shield of the republic), to the Inland Waterway Association (the inland waterway is a lifeline of the republic), to the small businessmen (the small businessman is the sentinel of the Republic).

Most of all there is Nixon, doom upon him, from the confident beginning, "Oh, I like sports," through the depressing middle, "Charles, I am not a natural politician," to the desperate end, "It's the millions of people that are buying new cars that have faith in America."

This painful, vulgar record evokes him again, but the mystery of his collapse taunts us yet. Still it was a terribly close election and who can say what small mistake cost him it?

There is one clue:

> Bill Henry, of NBC: I am so fascinated with that little kitten.
> Does the kitten have a name?
> Julie Nixon: Yes, it's name is Bitsy Blue Eyes.

Maybe Caroline saved the package when she held off naming the doll.

[January 9, 1962]

The Last Big Rally

John Fitzgerald Kennedy came back to the Boston Garden and the Boston Irish last night with a shudder that was visible from the topmost balcony.

There is a myth that Boston is his home. It is only the place where he went to college. He is a Cambridge man and he looks at Boston as Harvard looks at Boston in some middle distance between amusement and disgust.

They love him here because his name is Kennedy, and yet in point of fact the name could be Cabot or Bradford or Saltonstall. He is a changeling.

They are peculiarly afraid of him. The Massachusetts democracy has been caught stealing lately and the state ticket is contesting an evil hour, and its leaders might have expected to seize the opportunity provided by an audience of thirty-five thousand persons to flog its members with their message, but from simple awe they permitted no political speakers except himself.

So, be it recorded in the chronicles of Boston that John F. Kennedy came home to face a live audience of voters for the last time in the last, gasping hours of his stretch drive with no one else on the bill except The Pickerts, The Jackson Trio, Eva and Everett, The Kaynes, The Three Renouns and other tenants of the dark little Boston clubs where Harvard men since Oliver Wendell Holmes, Jr., have gone in search of real life. The campaign closed with Jack Kennedy at the Old Howard.

A RUMOR, A CHEER

It was hardly the proper audience for revels of this sort, since the teenagers had come early and by seven o'clock the Garden was full and men who had done some service to the party were beating like broken butterflies at the doors. To the children inside, these vaudevillians seemed like archaelogical specimens; they barely watched the acrobatic dancers; before their eyes, the male dancer ran his jaundiced hand under the armpit of the female dancer and winked disgustingly at the upper reaches of the balcony.

A wild cheer went up and died; but it had been for the rumor that Jack Kennedy was approaching. These poor players went through their obscenities unwatched thereafter; the audience had fixed its eyes on an attendant solemnly throwing bags of confetti into those balconies closest to where John Kennedy was to enter.

It was an enormous, fetid and hungry crowd; no man who looked upon it could escape the sense that the strongest argument against any candidate for public office is the condition of his partisans at the end of his campaign. Jack Kennedy came at last, forty minutes behind schedule; they stood and cheered him for ten minutes. The cheers came harder from the platform than from the hall. The Massachusetts ticket is all Irish; its members have the cold eyes and slack faces of IRA members who have gone into another line of work. Yet all those eyes were anxious; everything that happens today depended on what John Kennedy said about them last night.

He came in; the confetti came down; he said his piece about their elevated place in the political history of the Commonwealth; as though it mattered, a fat man in a blue suit on the platform stretched his arms and swung them as a signal to convert frenzy into hysteria. John Kennedy said his piece and left, as fast as he could; the police cars fairly scuttled through the worshipers in the iron New England air outside.

AMONG THE ANCESTORS

He had a date in Faneuil Hall to walk, for television, among the ancestors with whom he truly feels at home, the John Hancocks and the Samuel Adamses. There was a crowd in Faneuil Hall, a loud, wild, young one too, although no louder nor wilder than the one Sam Adams must have had 195 years ago.

It is a place where the history of America is buried. A police captain was saying that the word "cop" was invented there; it had been the initials for "constable on patrol." A politician said that the word "caucus" had been invented there, because Sam Adams's strongest base of support had been among the caulkers, the boat repairmen. A CBS camera was anchored in the aisles under the gilt clock, between the gilt Greek columns; a man came out and asked the ladies in the audience to take off their Kennedy hats so as not to detract from the dignity of the scene.

Jack Kennedy was downstairs somewhere in this holy precinct purging his trousers cuffs of the Boston Irish. He came at last with six minutes left of his television broadcast; as they stood and roared for him, he walked up the aisle and upon a platform empty of everything except blond wood school chairs all in a row, and lingered a second with his back to this, his very last audience, looking at the great panel of the Webster-Haynes debate.

His speech proceeded through, quiet violently broken at the end by applause; the words were tired and had been heard before — this old hall, the citizens of the great republic, the contest between the comfortable and the concerned — but they were, in a peculiar way, ennobled by his own weariness and this ancient scene.

CROSSING THE TAPE

He stood and swayed when he had finished; they rose. Behind the rostrum his knees were bending and jerking; Roger Bannister must have looked this way at the end of that first swift mile. A woman of great wisdom said afterwards that, on television, he seemed then suddenly very young, with the school chairs behind him as though he were saying that, having worked so hard, he must deserve an "A." But, in the flesh, there was only the sense of the blood running down through his shoes.

He went out into the street where the children were conducting a reprise of the Newport Festival riots. The Boston cops fell upon them with what fever was left after this long night; they clawed and bit back; be it recorded that, upon this last night, John Kennedy looked at the sovereign voters and the cops locked together in the combat which is older than reason. So, good-by, Fitz; whatever you may think, you're more Boston than Harvard; and, whatever the years ahead, you were one hell of a candidate.

[Boston, November 8, 1960]

VII

The Patriots

This is partly about a time when John Adams, an assistant to the Secretary of the Navy, begged Frank Carr, a keeper of Joseph R. McCarthy's disorderly house: "If you see J. Edgar Hoover, tell him I'm a good American."

Adams and Carr are gone now, who knows where; only Hoover endures to express the immutable national values.

It has become fashionable to say that Joe McCarthy was not a serious figure in our history. William F. Buckley, in reissuing his *McCarthy and His Enemies,* has composed a graceful introduction saying pretty much that; but if Mr. Buckley's introduction is correct, then how explain his decision to republish a serious book about McCarthy?

The temptation to laugh at Joe McCarthy endures still; that temptation explains why he was a serious figure. He was, for one thing, the cause of bad taste in others. These pieces, when they refer to him, are generally in rather bad taste; Mr. Buckley's own instances of bad taste — and he is unusually careful in these matters — will always be associated in my mind with occasions when he was inspired by McCarthy.

McCarthy's last months were so painful and sodden that no one could avoid being moved by the sight of him; I cannot really apologize to his ghost, but it is owed more dignity than these pieces give it. I can define that dignity only by saying that a little bit of what is bad in myself was a great deal of what was bad in him. There were moments when I enjoyed McCarthy. That is why he was a serious figure; in his twisted way, he explained to me how I was not serious enough.

The comedy ended and the question closed at the moment in the Army-McCarthy hearings when the Senator attacked an associate of Joseph Welch, the Army's lawyer, as a man with prior Communist associations. He was always doing this sort of thing; most of us who had been with him a long time were inured by now and barely listened. Welch's reaction was one of those classic occasions when a man, rising in shock, sorrow and anger, suddenly takes us back to first causes. There is a piece on that occasion here; it seems to me badly done, but its point is important. Only Welch among us that day was an outsider. I don't believe any of us there, Everett Dirksen or myself, was any longer capable of shock; we had all to that degree become co-conspirators of McCarthy's. I remember, most of all, being ashamed then of every moment when I had enjoyed McCarthy and laughed with him. At the end, I did not feel any cleaner than he was. I fixed my face, as Dirksen fixed his; and I pretended once again now and then that McCarthy was not a serious man; but I always knew that the devil in me and the larger devil in him were very consequential figures indeed.

These pieces are otherwise about those displaced persons Joe McCarthy found and left behind. The tone here more often than not wants to be comic; perhaps that is excusable when we consider that the people moved by his memory are less important than the people who appease them and who are not comic. These are persons who believed .once that Harvey Matusow should speak on high school platforms and believed later that he should be in jail. But it was government and not these persons which put Harvey Matusow on the witness stand and then into jail.

I have covered these displaced persons so long that we have rather become friends and once or twice, at their meetings, I have been asked to autograph their programs by young candle-bearers who feel that their services would be as incomplete without me as without Archibald Roosevelt. I do not think this relationship reflects much credit on me as a serious man — or upon them as a serious movement — but there it is. But I must confess that I was rather more shamed by all the advertising men who used to tell me they admired my assaults on McCarthy and who kept "Red Channels" for insurance purposes in their desks.

Bad Day at the Track

One of Washington's premature springs, false and treacherous enough, no doubt, to need all the protection of the Fifth Amendment but delightful in its way, suffused the Capitol yesterday afternoon. Joe McCarthy slouched off the Senate subway, like a wounded fox with the press pack close on his unshined shoes.

His eyes dripped, his baldspot glowed with humid phosphorescence, the gasping tick in his throat sank from its normal pulse of hysteria and softened to sound like the hart panting for some running stream. Joe McCarthy had spring fever.

"It is a crime," he said, "to be inside on a day like this." He was a-weary, and he wanted to lie somewhere safe in the shade.

As he lingered beside the elevator, Senator Flanders (R-Vt.) came walking towards him; without a moment's unease, Joe McCarthy said, "Hi Ralph" and threw a blue-serge arm around the shoulder of this old man who had accused him of trying to wreck the Republican Party and had been commended by the President of the United States for same. Flanders giggled a little and said he was glad to see Joe, and they rode up together and McCarthy said, with a smile and a trickle in his throat, that he'd been looking up Flanders's record.

It was not one of Joe McCarthy's good days. The President slapped him, the normally quiescent members of his investigating committee spat at him, the wind was rising and the track had come up mud. This race had been run, and Joe McCarthy was tearing up his mutuel tickets. He'll be back at the $50 window with a big bundle as soon as he can find a scratch sheet.

No day when Washington is obsessed with conversation about Joe McCarthy could ever be considered a total loss by Joe McCarthy, but there were signs yesterday that the new turn in the discussion sat heavy on him. As he walked into his committee hearings he looked no more swarm-haunted than usual. But, before very long, his wounds began to ache, and he was railing at the absent Senator Jackson (D-Wash.) because some friend of the Republic had heard Jackson speak at a club and had reported a heretic observation that McCarthy's detectives hadn't come up with much but "warmed-over biscuits." Senator Symington (D-Mo.) intervened on Jackson's side and, in a moment, McCarthy was pounding his ash tray like a gavel and shouting that he was sick and tired.

The hearing, thereafter, became the usual shambles; Roy Cohn made a handsome effort to inject Albert Einstein into the Federal Communications Laboratory; but McCarthy's own boredom hung over it all like the raven over the infected house. Someone had slipped him a note about President Eisenhower's press conference. This meeting adjourned; he began the wearisome day-long process of "no comment" on the President's statement. He ran into Jackson on the elevator and said, "Hi Scoop," with that delinquent choirboy's smile. There would be no great confrontations this day.

He went to the Pentagon and lunch with C. E. Wilson, coming out to announce that what he had called twenty years of treason in the Army had only been twenty years of softness; the adjectives were paling in the spring. He returned to the Senate to confront a rumor that Senator Potter (R-Mich.) was demanding that Roy Cohn be served up as a human sacrifice to the gods of mischance. McCarthy and Potter left Symington alone to conduct their hearing and spent forty-five minutes in Joe's office and came out to say (Potter) that nothing would happen today and (McCarthy) that Roy Cohn's future was as "counsel to my committee."

While they talked, McCarthy sent a message to Symington to keep the hearing going as long as he could and that as a reward Joe would guarantee him the Wisconsin delegates to the next Democrat convention. It was a day for rare public distemper and consistent private accommodation.

His bad day at the track ended, McCarthy sat in his office talking to the reporters, wearily, abstractedly, like a loser on election night, not so much grim as drained of his emotional capital, half wondering if it is all worth it. It is not a sensation likely to survive the night; tomorrow the scratch sheets will come up, the mutuel window will open, and Joe will be standing there ready to shoot the roll again.

[Washington, D.C., March 11, 1954]

The Wild One

No one could ever accuse John G. Adams of burning in the night; the mysterious oil that lubricates our political system is his fuel. He is one of those eternal gatekeepers who bar the doors of gentility from the barbarian — the room clerk who riffles through a pile of irrelevant paper and says that he is sorry, but there's no room at the inn for you tonight, Mister. The floorwalker who sniffs that if moddom is not satisfied, she will have to see the manager.

He is nasty enough to his inferiors to assure you that he never departs the presence of a superior without shoe polish all over his chin. He is a diplomat of the sewer side of politics, and Robert T. Stevens obviously hired him on because he was a familiar of the shadow world of Joe McCarthy, Karl Mundt, and other powers of darkness.

But John Adams has burned for the last three weeks. He doesn't mind abasing himself to his betters; but ever since last September, he had been toadying to Roy Cohn; there are social degradations a floorwalker cannot forgive. He said once that he would happily go to jail if Roy Cohn was in the next cell.

And yesterday, John Adams tried to destroy Roy Cohn, who is plainly the only enemy who has ever aroused his lackey's passions. He regards Joe McCarthy and Frank Carr as reasonable professionals. But Cohn is, by his standards, a wild one, breaking all the rules.

The story he told yesterday may be read for years by social pathologists interested in case studies of what happens when a young man of untamed passions becomes involved in a situation otherwise peopled by professionals.

Adams said that, when Roy Cohn was refused admittance to a secret project at Fort Monmouth, he began pacing the floor, wringing his hands, screeching this is war and demanding a car to carry him from this scene of unbearable insult. It took Adams, as Counselor to the Army, along with a colonel and a major to quiet him down.

By contrast, Joe McCarthy met Robert Stevens two days after Stevens had said there was no espionage at Monmouth, and observed "jovially" that "you've just called me a liar." At the bit of reminiscence, Joe McCarthy threw back his head and showed his zircon teeth in an unashamed guffaw at the suggestion that it might have been an insult to call him a liar.

During one executive hearing on Monmouth, Roy Cohn kept running over to Adams and muttering what about Dave's thing? What about Dave's thing? When Adams protested to McCarthy himself, he was warned to watch out, don't get Cohn mad at you. After that appeal, Cohn told Adams that he'd show him what it means to go over my head. He was most obscene about it, Adams said, and Roy Cohn lowered his eyes over his putty cheeks like a novitiate.

On December 17, they all went to Gassner's in New York for lunch, and Cohn began screaming (1) at Adams for abusing Schine and (2) at McCarthy for not supporting his staff. Very violent even over the ice cream, said Adams. Afterwards, Roy offered to drive Adams to his train. As in transit, Cohn continued his abuse; McCarthy and Adams heard him in subdued silence. Finally at 48th Street, Cohn said get out and get there however you can; and poor Adams had to run through the Park Avenue traffic for a taxi to Penn Station. Later Frank Carr told him that Cohn had kicked Joe McCarthy out of the car at the Waldorf.

When Adams was forced to tell him that Dave Schine might be sent overseas, Cohn leaned back in his chair and said Stevens is through; we'll wreck the Army, and, as soon as Dave has left Monmouth, we're going to get General Ryan, too. But Joe McCarthy was always nice about it. One night he invited John Adams to his apartment and surfeited him with cheese (free-loaded from his constituents), and explained that Roy had to be kept happy because otherwise he might quit the committee. Frank Carr was equally sympathetic; he kept advising Adams to do something for Schine or else expect a war with Roy for the next two years; once he snuck off to the Methodist Restaurant to have lunch with Adams — he didn't want Roy to catch them together at the Carroll Arms, the bucket of blood most favored by the McCarthy staff — and suggested that George Sokolsky, the East Coast Dirksen, might be helpful.

Each time Adams remembered how often Carr and McCarthy had confessed that Roy Cohn was a wild man, McCarthy made repeated television-geared gestures of affection for Roy's shoulders. Adams's obvious sense was that McCarthy was a professional with whom he could live, but that Cohn was one of those customers the store could never satisfy.

To hear him was to wonder why McCarthy didn't fire Cohn long ago. The answer must be that McCarthy is a mental and moral sloven, and whatever order and system his committee has comes from Roy Cohn's passion. Adams's only mistake was to assume that a wild one is not essential to Joe McCarthy's scheme of things. For, if one unhappy adolescent's spleen can produce the stuff of headlines, that is after all what we are after, isn't it?

[Washington, D.C., May 13, 1954]

Private Lives

By the standards of Everett McKinley Dirksen an obscenity is a cuss word.

By those standards, if by no others, the McCarthy-Army hearings were washed pure yesterday. Musty with delay, various telephone talks between Senators, McCarthy bravoes, the Secretary of the Army and his counsel, John Adams, were snuffled into the record by Ray Jenkins and other hot-potato-mouthed middle Southerners.

There had been general reports that those telephone calls were full of indelicacies, but they were puny stuff indeed. Even so, Jenkins, the Knoxville uplifter, laundered them with such moral passion as, on one occasion, to change the word "hell" to "devil."

Sometimes in the middle of these rites, Dirksen intervened to lubricate that, despite all previous testimony, he was relieved to hear that nothing in the telephone calls indicated either "indelicate language" or "vituperation." But in every sense but the Dirksen sense, those calls were obscene. They would have been unfit for the ears of children if they had been rewritten by the authors of the Book of Common Prayer.

In their course, the Army proved a great part of its case against Roy Cohn, out of the lips of his boss, Joe McCarthy, and his associate, Frank Carr. It was not a clear-cut proof and it was somewhat shadowed by the fact that McCarthy proved no small bit of his case against the Army, too.

For, after those calls, read to a drowsy hearing room in droning voices, there seemed little reason to question these assumptions:

(1) On October 21, Robert Stevens called David Schine to report that the Secretary of the Army and the Secretary of Defense had a deal cooking for Dave if only he would condescend to take basic training. This was just six days after poor Stevens says he told Schine that if he didn't pull his military service without fear or favor, "he would regret it the rest of his life." If Roy Cohn ever screeched that Stevens had double-crossed him, he would appear to have a point.

(2) In September, when Schine stood in peril of following Commando Kelly into the uniform of a private soldier, Roy Cohn clouded his allegiance to Joe McCarthy by repeated tenders of kindness to Stevens and the Army. At one crisis in Cohn's appeasement of Stevens, he told the Secretary that he would stick by a particular deal "regardless of Joe or anyone else." Once Cohn complained that, in one matter where he was trying to get the heat off Stevens, McCarthy had made a speech with his "usual string of adjectives." But, said Roy, "Don't worry about it."

(3) On November 7, McCarthy certified to Stevens that Cohn was "completely unreasonable" about Schine. "That," Stevens replied, "is where my problem has come right from the start." McCarthy suggested that the Secretary get Schine a few weekends, so "his girl friends won't be lonesome."

(4) In early March, when nobody was supposed to be speaking to anybody else, those two plastic characters, Frank Carr and John Adams, joked about how Schine had goofed off at Fort Dix. Adams told Carr that there was a chance that Schine, now reformed, might get into leadership training school at Camp Gordon. They agreed that Carr shouldn't tell Cohn until that was certainty; otherwise he would pester them and, in Adams's words, "blow the roof off the building."

In that long gone October, Roy Cohn and Robert Stevens were "working together 100 per cent." Cohn had saved Major-General Richard Partridge, the chief of Army Intelligence, from an embarrassing confrontation by the McCarthy committee. He accomplished that rescue once by suspending hearings in favor of a rehearsal of McCarthy's wedding. On October 28, Stevens told Cohn how he had trundled over to the Central Intelligence Agency to ask Allen Dulles about a place for Schine. ("Nice of you." — Cohn.) There were some "unusual things" he might do for Schine, Stevens said.

After that tender, Cohn told Stevens that McCarthy was talking about investigating the Army loyalty boards. Cohn said that it was just like the "Partridge thing"; don't worry about it.

On February 25, when the bloom was off all these peaches, the Army's John Adams began calling McCarthy's Frank Carr. They are not light fellows, and there was a deal of heavy badinage about who was tapping whose wire. (Adams was tapping Carr's.) On March 5, Adams told Carr that "something's happened to Dave." He's becoming a "good soldier."

Carr said he guessed Schine was "being discreet." Adams said that Schine had even given up his Cadillac and bought a secondhand Chevvy in Augusta, Georgia. They agreed that such was the way he should have behaved at Dix.

There was a chance that Schine might be in line for warrant officer. "Don't tell Roy," said Carr, and Adams said he wouldn't. They parted on March 8 with this tag on the script — Carr: "It's up to you, boy . . . it's my last offer, friend."

Roy Cohn says he is sure that Dave Schine was sitting up with a hot document on New Year's Eve and all those other nights he was on pass from Dix. Even Joe McCarthy and Frank Carr, on their own testimony, do not appear to believe Roy. Cohn is a little young for the experience of treason but Joe McCarthy is fat and balding with it.

And so there is no reason to believe that McCarthy was shocked to learn that Roy Cohn, one of the two finest young men in America, was making deals behind his back with the Secretary of the Army, and that Frank Carr, the other, was sneaking off to secret lunches at the Methodist Building with John Adams. They walk alone these boys, and there are rusty razor blades in all the beds in which they sleep together.

The long mumble from the depths of the sewer was almost at its end when they read a conversation in which John Adams told Frank Carr that either McCarthy or Cohn had relayed to J. Edgar Hoover some Adams crack indicating insufficient reverence for the FBI. Please, Frank, said Adams, if you see Hoover, tell him I'm a good American.

We should, I suppose, all be grateful that our children were protected and nothing in those transcripts was read over the air that might seem disgusting to Everett McKinley Dirksen. They were pure in word and rotten only at the core. It was left to Frank Carr to sum up the moral worth of all parties when he was trying to think of a private place to have lunch with John Adams. Let's go visit the Methodists, said Carr: "Nobody goes there."

[Washington, D.C., June 8, 1954]

Army Witness

Roy Cohn had almost run his course yesterday afternoon. He had run it well. He had lost a few feathers; no one in his right mind could now believe that David Schine had ever done any serious business in his life inside or outside the Army.

But no one cared much either. Joseph N. Welch had done some damage to Cohn and Schine. He had torn to tatters on television the paltry folder which Cohn described as David Schine's work record while he was away from Fort Dix saving the republic. He had run through the bills at all the restaurants where Dave and Roy had relaxed from the watch tower.

Welch had been sharp and deft and graceful, and he had done some damage; there was a moment when Joe McCarthy got up and walked out, which is always a sign that they are close to his neck. But it was not fatal; this had all gone on too long for anyone really to be very stirred by the petty sins of David Schine. Welch seemed a little tired; and Roy Cohn seemed almost home.

They were fencing, almost friends from so long a conflict, about why Cohn and McCarthy are accustomed to sit upon what they describe as evidence of immediate Communist peril until it is convenient for the fabrication of headlines. Welch expressed the hope, gentle and sardonic, that, whenever Cohn finds a Communist in a sensitive spot, he hurry up a little.

And then Joe McCarthy asked the chair's attention. He had a thing to say, an inconsequential thing, a passing flourish of tactics, a trick in the game. He was smiling as he began, and he smiled off and on throughout what he had to say. It was almost as though he were telling a joke.

He would like, he said silkily, to help Mr. Welch. He could give him the name of someone serving the Communist cause and still at large, still in fact in Welch's own law firm of Hale and Dorr. He is a young man named Fisher, who had been a member of the National Lawyers' Guild, "the legal bulwark of the Communist Party." Welch had tried to bring him down to Washington to help the Army's case. McCarthy went on, smiling and snarling; Roy Cohn shook his head, but McCarthy went on.

He has after all done that sort of thing day after day ever since he came up dank from the sewer four-and-a-half years ago. When he had finished, Joseph Welch began a sentence, "Senator McCarthy, I did not know until this moment —" and McCarthy interrupted him to turn and call upon Jim Juliana to produce the proper citations. Then Joseph Welch was allowed to continue.

"Until this moment, Senator, I think I never really gauged your cruelty and your recklessness."

Welch went on to talk about Fred Fisher and his hopes for his future as a lawyer. He said that he had brought Fisher down to Washington to begin the Army's case, and that at dinner the first night, he said to his assistants, "Boys, I don't know anything about you except that I like you, but, if there is anything funny in the life of either one of you, you speak up quick."

And Fred Fisher had said that he was a Republican now but that in law school he had belonged to the Lawyers' Guild. Then Joe Welch had told him that he had better go home.

"Little did I dream you could be so reckless and so cruel as to do any injury to that lad . . . I like to think that I am a gentle man, but your" — there was a pause — "forgiveness must come from someone else."

Roy Cohn sat there and shook his head. He shook for reasons deeper than a simple warning to McCarthy, because Roy Cohn was all alone, and his shock was over something more hideous than a blunder in tactics. Joe McCarthy was naked at that moment, and no man who ever clasped his hand and laughed with him could escape the sense that he had at that moment bathed himself in filth.

Roy Cohn had said that morning that Joe McCarthy is "a very good Senator," and Everett Dirksen had expressed a wish for ten minutes to praise the junior Senator from Wisconsin. There were no men in all that room who looked as stripped of every illusion they have ever held about themselves as Cohn and Dirksen; they will be back as though it had never happened today, but they have known, if only for a little while, what it will be to go to hell.

But Joe McCarthy went on sneering and snarling, alone as animals are alone and unconscious that he had done an evil thing. He ravened about the Lawyers' Guild until Joe Welch said: "You've done enough, Senator. Have you no sense of decency? At long last, have you no decency left?" McCarthy sneered about decency, and Welch said he would discuss Fisher no more. "If there is a God in Heaven, it will do you and your cause no further good." He would let Cohn go; let the chairman call the next witness.

There was a silence for perhaps ten seconds. And then people began to applaud. You can only measure what that applause meant when you knew that two press photographers were clapping, and I have never believed before that a press photographer cared whether any subject lived or died.

There was a recess, Joe McCarthy and his wife came out, and they were by themselves, as though all the people who cluster around them on these occasions expected the devil to come and snatch McCarthy away and were afraid to get too close. Where Roy Cohn went, no one can say. Only Joe McCarthy did not know what he had done. Once he spread his hands and giggled to show he could not understand the look on the faces around him.

He said afterwards that Joe Welch had put something over on him. Joe Welch did not care about that. He had ceased long ago to be a lawyer and, through everything he said, he had very plainly seen nothing but the face of Fred Fisher and his family in Newton, Massachusetts. He walked through the corridors, alone by choice and grieving for Fisher. He said once that he could take care of himself, but who could take care of his friends?

There were those, when the shock passed, who said that McCarthy had shown himself to all America as his worst enemy could never show him. There was a sense that those whom the gods would destroy, they give ten minutes for a statement. But Welch did not care about tactics; after the recess, he walked late into the hearing room, and sat with his pain-stricken eyes focused on nothing, unable to look at McCarthy. It does not seem possible that he can bring himself to cross-examine this man. The great case has ended for him.

It had ended for all of us I think; nothing else can happen now. The Army, stumbling, tired and shadowed, has been handed its best witness; his name was Joseph R. McCarthy. But the difference between Joe McCarthy and Joe Welch, two sons of poor farmers, is that Joe Welch would not choose to win a case at the price not of a friend but of a young man who is only a casual acquaintance. Welch had pulled a coup, and he was sick at heart. He could not bear the knowledge that the gods had chosen to destroy Joe McCarthy by sacrificing Fred Fisher.

In front of Joe Welch's sightless eyes, the Republicans were restoring the tableau. Roy Cohn, having thrown up in some secret corner of his soul, was back sitting beside McCarthy and coaching him. Ray Jenkins leaned forward to ask McCarthy to explain what us parents could do at home and hearth to teach our children how to save the American tradition.

McCarthy was desperately reclothing his scrofulous dead white self, a little while ago so naked; and Ray Jenkins was telling us all to rest awhile and listen to Joe McCarthy telling us how to raise our kids.

[Washington, D.C., May 1, 1954]

Duty

Back in the Twenties, at a low point of fashion for the combat soldier, Aldous Huxley observed that the dictionaries classify the word "intelligence" under two categories. They recognize, he noted, "intelligence, human" and then they recognize "intelligence, military."

Brigadier General Ralph Zwicker has a professional appreciation of the difference between military intelligence and human intelligence. He lives by a code which, to employ a word he favors, "delimits" notions of judgment. He was a hero in World War II because he stood and held against the odds in the Bulge. He would be the first to say that he was only acting under orders. He is a soldier of the book; he would die under orders. It is not inconceivable that he would also lie under orders.

We have had reason to be grateful to the copy-book soldier in the past; the enemies of Joe McCarthy have reason to be grateful to Ralph Zwicker now. For he is the rock upon which McCarthy broke.

McCarthy has been ebbing and falling ever since last February 18, when he assaulted Zwicker at one of his fire dances. Yesterday, at the end of a censure hearing that has been going badly for him, McCarthy's counsel, Edward Williams, made a desperate effort to grab the bundle by bringing Zwicker down and again he stood like a rock.

Last February, McCarthy had fought without success for two hours to get Zwicker to say who in the Department of the Army had ordered him to give an honorable discharge to Major Irving Peress, the Queens dentist who refused to say under oath whether he was or wasn't a Communist. Near the end, McCarthy had ravened that Zwicker was unfit to wear his uniform and threatened to put him on public display as a symbol of incompetence. Yesterday, Zwicker rehearsed the testimony which had led up to McCarthy's murkiest hour — narrowly, patiently, defining his duty in that soft, fogbound verbiage which is the occupational cloak of the modern Brigadier General.

George Patton appears to be the last American officer of general grade to function in four-letter Anglo-Saxon words. Zwicker's vocabulary is at once foggy and surprisingly precise; he does not "define," he "delimits"; he does not "use," he "employs"; he does not "describe," he "delineates"; he is firm in the soggiest words in the language.

This was the manner which Joe McCarthy described as the most arrogant, evasive and irritating he had ever known in a witness. And, when it was over, the source of McCarthy's fatal irritation remained unspoken. Nothing Zwicker looked or said explained it; the answer was below the surface: McCarthy had expected this rule-book soldier to mutiny and Zwicker had incited him most by loyalty. For the man who had brought McCarthy down should have been his friend and not an enemy target.

In August of 1953, Zwicker had taken command of Camp Kilmer. He had seen Peress's security file and been disturbed by it. In November of 1953, in accordance with an act extorted from Congress by the

American Medical Association, Peress had been automatically promoted to major and Zwicker had been disturbed by that.

Last January 23, C. George Anastos, a McCarthy committee investigator, called Zwicker to ask him about "a medical officer in your command who appears to have Communist connections." An hour later, Zwicker called Anastos back to say that the officer in question was apparently Peress, and that the information in his file indicated that Peress had been a Communist organizer, had a Communist wife, and last August had refused to answer questions on his loyalty questionnaire.

Anastos's testimony would indicate that, when he called, the McCarthy skulk did not even know Peress's name, and that its first solid information came from Zwicker. The day after Anastos called, the Department of the Army wrote Zwicker ordering an honorable discharge for Peress.

Zwicker said yesterday that he had "emphatic" opinions about Peress's right to an honorable discharge; he would not say what they were, but it seems safe to assume that he did not consider the order a blow against the witch hunters. In February, James Juliana, another McCarthy staff worker, went to see Zwicker; he seems to have reported back to Roy Cohn that the general was aroused and indignant.

So if McCarthy was briefed at all the day he first faced Zwicker, his aides must have told him that here was a friendly witness. For up to this point, Zwicker seems to have conducted himself in accordance with the traditions of McCarthy's good American underground. McCarthy must have expected nothing worse than personal evasion of responsibility and expression of the pious hope that the men guilty of this particular treason be brought to book.

But Zwicker had his orders and he chose to stand upon them, whatever the cost to himself. He had talked too much about Peress once; he would talk no more. He took the rap, calmly and coolly, because this is the duty of the copy-book soldier. McCarthy knew, or should have known, that Zwicker was exempt from any charge of kindness to Peress. But he was not seeking the guilty; he wanted only obeisance to himself from the innocent. The "arrogance" of Ralph Zwicker came down at the end to his acceptance of the chain of command and the orders of his superiors.

If he had said that he had to protect his own skin, McCarthy would have been gentle with him. The irritation was in his reference to orders; the arrogance was in his concept of a duty to someone except Joe McCarthy.

And so McCarthy visited upon Zwicker language he never used on Irving Peress. And, when it was over, Zwicker is reported to have observed that he had not before understood what McCarthy was all about. Joe McCarthy had been engaged in a great insurrection against the civil and military authority of the United States. The sin of his potential friend, Ralph Zwicker, was refusal to join McCarthy's mutiny.

Yesterday, McCarthy sat silent and sodden while Edward Williams tried to sully the image of Ralph Zwicker before his judges. Zwicker stood his ground stubbornly, replying in his fogbound verbiage; and, at every crisis, there was a sense that he was not dancing away for planting his feet. At the end, Ralph Zwicker arose, now eligible for his orders, which are to Korea.

Joe McCarthy was left, here behind, to await the new turns in his downward slide. McCarthy has defended his every infamy by saying that it was necessary to the preservation of the primary values of loyalty and duty. It is one of those ironies which history enjoys. That, if he is defeated and alone today, it is most of all thanks to a rule-book soldier who lives by the unfashionable virtues and no word but duty.

[Washington, D.C., September 14, 1954]

On and On and On

The McCarthy battalions descended upon Washington yesterday. There were pictures in the papers of their New York masses — 559 in all — trooping into the trains and it was impossible not to remember the Reverend Harry F. Ward and Howard Fast embarking on some Communist sortie to stop the Fascist horde.

They were around the corridors of the Senate all day. There were the usual empty rumors of violence; a high source said that there were ten Wisconsin lumberjacks waiting to smite any bolo who might threaten the Republic, but nothing happened.

They were an orderly and peaceful crew. A woman was reported to have fainted after gasping that she had touched Joe McCarthy and the Cossack forces stripped them of their "God Bless McCarthy" stickers without resistance. They had come to mourn and not to fight.

They ended up at Constitution Hall, where they had announced readiness for an overflow and where in point of fact some 350 seats remained empty all evening. To them, came Joe McCarthy as manna very late at night, quite gone as to flesh and looking altogether like a mole with the mange.

He leaned over them and said in his choked, low-registered scream:

"Regardless — and I make you this solemn promise — the fight will go on and on and on."

They tossed and shouted and waved their little American flags and their "For McCarthy, For America" posters and one of them swung a placard bearing the strange device "Give McCarthy What He Deserves: the Congressional Medal of Honor."

They are a party of memory and endurance. Rabbi Benjamin Schultz, the master of their rites, disinterred more often than he introduced. He found poor Ham Fish somewhere in the audience, and he made them roar for the ghost of Burton K. Wheeler in the back of the hall.

Westbrook Pegler was there, and they yelled so loud for him that Peg came to the microphone, his face touched by love, and growled his blessing which was that he wanted to know who promoted Peress.

Schultz introduced a fresh corpse in that "Midwestern hero, Representative Fred Busbey" foully murdered by the voters of Illinois last November 2, and they shouted as for a conqueror.

The McCarthy people are like all sects; they do not mourn their dead but greet them with glad cries of recognition.

Rabbi Schultz said that this was a great outpouring of grass-roots-America. The grass-roots Americans had upon them the dust of a thousand Roy Cohn dinners; there was the president of the Ancient Order of Hibernians, and that Minute Woman from Texas, and the Honorable Karl Mundt and Vivian Kellems and a man from the Chicago Committee to Fight Communism. There was Robert M. Harriss, of Queens, who claims to have been habitually defamed by the Anti-Defamation League and who, according to Rabbi Schultz, is devoting his declining years to interfaith work.

There were also a dozen people who were parents of men still missing in Korea and who wore blue ribbons across their chests attesting their loss. Rabbi Schultz brought numbers of them to the microphone and they all said that only Joe McCarthy had promised to bring their boys home.

One of the mothers said that she had gone to the UN to seek action to find her boy and that the UN had treated her like a spy. Rabbi Schultz smiled and the audience laughed.

A father of a missing soldier from Georgetown, Delaware, was asked by Rabbi Schultz who he thought was his friend in Washington and he said Joe McCarthy. He went back to sit down and then arose and told the audience not to forget that the UN is a cesspool of traitors and Communists. That knowledge, said Rabbi Schultz, was born of suffering.

Rabbi Schultz ceased his parade of corpses and introduced the speaker of the evening, the occasionally Honorable Herman Welker of Idaho. Welker is a man with an expression of habitual affront; he spoke for an hour and ten minutes.

He said he had been sitting in his little office in Idaho in 1950 and God had put in his hands the *Congressional Record* and he read there what Bill Jenner had said to Millard Tydings and he had said to himself that, regardless of personal sacrifice, he would go to Washington and be a Senator like Bill Jenner.

No man ever made out a better case against general circulation of the *Congressional Record*.

Welker was reminded that George Washington had once had to deal with a general who was a traitor and voices all over began shouting back "Zwicker." When did it all begin, he asked; and the voices shouted back that it had begun when they got Ham Fish.

Welker said that Martin Dies had been crucified too. And that it had really all begun with a man named William Wirt, who went to dinner in Washington in 1934 and was grievously insulted by a bunch of Communists.

By now, Ben Schultz was rushing around the stage and fluttering over the imminence of Joe McCarthy. McCarthy came in, and the crowd stood up and sought the sight of him, and Welker was suddenly all alone at the podium.

So Welker read the Psalm which begins "The Lord is my Shepherd," and Schultz gave McCarthy another plaque. McCarthy stood up and was cheered for a minute. He turned and gestured towards the women with their blue ribbons and apologized for opening up an old wound. "I hate," he said, "doing this but they must be described as the victims of massive appeasement."

One of the mothers cried all by herself. Joe McCarthy turned from them and said that what he had seen for the last two days made him sick down deep inside, and the crowd greeted that old familiar phrase as though Sophie Tucker had started on "Some of These Days."

McCarthy said he was oppressed by men of little minds and even less morals, but he was sustained by the knowledge that there is a God and every man has a soul.

When he finished, a young man named Vince Matthais — a sort of blend of Dave Schine and William F. Buckley — sang the song which goes "Nobody Loves McCarthy But the People, and We Just Love Our Joe," and we were back in the Wallace campaign. Rabbi Schultz said it was time to go home; there would be no resolutions.

"Joe McCarthy is our resolution. We're going home," he said; "we're going to write and telegraph; and we're going to have rallies like this in every town in this great land." Not with this customer, Schultz, not with this one.

[Washington, D.C., November 12, 1954]

The Big Change

The sun goes down upon the same man upon whom it rose not so long ago; we are the same people at our ends that we were at our beginnings.

Joe McCarthy crossed the shadow line yesterday; the American Senator, as institution and individual, crossed it with him. Each made the passage in character and each seemed to do what would be expected of him.

The Honorable Herman Welker bawled near the end that he had misunderstood the parliamentarian. Everett McKinley Dirksen trickled that there were only twenty-two days of forgiveness left until Christmas and that the "great sales manager of the faith, Paul of Tarsus" would counsel forebearance at this season of the herald angels.

The Honorable Styles Bridges sat all morning in the office of the

Honorable Richard Nixon conjuring up deals which turned to smoke before they left his bottle. The Honorable William Knowland climbed solemnly on board the sinking ship and met the Honorable Francis Case departing it. The Honorable Alexander Smith and Honorable Leverett Saltonstall huddled and trembled together, two aspen trees no longer able to pose as oaks, and cast the vote to censure they had forestalled so long.

Joe McCarthy stayed off the floor most of the day. He came in, still dripping contempt of his fellows, only after he had lost the first test vote wearing his arm in a sling that was like the rest of him, somehow all out of proportion and expending enough gauze to wrap a mummy.

He proposed, it seemed, to go on as he always had. He asked for two minutes and took four. Then he asked for thirty seconds and took a minute. He had much to do, he said, and must return to the sentry box at once; having proclaimed the emergency, loafed an hour upon the floor, and departed only when Welker said he must be in great pain.

He held in his hand a set of documents which he said proved that the Senate subcommittee that investigated him in 1952 had asked the Post Office Department to check the mail coming to a special McCarthy box in Kensington, Maryland, for evidence that he was playing the market with funds given him to fight communism. This was an illegal action, he said, and "somebody forged" the signature of Committee Chairman Gillette on the letter requesting the mail check. "We should put the proper persons under oath . . . We should call the staff of the Watkins Committee to find out about the suppression of this evidence."

This concerns, he said, the dignity of the Senate. "It makes me a little ill to hear what some of my colleagues have to say about dignity . . . We have gone through this farce to a point where I think the Senate is disgraced . . . (let us) get rid of this foul job and get back to work."

It was the customary diversion and the old language, and for just a little while he reeked the illusion of the old magic. Then John Stennis shouted a request for the regular order, and Karl Mundt rose on cue to suggest that there must be a middle way. McCarthy went over to talk to Knowland and crooked his finger to summon Lyndon Johnson, the minority leader; and Johnson came to the call. McCarthy was beaten and dying; but custom and habit can outlive reality.

The only proper medical examiner to certify the death of a politician is another politician. McCarthy had hoped for thirty-three votes in the last ditch; he got twenty. He lost every doubtful. Every Democrat, from Eastland to Lehman, joined to condemn him; and the Republican vote was twenty-two to twenty against him. Six of the eight Catholics in the Senate voted for censure, which ought to take care of that subject. Men who had feared for years to call against him the verdict of principle called against him now the verdict of expediency.

Only Welker said (dared now to say) that McCarthy was a man who deserved the gratitude of the Republic. The case for the defense was a confession of guilt. Dirksen observed, in the Christmas spirit, that "Joe McCarthy is something of an alley fighter." Mundt argued only that, "in spite of himself," McCarthy has become a symbol of opposition to communism. Even the friends of Joe McCarthy conceded that he was a dirty fellow and a bit of a fraud.

Everyone played himself to the end, and it was possible to look upon Dirksen shining like some damp and decaying bit of phosphorus in the swamp, and entertain the illusion that his long-deferred hour of judgment was not very important after all. But that illusion did not survive the moment when Arthur Watkins stood up to summarize for the prosecution.

He was thin and tired and his perspective may have been fogged by grievous pounding from such as Knowland, and Nixon and Bridges. He talked like a man who expected to lose, because what he was after was Republican votes; he wanted to beat Knowland and Bridges on their own ground. And Arthur Watkins said a thing which no liberal on the floor of the Senate has dared for five years.

He was talking about Ralph Zwicker and what McCarthy had done to him. He said that Zwicker was a wartime hero, and suddenly he was wondering aloud whether the principle was any different if he hadn't been. "We were given the power to investigate, not to try men and to blast them and to pillory them before the whole world." After all, said Watkins, the Senate protects its dignity best when it protects the ordinary citizen.

"The ordinary citizen of the United States has the right to claim the protection of the Fifth Amendment and we haven't any right to damn him for claiming the protections of the Constitution," he said.

Arthur Watkins, who was an ordinary Senator when he began to run his course with Joe McCarthy, will never be that again. The Senate seemed as it always had yesterday, but, if he has changed, it must have changed, too, more than we can yet assay. No man who lives in this country all his life can do it undiluted harm; and we can thank McCarthy at least for the education of Arthur Watkins, which is no little thing.

[Washington, D.C., December 2, 1954]

Kid Nickels

Harvey Matusow tells us that, in 1936, when he was still a little boy, his father used to draft him for service in the cigar store downtown. It was one of his duties to go to the box office of the theater next door and pick up rolls of nickels for change at the pinball machines. Around the theater they called him "Kid Nickels."

He never earned a nickname embodying a higher denomination. He joined the Communist Party in the Bronx in 1947, mainly because he was tired of hanging around street corners. For a while, thereafter, he made his living from that experience, but it cannot have been very important to him or he to it.

When the Party announced his expulsion in 1951, the *Daily Worker* could not even spell his name right.

At the time of his expulsion, Harvey Matusow was serving the FBI for $70 a month as an undercover informant. After his expulsion he went back into uniform and was sent to Dayton, Ohio, where he moldered as a security risk. There he decided to escape by way of the Un-American Activities Committee.

The committee was interested enough to fly an investigator out to see him. Harvey Matusow knew that the ground of disenchantment had been pretty well worked over by now, but he thought he had a new furrow to plough. He would be the expert witness on the Communist plot to subvert our children.

He went to Washington and testified; after that the Air Force gave him his discharge, and he went back to Dayton and $300 a month as a staff member of the Ohio Un-American Activities Commission.

The Un-American Activities Committee called him back to Washington in February, 1952. He opened headquarters at the Hotel Congressional and summoned the buyers from the Hearst Corporation. He says that Jack Clements, now publisher of the *American Mercury*, agreed that youth was a proper gimmick. The gimmick having worked, he went to New York and had his story done, complete to the picture of him kissing his mother, and then he flew off to Washington and the big stage.

On the great day, he was shocked to find that the death of King George VI of England had knocked his story off page one. "What a break for me," he wrote in his diary, "the King had to die on my day of 'triumph.' Pushed me right off the front page."

But the story he told had to make a few headlines — because there was sex in it. He told of wild parties at his Communist youth club. And hanky panky at Camp Unity. A *Daily News* editorial said that his reports on the Party's undercover social life "pose a new light on the brutishly immoral and completely conscienceless strategies of the Red traitors."

That qualified him as an expert. The *New York Times* paid him $300 for an affidavit swearing that Communists had fomented the 1949 student strikes. The New York City Board of Education paid him $250 for ten days' investigation of Communist teachers. To protect the Board he sold it a $24-a-year subscription to *Counterattack*, taking for himself a $9 commission. He was still "Kid Nickels."

When he favored the McCarran Committee with some tattered documents on the Communist plot against the Boy Scouts, Chief Scout Executive Arthur A. Schick alerted every cub pack to be "eternally vigilant." Harvey called up the Yankees fourteen times, using different voices, and finally bludgeoned them into taking Yogi Berra off a television program with a leftist actor. He spent the fall of 1952 as a speaker for the Republican Senate campaign.

With all this, he never made much more than nickels. It will be said that he is a punk of small importance and hardly a reliable witness. No one said such a thing when he was testifying against Communists; they only say it when you quit the mob.

Harvey Matusow did not meet Joe McCarthy until the summer of 1952. There is no indication that McCarthy ever took him very seriously except in public. It is a mark of the Joe McCarthys that they don't drink the stuff they sell.

But, if McCarthy were not otherwise a dedicated man, it would be impossible to read Matusow's recollections of their brief span together without hearing over and over again the voice of a numbers runner talking about the big boss.

Matusow does recall one serious moment after the elections when he claims that McCarthy told him there wouldn't be enough jails to hold all the people he was out to get. That sounds like apocrypha dictated by Matusow's recent assumption of the exterior of a left liberal.

But there is a Joe McCarthy in Matusow's memory who reeks with artistic credibility. It is the McCarthy who swore that he would never talk to a *Time* reporter because one such jackal had accused him in print of serving warm drinks. It is the McCarthy who Matusow says, threw him a big bill and said, "Go buy yourself a new suit."

It is the McCarthy who played wild Wisconsin card games all night, sent Harvey out in the street for drinks for the whole party, and stood up after everyone had gone home and said, "I'll show you my scar for a quarter." Matusow said he gave him the quarter and McCarthy showed him a scar which seemed almost to cut him in two.

This is an engaging McCarthy, a great rogue sitting out the night while his doctor pleaded with him to go to bed and then bouncing off to his wars again on three hours of sleep. But no one could say that here was a man who believed, right up to and including the moment he inscribed his book to "Harvey Matusow, a great American."

When McCarthy had won his primary, he gave Harvey to other beleaguered Republican Senators, Arthur Watkins in Utah, Harry Cain in Washington, Zale Ecton in Montana.

The entire student body of Pocatello High School sat for two hours and heard this juvenile delinquent explain the Communist peril in teenage terms. In Great Falls, Montana, Harvey made $50 plugging an anti-Communist movie in a drive-in theater. He made $1,000 speaking for Ecton. On election night he went to Washington and got drunk at the big colonial house of Mrs. Arvilla Bentley, who had an oil portrait of Joe McCarthy in her great hall. She later became Mrs. Matusow.

She took him to the Virgin Islands and paid his bills and married him. He took her to Texas, where he talked to the Rangers on how to spot a Communist. He told them that, off-guard, the underground Communist sometimes betrays himself by humming or whistling a revolutionary anthem. He hummed a few such into a recording tape which is still, I'm sure, in the Rangers' files.

Texas paid him $25 a day as an expert witness and nights he worked as a comedian in a Juarez ginmill. By now, McCarthy and the new Mrs. Matusow were privately disenchanted, although publicly McCarthy used him as a witness and commissioned him to investigate Communist influence in the press. After a while, he lost the faith he never had, a process he describes in a sort of wild parody of Whittaker Chambers's very real interior struggle, and now he is a counter-witness witness.

His was the life of a petty hustler, and the patriots presented him to us as a prophet worthy of the compulsory attention of high school students. He was able to make anti-Communism a racket, and to practice it unashamedly in the presence of Joe McCarthy, who was then its high priest.

His old friends tell us now that he is a liar, and psychopath. The Communists used to say, and not always without reason, the same thing about their apostates, because they wanted to distract our attention from themselves.

[February 8, 1955]

What Harvey Did

The Senate Internal Security Subcommittee apparently proposes to spend the next two years following up its suspicion that Harvey Matusow has got himself involved with Communists. Senator Eastland (D-Miss.), the committee's chairman, is a man so expert in the domestic conspiracy that he describes Communists as "Markits."

He can save us all a lot of money by stopping now. Of course, Matusow has thrown in with the Communists. He has a pro-Communist publisher. The Communists rejoice as none of the rest of us can in his disclosures. Before he came home to them, Matusow tried to peddle his story to four or five respectable publishing houses, all of which turned him down. It seemed inevitable that he would end up with the Commies, and I for one am glad he did.

I cannot think where else he could have done what he has done as thoroughly and as shockingly as he has done it in the last few weeks.

Domestic anti-Communism has an old and honorable history in the United States. In the last five years, it has become, when least malevolent, the flagellation of dead horses. Worse than that, it has become, on every level, a war on the weak and their children. Throughout the Fifties, as the American Communists have grown steadily weaker, their enemies in every camp have become more violent, more cruel and more irresponsible.

As an organized political group, the Communists have done nothing to damage our society a fraction as much as what their enemies have done in the name of defending us against subversion. The authors of this damage are named Harry Truman as well as Joe McCarthy. They are, if you please, you and I even to the extent that we simply kept quiet and rode with the times. There are few Americans who have no part in this shame and no hostage to the policy which produced it. It is a thing which has infected our whole society.

Comes now Harvey Matusow peddling his memories. Who can buy them all? For remember, Matusow's memory is flexible, but his documents are immutable. And the most damaging and most terrifying of those documents were written and signed not by Joe McCarthy but by respectable and decent men who, if they are not ourselves, could be our image.

Superintendent of Schools William Jansen wrote Matusow an abject letter begging him to go on the Board of Education payroll as an expert on Communist teachers. A representative of the Columbia Broadcasting System weighed in with an equally craven document apologizing for the use of a pro-Communist comedian on the Godfrey show and promising that it would never happen again.

Jansen is a liberal and CBS is the only network which stood up against McCarthy, even for a little while. They are not the worst of our society; in most ways, they are the best. To read those letters is to catch the scent of a national disease; it is to watch decent men running from the bullies; and I don't know publishers except Cameron and Kahn who could have afforded to print them.

And, thanks to Matusow, we are debating for the first time the techniques Harry Truman's Justice Department employed in order to send Communists to jail. The Smith Act trials rested on the proposition that the writings and speeches of Communist Party leaders were dangerous to our national safety because they could inflame the populace to armed revolution. This was nonsense on its face; and, to convict them, we had to substitute a malignant fantasy for reality.

We had to go even further. We could not even prove that the defendants had uttered the key words which, as the myth had it, would have triggered the assault on City Hall without using witnesses like Matusow who were anxious to invent the quotations as needed. The Smith Act trials rested on a fantasy which itself could only be sustained by a little lie.

And the script for that fantasy was written, not by Joe McCarthy, but by Harry Truman and J. Edgar Hoover. None of us could have done what Matusow has; each of us to a degree shared the sickness that made him possible. Only the Communists were outsiders and could have pointed out what we have become. Only a liar could tell us the truth about ourselves, and only our enemies could show us the disease which was destroying our way of life.

[March 9, 1955]

Until Sundown

I often forget, in my harsh, cruel way, that New York is a city of lonely people, and that I am paid to make them my sport, and that this is not a very honorable way to make a living.

That defacement of loneliness is especially conspicuous here this week because the Un-American Activities Committee is in town working over bones in the desert. Its victims, such of them as it can find, are thus made lonely, of course. But the committee is lonely too. It is not loved, and less and less can it hope for even that dreary substitute for love, the illusion that you are feared.

Yesterday, Aware Inc., "the anti-Communist organization in entertainment, communications, and the fine arts," held a reception to welcome the Un-American Activities Committee at the Sheraton-

McAlpin. It was part of a series of regular renewals of the spirit of Emma Goldman and Sascha Berkman which Aware offers under the general title: "Cocktails Against Communism."

The guests of honor were Representative Gordon Scherer; Representative William M. Tuck; staff director Richard Arens; Don Appell, visiting investigator, and Dolores Scotti, the committee's resident mandrake root. William M. Tuck is a former governor of Virginia, by appointment of Harry F. Byrd, that commonwealth's Trujillo.

Former Governor Tuck walked about saying vaguely to the attendant ladies that they all seemed to him like nice Southern girls, and then he went home early. He does not, of course, know why he is here; and if, because of the likes of him, some poor flautist is driven off the "The Telephone Hour" after today you cannot even say that William M. Tuck knew what he was doing. These are careless people.

There were perhaps a hundred persons there. A visitor, conscript, wandered among them, and, every now and then, the counter-revolutionary juices would beat in his veins so loud that it seemed impossible that they could not be heard in the room, and he would do his duty for his country by paying a dollar for a gin and tonic or bracing some other patriot to buy one for him, and, while he was thus at the barricades, the Congressman had shook hands and gone.

A man in search of hard facts came back to say that Don Appell reported that fifteen of the persons he had sought for subpoenas had vanished from the earth, and the committee would have to make do with culls and remnants. It seems to have been Appell's view that the Communists had ordered those missing to go underground; it is far, far more likely that they have merely passed into smoke, if they ever lived, gone like the fronts they adorned.

A few ladies, unattached — who at these things can be described as attached? — started a communal sing; it began bravely enough and then it died in the room, and there was nothing but the sound of the conversations people carry on when they have no place to go in company to dinner.

There was, behind the visitor, a little group talking about the case of a nearly forgotten actress who had been blacklisted for years and had now begun to work again. Someone said that he still could hardly trust the woman, and someone else said, "I think you're wrong; I know her very well, and you can trust her."

That is all the point of these poor people. It is enough for them to be able to call their victim by his first name for him to have earned his exculpation; they are confessors without churches; they do not say, "Go, my son and sin no more"; they say, "Okay, Jean or Kim, or whatever your name is, love me and let me say at cocktail parties that you love me, and I will swear that you sin no more."

They are the nicest people who ever, starved for love, went to a meeting with a tape recorder stashed under the armpit and, unobserved, for the good of those present, transcribed the proceedings.

The room was thinning and the visitor fell into conversation with a Latin, whose means of support are his business, who explained that a distinguished American academician of otherwise iron anti-Bolshevik kidney had turned against the benefactor of the Dominican poor because he had asked Trujillo for a payoff and Trujillo wouldn't shake. The victim of this defamation — I see no reason to spread it by identifying him — is perhaps eccentric but honorable in his way. The room was full of the defamed man's friends; and the visitor, who is technically his enemy, arose to the defense of his honor. No one present said a word.

I am sorry these people are lonely, but I am not surprised. A stranger can say in their presence that a friend of theirs is a taker, and they do not bother to object. Gin and tonic and the death of the heart; thus do we save a nation.

All these little things came to an end, and the Congressmen and Appell and Miss Scotti, their souls widened by these inspiriting associations, went home to bed to arise this morning and execute the holy office of protecting the fine arts from some chorus girl who shook for Henry Wallace. So kind a host is Aware: to find the victims and then send out for gin and tonic.

They shot Imre Nagy in Hungary some time go; we do not even know when. What we do know — what is real — is that moment when Khrushchev said, we have to show Tito; fish up that Hodge, Podge, whatever his name is, and shoot him. Thus, in some of the same way, all over the world does death condemn life.

The Congressmen will sit there today, and the Aware people will sit there watching them. There is a face you see in New York and nowhere else I know; it is the face that stares across the police barricades at the funerals of faded celebrities, to gaze with pleasure upon the face of death. Such are the faces at our trials; such are the faces that will welcome the Un-American Activities Committee.

Congressman Tuck comes here, a judge who does not even know the names of the defendants before him. He does not care; he eats what Dolores Scotti puts before him. No one cares any longer, except these poor lonely people.

It is all up with them. Their back is broken. Still are we condemned to stand and watch them as they wriggle on until sundown.

[June 18, 1958]

A Musical Offering

The House Committee on Un-American Activities began its researches into Communist subversion in music here yesterday. America is a richly comic nation, but I do not think the Un-American Activities Committee is funny any longer.

It is, in the increasing desperation of its rag-picking, now revealed as tawdry, stupid and malignant. Its conduct is no longer a matter of taste. It is ugly and dirty and we are all ugly and dirty with it, because we are degraded with the Congress which perpetuates its franchise.

It is also an investigative body of massive illiteracy. Its counsel, Richard Arens, arose yesterday to call Wallingford Riegger, the composer. He spelled his name aloud for the benefit of the visiting press — R-e-i-g-g-e-r. That misspelling prevailed on the AP ticker all day yesterday.

And Wallingford Riegger belongs among our few serious composers of substance, somewhere by himself with Roger Sessions. On Sunday, Jay Harrison of the *Tribune* ran a piece on him which began: "April is likely to go down as Wallingford Riegger month for no apparent reason other than his own extraordinary and controversial gifts."

His gifts are not described as "controversial" because he may have been or still be a member of the Communist Party. He is a composer of monumental integrity; he went on in his grain during the most savage period of Soviet attacks on the bourgeois formalism of music like his. He was not so much resistant as absolutely inattentive to the aesthetic theories of Andrei Zhdanov; and this is the man the Un-American Activities Committee presents to us as submissive to Communist dictation.

The committee called Riegger because he is president-emeritus of the Metropolitan Music School, its primary target. The proceedings opened with a dreadfully depressing example of the terror these people can visit upon persons whose position and presumed taste might be thought to give them some pride.

Arens read a letter from Abram Chasins, music director of WQXR, certifying that the Metropolitan Music School had continued to list him among its sponsors even though he had resigned two years ago. He had joined, he said, because he had thought "its musical objectives were worthy of encouragement." He wanted it understood that he loathed persons who use the privileges of democracy to overthrow it and that, if the committee can attain its objective, "every American will be in your debt." I cannot believe such self-degradation is absolutely necessary to the preservation of such WQXR contributions to *echt Kultur* as "Bright and Early" and "Cocktail Time."

The director and registrar of the Metropolitan Music School took the Fifth. Leonard Cherlin, a clarinetist on leave from its faculty, testified that he had been a Communist and left, naming in the process ten musicians who had been Communists with him. One was a violinist, another a bass player. The rest were all woodwinds; the brass section appears free of treason.

Arens asked Cherlin how the Communist line was sold in the music school, which presumably is the point of this investigation, if the word "point" can be used with reference to this committee any longer.

"I never saw any synthesizing of politics and music," said Cherlin. "It was understood that politics and music should not mix."

This answer is, of course, irrelevant because it refutes only the assumed point of these hearings; the real point is, of course, the degradation of unimportant little people.

The best musicians scuffle in this town; and most of the persons mentioned make their livings from a host of different employments which taken all together can barely carry them. Their citation cannot put them completely out of work; but the committee can cut their incomes $15 a week here and $20 there and reduce them closer to the ragged edge, which is certainly a noble work.

Wallingford Riegger, by the way, spit in the committee's eye with an elderly grace which would have suited Bach better in his relations with the Margrave of Brandenburg. "As an American," he said, "I fear the loss of my self-respect if I answered you." Riegger was standing on the First Amendment alone; the committee told him that he wasn't "being very smart." This means that he could expect to go to jail. I suppose he can go to jail, and that is perhaps not very smart. It is, however, in the lonely, noble tradition of this old man's life.

[April 10, 1957]

How the Other Half Lives

The friendship of Sherman Billingsley is generally considered beneficial to a man's social position. But I can't say the association has done much for Roy Cohn's.

Billingsley hired Cohn as his lawyer a few weeks ago, and has since cast him into the lower depths of the legal profession. The boy who discomfited Secretaries of the Army has become a man hectored by night court magistrates. He has already occupied weeks defending Billingsley on the barricades at the State Labor Relations Board, which, although its business is conducted with grace and dignity, is not precisely an appearance before Lord Coke in Westminster Hall.

The evening before last, Billingsley was dragged into night court like a common dishwasher (*plongeur*), and Roy Cohn was summoned from a high Roman feast in honor of George Sokolsky for his immersion in how the other legal half lives.

That afternoon, Billingsley, whose passion for inhospitability has been inflamed by his troubles with his striking cooks and waiters, had engaged in an altercation with three AFL painters who were resting on his stoop from their task of redecorating the Austrian Consulate next door to his 69th Street manse. Murray Beskin, the most conspicuous target of Billingsley's wrath, said that the suavest of hosts had pulled a gun on him, but Billingsley replied that he had simply run a caressing hand over the .25 in his pocket. Beskin left the O.K. Corral and fled for protection of the Austrian authorities, who, out of their ancient melancholy experience with refugees, suggested he call the police. He did and Detective Lieutenant William Nevins found Billingsley and booked him on a charge of felonious assault.

Yesterday, he and Roy came down to the complaint department in the Criminal Courts Building to face their judgment. It is one of those horrible bare places, reminding one of nothing so much as the sets upon which Ralph Kramden strides, and filled with the dreariest assortment of couples bespeaking the simple, happy togetherness of the poor, the scars, the bandages and the black eyes equally distributed among husbands and wives. They looked altogether like specimens at a Civil Rights Congress rally protesting police brutality.

Billingsley was wearing a blue ensemble and one of those not-of-this-world smiles developed by juveniles for Truman Capote fantasies about tender spirits who take refuge in trees. He said that he had a witness from the State Board of Meditation [sic] to the terror visited against him by union bravoes, which made this whole thing understandable.

Magistrate Martinis is forced by the brutal circumstances of this slum city to run what amounts to a pre-penal traffic court and the suavest of hosts was forced to wait his turn at the end of a despairing parade of losers who had pushed a cop when he tried to take the dice away from them.

Billingsley spent his time developing his interior sense of injury at the hands of Lieutenant Nevins, who, he later declared, had been the recipient from his hands of tankfuls of Sortilege and whisky and carloads of that soap with Arthur Godfrey's face embossed upon it. Nevins said afterwards that Billingsley must have flipped his wig. (He certainly left it home; when he took off his hat and in his benevolence he looked like Wyatt Earp with a Norman Thomas haircut.) Nevins is one of those new college cops, and the charge of freeloading seemed fantasy in his case although he smelled richly enough of bay rum to arouse the suspicion that, in celebration of Tuesday night's great event, the Kreindlers had forced a haircut on him in the 21 barber shop.

Cohn demanded an immediate hearing; and Judge Martinis granted one for the afternoon, by which time the social level of the courtroom was measurably raised.

Magistrate Martinis decided that, since no one knew the gun was loaded — Billingsley swore it wasn't — the charge should be reduced to simple assault and the prisoner released to Cohn's custody for future action in Special Sessions. Cohn demanded the right to file a cross complaint of trespass and assault. The laws of the lower purlieus seem as foreign to him as the procedures of a canonical court of the Middle Ages would be to a Mississippi Baptist, and the magistrate patiently explained that the law of trespass applies only to the erection of a shack on another man's property. Cohn was left with only the complaint of assault.

So Cohn made a futile effort to introduce evidence of threats to Billingsley's life and safety, and Billingsley, out of the poverty of his vocabulary, then went to work to tell his side of the story. (I don't know any other social arbiter who habitually says "so I come out of the door.") He said that Beskin had expressed his solidarity with the strikers, and suggested that Billingsley was the unregistered offspring of a pariah dog and that the best solution to the present problem was for someone to beat the waste from his intestines. He lingered lovingly over the short words Chaucer used in descriptions of this sort; it is plain that to him the ears of women are sacred only in the Cub Room.

He had fondled the gun, because he had thought of using it, unloaded, "to defend myself with." "You would use it only as a blackjack?" Melvin Cohen, Beskin's lawyer, asked. Roy Cohn protested despairingly, and the suavest of hosts answered, "Don't you think it's a good idea?" One wishes poor Roy Cohn didn't have this affinity for clients with the habit of public hara-kiri. Cohn made the hand signal for temperance, and Billingsley raved on unseeing at Beskin's lawyer: "You're a smart fellow . . . They looked like goons . . . You want to sue me," etc. Martinis endured all this patiently and dismissed the complaint.

Outside, two of the painters who had been with Beskin told the same story he had. I don't think anything they said could have shocked Billingsley as much as the fact that they did not know who he was. He thinks all the world knows him and these shocked strangers set him down simply as the mad hermit of 69th Street.

[June 13, 1957]

The Great Melting Pot

I will get Peter Quince to write a ballad of this dream: it shall be called Bottom's Dream, because it hath no bottom.—William Shakespeare.

The Congo hath no bottom. Which of us could have thought that this Christmas week a jet plane will almost certainly fly over Elisabethville and drop its bombs of pacification and kill some little colored girl on her way to hear whatever nonsense the Seventh Day Adventists are passing out and that upon its wings there will be the United Nations insignia?

Where else but where else in the world but the Congo could Moise Tshombe grow up black and then, in his trouble, find Senator Jim Eastland the most prominent American on his defense committee?

A Committee to Aid the Katanga Freedom Fighters was formed Wednesday. Its manifesto was a desperate improvisation from the slogans of the Spanish Civil War almost up to "Make Elisabethville the Tomb of Communism." Everett M. Dirksen, minority leader of the Senate, was among the signers. The manifesto, through the inadvertence of hyperbole, left the impression that its signers proposed to raise volunteers and send guns to save Tshombe.

Yesterday the Katanga Freedom Fighters Committee called the press in to explain its plans. It had begun as most causes end, from Thomas E. Dewey's to Joe McCarthy's, with the desertion of Everett M. Dirksen. Dirksen, having waked to find in the *Times* that he had called all lovers of freedom to arms, was shocked into the public announcement that he had done no such thing. The proceedings opened with the reading of a memorandum from William F. Buckley who had been delegated by his comrades to telephone Dirksen and find out why he had deserted his station. "An aide to the Senator replied," Buckley reported, that "he would call me back in twenty minutes to explain the confusion. He never called." Who deals with Dirksen walks on water.

This left the Freedom Fighters with no Senator except Jim Eastland. The mind summons the dialogue: The Committee: "Senator

Eastland, we would like you to sponsor the Katanga Freedom Fighters." The Senator: "Boy, did you say Fyetahs or Ryedahs?"

Still, Tshombe had made the great breakthrough. The chairman of his committee is Dr. Max Yergan, who was a YMCA secretary in Africa for seventeen years, and for a while a prisoner of the Commies on the Committee on African Affairs, from which he burst free, and all in all is a profound, if somewhat bruised, student of the problem. Dr. Yergan is of course a Negro. One ornament of his committee is Eastland; another is Tom Anderson, a Bircher and a Citizens Council member. What Jim Crow put asunder, Moise Tshombe has put together.

The press conference was the sort of shambles to be expected from the subject of the Congo. It was presided over by Dr. Yergan, by James Burnham, and by C. Dickerman Williams, who was there to explain that the Freedom Fighters would, of course, do nothing without an export permit from the State Department.

The questions were generally argumentative — the less we know about the subject the more intensely we can discuss it. Somebody asked Burnham about these mercenaries of Tshombe's and Burnham replied that Tshombe had shown great tolerance of and interest in Western techniques and every African country had imported specialists. Tommy-gunners are, I suppose, specialists. Tshombe, after all, is content to work with free enterprise. A lady from radio recalled that Tshombe had talked a few weeks ago about dealing with the Russians. "Well," said Professor Burnham, "if we forced him into a hole where he could do nothing else . . ."

Afterwards Yergan talked about Africa. He is a man of great kindness and great sadness; his memories are largely irony. After all, he is an American who went back to Africa and sat with an Ashanti chieftain who served champagne for breakfast and said to Yergan, "Do you suppose my ancestors sold your ancestors into slavery?" It is strange to think of this long journey's ending on a committee with Jim Eastland.

But the Congo turns everything to irony. What must it be to be a United Nations pilot bombing civilians? You think poor Yergan's mixed up? I think we are all pretty mixed up. This season we're all buying UNICEF cards and UN planes are strafing children.

[December 15, 1961]

Trudeau Was Here

Lieutenant-General Arthur G. Trudeau is chief of research and development for the United States Army and one of those rare moments in human existence when the man has become the caricature. He is gone in the haunch and looks like Stengel when he was managing Brooklyn.

Somewhere, in some lost time, he commanded the Good Soldier Schweik. There was a Trudeau at Agincourt, with the French, of course: they would have had the longbow but the Sieur de Trudeau was in Paris rousing the Alchemists Union on the internal peril of Anglo-Saxon barbarism and did not have time to approve the designs. Enlisted men have hated him since the Assyrians came down like the wolf on the fold, and only the angels can count the civilizations which have perished with a Trudeau as their shield.

The Senate called him yesterday to hear his complaints because his speeches had been censored by unknown conspirators at a lower echelon.

The vanity of writers is older than death or sin, but the vanity of Arthur Trudeau is something else. He is affronted when someone edits his ghost writer; to him the word you possess is more precious than any word you compose. The word for him is an item of government issue, along with rations and quarters.

He told the Senate that only the day before he had been in Athens studying the Greeks. He had gone among the Greeks asking if they would rather be dead than Red and they had said they would and he had therefore associated himself with these sentiments in a speech to the Greek General Staff. The Agora in 1962 moves with the spirit of General Trudeau, walking where Plato walked, asking the Socratic question, turning occasionally to his interpreter and saying: "Boy, what did you say the Greek was for 'Red' and what for 'dead'?" And he had arisen in the first sweet sleep of dawn and gone onto the balcony of the King George ($25 per room per night) and stood in his leather slippers ($48, counterpart funds, Morocco) and in his bathrobe (guaranteed Japanese silk, requisitioned, Korea) and remembered Alexander the Great, who had brought peace to the Middle

East, and thought of those marble gods who had so long looked down upon and protected Christian civilization.

And, he thought, he told the Senate: "If it's anathema to stand firmly against communism, or Marxism, then let them spell it out and tell us."

Some unknown party in the State Department had suggested that he soften an attack on "Fabian socialism"; a note of explanation had observed that "some of our best friends are Socialists." He said six times that he did not know whether his censors were good Americans, mistaken, or something worse ("whether it is in the best interests of the country or from some other shade of motivation"). Senator Bartlett (D-Alaska) asked him what a Fabian Socialist was and General Trudeau, from the depth of his studies at the London School, answered:

"I, uh, what was the date of the speech? [His ghost-writer handed him a note.] I don't know whether your definition agrees with mine . . . It has come down since 1884 to describe those people whose philosophy is toward communism but is not communism . . . those who lean toward that intermediate step which is socialism . . . some of those to the left who appear usually anonymously . . . the fellow travelers who sometimes raise questions as to where we should go . . . where they are I don't know . . . [Those of us in the center who believe in] the spiritual guidance of God . . . free enterprise within reason . . . are attributed to be an extreme right wing."

As for any man who would dare to censor any student of social forces of his dimensions, General Trudeau went on: "I don't care if he's a Ph.D.; the basic question is how does he feel about America and the question of communism."

General Trudeau was peculiarly distressed because he knew that America had been denied an absolute clear-cut expression of the truth before such groups pregnant with the fire of decision as the Retired Diplomats Association. The truth in full clarity was: the focus of the conspiracy is Moscow except to the extent that it is Peking.

Some unknown conspirator, for reasons unclarified, had denied General Trudeau the right to deliver this paragraph in public: "The Reds deliberately, unceasingly, fanatically strive to destroy the shreds of stability remaining as we enter the new frontiers of the Sixties. A tower of peace founded on anarchy and chaos cannot stand."

It is unpatriotic to suggest it, but could there be a copyreader lurking somewhere in the State Department? Is it possible, treasonable though the thought might be, that someone might object to Trudeau on merely aesthetic grounds?

[January 25, 1962]

The Young Americans

All that the selective eye remembers of last night at the Garden was the paper airplanes that the Young Americans fashioned in the distraction of their boredom, most often from American Nazi Party leaflets warning them against the Jew Goldwater, and sent forth some to plunge straight down, a few to swoop above the floor.

Paper airplanes are the escape of inattentive school children. Their languor is all that lingers in the memory, corrupting every effort to recall what was said and every impulse to think of the new conservatism as a thing of consequence. Barry Goldwater's welcome to New York was overproduced and overpicketed and, as entertainment certainly, overattended, but it was underfed at the heart. Can that death which always begins in the interior have come to them so soon?

Two years ago there was only the right wing. Today there is the respectable right wing and the disreputable one; the price of respectability is animal vigor. Last night's crowd was more a flock than a mob. Still, the young men in charge were plainly conscious that there is a beast even in these sheep. They abstained — with several lapses — from the noble tradition of reaching for boos; they were careful to avoid reference to Mrs. Roosevelt, Arthur Schlesinger and Senator Javits; the *Post* was booed once rather by accident, and the *Times* once. President Kennedy was faintly applauded the first time he was mentioned — in gratitude for his promise to pollute the atmosphere — but booed in larger volume later.

Three men in the gallery set up a call for the martyr Walker and were at once levitated from the premises by the special cops. Someone else set up a cry of "That's a lie" while a message from the martyr Tshombe was being read. He was allowed to stay after he assured the cops he had meant that Dean Rusk was a liar.

The crowd started willingly enough; it fairly roared for the phrase "the market economy." But for the next hour, very little music as mad was offered them. The Young Americans for Freedom consumed that time giving awards to those of their elders who had kept a particular shine on the Republic over the past year. Most of these were strangers to the audience; one of those honored was Professor Ludwig von Mises, the pearl of the Austrian economists, who stood among pigs in the marketplace and pronounced his gratitude for the reawakening of the intellect in the country of his adoption while cries of "Louder!" came down from the galleries.

The few who might have been familiar were absent. Herbert Hoover sent a message from a barricade labeled "Key Largo Anglers Club." A young man said that John Wayne would be honored for remembering the Alamo: "Out of our flabby moral horizons comes John Wayne, tall in the saddle." But there came instead George Murphy, a mere dancer, to plug Fred Schwarz's communism movie. John Wayne, of course, forgot the Alamo after it petered out in the drive-ins; his patriotism had been conquered by the old show business tradition that you can't get an actor for a free walk-on unless he has a current movie to shill.

The program was running an hour late and an outrider came back to report that Barry Goldwater was pacing like a damned soul in hell among the paper coffee cups in the dressing room and complaining that he had told these people that he would never come back if they kept him late the way they did last year.

The crowd by now could be roused only by the wildest slogans: Representative Donald Bruce read Patrick Henry's speech about our brothers being already in the field and it stirred a little, to be lulled again by Brent Bozell, who is back after a year in Spain and was thus full of the possibilities of Christian civilization and the peril of gnosticism. It awoke to hear him give his orders to the Executive: Invade Havana, tear down the Wall, stay until Africa is safe for the Tshombes.

They were ready for Barry Goldwater. He came at last, to stand amid his half-ration of balloons — the other half had been used for Senator Tower of Texas.

Goldwater said that the ADA has joined the Nazis in picketing him. "I speak as a man who is half-Jewish" (cheers). He went on to talk about the conservative revival which we must all take seriously. He said nothing about tearing down the Wall or landing in Havana; he said merely that the Republicans were gaining in Queens. There's a program for challenging Godless communism: win Queens.

It was near midnight; Goldwater stopped. A Young American for Freedom said: "Well, we filled the Garden." It was the tone of a small businessman. And that is all there is; there isn't any more.

[March 8, 1962]

Absurd Right, U.S.A.

[A California editor] . . . said extremism appeared to be tapering off in San Diego County. He said that 104 right-wing organizations were active in the county last year, but that fewer than thirty seem to be active now."—New York Times, July 15.

It may be graceless for this source to say so, but how unproductive is journalistic inquiry, with its care for the statistic and its lack of interest in the face. What have you said when you cite "104 right-wing" organizations without difference or distinction?

Have we grown so unconscious of the diversity of man?

Robert Welch seems rather to have fallen out of history, or at least out of journalism. This means, one suspects, that the far right, our most conspicuous example of the politics of the absurd, is falling toward the yellow leaf. The Minutemen were announced and a book describing their menace no doubt commissioned, and now they are gone, and we have one advance withdrawn and one book less. The politics of the absurd is like marijuana; there is more profit to be got opposing it than pushing it. Robert Welch's decline is a sad hour for those of us who looked forward to a profitable enterprise of exposing him. But, even here at the end, let us have some sense of the difference in men. It has always been a complaint of liberals that the right wing never distinguished between them and the Communists. The early prophets may tell us that it is only just for Barry Goldwater to find his critics unable to distinguish between him and the John Birch Society, but Micah would certainly argue that it is just for him to complain.

Every man who lives in a community has a right to complain when its casual visitors think him just like every one of his neighbors. And

Absurd Right is a community, the way Winesburg, Ohio, was, small, narrow, full of hatred for the man next door and for most men outside, but large as — to use one of its favorite expressions — all America.

It encompasses Ezra Pound, one of our great teachers; Ayn Rand, a young woman badly educated by Germans, and Taylor Caldwell, who writes novels for shop girls. It includes the poor who hate the rich and the rich who hate the poor. It includes the man who manufactures the Barry Goldwater sweatshirt and also George Lincoln Rockwell, who pickets all public assemblies where the "Jew Goldwater" appears. Its movie house specializes in horror films; Herbert Philbrick is its manager. It has its church, interdenominational, of course, where Fred Schwarz comes now and again to raise funds for his missions in Laos and India. It includes Senator Jim Eastland and a small population of Negroes, all of whom can report unspeakable sufferings from their experience in the rival city of Absurd Left. The Negroes seem to have shined shoes in both locations: each has two watches, given him by grateful customers in each town. Absurd Left wants its watch back.

Absurd Right has a small Jewish community, which is widely respected by the middle class although detested in the poolrooms. George Sokolsky is its rabbi, but he is lately suspected of reform tendencies. Marvin Liebman, proprietor of the Committee of One Million, a small neighborhood improvement association, is manager of the Chamber of Commerce. Absurd Right has cops, whose duty it is to keep an eye on strangers; as happens with small towns, a few of them seem to be on the take. It has its high school, Young Americans for Freedom: all students wear the top buttons of their jackets buttoned and are training for jobs with the Milwaukee Manufacturers Association.

There is a military post just outside of town: Absurd Right is disturbed because it has been declared off limits for enlisted men. Occasionally an officer of rank drops by: Absurd Right is especially favored for military retirements. But no respectable citizen plays bridge with General Walker any more; his shell is seen, lonely and absorbed at the bar in Robert Welch's saloon.

For Absurd Right, like most small towns, is divided along class lines. It even has a cosmopolitan set, whose major ornament is William F. Buckley, Jr., who went to Yale, but who is especially cherished because, for all his travels, he retains his loyalty for the town where he was born. Some of the publicans wish he didn't: he has a civic reform streak and has on occasion gone to the city commissioners to demand the lifting of Robert Welch's license: and Welch blames him for the decline of his trade among the respectable.

Absurd Right, in truth, is just that small and just that complicated. I should not suggest that it is a good place to live; and, like most small towns, it is tiresome to visit unless you happen to have a friend like Buckley. But it does seem fairly unproductive to keep saying that all its citizens are alike.

That is not the way novels are written.

The Schwarz Rally

A tag team of Fred C. Schwarz, Pat Boone and Herbert Philbrick wrestled the Mongol Horde in the Garden last night. Wrestling is not a sport but an exhibition and its results are judged by the gate receipts. Schwarz, Boone and Philbrick drew less than half as many customers as Antonio Rocca and Nature Boy Buddy Rogers had the week before.

The returns are not heartening, but the spirit is strong. Fred Schwarz stood up near the end and remembered that his enemies had accused him of making a fortune out of the struggle. He counted the house. "That's a joke," he said.

A young man who had been engaged in the preliminaries of this event was saying later that he had come into the office and one of the volunteers had gotten down on her knees and kissed his hand. "Let us," she had said to the assembled faithful, "pause for a moment and pray for this young man." I am afraid that Fred Schwarz would have found this moment of communion a distraction from the licking of envelopes and the mailing of appeals. Still his calculation is engaging and the piety of his disciples is affecting, and, in combination, I would not bet that they will not altogether ignite the Hudson yet.

It was a quieter evening than anyone had expected. The pickets were there at five and gone by eight-thirty. There was, as always happens, little passion in their performance; by nine the police had left the streets and were sitting in the Garden locker room reading their free copies of *I Led Three Lives*, which, under the circumstances, constituted all the tip Fred Schwarz could afford.

Still, it was a better show than we are used to from these quarters. It was a better show mainly because of Schwarz. He is a live one. He sat down on his stool and asked any member of his audience to raise his hand if he knew as much as he wanted to know about dialectical materialism. No hands were raised outside the press section. He asked everyone who wanted to learn more at his school next August to raise his hand, and there was a brave and encouraging show. One thought of the men who sell magic potato peelers in Union Square, harried and derided, and never dream that there is a world where the pitchman can stand up, assured that cops are off the premises reading Philbrick, and explain to the customers how one goes about writing a check.

"The grim and ugly truth," said Dr. Schwarz, "is that the tide is running against us." He looked at his watch. He had, he said, to hurry. "We have a special treat tonight." Pat Boone was coming.

Pat Boone arrived wearing a dark blue shirt and a white jacket, and apologizing for his white shoes.

Many of his friends, said Pat Boone, had begged him not to come to this meeting. "It may hurt your record sales," they had said. "It may cost you the people who want to go to your pictures." But then he had thought of his responsibility as a citizen. "We cannot be so petrified by the fear of being labeled that we do nothing."

"I have four lovely daughters. I would rather that Cherry, Debby, Wendy and Laurie be lined up and shot down before my very eyes than for them to grow up in a Communist United States. I would rather have them blown to heaven by an atom bomb than taught to hell by the Communists."

These are brave words at a moment when the Commies have gotten Skouras and none of us is safe. Let us hope that every American patriot will tell Pat Boone that we are as ready to buy his records and to go to his movies as we were before last night when he chose freedom.

In sum, though, Schwarz is in the slack season. He came back again and again to the statements of his enemies that his Christian Anti-

Communist Crusade grossed a million dollars last year. "Some people," he said, "don't know the difference between total sales and profits. Yesterday I had to borrow $10 from my secretary."

But he will pay it back a thousandfold. We are a city generous to strangers. No man has ever come here before with Fred Schwarz's deep understanding of the operations of the free enterprise system and left poorer than he was when he arrived. School keeps at $20 a head next August at Carnegie Hall. It was for this that Isaac Stern loved and sang.

[June 29, 1962]

Wonders

In 1951, Miss Kim Hunter appeared in *Darkness at Noon*, Arthur Koestler's intuitive leap into the minds of the Soviet policemen who persuaded men to confess crimes which they had begun knowing were not crimes. Miss Hunter played Arlova, their most innocent victim.

The great symbol in *Darkness at Noon* is Gletkin, the examining magistrate, Kim Hunter began dealing with her own Gletkin in 1954; he was Vincent Hartnett, a gray, earnest little man in most ways the other Gletkin's opposite, anxious to assist the fallen, but like Gletkin, with his own particular formula for recantation.

Vincent Hartnett was the compiler of Red Channels and an expert in the arraignment and clearance of actors whose identification with Communist fronts barred them from employment. Kim Hunter had won an Academy Award in 1952. For three years thereafter she never got a movie offer and her once-steady television engagements dropped down to one or two a year. Kim Hunter had attended a meeting for the Hollywood Ten, had signed the call for the Waldorf peace conference, and had her name on a telegram dispatched by the Civil Rights Congress to the Supreme Court asking a new trial for Willie McGee, a Negro later executed in Mississippi.

In 1953, when her case was desperate, Kim Hunter's press agent wrote Vincent Hartnett and asked what she might do to clear herself. Hartnett wrote back that "if she really wished to correct her history, she will have to review her entire record." Hartnett would produce the record and charge her $200; the fees of his competitors were, he said, a bit higher.

Kim Hunter came to Judge Abraham Geller's court yesterday as a witness for John Henry Faulk, who is suing Hartnett, among others, for driving him from the radio. She told how she had finally talked with her Gletkin directly and how he had rehabilitated her.

She had gone at last in 1953 to see Roy Brewer, another ritual purifier, and he had suggested that she give Hartnett an affidavit of pro-Americanism. She submitted three drafts before arriving at a satisfactory tone in 1955 and then Hartnett seems to have passed her for a show sponsored by Borden's, a company from which he had earned $10,000 as a clearance expert that year.

The acceptable tone perfectly fitted Gletkin's notions of propriety:

"It was only after I had made several errors in judgment, which regrettably may have served the Communist cause, that I was finally alerted to a clearer and more intelligent understanding of the insidious workings of the Communist conspiracy. Without the benefit of a well-rounded political education, my ability to probe beneath surface appearances was limited."

In May of 1955, Vincent Hartnett called her to say that the affidavit had not been quite enough. The New York local of her television actors union was debating a resolution to condemn Aware, Hartnett's action squad. "He said one way I could show a strong anti-Communist position would be to go to the meeting and support Aware. I said that would be difficult because I didn't support Aware."

In his tolerance, Hartnett conceded that a telegram would be enough. She sent the telegram — warning her union "against placing itself on the record as protecting and aiding the Communist conspiracy" — with a copy to Vince Hartnett, who dropped a note to Larry Johnson, his fellow worker from Syracuse, saying that now "you will hear the comrades screaming."

"You and your associates," he said, "have done wonders." Wonders. Beating proud and defenseless women to their knees. Extorting confessions from people who know they have done no wrong. It is our saving grace that there is something in the Kim Hunters and the Johnny Faulks that such wonders can sometimes bend but never break. She sat there yesterday, in a place which could hardly be convenient to her yet, and Louis Nizer asked if she regretted signing a petition for Willie McGee. All our saving grace came strong and clear in her answer. "I certainly do not."

[May 17, 1962]

The Lonely Cop

Engaged professionals, I suppose, doodle the symbols of their trade. Naturally then, when Vincent Hartnett, compiler of Red Channels, has occasion to doodle he takes down names.

Yesterday, he wound up three weeks as a witness in John Henry Faulk's suit against him and others for alleged libel, blacklisting and career destruction. In its course, Louis Nizer, Faulk's attorney, asked Hartnett why, in moments of repose during the trial, he engaged himself in writing on small cards. Hartnett answered that he was writing down the names of persons he has seen among the spectators. There will be, one assumes, on his roster of the fallen, a new category: "Attended Faulk trial."

A man is blacklisted; he protests. That provides a new reason to blacklist him. He remembers and bears a grievance. That is another reason to blacklist him, up until death where attendance at his funeral is a further reason to blacklist the mourners.

Near the end of his last day's testimony, Hartnett's attorney asked him to recall some of the names he had taken down. "Well," Hartnett answered, "Elliott Sullivan, who was sitting next to Mrs. Faulk, one day," and then three others, all unfriendly witnesses before the House Committee on Un-American Activities, and all still unemployable on television.

Poor Hartnett is a man in whom may be found a malice, with which he is charged by the suit, mixed with a desire to be liked in degrees uncomfortably larger than in most of us. It was a hot day. No one's temper was comfortable. Hartnett placed Sullivan next to Mrs. Faulk in his memory with the faintest of smiles; he had discovered the newest sin: guilt by accidental proximity.

Louis Nizer arose a little later. Could Hartnett point out Mrs. Faulk in the courtroom now?

Vincent Hartnett looked carefully and precisely about the chamber and then pointed to a lady with dark red hair on a side bench.

"I believe she's the lady there," he said. The visitor thus identified stood up, distressed by this sudden attention, and expostulated, "I am Mrs. Sopher."

"Would you like," smiled Louis Nizer, "a second chance at Mrs. Faulk?" The witness declined. He went on to say that the lady he had identified looked like the one who had been pointed out to him as Mrs. Faulk and whom he had seen later sitting with Elliott Sullivan.

Somebody thought he saw an actress at a meeting of a Communist front. Therefore the actress was at the meeting. Somebody looks like somebody; *ergo* the first somebody is the second somebody. Mrs. Sopher is Mrs. Faulk. Just how many reports must Vincent Hartnett have made to how many advertising agencies which contained the confident sentence that so-and-so was reported at such-and-such a meeting and that cost so-and-so a job?

What counts for a mind like this is not the judgment but the power to judge and dispose. Hartnett dispensed convictions on evidence not always better than this; and, since he wanted to think himself a fair man, he granted indulgences on evidence as thin. He explained yesterday that he had cleared one radio announcer because a source he accepted as reliable had told him that the subject was now anti-Communist. We can be grateful for Hartnett's mercies, and still wonder, after his confrontation with Mrs. Sopher, if he knows a reliable source when he hears one.

And then there is that terrible empty impersonality. We seem to watch a man detached from all inner feelings except the sense of continual affront at being undervalued and misunderstood. Faulk sued him six years ago; he did not know Faulk when he began and he cannot even now identify the wife of a man whose destroyer he is alleged to be. He could hardly be incurious because he is embarrassed; a man capable of embarrassment would not have said what he said about her yesterday. The fact must be that he is simply not interested in people except as cardboard models for a private drama of Hartnett, the cop alone. Faulk charges him with malice; if the charge is true, not often was malice as blind as this.

[June 20, 1962]

Inside the FBI

Our Mr. Wechsler yesterday took notice of the public emergence of Jack Levine, the first apostate alumnus of the Federal Bureau of Investigation to tell his story to the free world.

Levine's recollections have the irresistible appeal of all reports from closed societies. We honor Djilas the man, but we listen with real fascination to Djilas the gossip. And what we know about the operations of the FBI is quite like what we used to know about the operations of Joseph Stalin, since in both cases the prior first-hand sources are idolatrous.

The very nature of closed societies — their habit, for example, of burning documents and assassinating the character of heretics — makes it necessary for us to take most of the reminiscences of their refugees on trust. You trust a man if you find his story artistically credible. That was the ultimate reason for trusting Whittaker Chambers on Alger Hiss; and Levine passes the test on J. Edgar Hoover just as well.

He will talk on his memories over WBAI tonight at eight-fifteen for two hours and a half. His recollections of J. Edgar Hoover as sacred object are the most formidable of these memories.

He describes, for example, the preparations each class of FBI trainees endures for its first group audience with the Director:

"The duration of this preparation was approximately eight hours. A bureau official who had a familiarity with the physical layout of the Director's office lectured to us for close to an hour, using maps and sketches as visual aids.

"It was explained to us that such a briefing was necessary because in the past there had been incidents in which new agents had walked in and out of undesignated doors, stumbled into desks and had tripped over door saddles, all in the presence of the Director. These new agents did not graduate from the training program.

"We were then briefed for about an hour on our personal appearance. We were instructed to wear dark suits with a folded handkerchief in our breast pocket. We were told what kind of ties were acceptable to the Director and what were not. We had to wear shirts with French cuffs . . . The Director considers short haircuts a sign of immaturity. Even the style of socks we were to wear was dictated.

"We were instructed to carry an extra handkerchief with us for the purpose of drying our palms before entering the Director's office . . . S. A. Victor Turin, class counselor, told us in past years several new agents were fired for shaking hands with the Director with moist palms. It was explained that the Director distrusts persons with moist palms, as he considers this an indication of weak character."

This kind of thing indicates the essential character of the FBI as an institution. No one, for example, would think of this sort of briefing for an audience with the Pope. The Church has on its side the dignity of history; His Holiness represents not himself but the body of the Church. Hoover and Stalin were, of course, usurpers; they therefore have no presence but themselves. They cannot afford to trust anyone; Stalin was annoyed at tall people; Hoover is uneasy to discover a wet palm.

Unfortunately, all paranoid societies lend themselves to this kind of lay analysis. That the FBI is a paranoid society, Levine leaves us no ground to doubt. Most agents hate headquarters; most plot to cheat Hoover, who spies back on them. They are afraid to quit only because they can't get jobs without the proper reference from the FBI, and believe that Hoover would not scruple, if affronted, to destroy their characters. (For the employment of this technique by Communists, see *Masters of Deceit*.)

By one of those gloomy coincidences, Levine tells his story the same week the *Wall Street Journal* runs the headline: "More Companies Find Management Talent Among Ex-FBI Agents." One reason why Hoover is so immense a force in our society is that he has the quality of infection.

[October 18, 1962]

VIII

The Name of the Game

My method in these columns seems peculiarly deficient as an instrument of celebration. No public man has ever touched me more personally than Adlai Stevenson and no labor leader more than Philip Murray; yet when I read over what I had written about them, it seemed useless for reminding even myself how I had really felt. Fortunately, I had watched Stevenson in New York one rainy afternoon in the last week of his last campaign for President, and it seemed that for once I had almost said there what this man meant to us then and means to so many of us still.

It is in this section because it is about a man and his conduct with honor at the trade of his choice.

Paul Hall, of the seafarers union, is in some ways our last active labor leader. Hall succeeded the late Harry Lundeberg, and is, like him, a passionate Commiephobe. I was surprised a few years ago to find him in tandem with Lee Pressman, who is lawyer for one of the other maritime unions.

Lee Pressman was counsel for the old CIO and a terrible eminence in his time as representative of those pro-Communist unions I have mentioned before as the wicked giants in the fairy tale of my apprenticeship as a labor reporter. Pressman had long ago left the party and descended to obscurity, except as general counsel for the Marine Engineers Beneficial Association. He and Hall had met there and had found themselves on the same side in one of those Middle Eastern wars which are the history of the waterfront.

Pressman's union was preparing to strike the big passenger ships. It represented their licensed engineers, only a minority of the crews controlled by Joseph Curran's National Maritime Union. The day before their strike was to begin, Pressman went to talk to the shippers and Hall went with him.

"We were on one side of the table," says Hall, "and sitting across from us was Casey of U. S. Lines and Curran. Curran didn't say anything; he sat there and let Casey talk. Casey said, 'Pressman, you call your men out and we'll crew your ships just the same and we're gonna break your union. You can sign now or get broke; we don't care.' "

"And Pressman looked at him and stuck his finger on the table and then he said, 'If that is the name of the game, that is the game we will play.' We went down to the pier and he pulled them out and the longshoremen wouldn't move the cargo and they won that strike, and you ask me why I position with Lee Pressman."

These are people who, having been told the name of the game, played it, alone most of the time, on their honor always — quite different people but alike faithful to the rules and the standards. Eminent Victorians, each able to pitch the sort of game Sal Maglie pitched the day Don Larsen didn't let a Dodger get on base.

Name Your Weapons

The shadow of Joe McCarthy hangs like a great pall over the Democrats of Massachusetts.

At Joe's lightest breath, they button their coats to the chin and shiver. John Kennedy, the Massachusetts Democracy's great hope for the Senate, never mentions Joe's name.

It is Kennedy's view that the Irish core of his party likes Joe McCarthy and will grievously punish any man who traduces him.

The Democrats of Massachusetts sent that message to Harry Truman just before he went into New England week before last. Take it a little easy with McCarthy, they said; talk about Hoover. The people up here don't have to be told why they hate Hoover.

A few weeks ago, the Republican National Committee gave Dwight Eisenhower the lay-off-McCarthy warning for Wisconsin. Eisenhower took their orders like a soldier.

But Harry Truman marched into Boston's Symphony Hall last Friday with his lips tight and his eyes hot. Just before he got there, Jack Kennedy had completed a nice, alliterative, inoffensive assault on the "Capeharts and the Cains, the Brickers and the Butlers." The possibilities of juxtaposing "the McCarthys and the Malones" were very far from his mind.

Mr. Truman looked Boston in the face and read it a lecture about Joe McCarthy. He could speak without shame, he said, of his administration's record against communism.

He told them what McCarthy had done in pillorying the innocent. He spoke of "those moral pygmies, Senators Jenner and McCarthy," and he fairly spat their names. He reminded them that in a choice between McCarthy's favor and his debt to George Marshall, Eisenhower had gone with McCarthy.

"I stand by my friends," said the President, and suddenly Boston's cheers came pounding back at him. He spat out McCarthy's name again, and they were booing it. Mr. Truman had taken his chances on Boston and Boston had come through.

For Harry Truman, wherever he goes, is campaigning unafraid against the McCarthys and the Jenners. He is telling his party to meet them beard to beard. He singed the Connecticut Republicans for coddling them. In New Jersey, last Tuesday, he singled out that ancient fraud, Senator Smith, for "his sad lack of backbone" in caving in before McCarthy.

Not even for campaign purposes would Harry Truman blanch or quail. Yesterday in Cumberland, Maryland, where McCarthy is generally credited with deciding the 1950 Senate election, the President called Joe a "political gangster," a denizen of the "political underworld," a dealer in the "big lie." His audience listened open-mouthed and then applauded.

The President of the United States, a man nobody writes off as a political scientist, is gambling that McCarthy is an overrated punk. And, even if he isn't, Mr. Truman will not bow before him and none of the faint-hearted can tell him to.

You cannot write about this little man with the thick glasses in the language of politics. The words are the sparse words of a military citation — the citation for example of a soldier named Charles Kelly who stood off a German battalion in Italy. The sergeant who wrote it remembered leaving Corporal Kelly with his machine gun burned out and rifle useless.

"When last seen," the sergeant said, "Corporal Kelly was observed loading and firing a rocket launcher at the advancing enemy." A soldier like Harry Truman fights the enemy on ground of the enemy's choosing. He'll run on your own terms — any track, anywhere any time and distance and who in the hell are you?

[Washington, D.C., October 15, 1952]

The Kicks

Louis Armstrong blesses New York these nights at a place in the Fifties called Basin Street.

Armstrong carries his unique imperial scepter with him wherever he goes, and his court chamber, here as everywhere else, is a narrow dressing room unprotected against any man who wants to walk in and ask him for the gift and the secret of laughter.

He sits there at midnight between sets in his shorts and with a handkerchief on his head rubbing his scarred and ravaged lips with a special salve he discovered in Germany during some royal tour in the Twenties.

No man is denied the balm of his touch, for he is alone and walks by himself only in those moments when he looks at the ceiling and plays his slow, sweet song of memory and loss and desire.

A man walked in and said he hadn't known "Pops" was in town until he had seen the marquee and he had come in because he had told his kid that he would listen to Armstrong whenever he could.

When was Louis coming out to teach his kid the trumpet? And Armstrong said he was afraid he couldn't make it this trip, but he'd send a book of his old choruses like "You're Next" and "Cornet Chop Suey."

Someone had written the notes down from listening to the old records and made a book out of them, he said.

It was as though it were the most normal thing in the world to have stood in a barn in Chicago thirty years ago and blown a notion into a low fidelity recording machine and then had some musicologist come along now and listen to the old records and set them down in a book.

It is a rare thing to have written the book when all you thought you were doing was making $50 at a recording date. Louis Armstrong knows that he is history, but he is arrogant only with the gravediggers who come around and ask him to conform to his stature with the ages.

"They ask me my favorite band," he says, "and I tell them Guy Lombardo. They say you don't really mean that. And I say you asked me, didn't you."

The legend of jazz is death and defeat; its saints died beaten and broke; the legend says that it should be that way. They should drink like Bix Beiderbecke or be cheated and broken and lose their teeth like Joe Oliver, because the legend says they should be destroyed seeking notes that aren't in the registers of their horns.

But Louis Armstrong defies that invented destiny of destruction; he endures and to mix in his own person all men, the pure and the cheap, clown and creator, god and buffoon.

"You got to take care of yourself. You got to flush yourself out and you got to watch those germs. You got to keep before the public. Don't let them tell you you got to take top billing or nothing. Your instrument's your billing.

"I done everything in my time, and there were kicks all the time. I got kicks on that coal cart when I was fifteen. In fifty-four years you get lots of kicks. I've played with everyone.

"There's kicks anywhere. When I first came to New York, I stood up with the Vincent Lopez band and some old man stood up in front and played the same thing an octave higher. I went home that week and that's when I made 'When You're Smiling.' "

The name Vincent Lopez does not appear in the legend, but it is part of Louis Armstrong's life, and no part of his life is devoid of kicks because it does not fit the legend.

His vocalist, Velma Middleton, came in and said, "Pops, I never can get to you for the chicks," and he laughed and some boys came in and he said, "Ah, the cats," and everyone laughed. "My disciples," he said.

His soiree was over and he put on his pants to have his picture taken, as a favor to a press agent, picked up his handkerchiefs and went back on the stand. His band was loose and careless, for that's how Armstrong feels these nights.

They clowned awhile and then, of a sudden, he put up his horn and played "When You're Smiling," as he had heard that nameless forgotten old man do it thirty years ago, on the melody, the notes high, a little slow and longing, and he was walking on that plain alone.

The press agent at Basin Street was saying that he came down every night, which was more, after all, than anyone owes a client, because he could not stop listening to Louis.

He was saying I suppose that after all these years, Louis Armstrong has become the River Mississippi, pure like its source, flecked and choked with jetsam like its middle, broad and triumphant like its end. It is never the same river, but its ends are like its beginnings, and there aren't many rivers left like it.

[August 20, 1954]

The Doorkeeper

Arthur Watkins was selected to try Joe McCarthy by William Knowland and Richard Nixon, who cannot have known precisely what result they wanted at the time. They picked a narrow man of fixed principles, all of them orthodox Republican, limited, humorless and indifferent to theater.

They knew what they wanted yesterday and it was too late. Partly through fear and partly through craft, they wanted McCarthy kept on as a guest in the house he had profaned so long and Arthur Watkins, the creature of their choice, slammed the door in their faces and McCarthy's.

He seemed the least formidable of men when he took the floor yesterday morning to say his piece. He had behind him two weeks of memory of the times McCarthy had called him a coward and dishonest and the unwitting handmaiden of the Communist conspiracy.

He said, when he began, that he hoped the galleries would be quiet because, when he raised his voice, he tended to sound angry and he wanted most of all to be dispassionate, even though this was a matter involving his honor.

He said the word "honor" as though he were talking about his trousers. He would like to talk as a judge talks in a quiet chamber.

"I am human," he said, "and I will not say that what I feel this day is righteous but I will say it is human and justifiable." He would remind the Senators that, when McCarthy attacked him, "he is attacking you because I am your agent."

He read into the record the wire story of McCarthy's words about him in Milwaukee: "Most cowardly thing I've heard of." He supposed he should be indignant, but he was more sorrowful. It was after all a stigma to be called a coward.

He read the long record of McCarthy's paper war on the 1952 Gillette subcommittee which was investigating his fitness to sit in the Senate. No other man among them, said Arthur Watkins, "whose honor and integrity was under serious charges" would have shrunk from a public opportunity to refute them.

McCarthy chose "from the safety of his office" to attack the committee by letter. "I'm not saying he was a coward," said Arthur Watkins again and again. William Knowland moved a recess for lunch.

Watkins came back and began to read the questions that McCarthy had refused to answer. "I am not saying he was a coward. McCarthy said you were a lynch mob," he reminded them, "but he didn't come into the Senate to say it. He's not a coward! You say what he is."

Arthur Watkins went on to remember the times he had praised McCarthy in the past. He had his own credentials in the Communist hunt, and he read in his flat voice a letter of recommendation from Pat McCarran. No one could have thought that the rock upon which Joe McCarthy broke would be a man proud of a reference from Pat McCarran.

Then the passion, long deferred, came into his voice. All over the country, McCarthy and his journalistic satellites have defiled the honor of Arthur Watkins. "In your own presence you have seen this hit-and-run attack on my courage and intelligence."

He turned to the Republican side and his finger danced among the white faces in front of him. "I'm asking you and you and you, what are you going to do about it?"

"I may be a coward, but I am not going to compromise with that kind of indecency." He turned again and asked the Republicans how they could hold their heads up among the free bodies of the world if they compromised with it. He had listened in vain for a protest for all these insults or for a word of commendation for the committee which had had to endure them.

He hoped some member of the Senate would move to add another sentence to the resolution of censure "for the contempt which has taken place in your very presence."

He turned again to the Republicans. "I don't think you can skip it, gentlemen. If no one else will move the man who has been called a coward from Utah will do it."

In that moment all hope of compromise had died. Arthur Watkins took a drink of water and turned once more to his papers. McCarthy had been off the floor all day; it was his fate near the end to be first a minor actor and then not even a spectator; he was not in at his own death.

Edward Williams, his lawyer, left the chamber for a cloakroom phone. Francis Case of South Dakota, who had gone over the side, stared aghast at the ship still watertight and the captain still erect at the helm.

Arthur Watkins had lost a note and was fumbling again in the old dry tone. He stood, with the center light upon him, and just before the peroration, almost deliberately, he dropped theater. He was searching the committee report for some words; he found them and suddenly glowed with a fierce pride in them; they would, he said, go down in history.

They were words about McCarthy's defiance of the Gillette committee: "When persons in high places fail to meet and set high standards, the people lose faith. If our people lose faith, our form of government cannot long endure."

Those words, he said, go to the heart of the living Constitution. When a Senator disregards them, "he is violating his oath to the living Constitution of the United States."

Mike Monroney clapped his hands in the silence, that violation of custom went ungaveled. The galleries were empty in anticipation of the Honorable Herman Welker, and suddenly Watkins was gone to the cloakroom.

A Senator came to congratulate him and found Watkins sitting with his hand on his stomach. He had finished his speech through one of those spastic attacks against which his doctor had warned him. They come and go, said Arthur Watkins, but they pass.

All passes and Arthur Watkins remains. He had endured and he had spoken the last judgment. The debate was over; only the words remained; Arthur Watkins had closed all doors but censure. Dick Nixon had made the mistake all cynics make: He had selected an instrument and he was stuck with a man.

[Washington, D.C., November 17, 1954]

Sal Maglie . . . A Gracious Man

There was the customary talk about the shadows of the years and the ravages of the law of averages when Sal Maglie went out to meet the Yankees yesterday afternoon. It was the first time, after all the years, that he had ever pitched in Yankee Stadium, the home of champions.

He threw that hump-backed let-up pitch that is last in the warm-up, and then for the first time looked at Hank Bauer. He threw the curve in; Hank Bauer made a gesture at bunting; and the strike was called.

The hitter leaned over a little; the pitch was high; Hank Bauer skittered back in haste and the ball went by the catcher's mitt and back to the wall.

"If I know Sal," the old Giant writer in the stands said, "he threw that to tell 'em off. He knows the Yankees probably think he's a little tired. He's saying to them, look fellas, I'm still around. You've got to come and get me."

"The call was for an inside pitch," said Sal Maglie later. "I threw it too high and it got away." He is a gracious man who takes no pride in the legend of special, professional venom.

He worked his arm a little and blew on his hands as though he came from a world no sun could warm. And then Bauer plunked it up to Reese; Maglie looked once at the ball and then at the fielder, and, without needing to see the catch, bent over and worked his long, brown, dealer's hand into the resin bag.

He got Joe Collins to hit on the ground to the wrong field; Mickey Mantle went all the way around; Sal Maglie heard the sound and judged it. The left fielder was still circling under it when Sal Maglie crossed the foul line on his way to the dugout. He gives very little and can afford to spend less.

He went that way through the line-up for the first three innings. It seemed a memorable incident when the first pitch to the eighth Yankee batter was a ball. The utility infield of the fifth-place team in the Westport Midget League would have eaten up anything hit by either side in those three perfect eighteen outs. "I figured," said Pee-wee Reese, "that both you guys weren't giving anybody anything, and we'd have to call it at midnight."

Sal Maglie ended the third for the Dodgers, walking out slowly carrying one bat, digging his spikes in as though anything is possible in this game, driving the first pitch straight to Mickey Mantle and walking over towards third base to change his cap and get his glove.

He threw the warm-up pitches; Roy Campanella was standing up and almost dancing at the plate.

Maglie got the two quick strikes on Bauer who hit to Jackie Robinson; Maglie did not look at the play; he was busy with the resin. He pushed the curve by Joe Collins; it was the third strike. Mantle was back.

The first strike was a curve and called. There were no times intruding upon the memory when he had seemed more sharp. He threw the next pitch outside, and then hit the corner again. He waited awhile, rubbing his fingers on his shirt, wiping the afternoon's first sweat off his forehead. He threw a pitch on the corner that was low by the distance of a bead of sweat from the skin; it was that close and it was called a ball.

Mantle hit a foul; Sal Maglie knew it was out of play; the left fielder was still running and he was working on a new ball. The next pitch he threw Mantle was down the middle a little inside. Roy Campanella said later that it hit his fists. Sal Maglie watched it almost curve and then stay fair in the stands; with the unseeing roar all around him, he walked back to the rubber and kicked it once.

"He'd been fouling off the outside pitches," he said later. "I thought I'd try him inside once." He stopped for a minute, naked and dry beside his locker, the skin showing through the thin hair above his forehead. "That shows what can happen when you're thinking out there and the other guy isn't." That was as close as he came to suggesting that God is too tolerant with the margin of error he assigns the very young.

Then Yogi Berra hit one hard to the wrong field; Duke Snider ran the distance of years, and tumbled up with it. Sal Maglie had no reason to know it then, but that was the inning and the run.

In the fifth Enos Slaughter was walked very fast. Billy Martin bunted. Sal Maglie came scuttling onto the grass and snatched the ball and turned around and fired it high and smoky to second just in time, a forty-year-old man throwing out a 40-year-old man and knowing he had to hurry. He was sweating hard by this time. Harold Reese went up half his height, met McDougald's drive and knocked it into the air, and recovered it for the double play. Sal Maglie was watching the way the ball went now; the sound was different; for the first time today he had to think of the fielders.

Don Larsen went on making the rest period painfully short. Sal Maglie took his warm-ups for the sixth; he was throwing the last one in hard now. Andy Carey hit one over his head into center and the old remembered tightrope walk had begun.

Larsen bunted the third strike; Maglie and Campanella scrambled off too late to get the runner at second; they had made their mistake. Carey went far off second; Bauer slapped the ball to left. Sal Maglie drove himself over to back up third, but the run was in and safely in. Walter Alston came out; the conference went on around Maglie. A man in the stands said that if Labine was ready, it was time to bring him in. "Take Sal out?" Campanella said later, "the way he was pitching?" Joe Collins hit a low, hard single; Maglie went over to cover third again and came back slamming the ball into his glove. Mantle was up.

The first pitch was out of control; then he threw two strikes, one called, one swinging. Mantle hit the ball to the first baseman who threw to the catcher, who threw not well to the third baseman, who fell away and threw around Bauer to get him. After the game, Sal Maglie looked at Jackie Robinson sitting sombre across the dressing room; in a moment of surprise, Robinson's hair was gray. "That was a throw," he said. "Him falling away like that." Maglie saw it, and walked to the third base line and waited for the rundown, so as not to interfere, like a waiter at his station, and then walked slowly back to the dugout.

He was the last to come out after the swift Dodger half of the seventh. That appears in the boxscore to have been all it was, except that in the bottom of the eighth, Don Larsen was the first to bat. Sal Maglie went on with his warm-ups; alone in that great park, he and Campanella were not looking at the hitter. He struck out Larsen; he struck out Bauer; he struck out Joe Collins swinging. When he walked back, the crowd noticed him and gave him a portion of its cheers. It was the last inning of the most extraordinary season an old itinerant, never a vagrant, ever had. "I figured," he said later, "that for me, either way, it was the last inning, and I didn't have to save anything."

"I would like to see him," he said later, "pitch with men on bases." Someone asked him if he had minded Larsen getting his no-hitter. "I might have wanted him to get it," he answered, "if we hadn't had a chance all the time."

They asked him was he satisfied with the game he pitched. "How," said Sal Maglie, "am I to be satisfied? But you got to adjust yourself." To time and to ill-chance, and the way they forgot, you got to adjust yourself. Someone asked if you knew when you had a no-hitter, and he said, of course, you do. You remember who had hit, for one thing. "If you ask me two years from now," said Sal Maglie, "I'll be able to tell you every pitch I threw this year." He said it, in passing, naked, his body white except for the red from countless massages on his right arm, tearing his lunch off a long Italian sausage.

"They are pros," he said. "The way we are. You make one mistake with them and you're in trouble."

On the other side of the room, somebody asked Campanella if Maglie had made any mistakes out there. "Sal make mistakes?" said Campanella. "The only mistake he made today was pitching." He pulled on his jacket and turned to what was left of the assemblage. Maglie was going now, as losers are required to go, to get his picture taken with Don Larsen in the Yankee dressing room.

"I told you," chided Roy Campanella, as Sal Maglie went out the door, "That there would be days like this."

[October 9, 1956]

Last Sight

Very few persons within the sight of these words will see Adlai Stevenson again before next Wednesday, and all too few saw him yesterday. It was raining when he came a little before noon, and it did not cease until precisely the moment he got into his car six hours later. Adlai Stevenson is not a lucky man in the little things.

And so the great surging assemblages of the garment unions were washed out, and he made his speeches in crowded halls, and the streets through which he drove in a covered car were half deserted except for brave and loyal spirits under umbrellas. The great rallies do not, after all, decide elections. Adlai Stevenson's loss was not in votes but in heart balm. Somehow, it seems unfair that a tired man to whom peace and satisfaction so seldom come should have been denied the sight of Seventh Avenue bulging to the horizon with upturned faces.

He ended his day near dark on the loge of the Amalgamated Bank near Union Square, the room crowded with as many bodies as the fire laws would permit, standing under horrible heat, gazing into horrible lights, this quiet, delicate, shy man wearing a shirt wet with sweat and rain. Such are the barbarities of the democratic mandate; and Adlai Stevenson apologized later only because all this made it so hard for him to find time to compose the sort of speech that would satisfy his own sense of his own high calling.

An hour before Stevenson arrived yesterday, David Dubinsky, master of his garment district ceremonies, prowled the platform of Manhattan Center, setting up the seats, adjusting the microphones, juggling the cards of the honored guests, helping haul up the Liberal Party banner and driving his business agents to prodigies of emergency preparation. When Stevenson got there, there were 4,000 persons in the hall — the standees barely restrained by Dubinsky's admonitions to shut up; and there was also Herbert Lehman, who is quite an old man now and retired from politics and raising his earnest old voice all over town for Adlai Stevenson.

It was somehow moving to see Lehman and Dubinsky and Stevenson standing together here in this desperate hour, because each in his way is a man not without fault but each has tried, in good times and bad, to be true to the vision with which he began his life.

The Middle East hung over the day. It is an easy subject for passion here in New York, as Jacob Javits very well knows, because from it he is taking the punishment which essentially cynical men deserve. It is Adlai Stevenson's great quality that, for his own advantage, he would not rejoice in it all day yesterday.

In Manhattan Center, they roared and yelled and bellowed, even more than is their custom; yet there was a kind of sadness about Adlai Stevenson. There are two ways to react to the sudden shocking realization that everything you have said is true and that our foreign policy is in the hands of an incompetent and frightened man and the proof cries forth from the headlines. A petty man enjoys it, and a great man is terribly sad. I suspect that Adlai Stevenson, with all his wounds and troubles, is a great man.

"The United States," he said, "can never condone an unprovoked attack by any nation on another." He went on to say that what America has done in the Middle East has been no service to the Arabs.

"When our foreign policy fails, all of us suffer — Democrats and Republicans alike.

"In its conduct in the Middle East, the Eisenhower-Dulles Administration has been consistent in one respect only — it has not told the people the truth."

His words always read much tougher than they sound. He seemed yesterday morning trying not so much to arouse his audience's indignation as to plead for a policy which would base itself on trust in the people's right to know the worst of real life. That trust did not serve him well in 1952; he has no assurance that it will serve him well now but, for good or ill, he will carry on with it.

He was talking late in the afternoon at Erasmus High School, in front of a peeling plaster wall which was a living instance of how badly the old-fashioned Democrats and all-fashioned Republicans have met their responsibilities to our society. He said that the Republicans are running on their record. He wondered aloud if it was their foreign record, and there was the expected laughter from the partisans in his audience.

Adlai Stevenson looked troubled. "We can have a lot of fun," he went on, "but these are trying days and perilous ones." There is, he went on, no extricating yourself from error; there is only reformation. "They have not been telling us the truth; America can live no more on a diet of beatitudes and platitudes; we must offer the world something more than slogans; it is not enough to recite."

It is not enough to recite; it is not enough to stir partisan passions; it is not enough, I suppose he was trying to say, to bow down before any single human being, because man's destiny is in the hands of millions of complex, blundering human beings, and a piece of America dies every time a politician lies to them. The Republicans ask us to trust a man; Adlai Stevenson asks us to trust ourselves.

There is a temptation in many of us to want him to win so badly as not to care what he says; we want only to know how it is going over. He is alone among us here in the last week of the campaign; will any of us ever again look upon a politician who yet will not pander in an hour like this one?

He has been overmanaged; he has been forced through every assault upon his own sense of genteel conduct; he has been pelted with lights, and suffered through the inanities and hopeless bores, and been

pushed by crowds of gate-crashers, and indorsed for election by men
he would not have in his own house; his old exterior posture has been
dreadfully flawed, and, in addition to all that, he has suffered the
slights of purists like myself who undoubtedly would have knocked
Lincoln.

And he has come through all this to stand up here with his dignity
intact yesterday to remind us again that he will not cheapen his vision
of our duty to our tradition or of our limitless possibilities as a people
or his faith that, if he cannot trust us, he can trust no one. A great
garment rally would have been pleasant, but it was not essential.
What is essential is that the worst process known to an American has
left him intact; he is a man and a gentleman.

[November 1, 1956]

The Mercenary

They will, in our lifetime, run excursion trains to Washington so
that young lawyers can watch Edward Bennett Williams postpone
the frying of some damned soul. It is a good use for trains. To watch
Williams and then to watch a Department of Justice lawyer contend-
ing with him is to understand the essential superiority of free enterprise to government ownership. The Justice Department used forty
FBI agents to sew Jimmy Hoffa in a sack last March; yesterday Edward Bennett Williams almost had him out.

He had two members of the jury sniffling when he had finished his
two-and-a-half-hour summary yesterday. Prosecutor Edward Roxell
went to the bench afterwards and asked the presiding judge to explain
to the jury that this was not a capital offense and that a conviction
would not mean that Hoffa would be hanged.

I think that, if it were in James Hoffa's power to look penitent,
Williams would have saved him yesterday. He cannot, of course,
because he has not the grace to be hypocritical. Strangers came up
to Williams when it was over yesterday to say that what he had done
belonged in the literature of the great trials. His client didn't even
thank him, being a man who expects value received for money laid
out. Jimmy Hoffa is Sam Hall; on the very scaffold, with the priest

beside him, he will say: "I hate you one and all; you're a lousy bunch of bastards and damn your eyes."

The government rushed this trial into August in the hope that, by convicting James Hoffa, it could stop him from becoming president of the Teamsters Union. That is not a proper aspiration of government; society has no right to deny a man his own damnation. We cannot expect government to prevent the Giants from going to San Francisco or to prevent the Teamsters from going to Hoffa.

James Hoffa, by the mere fact of his demonstration yesterday that he is incapable of appreciating what Williams may have done for him, makes it plain that he has another destiny — a gaudier doom — than going to jail for a crime which by his lights is no more than spitting on the sidewalk. Edward Bennett Williams is one of the glories of our time because he saves the rascals he represents from the feeble malignity of the state and reserves them for the majestic vengeance of God.

Every proper man should be grateful for the spectacle of talent used to keep a guilty man out of prison rather than to put an innocent one in. Ed Williams prowled like a great cat in front of that jury yesterday, by himself, alien to his client, beyond help of friend or damage of enemy, in the bottom of the ninth, with two outs and a tide of runs against him. He talked for an hour; there was the silence of total attention, while he tried to destroy the character of John Cye Cheasty, the witness who swears Jimmy Hoffa tried to plant him as a spy on the Senate Labor Committee staff.

When Judge Matthews broke in to announce a recess, there was a low sigh of appreciation from the audience — Williams draws Washington audiences who understand each nuance of his work the way the Milanese do La Scala — and Ed Williams, saving himself, walked back. Jimmy Hoffa did not even look at him.

"Is that all," he said querulously, "he's going to say about this fraud and deceit?" One of his retainers said: "Relax, Jimmy."

To have no sense of sin is to have no taste, and to have no taste is to be a loser at the end; Edward Bennett Williams can save you only in the non-essentials.

Williams came back and went on making little chinks in the government's case look like great holes. He bowed his head before the

jury and reminded them that a man's life was at stake. One of the
jurymen was crying; Ed Williams paused to let him collect himself
and begin to listen again. Everyone in the room with one exception
seemed to feel the terrible burden that every man should feel when
he assumes the right to judge another man. The exception was James
Hoffa, who looked about the room and counted the house and his
chances. The whole world will weep for James Hoffa before he weeps
for himself.

When Williams had finished, there was another recess. Williams
sat down; Hoffa said something absolutely matter-of-fact to him; he
would treat Saint Peter like a headwaiter. His enemies came up with
a kind of awe to tell his lawyer what a job of work he had done.
Troxell got up lame and halting with the truth; it seemed a kind of
affront to art that truth should summon to her side a spokesman so
inept; right does not deserve to triumph if it has no better voice than
this.

It goes to the jury today; I cannot, even after Williams, quite believe that Hoffa will not be convicted. I doubt if Williams believes it
either; having done his job, with the room full of its memory an hour
later, he was laughing at the bench. There is a kind of wonder at the
sight of the pro when his day's work is done. It is the dignity of a man
who brings to his job the best that is in him for a team that is going
nowhere, who expends himself with no thought of another game and
another day. He was laughing but he was used up, having spent himself for a man who does not appreciate him and whom he could
hardly like.

There is a poem by Housman about the army of mercenaries who
died to save England at Mons:

> *What God abandoned, these defended,*
> *And saved the sum of thing for pay.*

Nothing better could be said of the pro; Edward Bennett Williams
needs nothing better said of him.

[Washington, D.C., July 19, 1957]

Farewell the Banner

John L. Lewis has departed, and now the nineteenth century is officially closed, as the eighteenth century can be said to have ended only when Lord Melbourne retired as the Queen's first minister in 1839.

The nineteenth can hardly be anyone's favorite century; it is after all the parent of the twentieth. But it was at worst a time of active virtues and active ambitions. You think of John Lewis as a child reading Carlyle on the hero, or looking at the chromos of Samson at the pillars or Ajax defying the lightning and being infected permanently by the notion that man is the master of his fate.

The chromos were better and closer to reality. What is Samson now but Victor Mature, as what is Solomon but Yul Brynner? Can anyone grow up conceiving a member of the Screen Actors Guild defying the gods when Kim Novak wouldn't even defy Harry Cohn?

Lewis was a child of the nineteenth century because the dancer never stopped being the dance. There does not exist among all the thousands of pictures which the editors fished over so happily this week a single one in which he ever made the slightest attempt to look like an ordinary human being. Put a dinner jacket on him and set him somewhere to condescend to Congressmen or corporate directors and sneak a cameraman upon him unawares and he would come out looking like Samson among the Philistines.

He departs among clouds of the warm steam of public affection, which would have been surprising ten years ago, although it was foreshadowed in 1952, at a House hearing on mine safety, when Congressman Thruston Morton, now chairman of the Republican National Committee, went running after him like a little boy for his autograph.

Scattered among the tributes, like chunks of plaster ripped off a baroque façade, there were quotations from his old speeches, which, without the majesty of his presence and the grandeur of the occasion, seemed comparatively poor stuff, almost contrivances. It was like asking people to judge Samuel Johnson without reference to his conversation. Already the image grows a little dim; from now on it will be necessary to tell people what he was like.

Then he was harsh, violent, in a measured way, unpitying. At heart, I do not think he liked the poor, although, in the nineteenth century habit, he seems to have hoped for rather better things from their children. One of my least favorite authors once said that Lewis in the Thirties conceived himself as the sun and of everyone else, even Roosevelt, as a minor planet, and I think that has stood up better than most of that man's estimates.

In most of what has been collected from Lewis in the summit of his powers, there is very little that brings close to the heart the suffering of his people.

The phrase "shrunken bellies" was, as an instance, not an image but an empty rhetorical figure. This is a weakness, I suppose, but you cannot condemn a man for being true to himself; who would demand of Lear that he stand on that windy plain and complain that Goneril is soaking the poor?

The image of the workers which Lewis embodied was one not of suffering but of power. His highest peaks of rhetoric were the moments when he assailed a President of the United States for insufficient appreciation of the awe and majesty of John L. Lewis. He talked about the miners the way Hercules might have talked about the club he carried on his shoulder.

And yet, in his worst moments, he never lost his dignity because he never lost his respect for that club. Is not the thing we miss most the awful grandeur of those marching syllables, "The United Mine Workers of America"? For now, with him departing, we are condemned to live with a President who cannot even muster the sense of history to say "The United States of America" but can only mumble Yewnytedstates.

And now he is going, but in the official, accepted sense, hadn't he gone quite a while ago? The unions left him after the Thirties for drearier but softer men; no one has asked very seriously who was his candidate for President since 1944. I suppose the Lewis of the Thirties would have railed against this condition; the Lewis of the Fifties seemed rather pleased by it. He had reached, by some interior miracle, a stage where the things that are on the front pages of newspapers had lost any real interest for him; he had come to that wonderful period where man looks for no judge but himself.

He had become, outside the business of the United Mine Workers, a magnificently detached observer. There is a story that one day, in the Carlton, he met Al Hayes, chairman of the AFL-CIO Ethical Practices Committee. "Hello, Al," he said, "found any Ethical Practices lately?"

He attended with nineteenth-century devotion to building his own memorial. It was the United Mine Workers, its pension program, its hospitals, its banks.

Not long ago, he was talking to a *U.S. News* reporter about his program to put machines in the mines. The effect has been to cut the number of men paying him dues almost in half in the last ten years. His interlocutor asked him if this program for contracting his population was not an odd one for a man whose aspirations were once so imperial.

John Lewis answered that he hoped some day that there would be no miners at all.

"It will be a millennium," he ended, "if men do not have to work underground, but can all work in God's sunshine."

John Lewis is the most fortunate of men. There is nothing that he ever said in his great days so warm and winning as this. In the great days, there was always this painful reminder of Dostoevski's remark that hell is being unable to love. He has passed from that private hell; if he had quit in 1940, he would have departed with honor; now he retires with grace and glory.

[December 17, 1959]

Final Returns, Final Night

Carmine DeSapio came to rest a little while last night at the Fifth Avenue Hotel, an hour before the polls closed.

Someone had chalked on the blackboard that "Now Is the Time" and "This Is D-Day" and "What Can You Do for Him?" Mrs. De-Sapio was still working the phones; DeSapio sat at a long table, de-

tached from pain or blame or rancor, and said that there were so
many conflicting views of what a big vote meant that an outsider
could not possibly make an estimate.

"Some of them say try for a light vote, some say try for a heavy
one." The Village, he observed, was so quiet; a visitor, searching for
consolation, said that he had heard a shout when Roger Maris hit a
home run just now. Carmine DeSapio smiled politely. With all his
other troubles, can he be a Ruth man too?

He doodled with his pen. He doodled the initials "V. I. D." and
scratched them over. The visitor asked how big the vote was, and
Carmine DeSapio rose, with the grace that will never leave him in
life, and said he would find out. He called. "What do you hear
around?" he asked into the phone. He came and said that up at the
Biltmore they said it would come close to a million and what did that
mean? The visitor said they must be crazy.

AT THE SCHOOLHOUSE

It was time for him to go, a field marshal on lonely patrol in the
enemy country. He said he would try the South Village; there had
been complaints about the machines there. He came to the Little
Red Schoolhouse; the line out to the door looked like a convention
of folk singers. He went inside; there was a sense that, although he is
a man too polite ever to suggest it, he did not want company on this
pilgrimage. He was there a long time. The visitor moved in to find
him; DeSapio was standing by himself on the side watching the
enemy challenge every vote. He clapped his hands once and said:
"Come on; these people have to vote."

The tables rustled and stirred a moment with the habit of discipline; then they went back to their slow quarrel, the illusion of authority having passed. Carmine DeSapio walked out past the long
line of assassins, stopping now and again to shake the hand of a
middle-aged man with a necktie. "How are you; it's nice to see you."
Most of the line — insurgents don't wear neckties in public — would
not look at him; the visitor remembered the old rule about juries and
the defendants they cannot bear to look upon.

Carmine DeSapio smiled and said that he supposed it was time to
go and get the results.

Tamawa was as chaste as ever, and as ever a dedicated citadel of respectable upper mobility. The captains were not back yet; their ladies sat in a row on the side; Tamawa has always had the good old rule about the silence of women in church. There was a long table for taking returns; DeSapio went to a cubicle at the side of the room, which began to fill, horridly silent; every now and again a man would come in with his bundle of tally sheets and hand it over to the captain as though it were a secret document. The attendant would look at it, check the election district and send it back to the cubicle.

'EVERYBODY CAN'T WIN'

A half hour went that way. There was by now a crowd of the sort which shows up at disasters. DeSapio came out to talk on the radio. The smile on the face of the tiger was a wound. Downtown the police reported Lanigan leading by a thousand votes; DeSapio said his figures showed him slightly behind. He was asked about the mayoralty. "I really don't know," he answered, "I haven't had an opportunity to talk to any of the county chairmen."

By eleven fifteen he came out holding the tally sheets. He said that he was behind 5,210 to 4,093 with five electoral districts missing. "I would say at this stage Lanigan is the victor. The results in the city are not encouraging."

"Has everybody got the figures?" he asked. It was the tone of a host searching for the last lonely guest whose glass is running dry. He went back to the cubicle. His people stayed; when he came back to dismiss them, they applauded.

"I can't tell you how grateful I am. We're not going to close the club. Things will adjust themselves as we go along. That's the democratic form of government. Nobody likes to lose but everybody can't win."

I sometimes think if Carmine DeSapio were running against Lucifer he would consider it ungentlemanly to mention that little trouble in heaven.

"It's not easy for me, but try to accept it as graciously as you possibly can." He stopped; the wistful, disembodied smile played on. "I know you are going to say that fellow DeSapio is too soft; he wants to forgive everybody."

This was too much for even the habitual docility of the ladies along the wall.

"You are, you are," they cried.

"Let me please once again say to you from the bottom of my heart," Carmine DeSapio began again. "We tried and we lost. Don't let's get sick about it."

He adjourned them and loyally they went home.

Carmine DeSapio's father was standing patiently and without rancor, twisting a discarded tally sheet in his old longshoreman's hands. What must it be to raise a son who believes in every virtue in the book and see him defiled and brought down like this? The De-Sapios keep such reflections private. Carmine DeSapio began introducing the stray guests to his father, the distant relative who is the rock of all occasions of family sorrow, welcoming the stranger, consoling the mourner.

He had to go back to the Fifth Avenue Hotel, the command post for the genteel among his supporters. There were perhaps ten persons who had risen in the world with him; there was a piano and a lady wondering whether anyone could play it so that we could sing "East Side, West Side."

No one felt like playing and Carmine DeSapio rose and talked interminably about not being indispensable and not being immortal and about being very sorry if I have let you down; I'll call you in a day or two and we'll have a little party and a little celebration in the climate of friendship that's endured for many years.

There was nothing to do then but wait for Mike Prendergast, the state chairman, who came to say that he was proud to have his picture taken with Carmine DeSapio. It was then one o'clock; Sydney Baron said that Carmine was tired and hadn't eaten and someone should get him a sandwich. Carmine DeSapio roused himself as though he had lost his manners, and said he was sorry, they must be hungry; could he get them a sandwich?

That way his visitor left him and walked into the streets and noticed that there were no slums any more, and no landlords, and the Age of Pericles had begun because we were rid of Carmine DeSapio. One had to walk carefully to avoid being stabbed by the lilies bursting in the pavements. I wish the reformers luck — with less Christian sincerity than Carmine DeSapio does. I will be a long time forgiving them this one.

[September 8, 1961]

Visiting Hours

Mrs. Martin Luther King brought her children, Yolanda, 6, Martin Luther III, 4, and Dexter Scott, 18 months, to the city jail to visit their father a little after noon yesterday.

They had never seen their father in jail before; and he, rather than Mrs. King, had suggested that it would be better if they did not see him behind bars.

"They're so active," she said. "And the cell's so narrow." She and they waited outside the chief's office while the Albany police arranged for King to receive his family in the narrow hall between the cells and the booking desk.

Someone asked how long she thought her husband would stay there. Her face was suddenly painful and she said she didn't know, but she hopes very much that it might be coming to a close. She and he are essentially such reserved people, and to be conspicuous is such an embarrassment to them, and the police court so alien. They are actors with a particular talent for reconciliation; yet they have been assigned the part of active resistance; it is one of the strangest twists of this strange country that Martin and Coretta King, of all people, should have become symbols of militant disturbance to the official South.

The children had precisely fifteen minutes. They came out to play in the lobby through which so many children, not really much older, have marched off to jail in the past six months. They asked for Cokes and were firmly overruled; Martin III reached up to try the water fountain.

Mrs. King was undisguisedly relieved that it had all been so easy. "I told Martin," she said later, "that if you stay away much longer the baby won't know you." But that worry, like so many others, had not come true. Yolanda, she said was the only one of the children who was beginning to ask the sort of questions to which fruitful answers can be given.

"I told her and Marty too this time that Daddy had gone to jail to help the poor people, that there are people different from ourselves who don't have good homes to live in or enough food to eat.

"The first time Martin went to jail in Atlanta, Yolanda heard about it on television. She started crying. I told her, 'Yorky, Daddy's gone to help the people. He's already helped some people; he has to help some more. He'll be back.' And then she stopped crying."

She has tried, as mothers must, to protect Yolanda as long as she could. "When they built Fun Town for children in Atlanta, she was after me to take her there. I put her off as long as I could and finally I had to tell her that some of the people who built Fun Town are not nice Christian people and unfortunately they didn't want colored children. She started crying. And I told her: 'It won't be long before Fun Town is open to all the people. That's what your Daddy's working for.'

"And this time Yolanda said, 'I want Daddy to come home.' And then, 'Tell him to stay until he fixes it up so I can go to Fun Town.'"

Fun Town had been the first time Mrs. King had to tell Yolanda. "I want her to have a healthy attitude toward white people. She will have her bitter time, but I think that we have protected her enough so it will pass."

But Yolanda hears things, as children will. One of their friends told her that there were people who hated her father. "You wonder why people say things. She went to Martin and he told her, 'I don't think a lot of people hate me. But a lot of people don't like what I'm trying to do.'"

But young Martin is four, and cannot see enough of his father. "Boys are different; he needs that firm hand." A visitor asked just how many more times her husband would have to go to jail and for how many more years they would live as they do now.

"I think five years," she said with that familiar sudden sadness. "After that, it will not be all perfect but it will be different." Her largest hope is that the term to which they have been called will only be five years. They are five years to be accepted as prescribed and to be endured in infrequently broken measures of pain and worry.

[Albany, Georgia, August 6, 1962]

Peg

Westbrook Pegler has departed as he worked, faithful to his original vision of himself and to his class and to his kind.

He was true to us at the end, truer than we are to ourselves, because his last words were a curse on his employer for defiling the product. Which of us has not sat one lonely night in the dirty lofts where we work and just once cursed the owner of the property?

And which of us before Peg has ever said these words in a public place? He should have said what he said before some convention of the American Newspaper Guild. It was, after all, the protest of the craftsman against the distributor, which used long ago to be a concern of unions. But Peg, by one of those peculiar distortions of his real complaint which are so much the story of his life, had to deliver his judgment on his boss to the Christian Crusade Against Communism.

There are two Americas as there are two parts of every country. There are those who own property and those who work for them. The last words of Peg's which are likely to appear on the front page of any newspaper were spoken by a man who knew that he was one of those who worked for a living and that had nothing in common with the owner. Walter Reuther is a more responsible man; but only on the day when Walter Reuther complains about the kind of cars the auto companies build can we think him as fundamental a radical as Peg is.

Peg, of course, was unkind to William Randolph Hearst, Jr. There is a temptation, merely because we have overcome it, to think the past more pleasant than the present. William Randolph Hearst, Jr., is every bit as good a citizen as William Randolph Hearst, Sr.

But Peg was right about the Hearst team. It is, whatever its skills, by necessity a mere traveling collection agency for the mendacities of the powerful. It goes about the world, listening to and recording the lies which the owners of states tell their poor, and transmitting them to the uncritical. Franco, Salazar and Khrushchev all lie to the Hearst team. After which the journalism schools give it prizes for contributing to the public enlightenment. The Hearst team is, of course, Mr. Hearst's effort to run a serious and respectable journal.

Peg was cheated, but he was never a cheater. He is a large man and his delusion was worthy of his size. He believed, quite simply, that America was a classless society and that he was an owner of property. He wrote as honest owners of property should: he hated unions and income taxes and all useless citizens. Real owners of property, of course, can afford to be tolerant: they don't pay income taxes; they can buy unions for a cup of coffee; and useless citizens are inexpensive to them, and, quite often, relatives.

But Peg, as he was a kind man at the core, was also a man incapable of indifference. There has always been a part of him which understood that he really just worked for a living.

That part of him could not be controlled, but it could be distracted. No work of Peg's has ever been without art, but it was sad to see how much of his passion has been exercised on the inconsequential. A year at least on Winchell. But, if there had never been a Walter Winchell, would the decay of Peg's craft have been any slower? Would one less of his old colleagues have become a press agent or a ghost writer or a figure on television or otherwise lost the vision of his youth? Would there still have been anyone left but Peg?

So many American lives, even those noblest of impulse, have been wasted by missing the point in just this way. Our enemy is not the man who makes bad goods but the man who sells them. This late in the game, there is enough of Peg left to see that point. The day he sees it clear and utters it, he is fired. He has finally gone too far; he has violated the laws of property and history. He leaves us in a moment of revelation, like a Bolshevik at the execution wall.

He goes with honor as he has lived with honor. There is a poem of Yeats which begins: "And why should old men not be mad?" It is Peg's and he has earned the high compliment of it.

[August 17, 1962]

Willie Mays

There was this moment when Willie Mays caught the last ball hit in the National League in 1962 and turned and laughed and threw it at the right-field foul pole. It was his ball and he could do what he pleased with it.

All of a sudden, you remembered all the promises the rich have made to the poor for the last thirteen years and the only one that was kept was the promise about Willie Mays. They told us then that he would be the greatest baseball player we would ever see, and he was.

Charles Einstein, who left New York when the Giants did, only to follow Willie Mays, once looked up all the games the Giants have played since he came back from the Army in 1954 and found out that they have not won a game in which the name of Willie Mays did not appear in the box score.

Is there a single other American in this slack decade who can look his employer in the eye and tell him that?

A little boy once confessed to me that he was only a Willie Mays fan and that if Mays left the Giants, he would go to the team that Mays went to. I was, as Whittaker Chambers once said, an *org* man at the time and this seemed childishly irresponsible.

Yet suddenly one gets old and one learns if nothing else that there are no teams but only men. I, to be personal, am not a Democrat; I am only an Adlai Stevenson fan. And the team is out of my system now; I am only a Willie Mays fan.

It began a long way back here in New York, when the Giants were always sixth and would have been eighth without him. By July, there was very little reason to look at the box score, except to see how Mays had done. He was all the pride that was left us. Now they have won a pennant again; yet all that mattered at the end Wednesday, when he came up in the last inning, was not whether the Giants won but whether Willie Mays would get a hit. He had brought them this far, but it is his special touching quality that he is not really superhuman; he fails occasionally.

In the first inning against the Dodgers, Johnny Podres fooled him

with a pitch which one doubts would have fooled Musial or Ted
Williams. Ed Roebuck may have fooled him again in the ninth; it
looked like the pitch Roebuck wanted to throw and as if Mays had
simply overpowered it. Willie Mays is universally regarded as one of
the smartest baseball players alive, but he can be fooled; and that, I
think, is the secret of his charm. He is unlikely to hit .345 when he
is forty-one, because he will never lose the desire he had when he was
twenty, and pitchers fool not his head but his desire.

It would have been simpler, one supposes, if Willie Mays had hit
seventy-five home runs one year and over .350 every other, but he
would not be what he is if he did. But, if you are to go with one ballplayer all through his career, let him be a human ballplayer and
watch him fail when he has to. The one thing the greatest athlete of
our generation could not do to us was to quit on himself and his
team for as much as one second of his professional life, and that is
the promise Willie Mays has kept.

This is peculiarly his pennant, as neither of the other two could
be said to have been. The Giants almost lost it when he got sick;
they almost lost it again when he stopped hitting; they won it because he broke free at the end. It is also his pennant because without
him they would have finished third; no matter where this team has
been since 1954 it was always two places higher than it had much
right to be, and only because of him.

He went three for four against Whitey Ford yesterday, striking out
of course just when it seemed that Ford really never would get him
out. Mays batting against Ford, in the private world of our cult, is
the only interesting thing in this Series. Mays hits Ford the way he
would hit me; he hits Warren Spahn too. Yet once last summer,
Willie Mays struck out five times in a row against the pitching staff
of the New York Mets. Could anyone conceive of Ted Williams doing
that? We describe Whitey Ford as a pitcher when we say that the
only hitter who owns him is Willie Mays. And we describe Willie
Mays and the pleasure of his company when we say that the only
pitcher he owns is Whitey Ford.

[October 5, 1962]

He Loved Us

Saxe Commins, who was the great editor at Random House, has been dead nearly three weeks now, and, if there has been a satisfactory published obituary, it has escaped me. Our journalism will do handsomer by Senator Bricker.

And so, I am afraid, it falls to me, who could not be less satisfactory at the job, because I am a harsh and malignant man in many ways, and Saxe Commins was in absolutely none. The good acts he has done for writers are unlikely to have ended when our children have children, and he performs in memory one more good act for me just because, if only for one day, the thought of him has softened my sullen nature.

The obituaries said that he had been William Faulkner's editor, and Eugene O'Neill's editor, and there could not be a more handsome flourish of Nobel laureates. What they did not say was what Saxe did for every writer whose life ever touched his.

I remember once that a publisher came to him with a manuscript of the memoirs of a public figure who had been involved in a great sensation. He was a man about whom Saxe and I had one of our few disagreements. Saxe read the manuscript and sat down and wrote a critique which came as close to savagery as he could ever get. The publisher called and said that he agreed completely, but that this was a book that would sell a million copies. It was published, and, if it did not sell a million copies, it was a handsome success, and the company ordered another book from the author.

When it came in, it was gloomy, abstract and altogether a prospective commercial disaster. The publisher conferred with the sales department and called Saxe and said that this was a desperate case and that something drastic had to be done to convince the man that the book simply had to be more "upbeat." I have never seen Saxe more indignant.

"They would do a thing like that to a man? Talk about him to the sales department? He is a writer and this is his book."

He began with Horace Liveright in the Twenties, and he was the father of children and Maxwell Anderson's editor and O'Neill's and Theodore Dreiser's and he made less than $75 a week. It is hardly a secret that Dreiser was in some ways a pig, and once, when Saxe came into a cocktail party, Dreiser turned and said in a voice that filled the room, "Here comes a publisher, which is another word for thief." Saxe told that story twenty-eight years later, as though it had been yesterday afternoon. No wound of his ever healed, and none bled longer than the wound of a decision that he had to dislike a man.

Liveright went bankrupt, and Saxe Commins was out of a job at the beginning of the depression. He went to Random House, because Eugene O'Neill wrote into his contract with that new firm that he would never have any other editor but Saxe Commins. That was his only capital; it remained his only capital until he died: No writer who ever had him for an editor would ever take another.

Clifton Fadiman has said that we now have an "unedited generation." I suspect this condition arises from the false conception of love and tolerance which afflicts us so generally these days. Saxe Commins knew that the duty of the man who loved the writer was to make sure that the writer always did nothing less than the best that was in him. He consumed himself, sick as he had been for four years, sitting up all night forcing whatever man came to him to do that best.

The week after his last heart attack, dying of pleurisy, he finished editing two books. The galleys for one came to his home while he was in the hospital less than a week before he died. His wife, Dorothy, though it best not to tell him. He turned to her that afternoon and asked if the galleys had come.

"I could not lie to Saxe," she said afterwards. She knew the price, and he did, and she went home and got the galleys and he finished them. The afternoon before he died, he remembered a correction and he phoned Random House and delivered it. The author for whom he performed this service is a gentleman, and I am afraid this story will pain him, because he may think that no book is worth that suffering by a friend. But Saxe knew it was.

That was a life. And it does have its obituary for time beyond the *Times*. There was a telegram from William Faulkner. I do not work my trade when I go to say good-by to a friend, and I did not copy it down. But what it said approximately was that, if every man who ever knew Saxe Commins had to testify at the end, he would say, "He loved me."

[August 1, 1958]

Index